SUPERMAN
THE COMING OF THE SUPERMEN

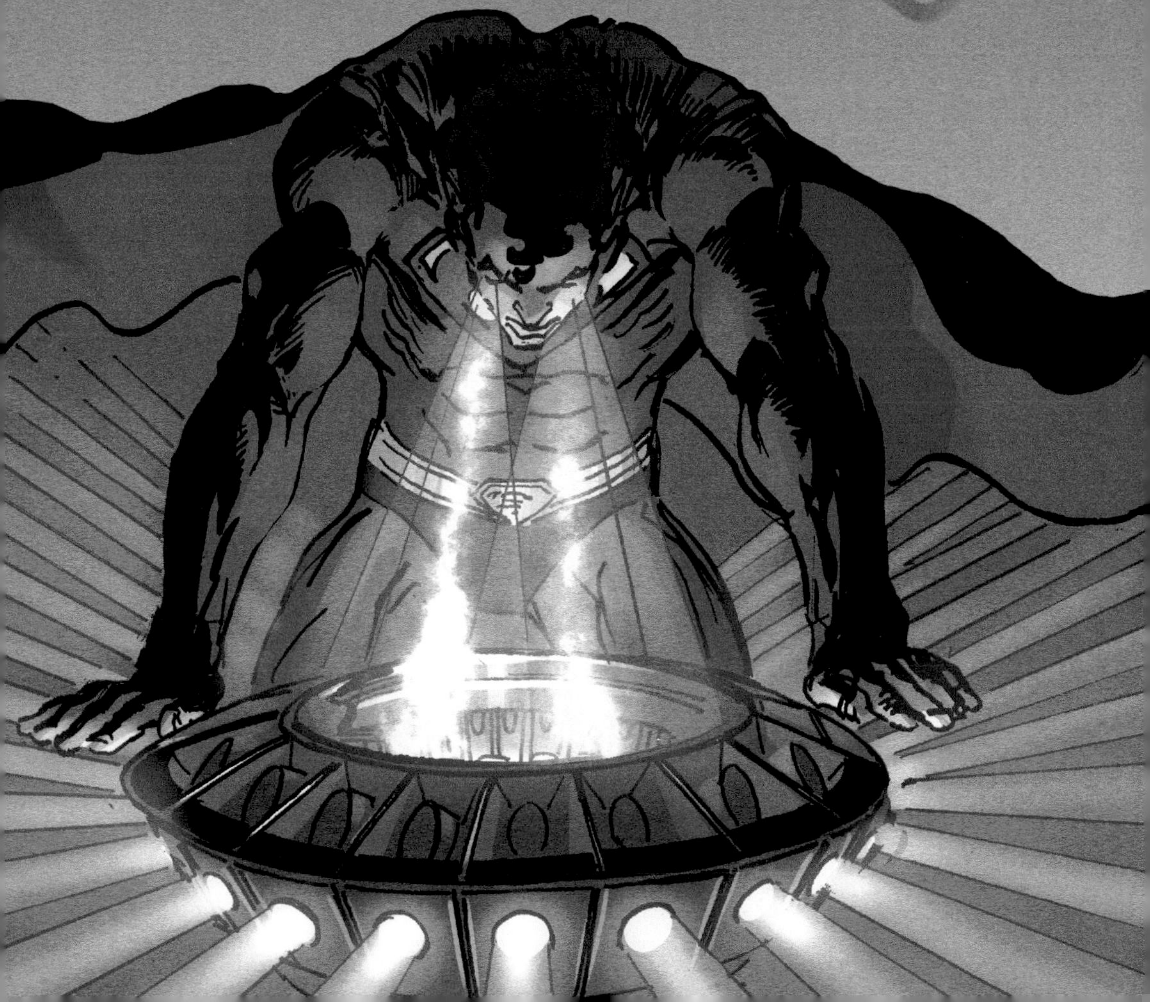

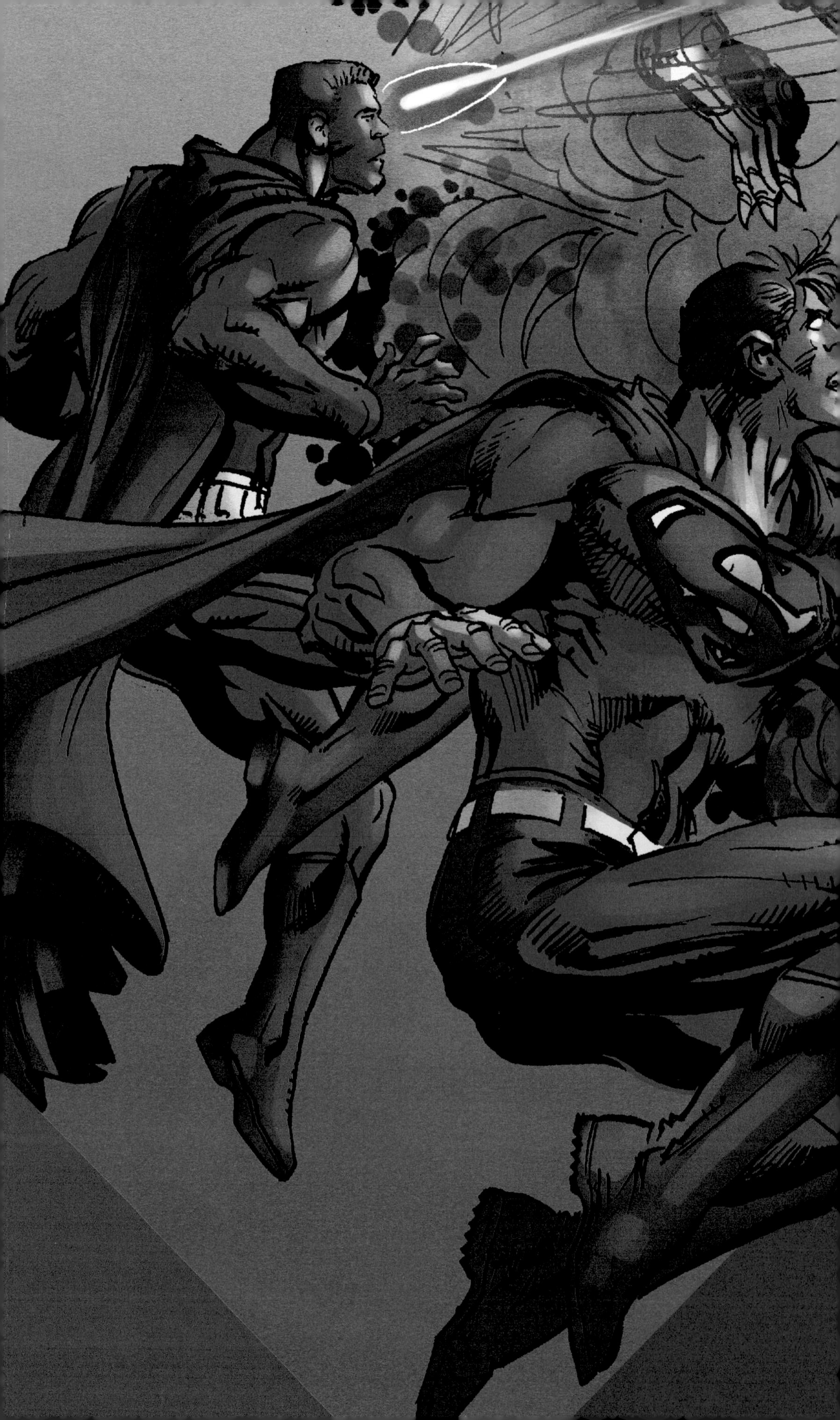

SUPERMAN
THE COMING OF THE
SUPERMEN

Neal Adams
Writer & Artist

Tony Bedard
Script Co-Writer, issue #1

Tony Aviña
Alex Sinclair
Colorists

Buzz
Josh Adams
Additional Inks

Cardinal Rae
Saida Temofonte
Erica Schultz
Letterers

Series and Collection Cover Art
by **Neal Adams** & **Alex Sinclair**

SUPERMAN created by **Jerry Siegel** and **Joe Shuster**
By special arrangement with the **Jerry Siegel family**

Eddie Berganza
Editor – Original Series

Andrew Marino
Assistant Editor – Original Series

Jeb Woodard
Group Editor – Collected Editions

Liz Erickson
Editor – Collected Edition

Steve Cook
Design Director – Books

Chris Griggs
Publication Design

Bob Harras   Senior VP – Editor-in-Chief, DC Comics

Diane Nelson   President
Dan DiDio and **Jim Lee**   Co-Publishers
Geoff Johns   Chief Creative Officer
Amit Desai   Senior VP – Marketing
                        & Global Franchise Management
Nairi Gardiner   Senior VP – Finance
Sam Ades   VP – Digital Marketing
Bobbie Chase   VP – Talent Development
Mark Chiarello   Senior VP – Art, Design &
                        Collected Editions
John Cunningham   VP – Content Strategy
Anne DePies   VP – Strategy Planning & Reporting
Don Falletti   VP – Manufacturing Operations
Lawrence Ganem   VP – Editorial Administration
                        & Talent Relations
Alison Gill   Senior VP – Manufacturing & Operations
Hank Kanalz   Senior VP – Editorial
                        Strategy & Administration
Jay Kogan   VP – Legal Affairs
Derek Maddalena   Senior VP – Sales &
                        Business Development
Jack Mahan   VP – Business Affairs
Dan Miron   VP – Sales Planning &
                        Trade Development
Nick Napolitano   VP – Manufacturing Administration
Carol Roeder   VP – Marketing
Eddie Scannell   VP – Mass Account & Digital Sales
Courtney Simmons   Senior VP – Publicity & Communications
Jim (Ski) Sokolowski VP – Comic Book Specialty
                        & Newsstand Sales
Sandy Yi   Senior VP – Global
                        Franchise Management

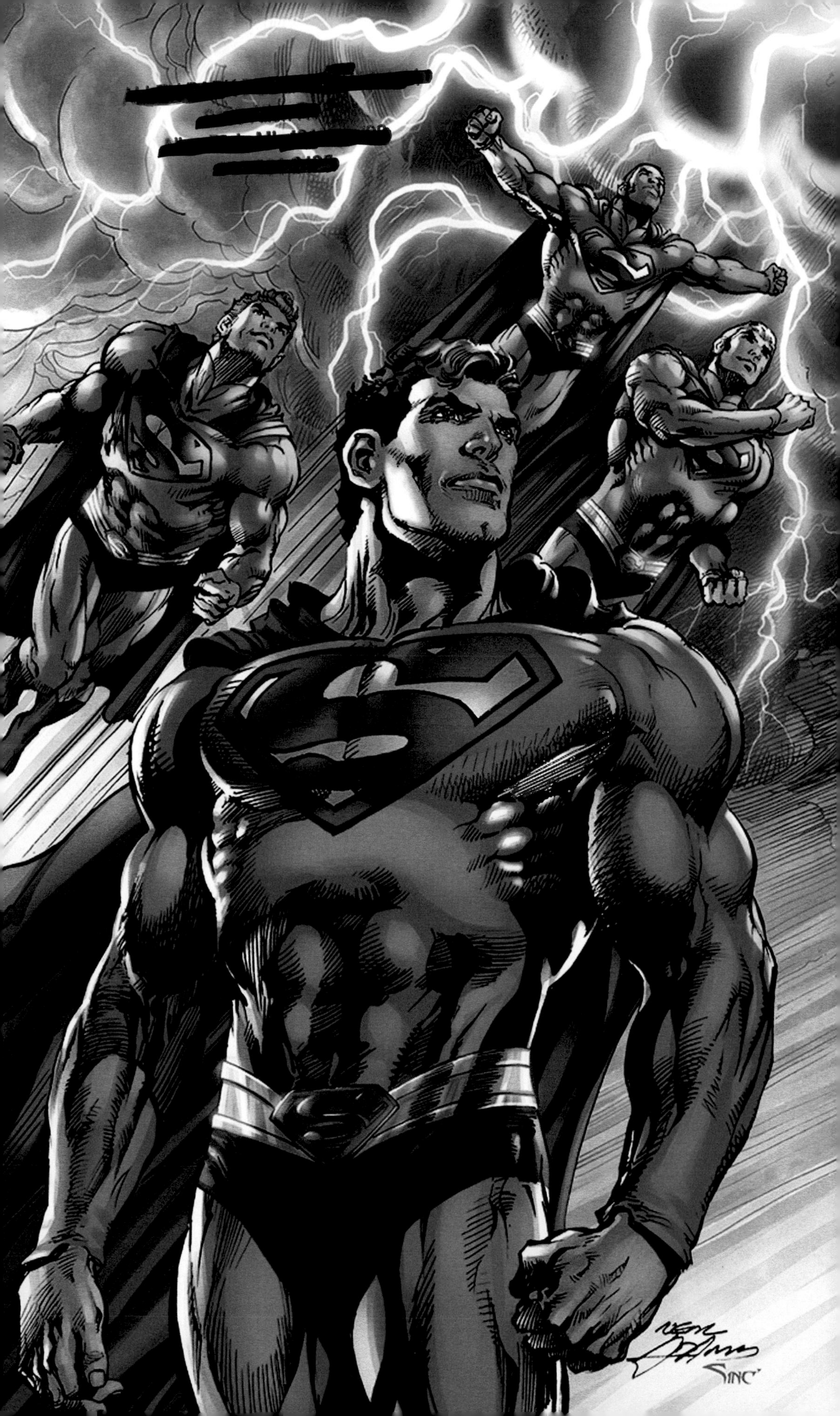
[redacted]

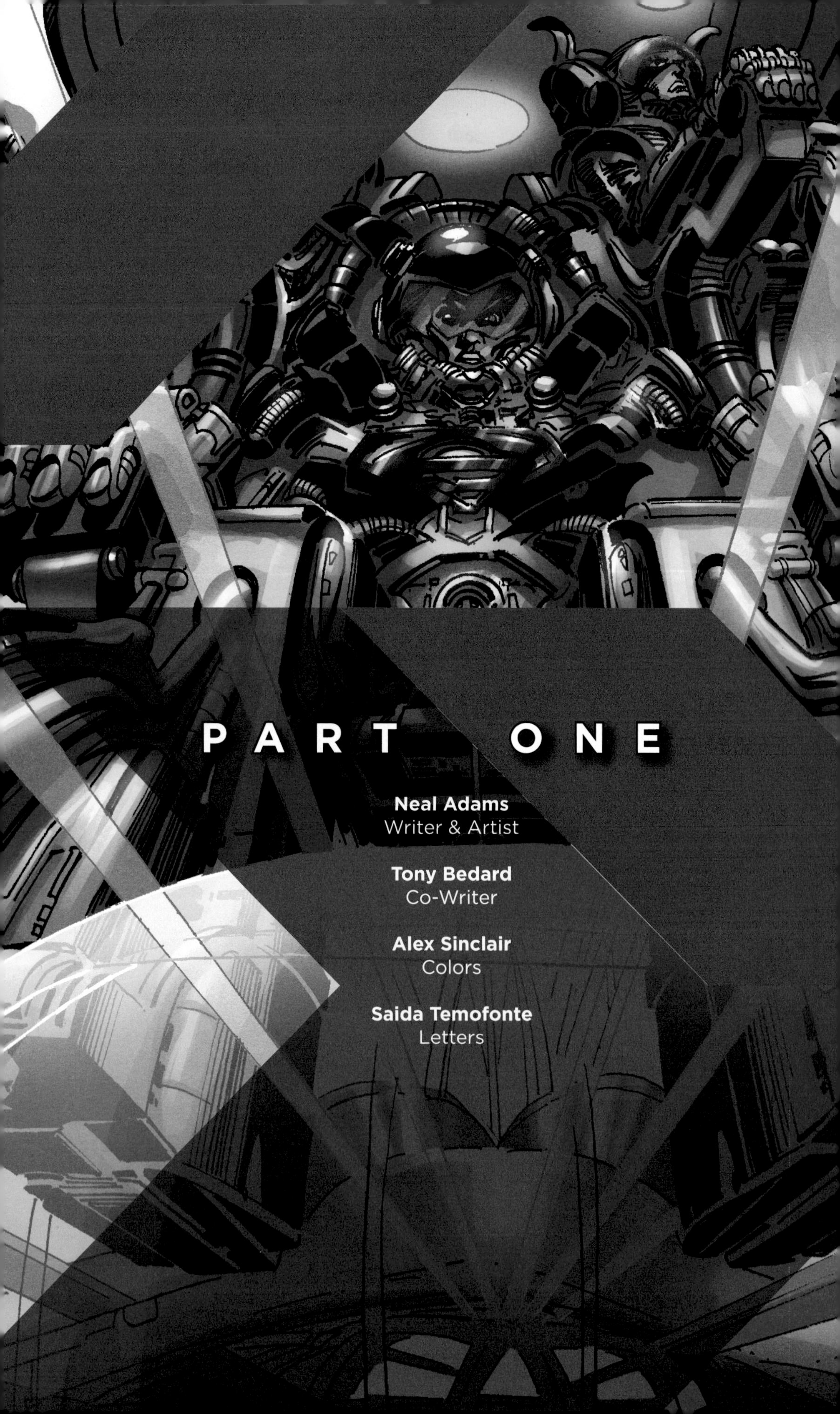

PART ONE

Neal Adams
Writer & Artist

Tony Bedard
Co-Writer

Alex Sinclair
Colors

Saida Temofonte
Letters

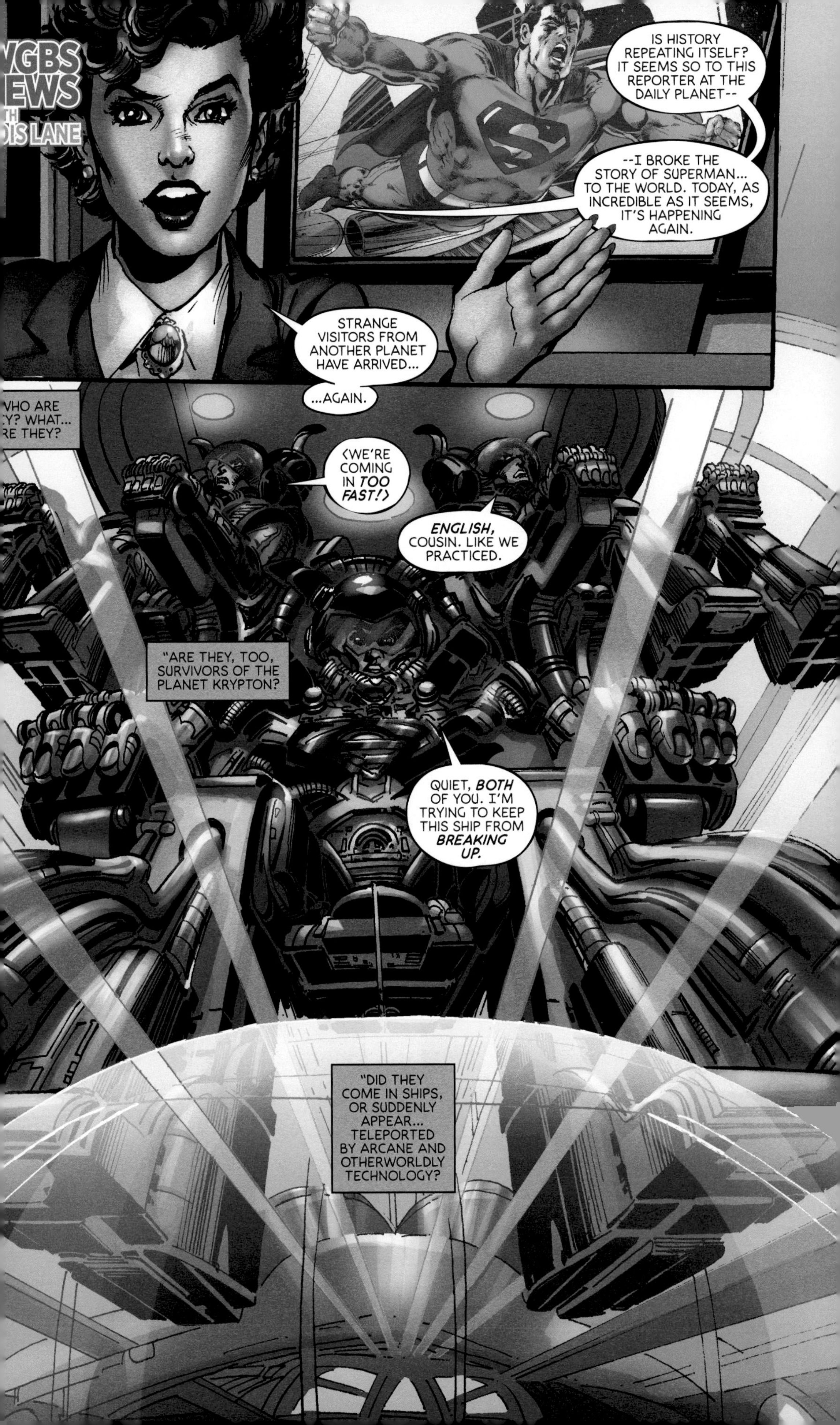
WGBS NEWS WITH LOIS LANE
IS HISTORY REPEATING ITSELF? IT SEEMS SO TO THIS REPORTER AT THE DAILY PLANET--
--I BROKE THE STORY OF SUPERMAN... TO THE WORLD. TODAY, AS INCREDIBLE AS IT SEEMS, IT'S HAPPENING AGAIN.
STRANGE VISITORS FROM ANOTHER PLANET HAVE ARRIVED...
...AGAIN.
WHO ARE THEY? WHAT... ARE THEY?
<WE'RE COMING IN *TOO FAST!*>
ENGLISH, COUSIN. LIKE WE PRACTICED.
"ARE THEY, TOO, SURVIVORS OF THE PLANET KRYPTON?
QUIET, *BOTH* OF YOU. I'M TRYING TO KEEP THIS SHIP FROM *BREAKING UP.*
"DID THEY COME IN SHIPS, OR SUDDENLY APPEAR... TELEPORTED BY ARCANE AND OTHERWORLDLY TECHNOLOGY?

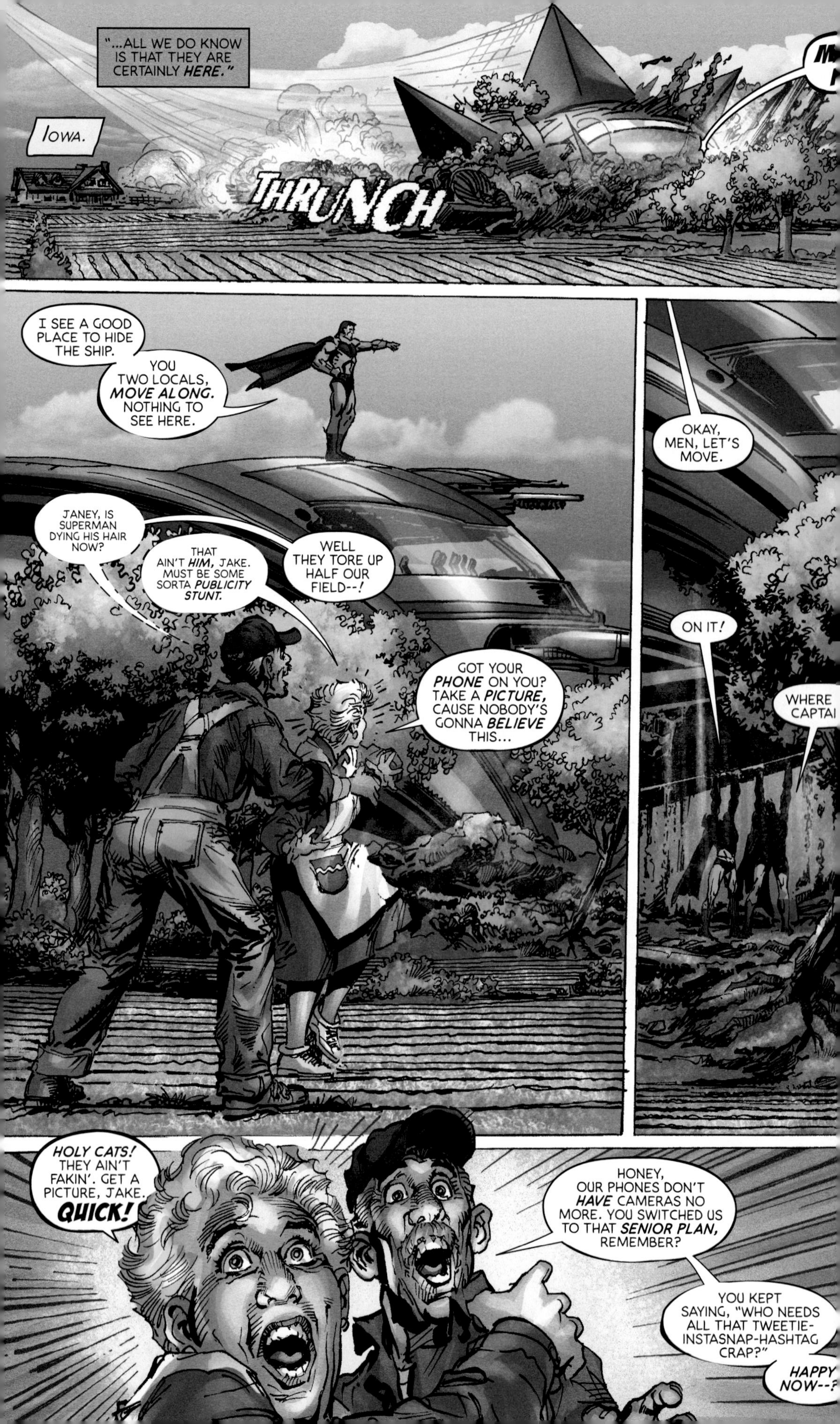

"...ALL WE DO KNOW IS THAT THEY ARE CERTAINLY *HERE.*"
IOWA.
THRUNCH
I SEE A GOOD PLACE TO HIDE THE SHIP.
YOU TWO LOCALS, *MOVE ALONG.* NOTHING TO SEE HERE.
JANEY, IS SUPERMAN DYING HIS HAIR NOW?
THAT AIN'T *HIM,* JAKE. MUST BE SOME SORTA *PUBLICITY STUNT.*
WELL THEY TORE UP HALF OUR FIELD--!
GOT YOUR *PHONE* ON YOU? TAKE A *PICTURE,* CAUSE NOBODY'S GONNA *BELIEVE* THIS...
OKAY, MEN, LET'S MOVE.
ON IT!
HOLY CATS! THEY AIN'T FAKIN'. GET A PICTURE, JAKE. ***QUICK!***
HONEY, OUR PHONES DON'T *HAVE* CAMERAS NO MORE. YOU SWITCHED US TO THAT *SENIOR PLAN,* REMEMBER?
YOU KEPT SAYING, "WHO NEEDS ALL THAT TWEETIE-INSTASNAP-HASHTAG CRAP?"

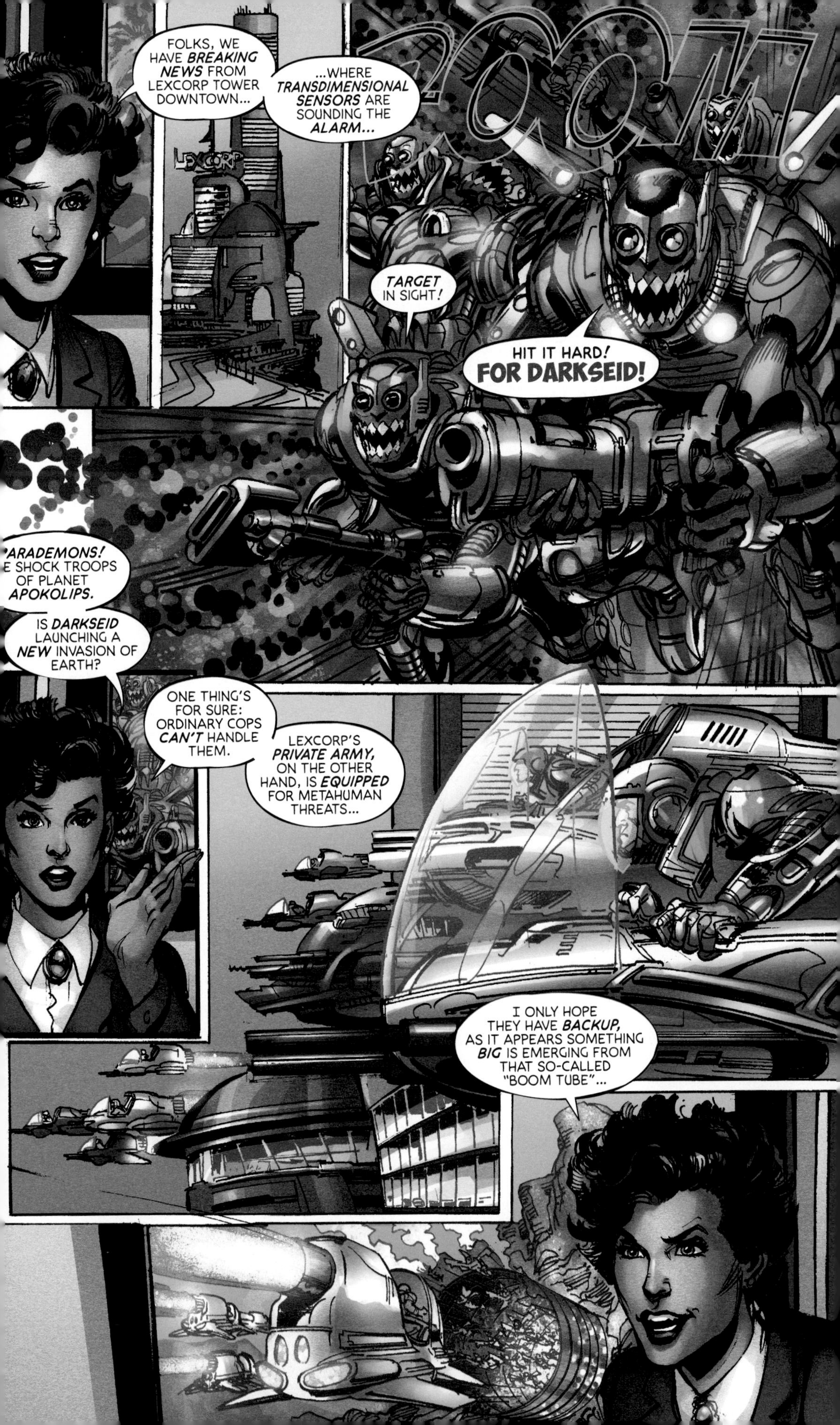
FOLKS, WE HAVE BREAKING NEWS FROM LEXCORP TOWER DOWNTOWN...
LEXCORP
...WHERE TRANSDIMENSIONAL SENSORS ARE SOUNDING THE ALARM...
ZOOM!
TARGET IN SIGHT!
HIT IT HARD! FOR DARKSEID!
'ARADEMONS! E SHOCK TROOPS OF PLANET APOKOLIPS.
IS DARKSEID LAUNCHING A NEW INVASION OF EARTH?
ONE THING'S FOR SURE: ORDINARY COPS CAN'T HANDLE THEM.
LEXCORP'S PRIVATE ARMY, ON THE OTHER HAND, IS EQUIPPED FOR METAHUMAN THREATS...
I ONLY HOPE THEY HAVE BACKUP, AS IT APPEARS SOMETHING BIG IS EMERGING FROM THAT SO-CALLED "BOOM TUBE"...

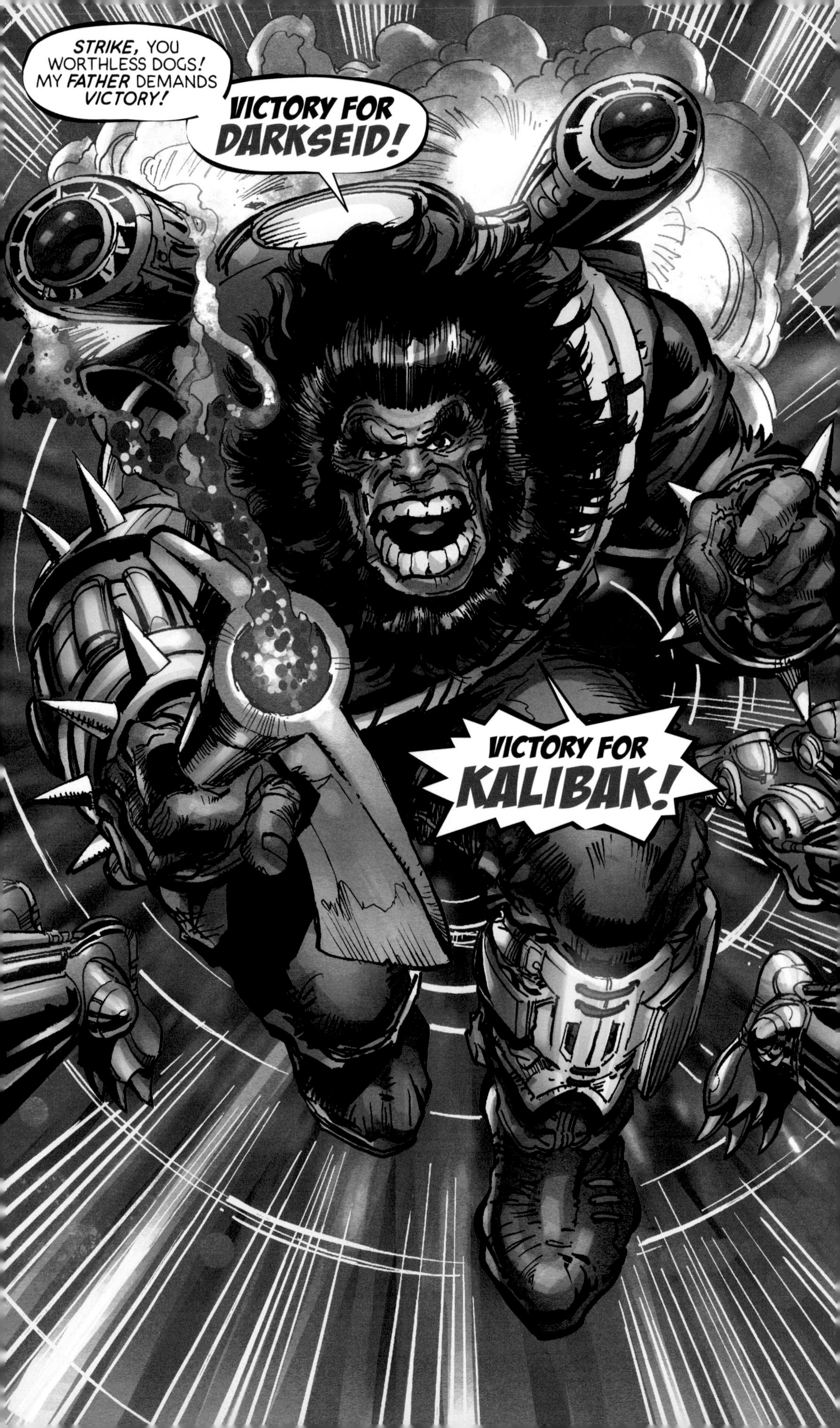
STRIKE, YOU WORTHLESS DOGS! MY FATHER DEMANDS VICTORY!
VICTORY FOR DARKSEID!
VICTORY FOR KALIBAK!

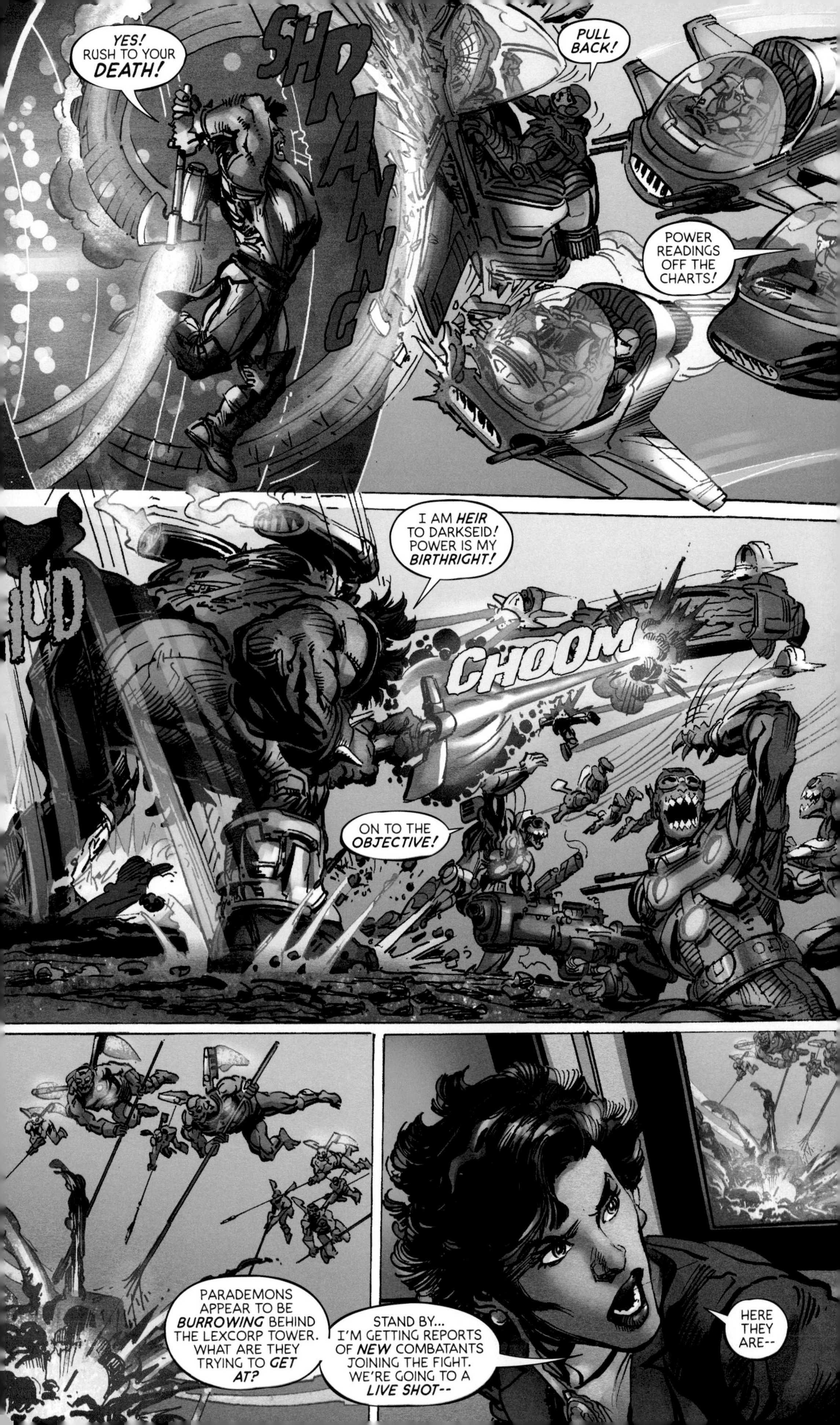

SHRANG
YES! RUSH TO YOUR DEATH!
PULL BACK!
POWER READINGS OFF THE CHARTS!
HUD
I AM HEIR TO DARKSEID! POWER IS MY BIRTHRIGHT!
CHOOM
ON TO THE OBJECTIVE!
PARADEMONS APPEAR TO BE BURROWING BEHIND THE LEXCORP TOWER. WHAT ARE THEY TRYING TO GET AT?
STAND BY... I'M GETTING REPORTS OF NEW COMBATANTS JOINING THE FIGHT. WE'RE GOING TO A LIVE SHOT--
HERE THEY ARE--

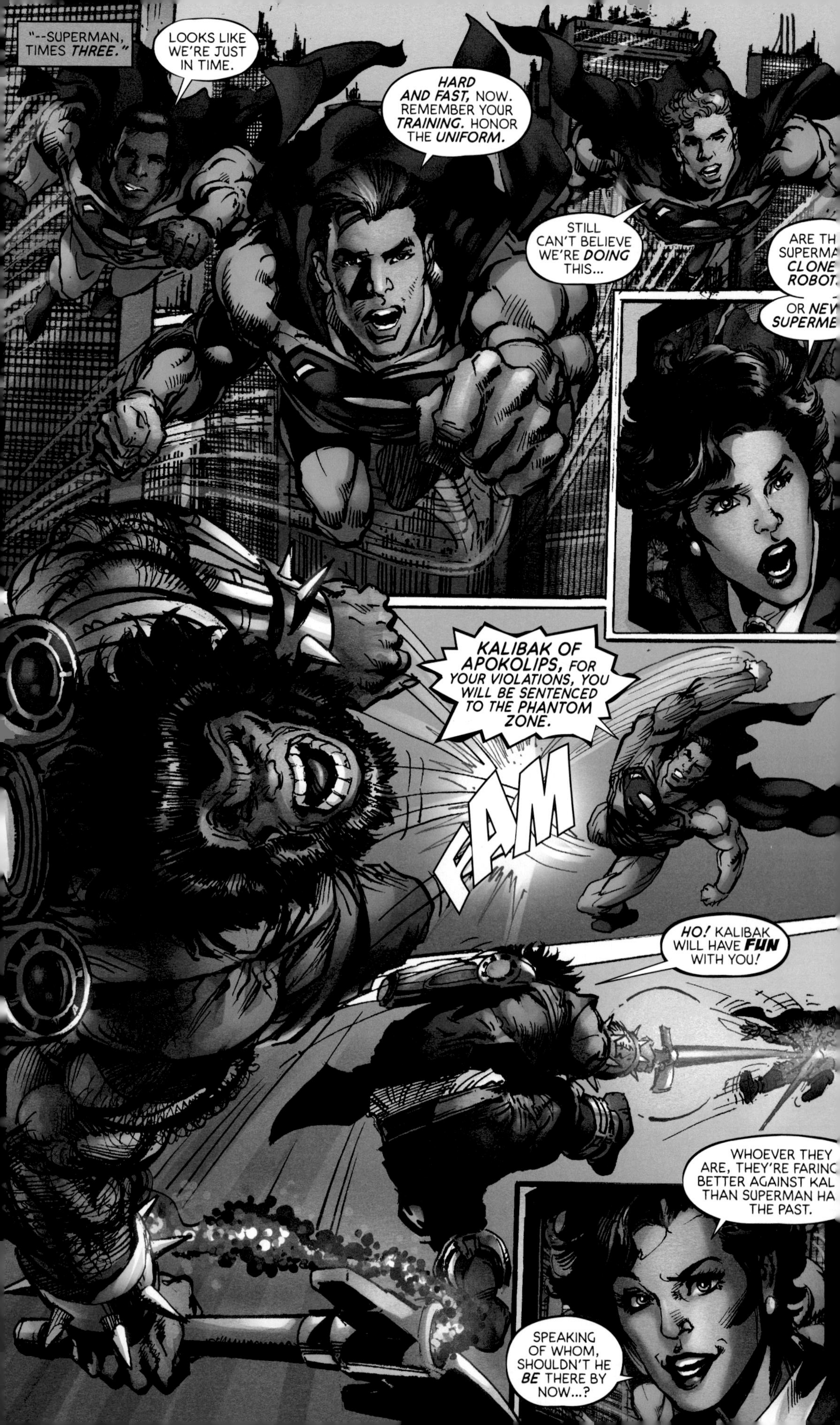
"--SUPERMAN, TIMES *THREE.*"
LOOKS LIKE WE'RE JUST IN TIME.
HARD AND FAST, NOW. REMEMBER YOUR *TRAINING.* HONOR THE *UNIFORM.*
STILL CAN'T BELIEVE WE'RE *DOING* THIS...
ARE TH SUPERMA *CLONE ROBOT*
OR *NEV SUPERME*
KALIBAK OF APOKOLIPS, FOR *YOUR VIOLATIONS, YOU WILL BE SENTENCED TO THE PHANTOM ZONE.*
FAM
HO! KALIBAK WILL HAVE ***FUN*** WITH YOU!
WHOEVER THEY ARE, THEY'RE FARINC BETTER AGAINST KAL THAN SUPERMAN HA THE PAST.
SPEAKING OF WHOM, SHOULDN'T HE *BE* THERE BY NOW...?

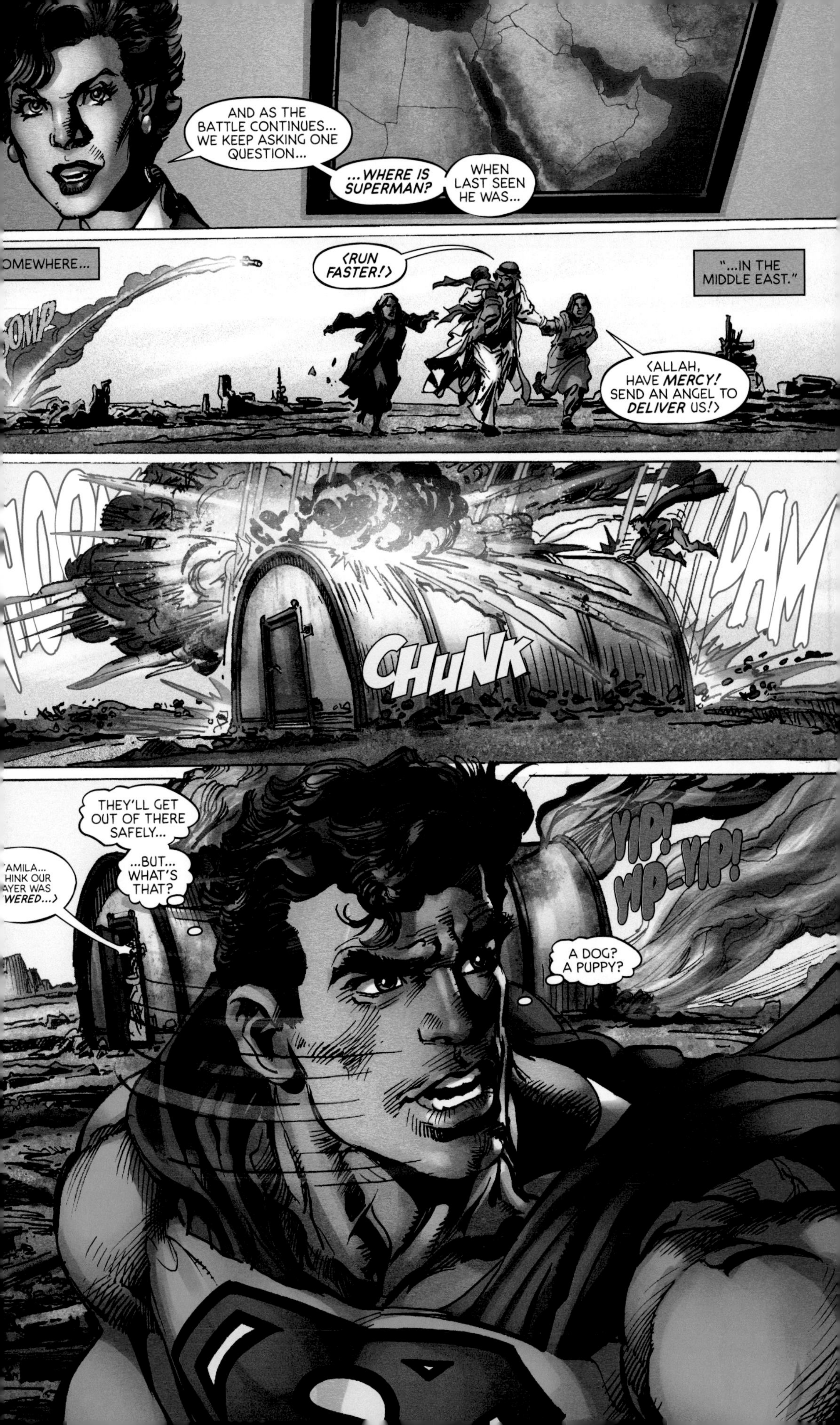
AND AS THE BATTLE CONTINUES... WE KEEP ASKING ONE QUESTION...
...WHERE IS SUPERMAN?
WHEN LAST SEEN HE WAS...
OMEWHERE...
<RUN FASTER!>
"...IN THE MIDDLE EAST."
OOMP
<ALLAH, HAVE MERCY! SEND AN ANGEL TO DELIVER US!>
DAM
CHUNK
THEY'LL GET OUT OF THERE SAFELY...
...BUT... WHAT'S THAT?
AMILA... HINK OUR AYER WAS WERED...>
YIP! YIP-YIP!
A DOG? A PUPPY?

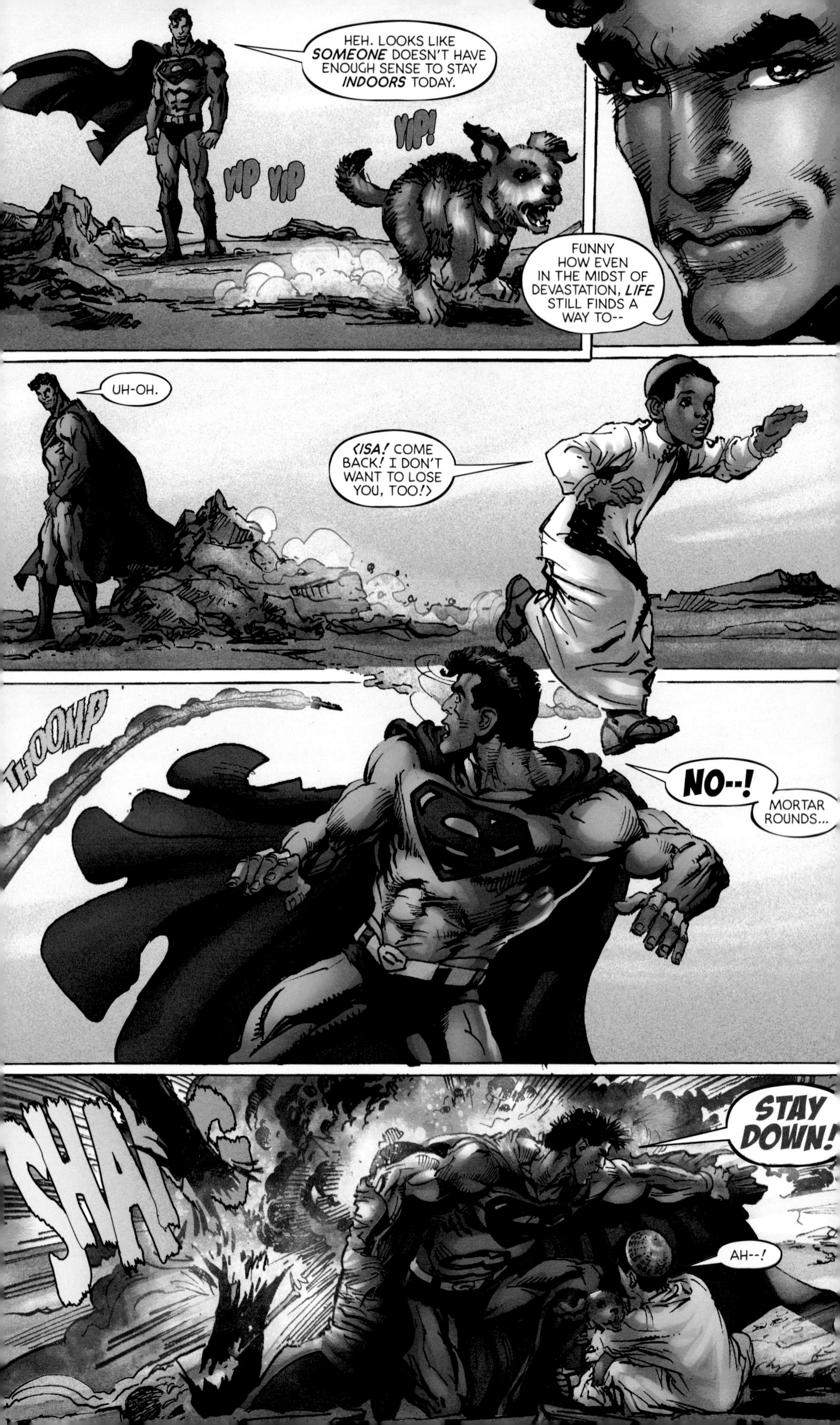
HEH. LOOKS LIKE SOMEONE DOESN'T HAVE ENOUGH SENSE TO STAY INDOORS TODAY.
YIP YIP
YIP!
FUNNY HOW EVEN IN THE MIDST OF DEVASTATION, LIFE STILL FINDS A WAY TO--
UH-OH.
<ISA! COME BACK! I DON'T WANT TO LOSE YOU, TOO!>
THOOMP
NO--!
MORTAR ROUNDS...
STAY DOWN!
AH--!

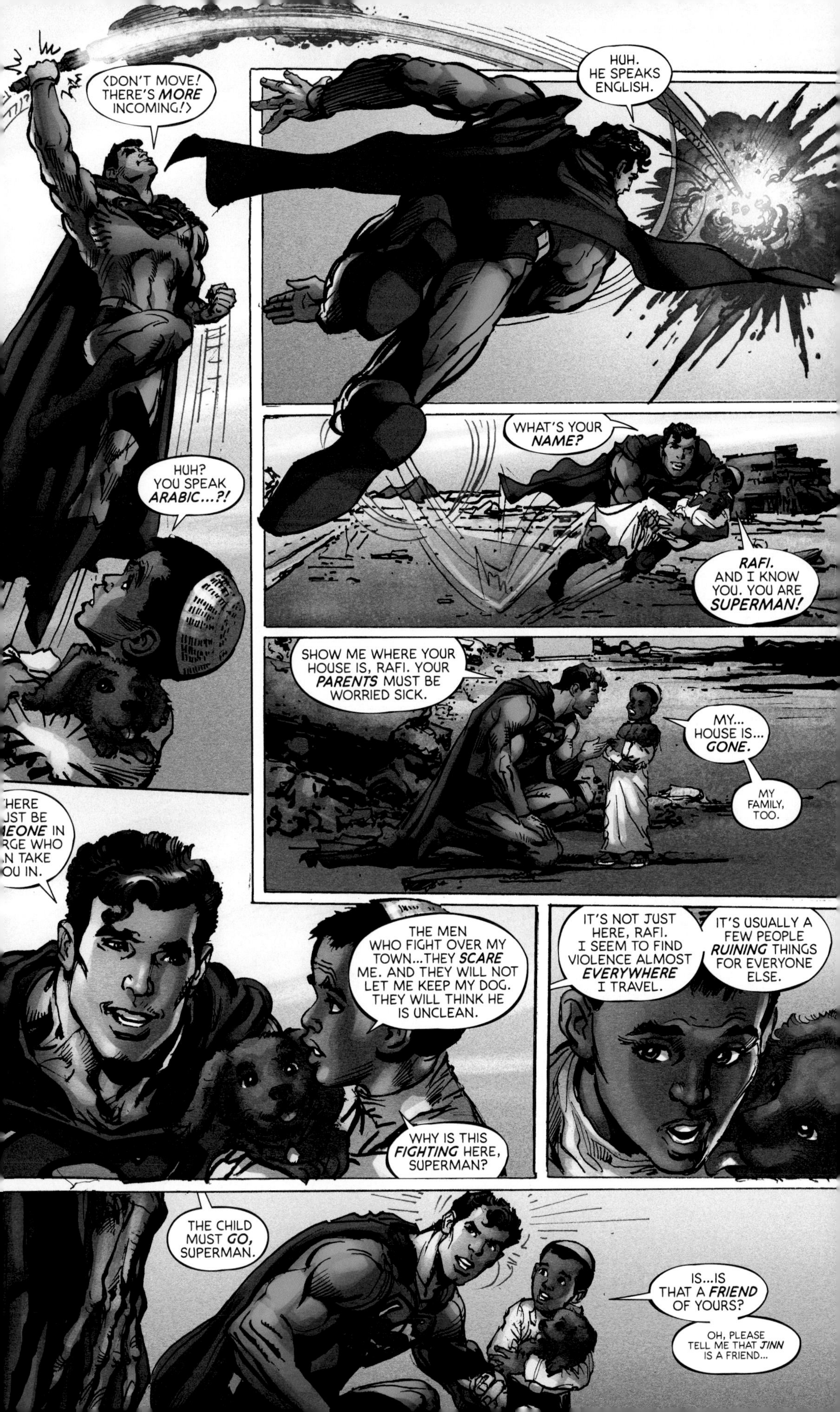

‹DON'T MOVE! THERE'S MORE INCOMING!›
HUH. HE SPEAKS ENGLISH.
HUH? YOU SPEAK ARABIC...?!
WHAT'S YOUR NAME?
RAFI. AND I KNOW YOU. YOU ARE SUPERMAN!
SHOW ME WHERE YOUR HOUSE IS, RAFI. YOUR PARENTS MUST BE WORRIED SICK.
MY... HOUSE IS... GONE.
MY FAMILY, TOO.
HERE UST BE EONE IN RGE WHO N TAKE OU IN.
THE MEN WHO FIGHT OVER MY TOWN...THEY SCARE ME. AND THEY WILL NOT LET ME KEEP MY DOG. THEY WILL THINK HE IS UNCLEAN.
WHY IS THIS FIGHTING HERE, SUPERMAN?
IT'S NOT JUST HERE, RAFI. I SEEM TO FIND VIOLENCE ALMOST EVERYWHERE I TRAVEL.
IT'S USUALLY A FEW PEOPLE RUINING THINGS FOR EVERYONE ELSE.
THE CHILD MUST GO, SUPERMAN.
IS...IS THAT A FRIEND OF YOURS?
OH, PLEASE TELL ME THAT JINN IS A FRIEND...

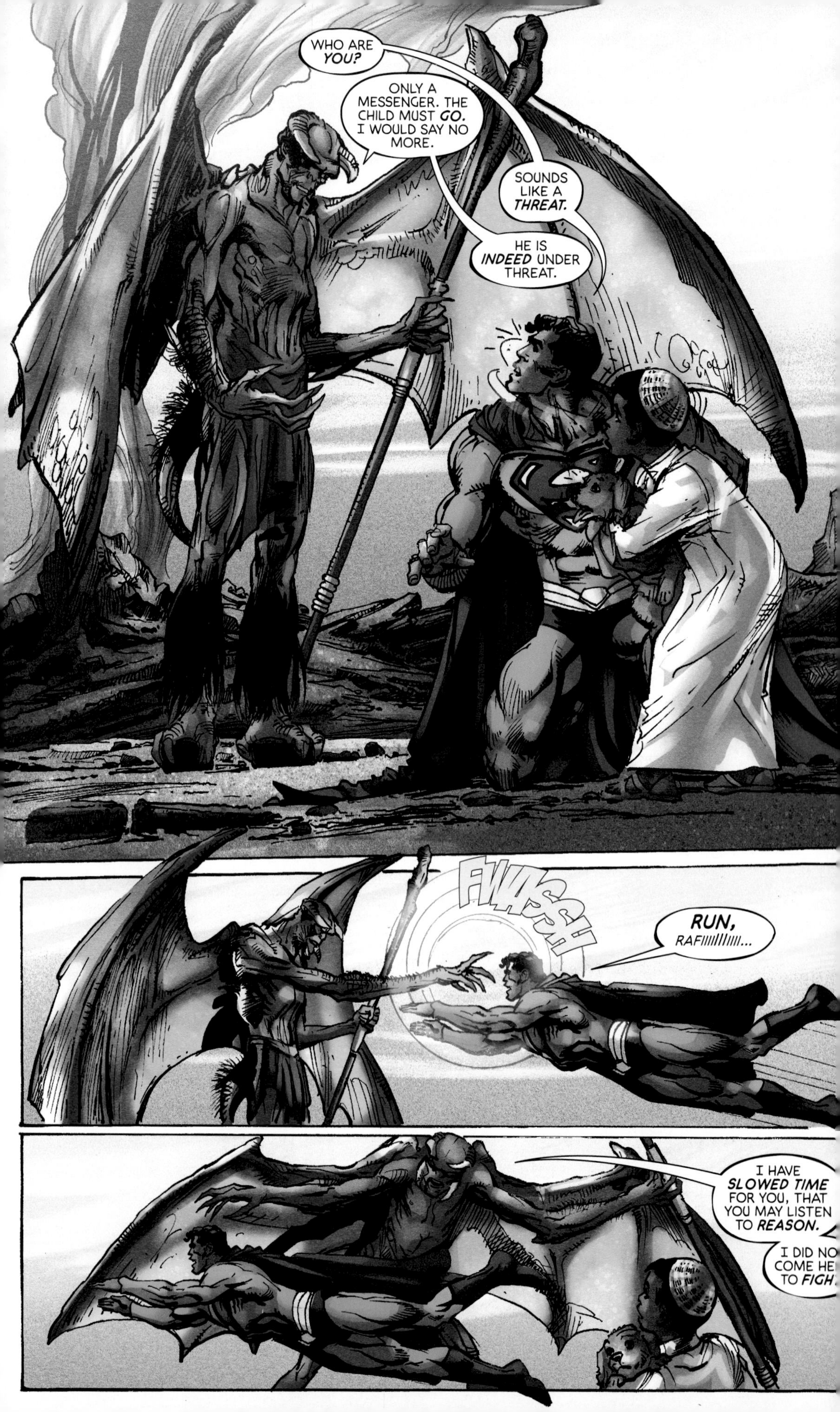
WHO ARE YOU?
ONLY A MESSENGER. THE CHILD MUST GO. I WOULD SAY NO MORE.
SOUNDS LIKE A THREAT.
HE IS INDEED UNDER THREAT.
FWASSH
RUN, RAFIIIIIIIIII...
I HAVE SLOWED TIME FOR YOU, THAT YOU MAY LISTEN TO REASON.
I DID NO COME HE TO FIGH

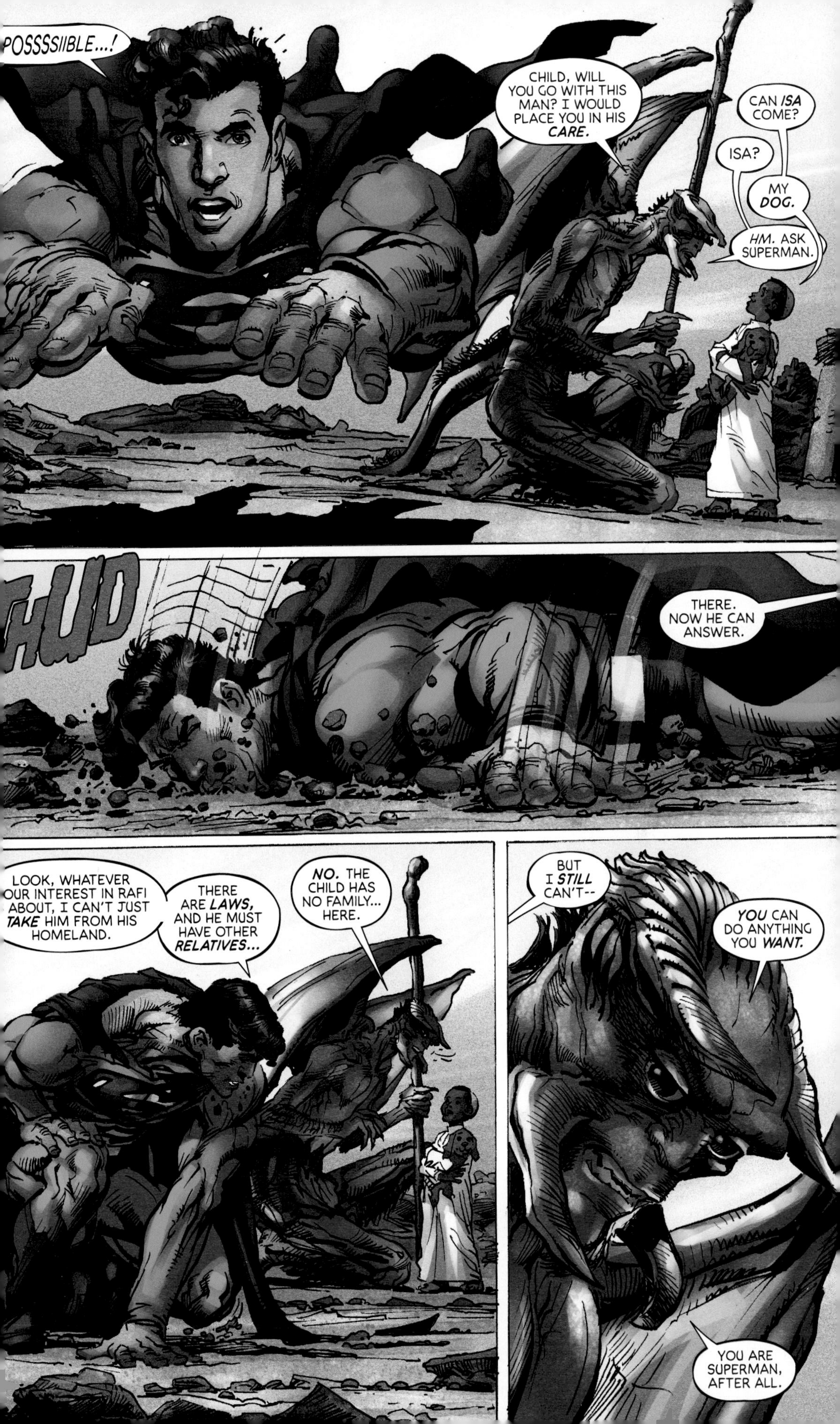
POSSSSIIBLE...!
CHILD, WILL YOU GO WITH THIS MAN? I WOULD PLACE YOU IN HIS CARE.
CAN ISA COME?
ISA?
MY DOG.
HM. ASK SUPERMAN.
THUD
THERE. NOW HE CAN ANSWER.
LOOK, WHATEVER OUR INTEREST IN RAFI ABOUT, I CAN'T JUST TAKE HIM FROM HIS HOMELAND.
THERE ARE LAWS, AND HE MUST HAVE OTHER RELATIVES...
NO. THE CHILD HAS NO FAMILY... HERE.
BUT I STILL CAN'T--
YOU CAN DO ANYTHING YOU WANT.
YOU ARE SUPERMAN, AFTER ALL.

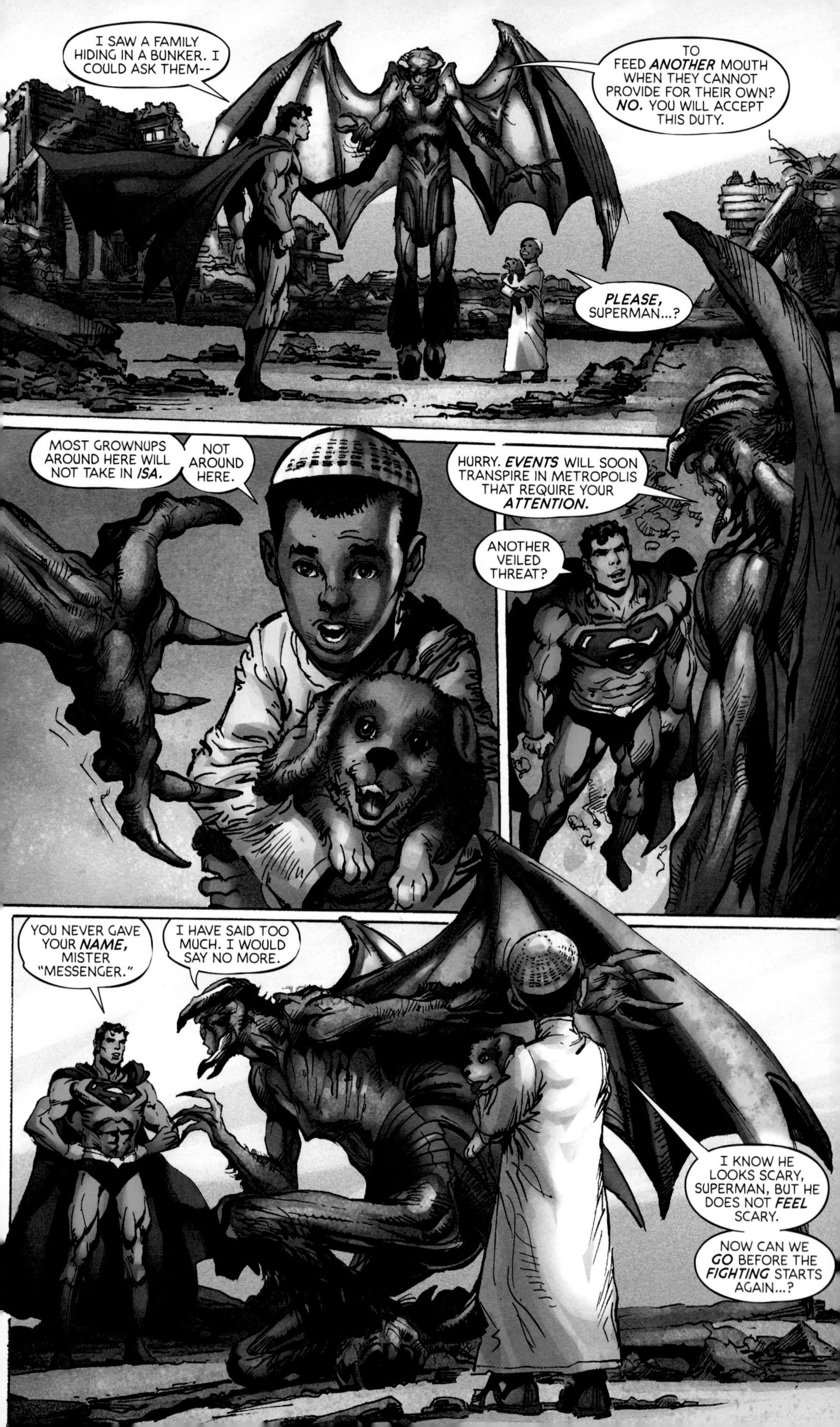

I SAW A FAMILY HIDING IN A BUNKER. I COULD ASK THEM--
TO FEED ANOTHER MOUTH WHEN THEY CANNOT PROVIDE FOR THEIR OWN? NO. YOU WILL ACCEPT THIS DUTY.
PLEASE, SUPERMAN...?
MOST GROWNUPS AROUND HERE WILL NOT TAKE IN ISA.
NOT AROUND HERE.
HURRY. EVENTS WILL SOON TRANSPIRE IN METROPOLIS THAT REQUIRE YOUR ATTENTION.
ANOTHER VEILED THREAT?
YOU NEVER GAVE YOUR NAME, MISTER "MESSENGER."
I HAVE SAID TOO MUCH. I WOULD SAY NO MORE.
I KNOW HE LOOKS SCARY, SUPERMAN, BUT HE DOES NOT FEEL SCARY.
NOW CAN WE GO BEFORE THE FIGHTING STARTS AGAIN...?

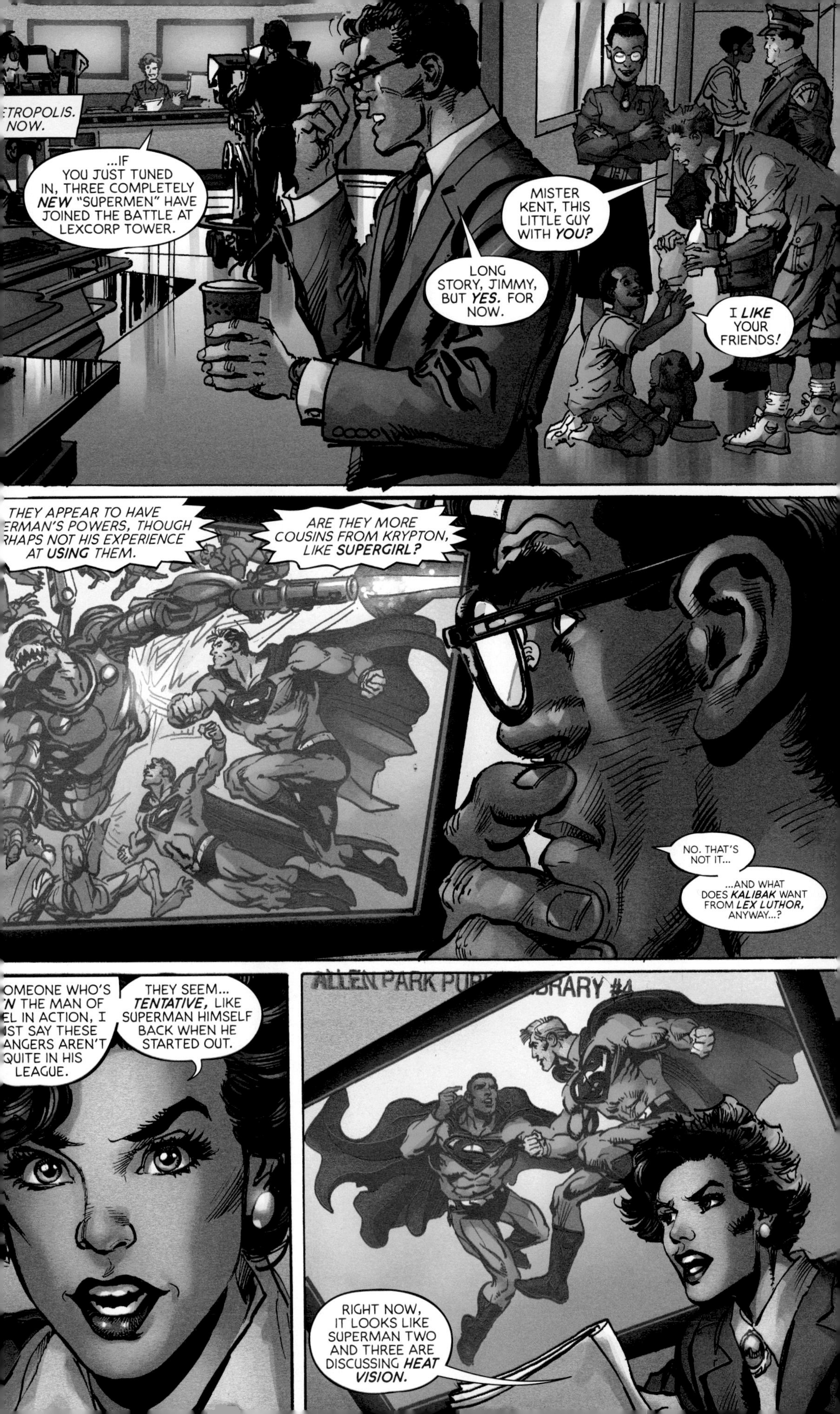
ETROPOLIS. NOW.
...IF YOU JUST TUNED IN, THREE COMPLETELY *NEW* "SUPERMEN" HAVE JOINED THE BATTLE AT LEXCORP TOWER.
MISTER KENT, THIS LITTLE GUY WITH *YOU?*
LONG STORY, JIMMY, BUT *YES.* FOR NOW.
I *LIKE* YOUR FRIENDS!
THEY APPEAR TO HAVE ERMAN'S POWERS, THOUGH RHAPS NOT HIS EXPERIENCE AT *USING* THEM.
ARE THEY MORE COUSINS FROM KRYPTON, LIKE *SUPERGIRL?*
NO. THAT'S NOT IT...
...AND WHAT DOES *KALIBAK* WANT FROM *LEX LUTHOR,* ANYWAY...?
OMEONE WHO'S N THE MAN OF EL IN ACTION, I IST SAY THESE ANGERS AREN'T QUITE IN HIS LEAGUE.
THEY SEEM... *TENTATIVE,* LIKE SUPERMAN HIMSELF BACK WHEN HE STARTED OUT.
ALLEN PARK PUB BRARY #4
RIGHT NOW, IT LOOKS LIKE SUPERMAN TWO AND THREE ARE DISCUSSING *HEAT VISION.*

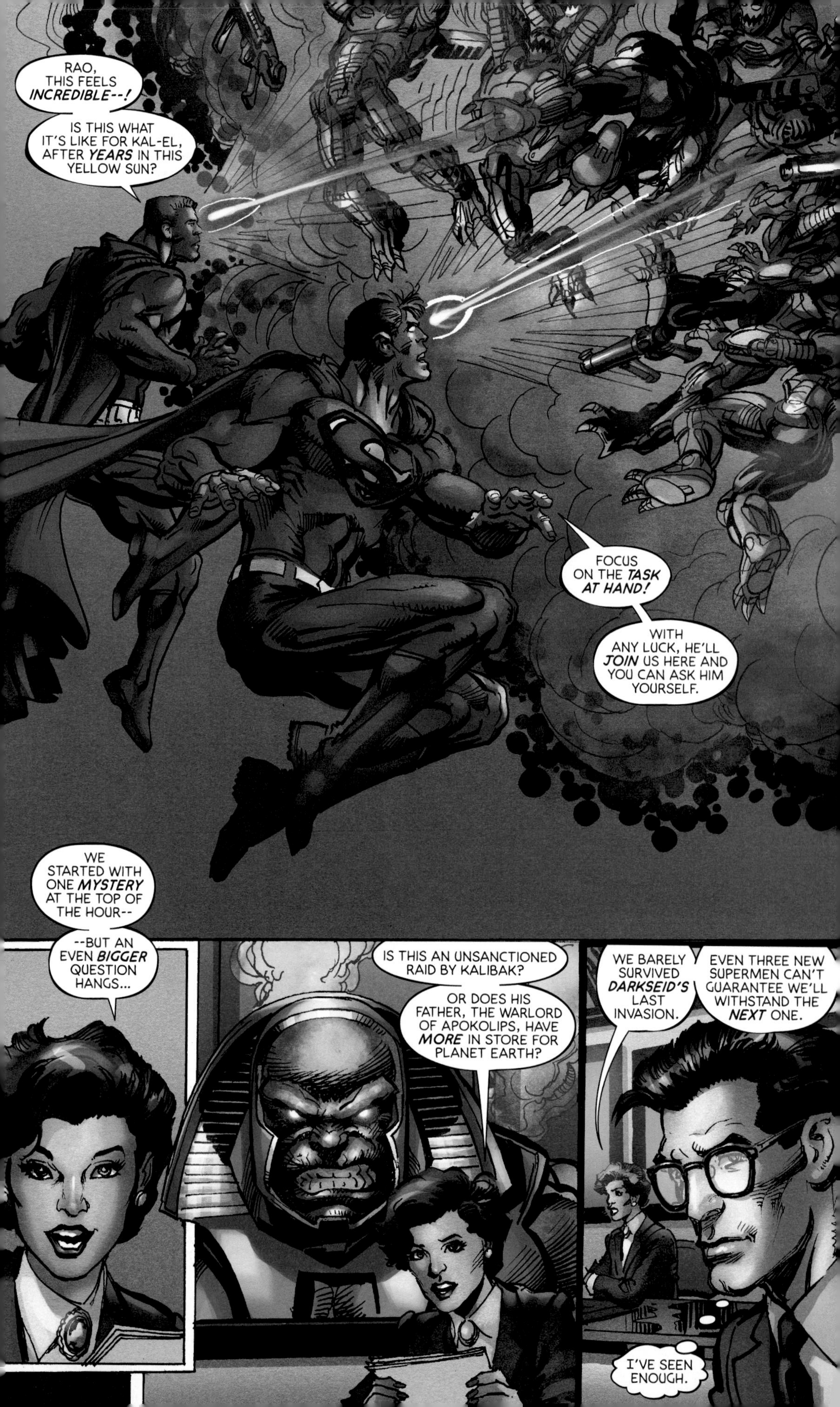
RAO, THIS FEELS INCREDIBLE--!
IS THIS WHAT IT'S LIKE FOR KAL-EL, AFTER YEARS IN THIS YELLOW SUN?
FOCUS ON THE TASK AT HAND!
WITH ANY LUCK, HE'LL JOIN US HERE AND YOU CAN ASK HIM YOURSELF.
WE STARTED WITH ONE MYSTERY AT THE TOP OF THE HOUR--
--BUT AN EVEN BIGGER QUESTION HANGS...
IS THIS AN UNSANCTIONED RAID BY KALIBAK?
OR DOES HIS FATHER, THE WARLORD OF APOKOLIPS, HAVE MORE IN STORE FOR PLANET EARTH?
WE BARELY SURVIVED DARKSEID'S LAST INVASION.
EVEN THREE NEW SUPERMEN CAN'T GUARANTEE WE'LL WITHSTAND THE NEXT ONE.
I'VE SEEN ENOUGH.

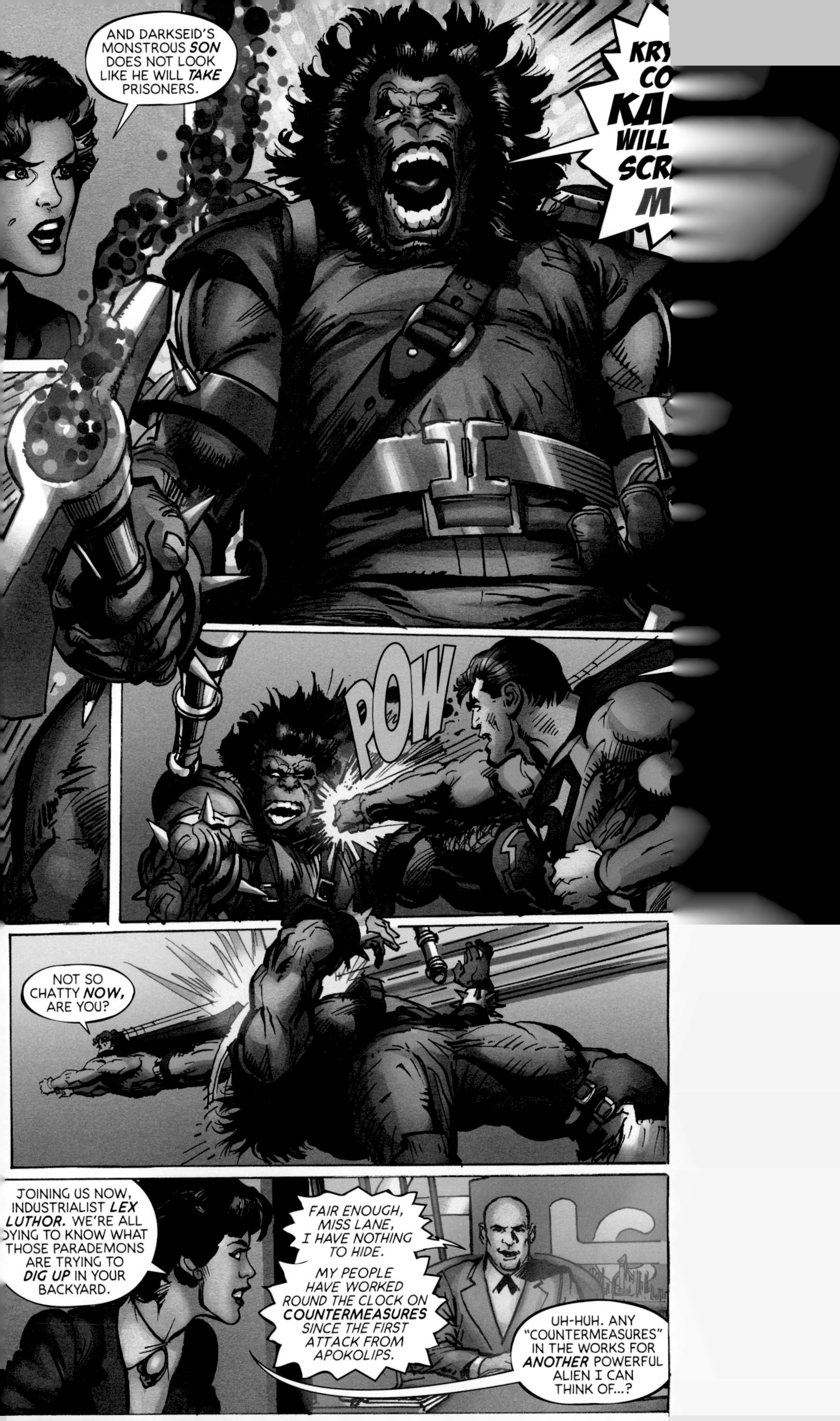
AND DARKSEID'S MONSTROUS *SON* DOES NOT LOOK LIKE HE WILL *TAKE* PRISONERS.
POW
NOT SO CHATTY *NOW,* ARE YOU?
JOINING US NOW, INDUSTRIALIST *LEX LUTHOR.* WE'RE ALL DYING TO KNOW WHAT THOSE PARADEMONS ARE TRYING TO *DIG UP* IN YOUR BACKYARD.
FAIR ENOUGH, MISS LANE, I HAVE NOTHING TO HIDE.
MY PEOPLE HAVE WORKED ROUND THE CLOCK ON ***COUNTERMEASURES*** *SINCE THE FIRST ATTACK FROM APOKOLIPS.*
UH-HUH. ANY "COUNTERMEASURES" IN THE WORKS FOR *ANOTHER* POWERFUL ALIEN I CAN THINK OF...?

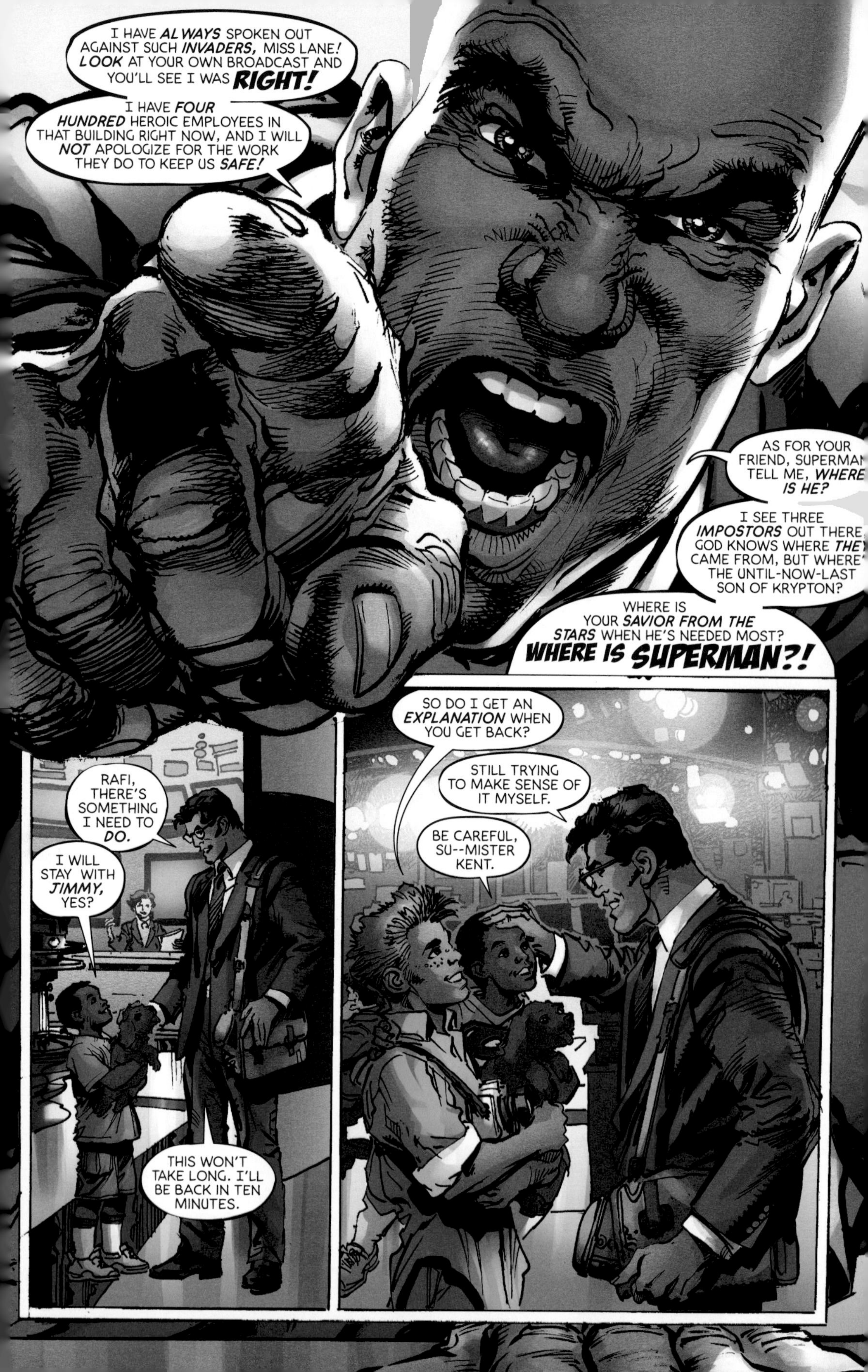
I HAVE ALWAYS SPOKEN OUT AGAINST SUCH INVADERS, MISS LANE! LOOK AT YOUR OWN BROADCAST AND YOU'LL SEE I WAS RIGHT!
I HAVE FOUR HUNDRED HEROIC EMPLOYEES IN THAT BUILDING RIGHT NOW, AND I WILL NOT APOLOGIZE FOR THE WORK THEY DO TO KEEP US SAFE!
AS FOR YOUR FRIEND, SUPERMAN TELL ME, WHERE IS HE?
I SEE THREE IMPOSTORS OUT THERE GOD KNOWS WHERE THEY CAME FROM, BUT WHERE THE UNTIL-NOW-LAST SON OF KRYPTON?
WHERE IS YOUR SAVIOR FROM THE STARS WHEN HE'S NEEDED MOST? WHERE IS SUPERMAN?!
RAFI, THERE'S SOMETHING I NEED TO DO.
I WILL STAY WITH JIMMY, YES?
THIS WON'T TAKE LONG. I'LL BE BACK IN TEN MINUTES.
SO DO I GET AN EXPLANATION WHEN YOU GET BACK?
STILL TRYING TO MAKE SENSE OF IT MYSELF.
BE CAREFUL, SU--MISTER KENT.

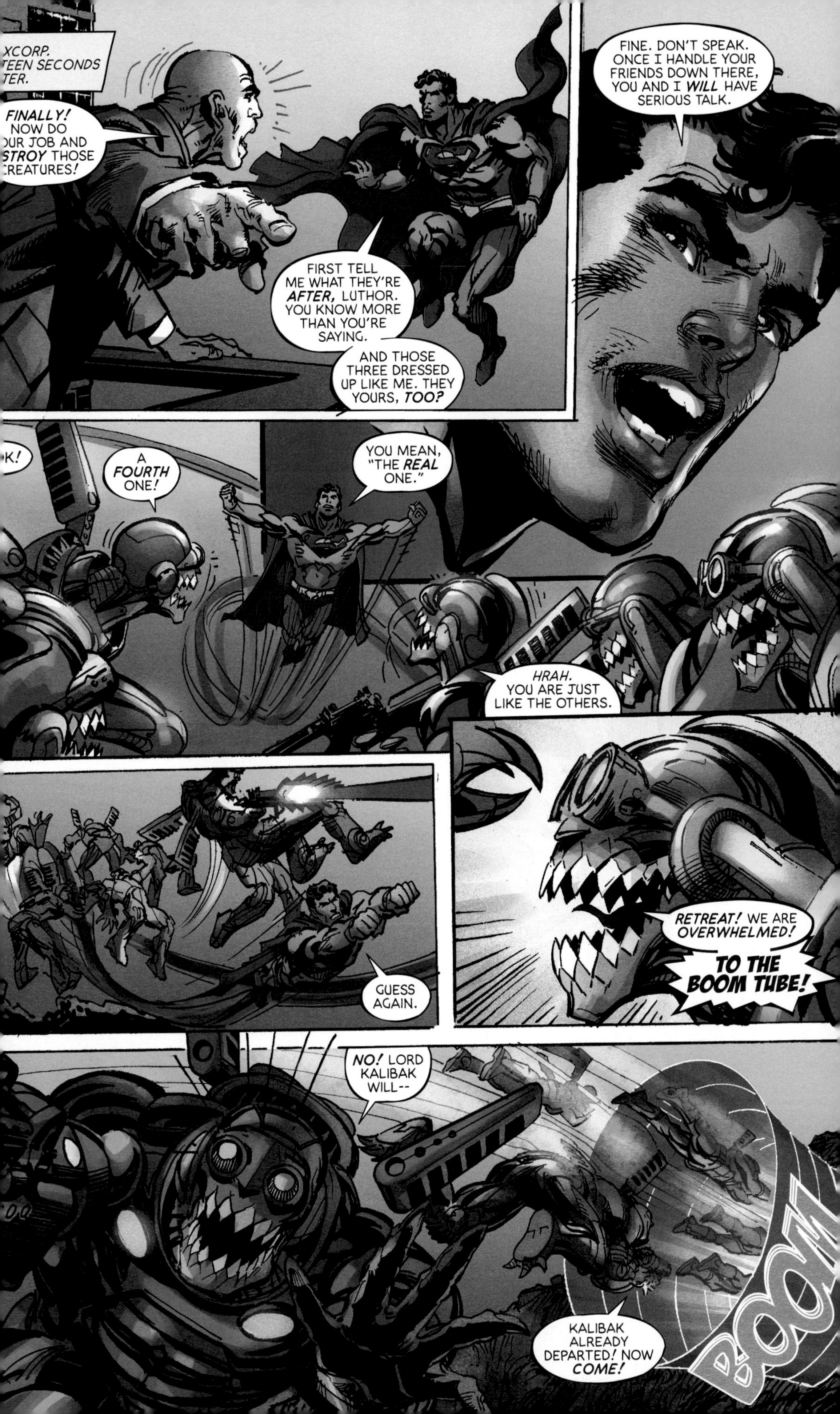
XCORP.
TEEN SECONDS
TER.
FINALLY! NOW DO
UR JOB AND
STROY THOSE
CREATURES!
FIRST TELL ME WHAT THEY'RE AFTER, LUTHOR. YOU KNOW MORE THAN YOU'RE SAYING.
AND THOSE THREE DRESSED UP LIKE ME. THEY YOURS, TOO?
FINE. DON'T SPEAK. ONCE I HANDLE YOUR FRIENDS DOWN THERE, YOU AND I WILL HAVE SERIOUS TALK.
K!
A FOURTH ONE!
YOU MEAN, "THE REAL ONE."
HRAH. YOU ARE JUST LIKE THE OTHERS.
GUESS AGAIN.
RETREAT! WE ARE OVERWHELMED!
TO THE BOOM TUBE!
NO! LORD KALIBAK WILL--
KALIBAK ALREADY DEPARTED! NOW COME!
BOOM

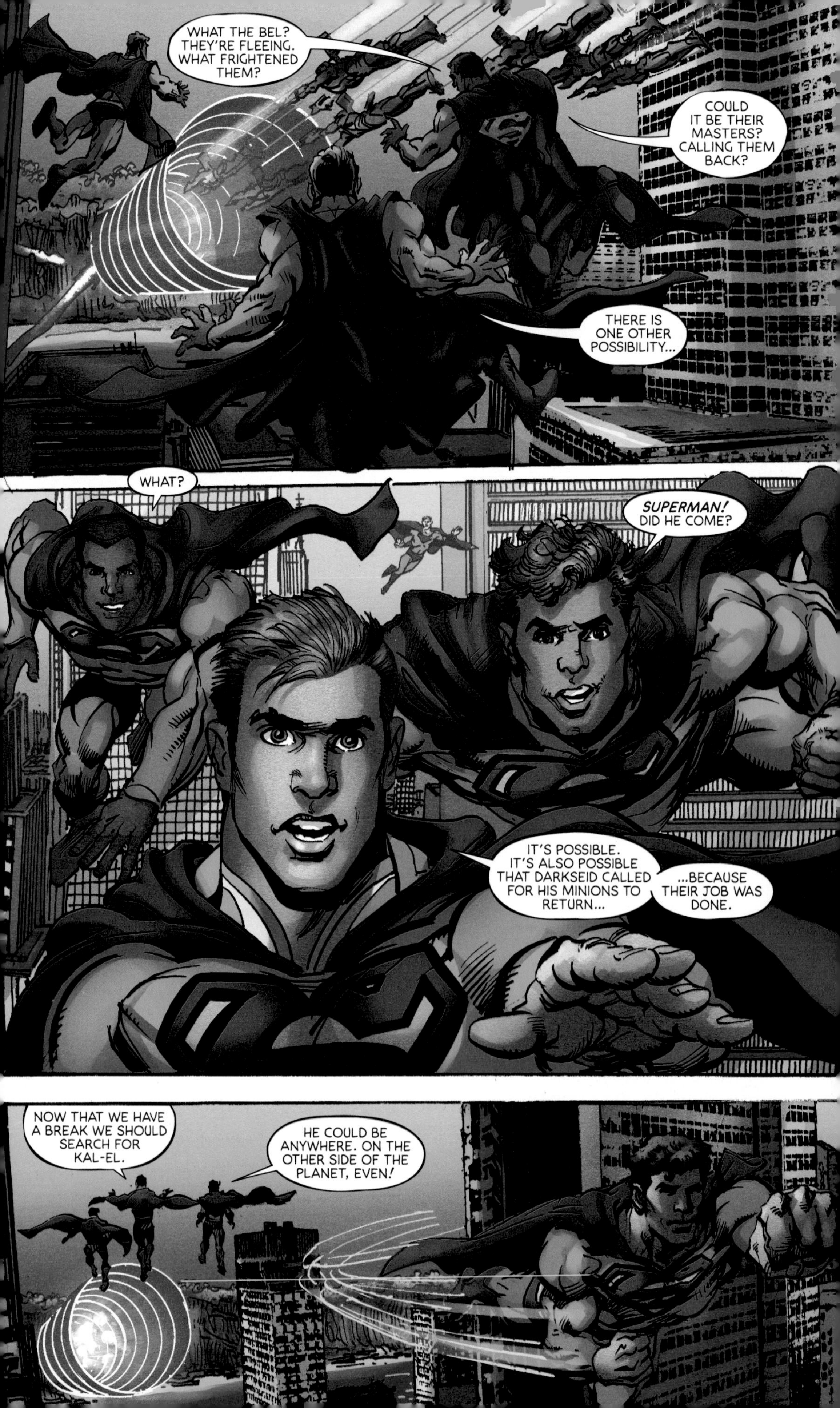
WHAT THE BEL? THEY'RE FLEEING. WHAT FRIGHTENED THEM?
COULD IT BE THEIR MASTERS? CALLING THEM BACK?
THERE IS ONE OTHER POSSIBILITY...
WHAT?
SUPERMAN! DID HE COME?
IT'S POSSIBLE. IT'S ALSO POSSIBLE THAT DARKSEID CALLED FOR HIS MINIONS TO RETURN...
...BECAUSE THEIR JOB WAS DONE.
NOW THAT WE HAVE A BREAK WE SHOULD SEARCH FOR KAL-EL.
HE COULD BE ANYWHERE. ON THE OTHER SIDE OF THE PLANET, EVEN!

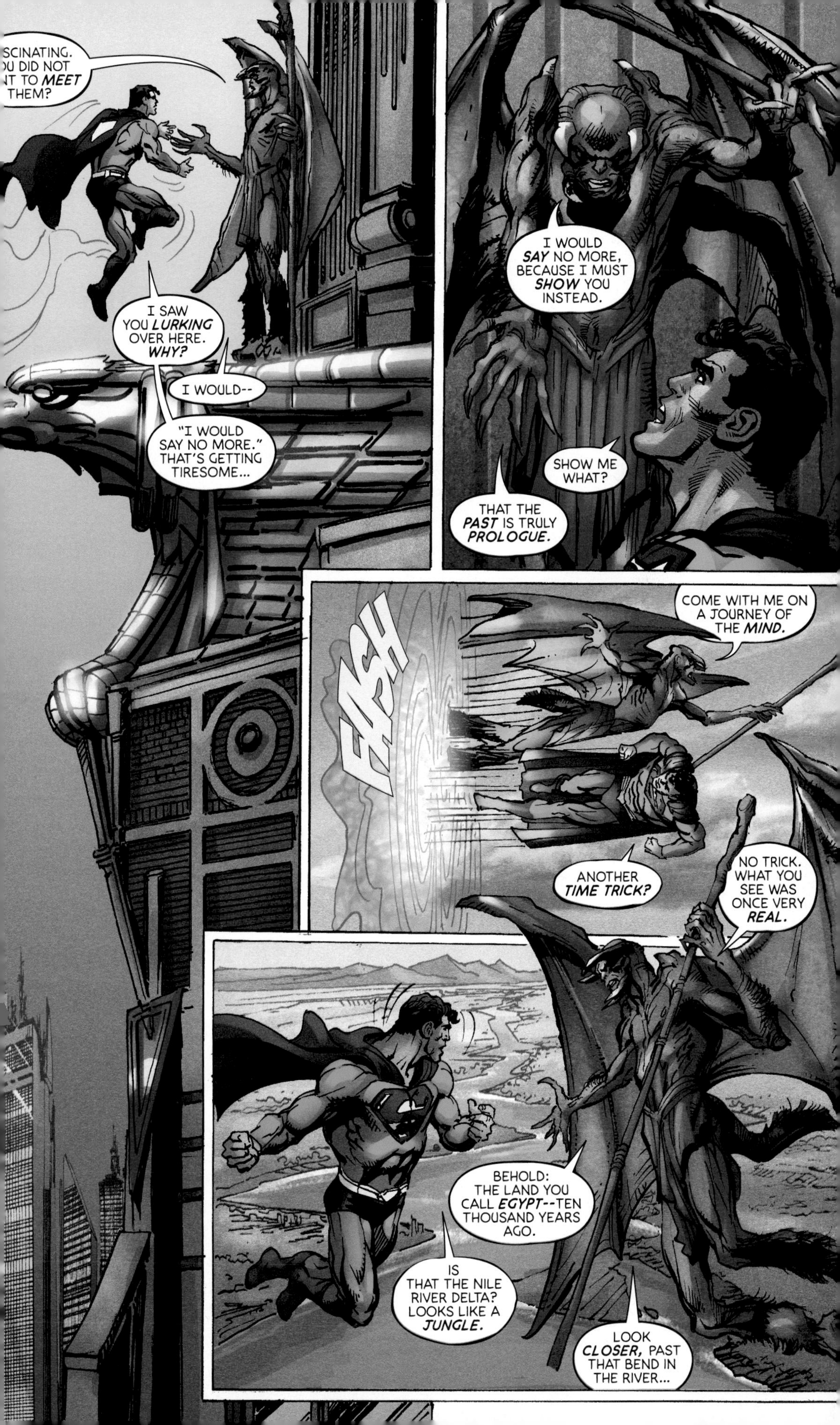
SCINATING.
OU DID NOT
IT TO MEET
THEM?
I SAW YOU LURKING OVER HERE. WHY?
I WOULD--
"I WOULD SAY NO MORE." THAT'S GETTING TIRESOME...
I WOULD SAY NO MORE, BECAUSE I MUST SHOW YOU INSTEAD.
SHOW ME WHAT?
THAT THE PAST IS TRULY PROLOGUE.
FASH
COME WITH ME ON A JOURNEY OF THE MIND.
ANOTHER TIME TRICK?
NO TRICK. WHAT YOU SEE WAS ONCE VERY REAL.
BEHOLD: THE LAND YOU CALL EGYPT--TEN THOUSAND YEARS AGO.
IS THAT THE NILE RIVER DELTA? LOOKS LIKE A JUNGLE.
LOOK CLOSER, PAST THAT BEND IN THE RIVER...

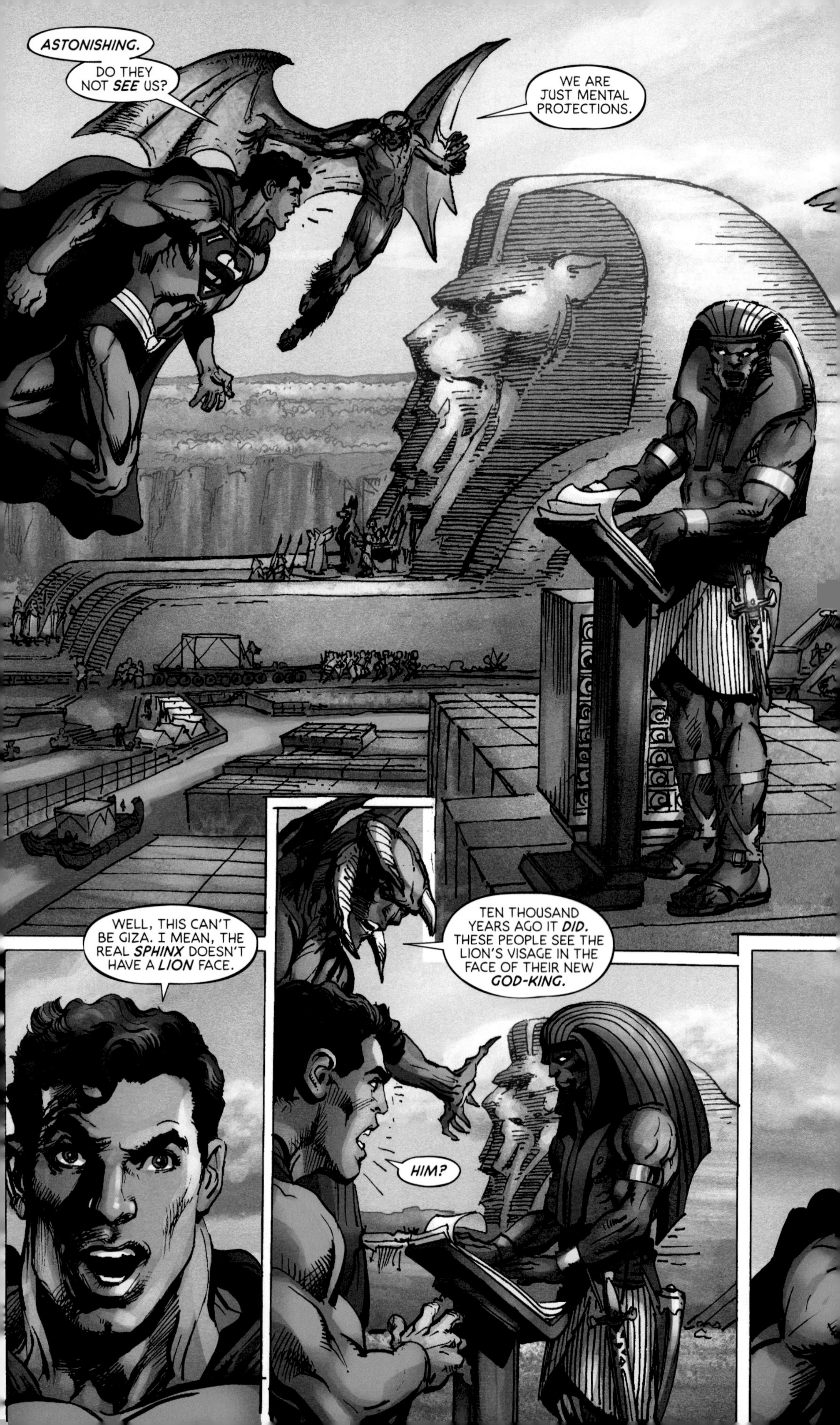

ASTONISHING.
DO THEY NOT SEE US?
WE ARE JUST MENTAL PROJECTIONS.
WELL, THIS CAN'T BE GIZA. I MEAN, THE REAL SPHINX DOESN'T HAVE A LION FACE.
TEN THOUSAND YEARS AGO IT DID. THESE PEOPLE SEE THE LION'S VISAGE IN THE FACE OF THEIR NEW GOD-KING.
HIM?

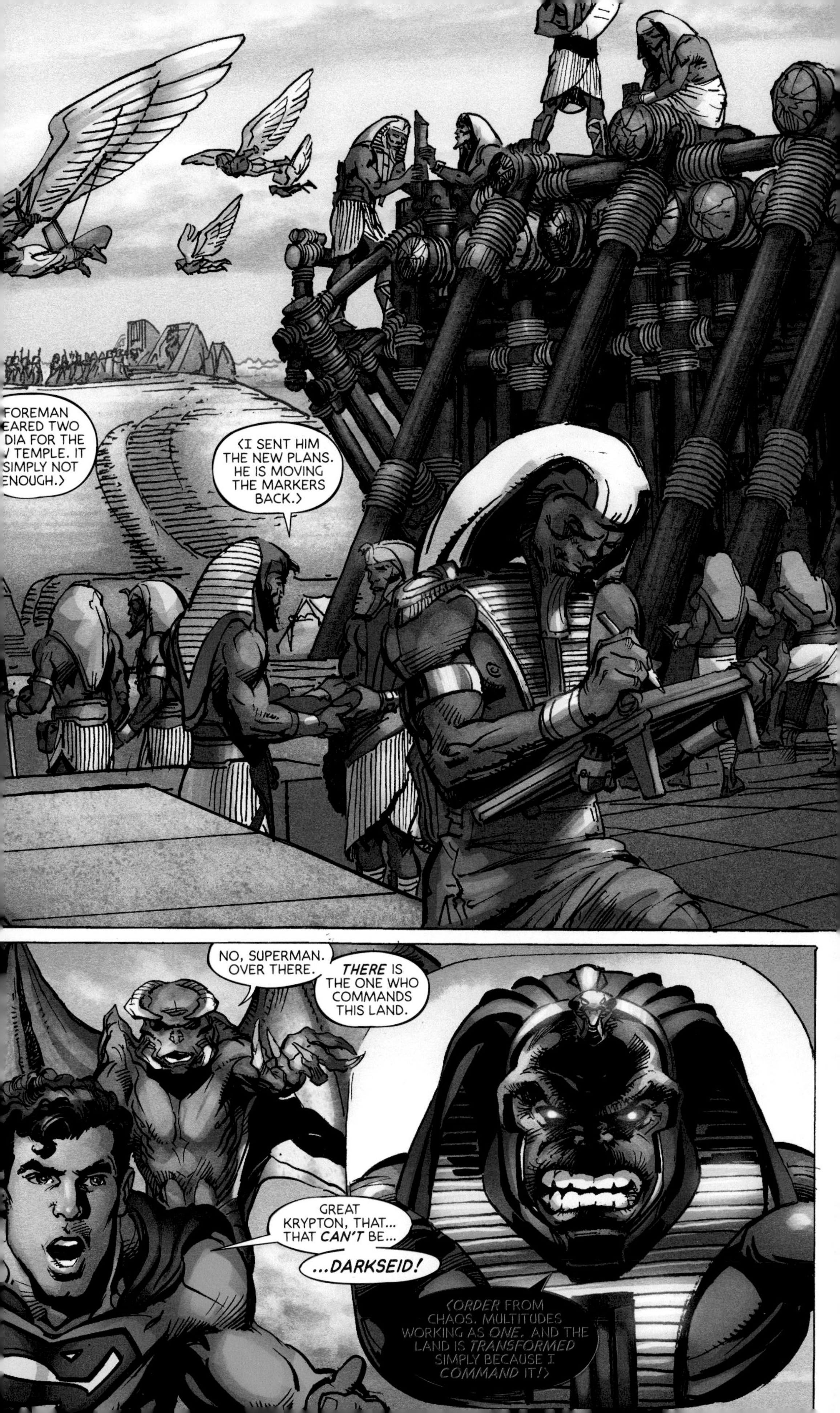
FOREMAN EARED TWO DIA FOR THE TEMPLE. IT SIMPLY NOT ENOUGH.>
<I SENT HIM THE NEW PLANS. HE IS MOVING THE MARKERS BACK.>
NO, SUPERMAN. OVER THERE.
THERE IS THE ONE WHO COMMANDS THIS LAND.
GREAT KRYPTON, THAT... THAT *CAN'T* BE...
...*DARKSEID!*
<*ORDER* FROM CHAOS. MULTITUDES WORKING AS *ONE*. AND THE LAND IS *TRANSFORMED* SIMPLY BECAUSE I *COMMAND IT!*>

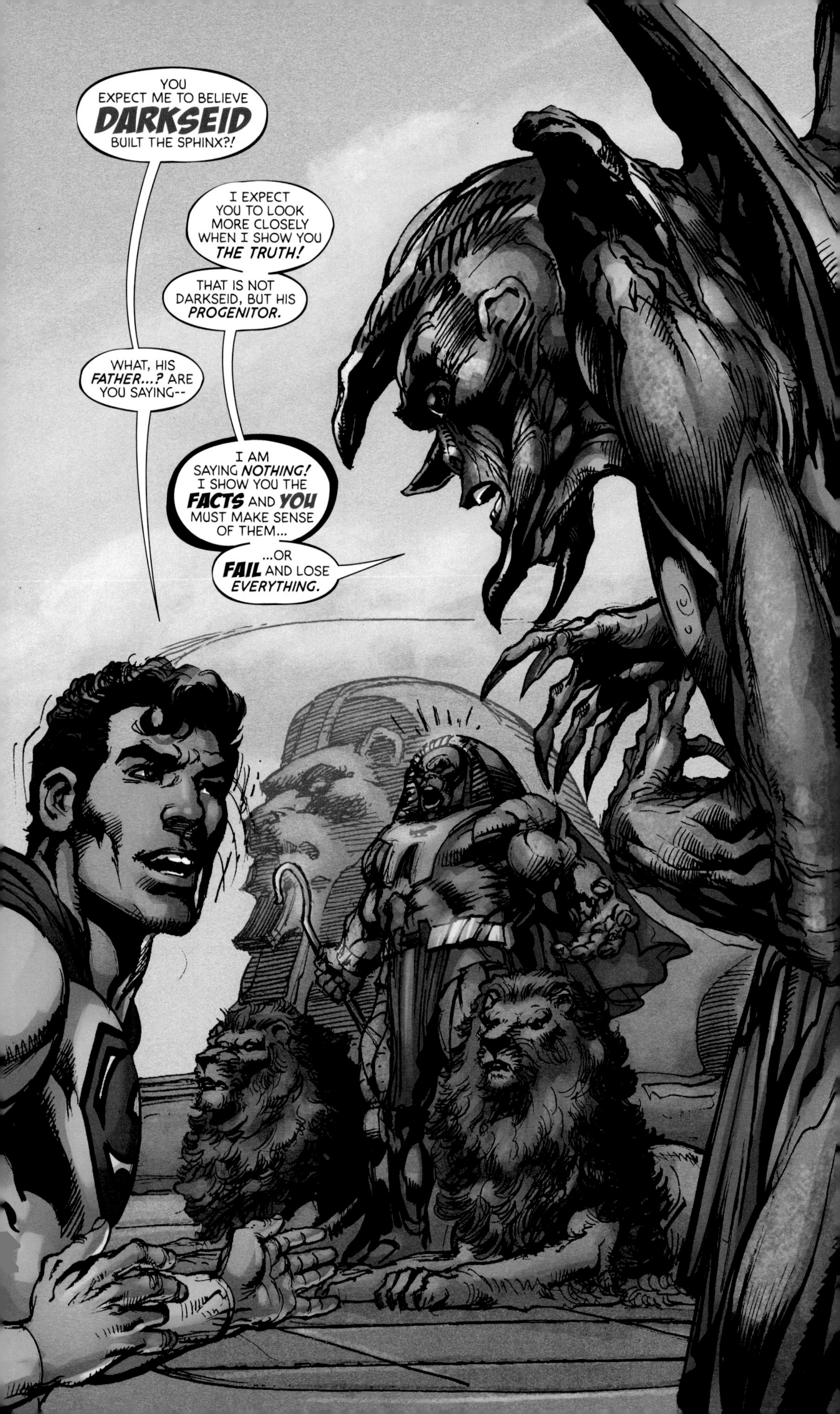
YOU EXPECT ME TO BELIEVE DARKSEID BUILT THE SPHINX?!
I EXPECT YOU TO LOOK MORE CLOSELY WHEN I SHOW YOU THE TRUTH!
THAT IS NOT DARKSEID, BUT HIS PROGENITOR.
WHAT, HIS FATHER...? ARE YOU SAYING--
I AM SAYING NOTHING! I SHOW YOU THE FACTS AND YOU MUST MAKE SENSE OF THEM...
...OR FAIL AND LOSE EVERYTHING.

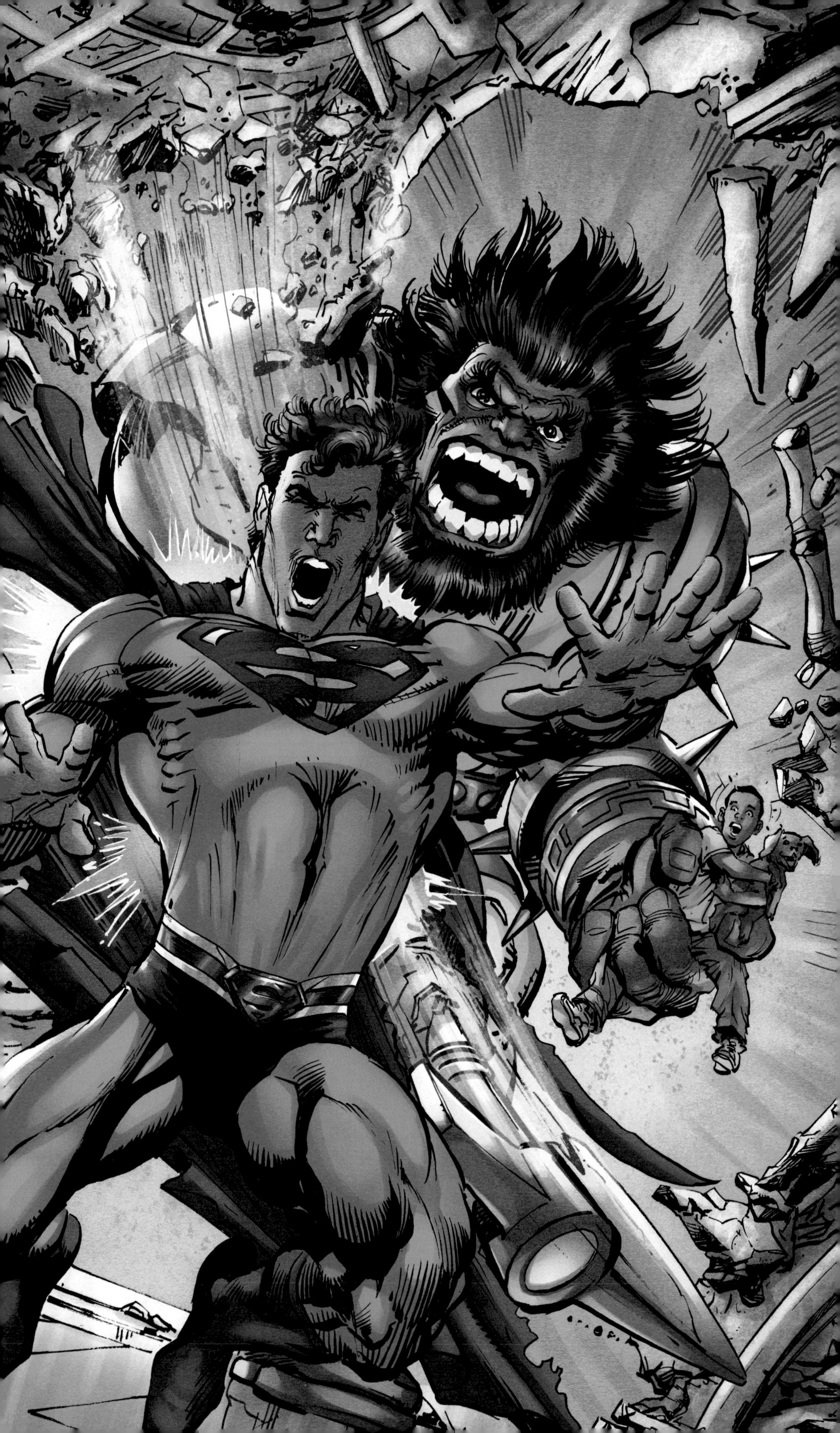

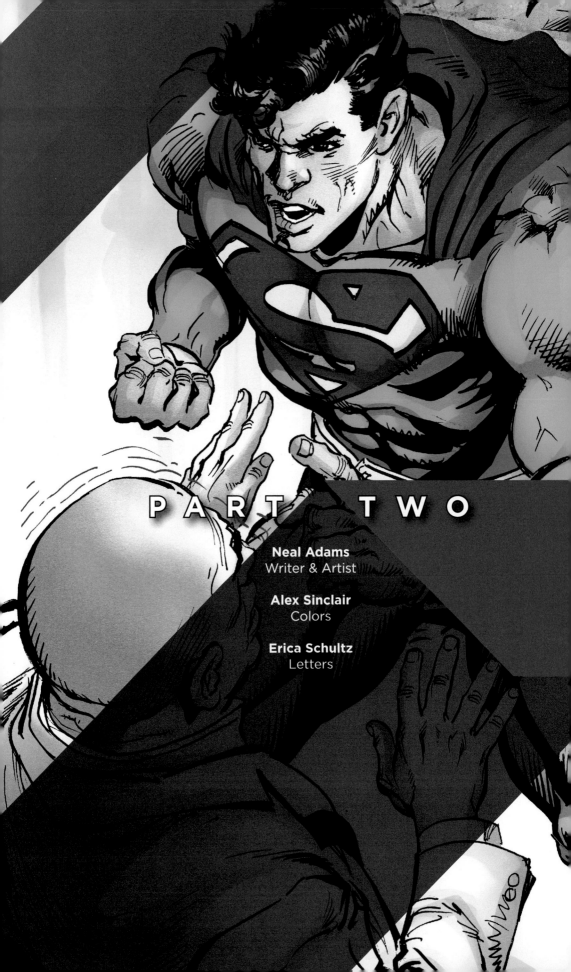

PART TWO

Neal Adams
Writer & Artist

Alex Sinclair
Colors

Erica Schultz
Letters

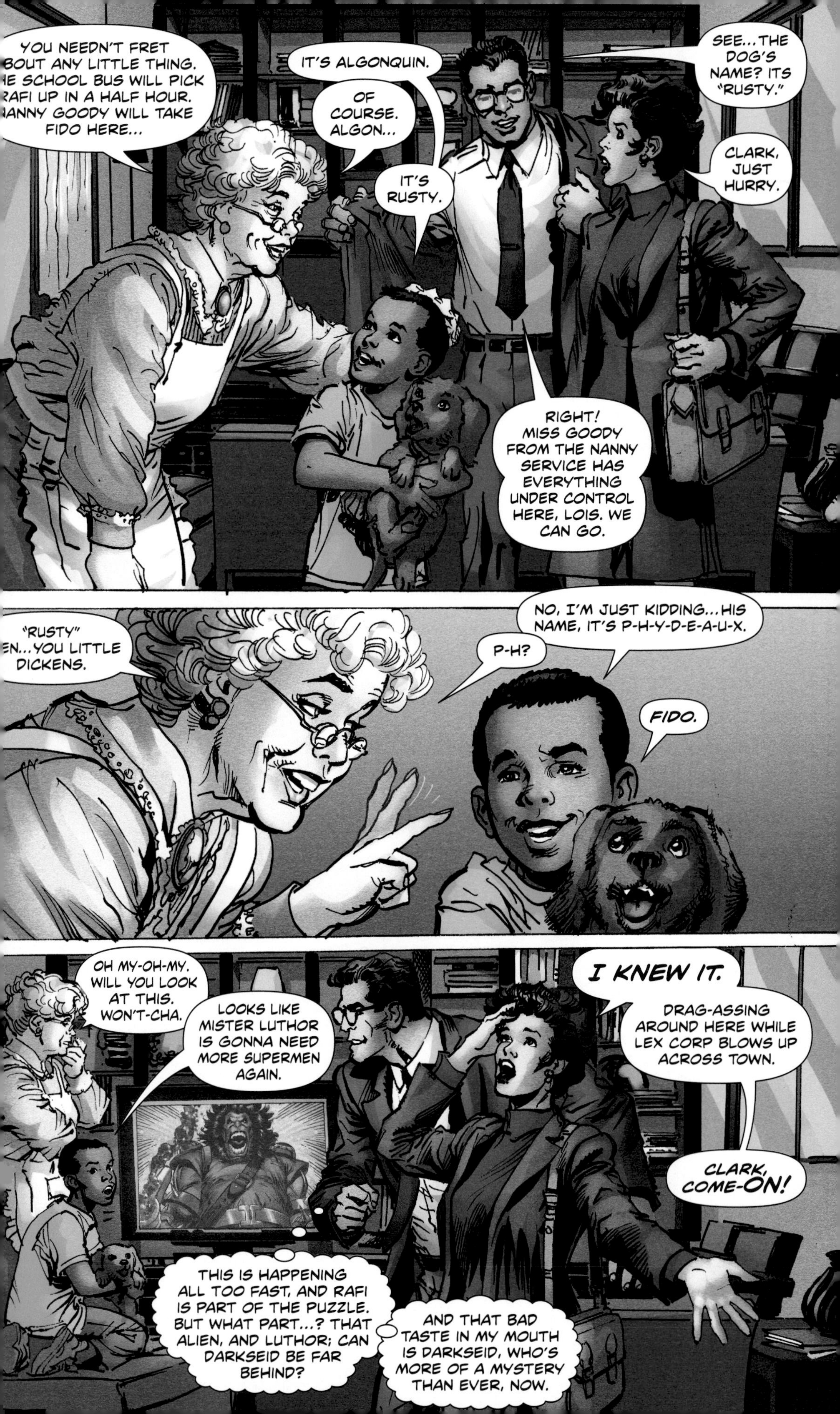

YOU NEEDN'T FRET BOUT ANY LITTLE THING. HE SCHOOL BUS WILL PICK RAFI UP IN A HALF HOUR. NANNY GOODY WILL TAKE FIDO HERE...
IT'S ALGONQUIN.
OF COURSE. ALGON...
IT'S RUSTY.
SEE...THE DOG'S NAME? ITS "RUSTY."
CLARK, JUST HURRY.
RIGHT! MISS GOODY FROM THE NANNY SERVICE HAS EVERYTHING UNDER CONTROL HERE, LOIS. WE CAN GO.
"RUSTY" EN...YOU LITTLE DICKENS.
NO, I'M JUST KIDDING...HIS NAME, IT'S P-H-Y-D-E-A-U-X.
P-H?
FIDO.
OH MY-OH-MY. WILL YOU LOOK AT THIS. WON'T-CHA.
LOOKS LIKE MISTER LUTHOR IS GONNA NEED MORE SUPERMEN AGAIN.
I KNEW IT.
DRAG-ASSING AROUND HERE WHILE LEX CORP BLOWS UP ACROSS TOWN.
CLARK, COME-ON!
THIS IS HAPPENING ALL TOO FAST, AND RAFI IS PART OF THE PUZZLE. BUT WHAT PART...? THAT ALIEN, AND LUTHOR; CAN DARKSEID BE FAR BEHIND?
AND THAT BAD TASTE IN MY MOUTH IS DARKSEID, WHO'S MORE OF A MYSTERY THAN EVER, NOW.

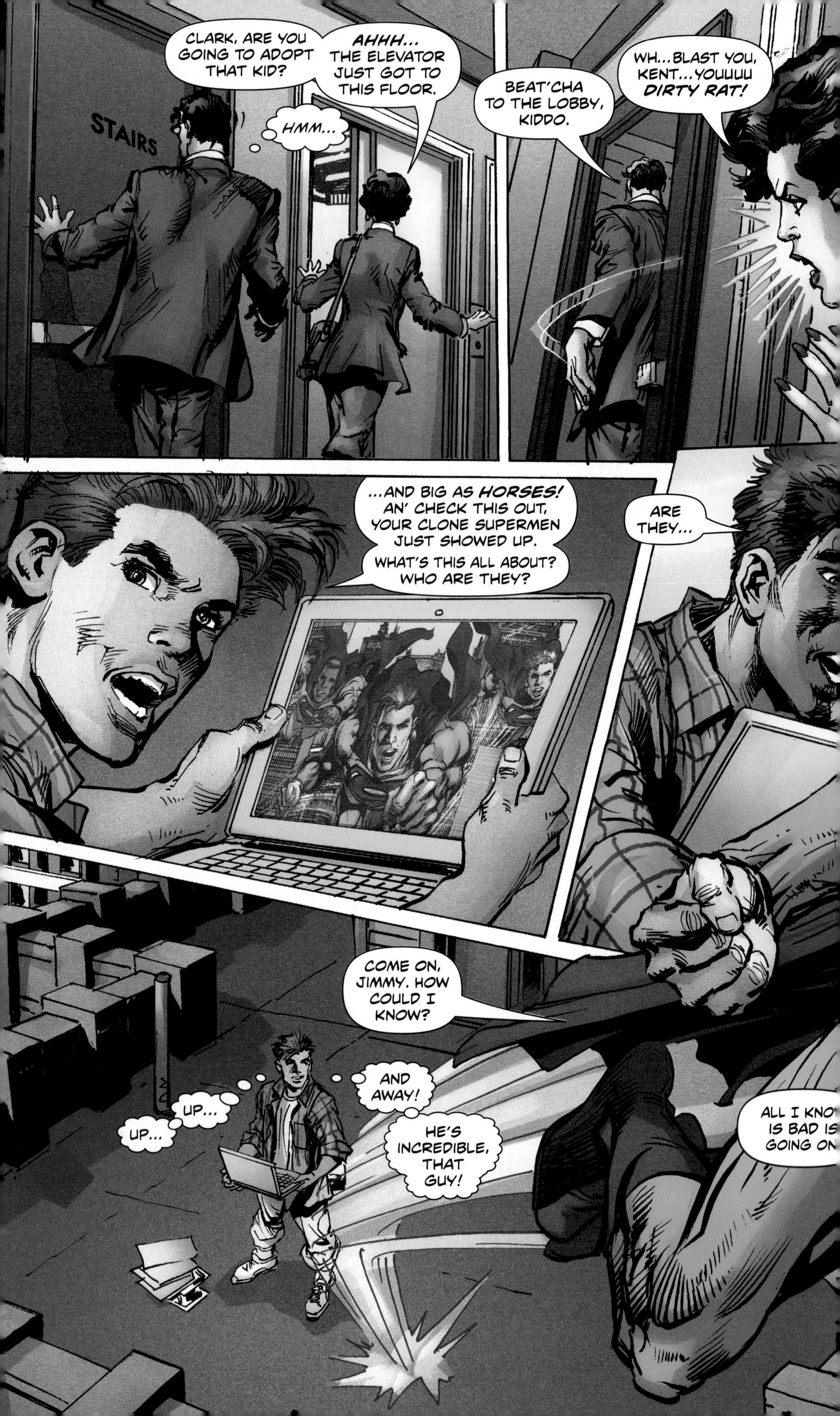
STAIRS
CLARK, ARE YOU GOING TO ADOPT THAT KID?
HMM...
AHHH... THE ELEVATOR JUST GOT TO THIS FLOOR.
BEAT'CHA TO THE LOBBY, KIDDO.
WH...BLAST YOU, KENT...YOUUUU DIRTY RAT!
...AND BIG AS HORSES! AN' CHECK THIS OUT, YOUR CLONE SUPERMEN JUST SHOWED UP.
WHAT'S THIS ALL ABOUT? WHO ARE THEY?
ARE THEY...
COME ON, JIMMY. HOW COULD I KNOW?
UP...
UP...
AND AWAY!
HE'S INCREDIBLE, THAT GUY!

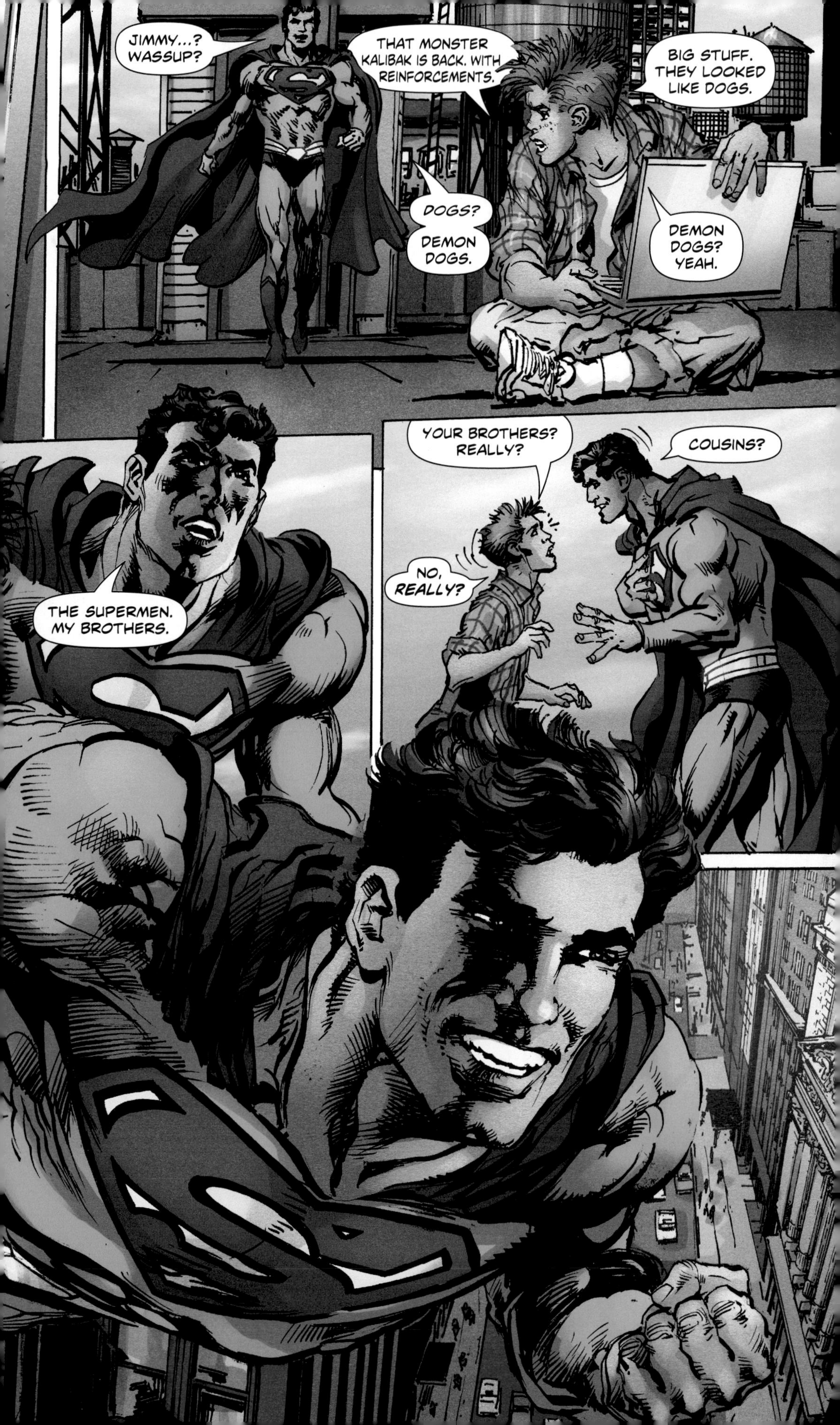
JIMMY...? WASSUP?
THAT MONSTER KALIBAK IS BACK. WITH REINFORCEMENTS.
BIG STUFF. THEY LOOKED LIKE DOGS.
DOGS?
DEMON DOGS.
DEMON DOGS? YEAH.
THE SUPERMEN. MY BROTHERS.
YOUR BROTHERS? REALLY?
COUSINS?
NO, REALLY?

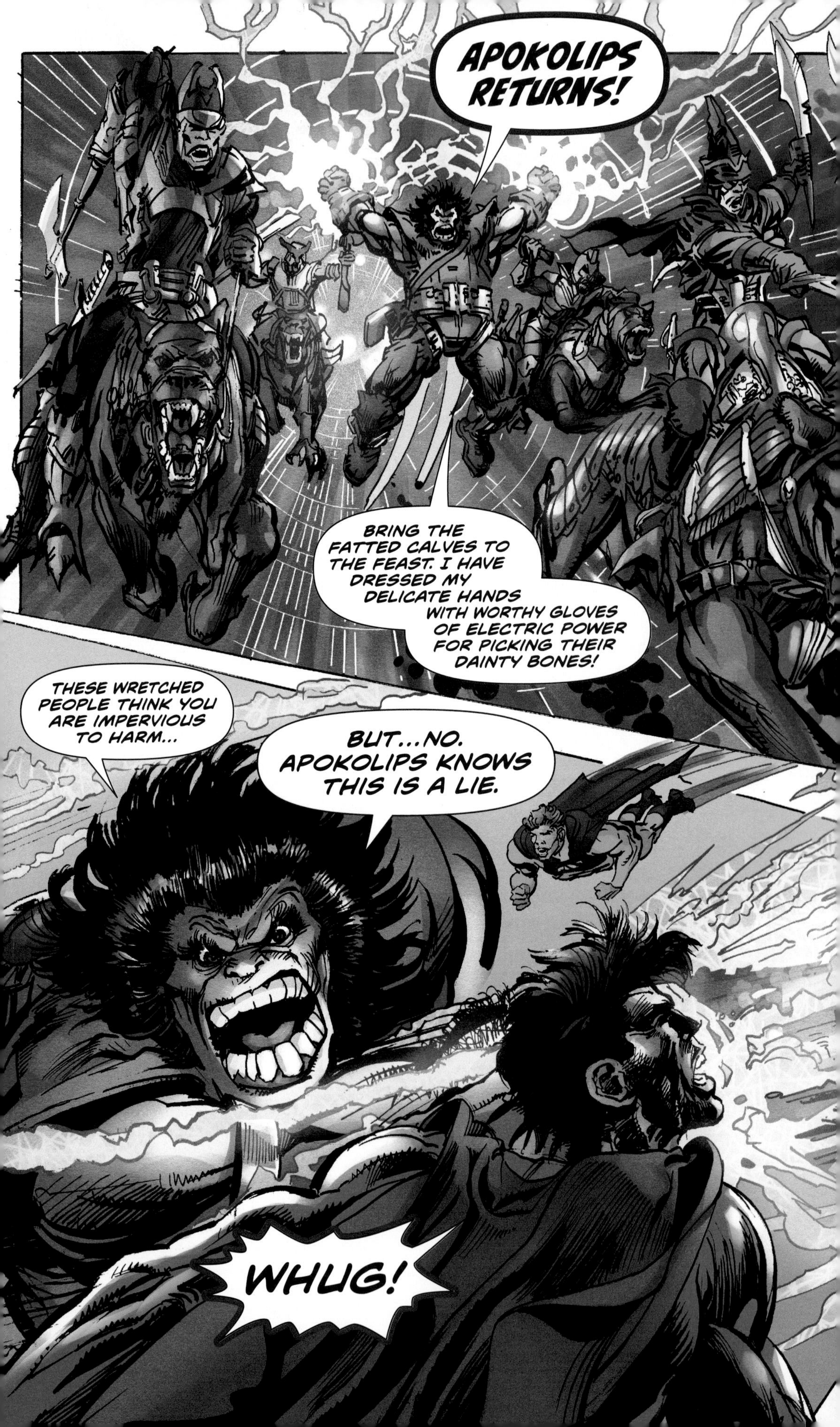
APOKOLIPS RETURNS!
BRING THE FATTED CALVES TO THE FEAST. I HAVE DRESSED MY DELICATE HANDS WITH WORTHY GLOVES OF ELECTRIC POWER FOR PICKING THEIR DAINTY BONES!
THESE WRETCHED PEOPLE THINK YOU ARE IMPERVIOUS TO HARM...
BUT...NO. APOKOLIPS KNOWS THIS IS A LIE.
WHUG!

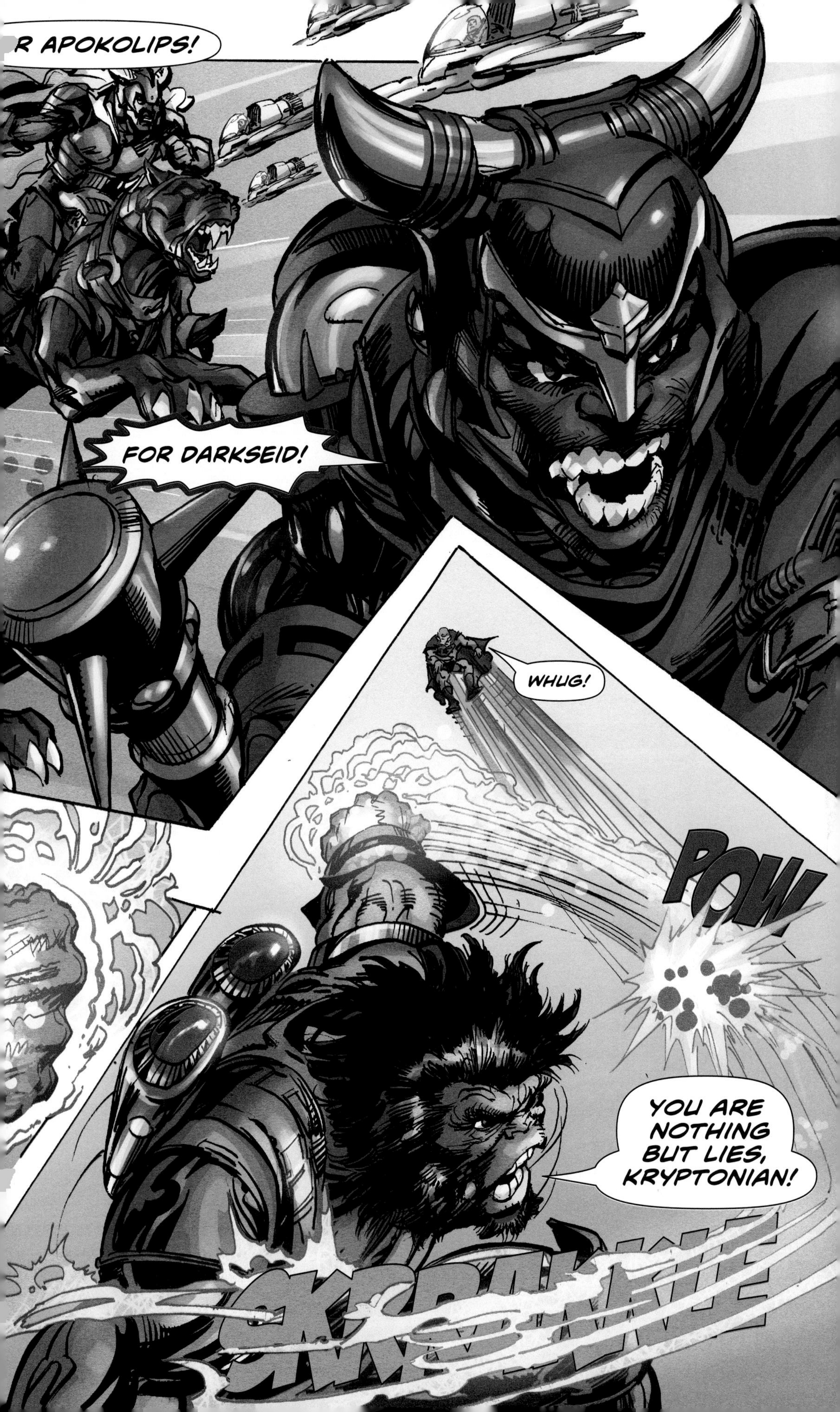
R APOKOLIPS!
FOR DARKSEID!
WHUG!
POW
YOU ARE NOTHING BUT LIES, KRYPTONIAN!

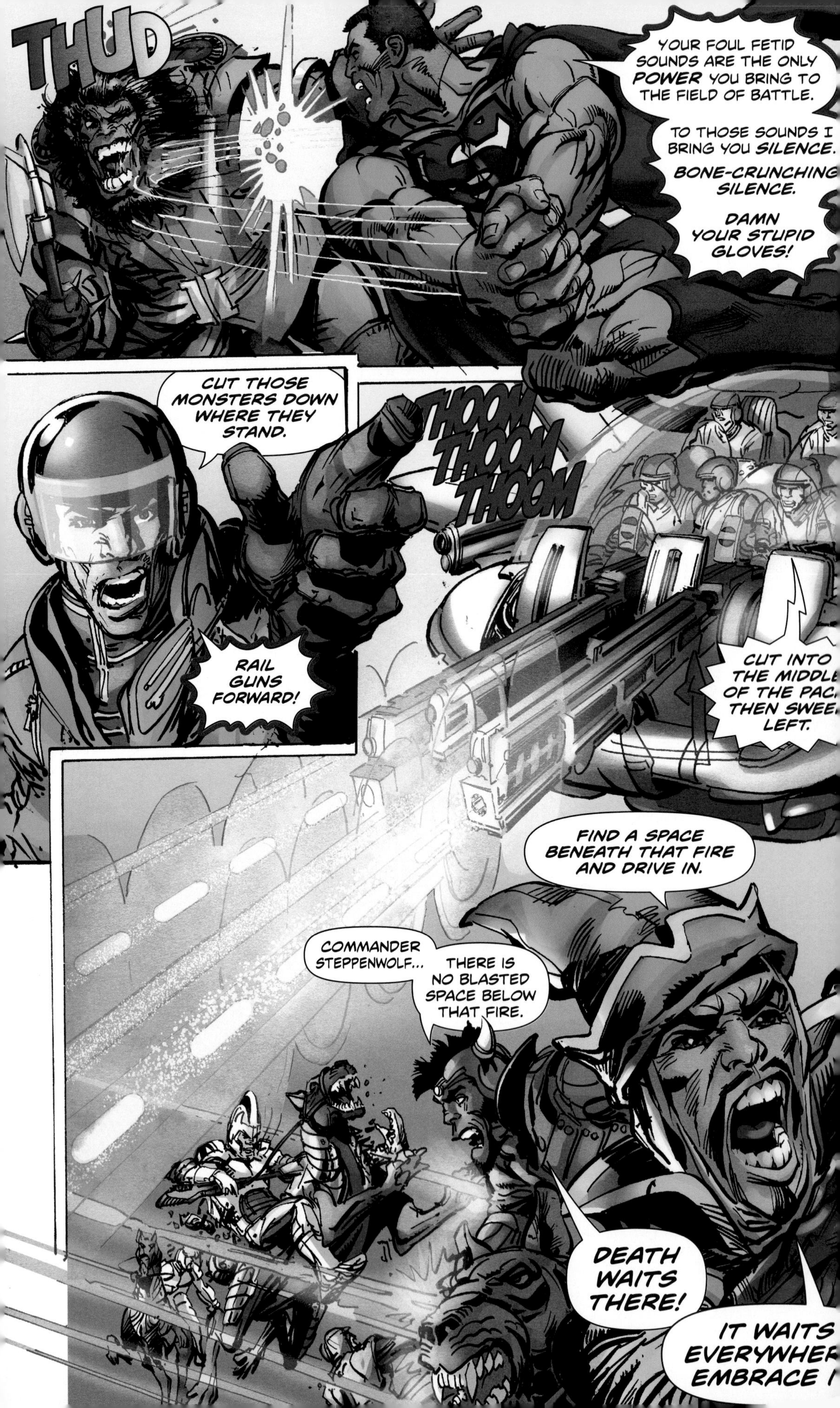
THUD
YOUR FOUL FETID SOUNDS ARE THE ONLY POWER YOU BRING TO THE FIELD OF BATTLE.
TO THOSE SOUNDS I BRING YOU SILENCE.
BONE-CRUNCHING SILENCE.
DAMN YOUR STUPID GLOVES!
CUT THOSE MONSTERS DOWN WHERE THEY STAND.
RAIL GUNS FORWARD!
THOOM THOOM THOOM
CUT INTO THE MIDDL OF THE PAC THEN SWEE LEFT.
FIND A SPACE BENEATH THAT FIRE AND DRIVE IN.
COMMANDER STEPPENWOLF... THERE IS NO BLASTED SPACE BELOW THAT FIRE.
DEATH WAITS THERE!
IT WAITS EVERYWHER EMBRACE I

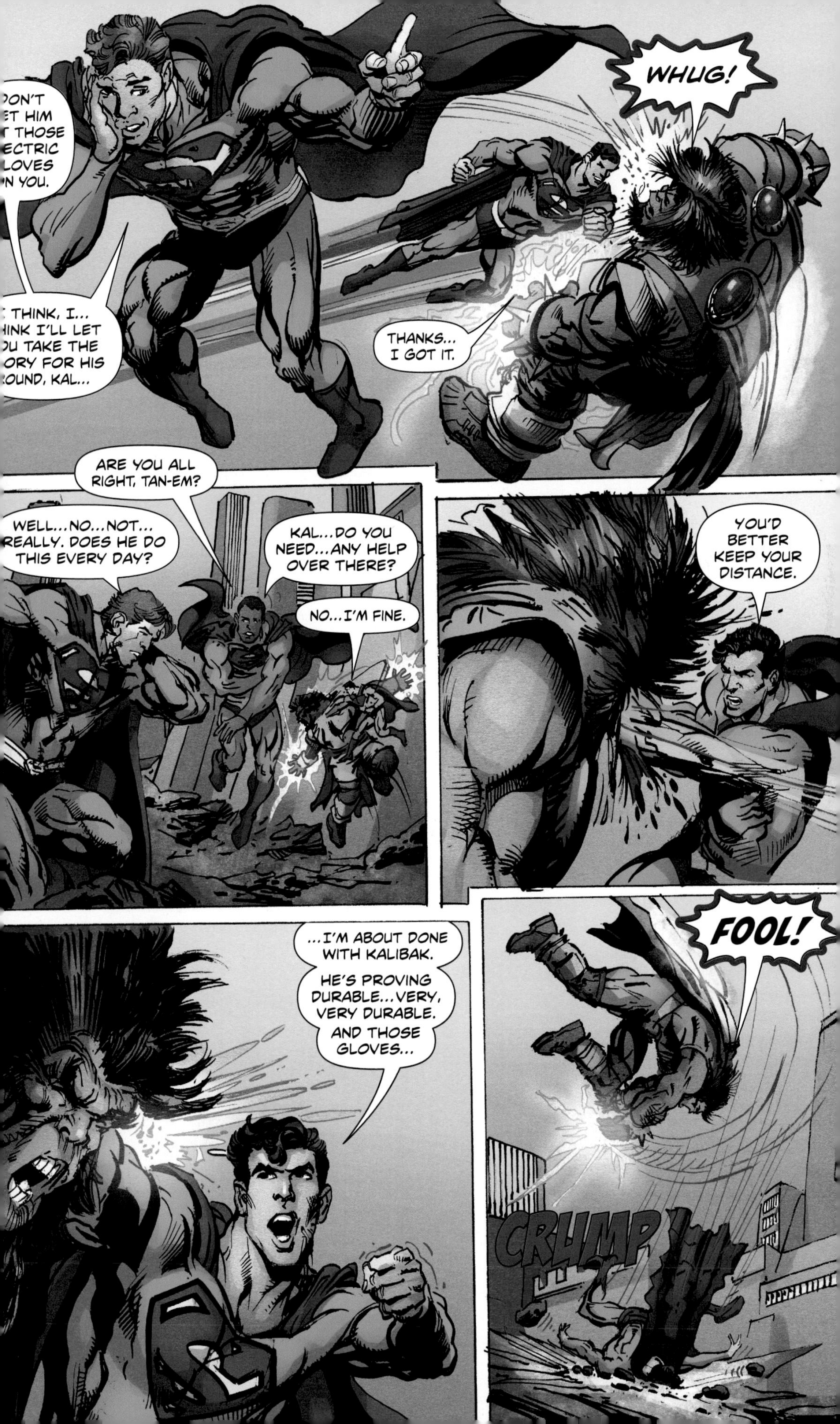

ON'T ET HIM T THOSE ECTRIC LOVES N YOU.
THINK, I... HINK I'LL LET OU TAKE THE ORY FOR HIS OUND, KAL...
WHUG!
THANKS... I GOT IT.
ARE YOU ALL RIGHT, TAN-EM?
WELL...NO...NOT... REALLY. DOES HE DO THIS EVERY DAY?
KAL...DO YOU NEED...ANY HELP OVER THERE?
NO...I'M FINE.
YOU'D BETTER KEEP YOUR DISTANCE.
...I'M ABOUT DONE WITH KALIBAK.
HE'S PROVING DURABLE...VERY, VERY DURABLE. AND THOSE GLOVES...
FOOL!
CRUMP

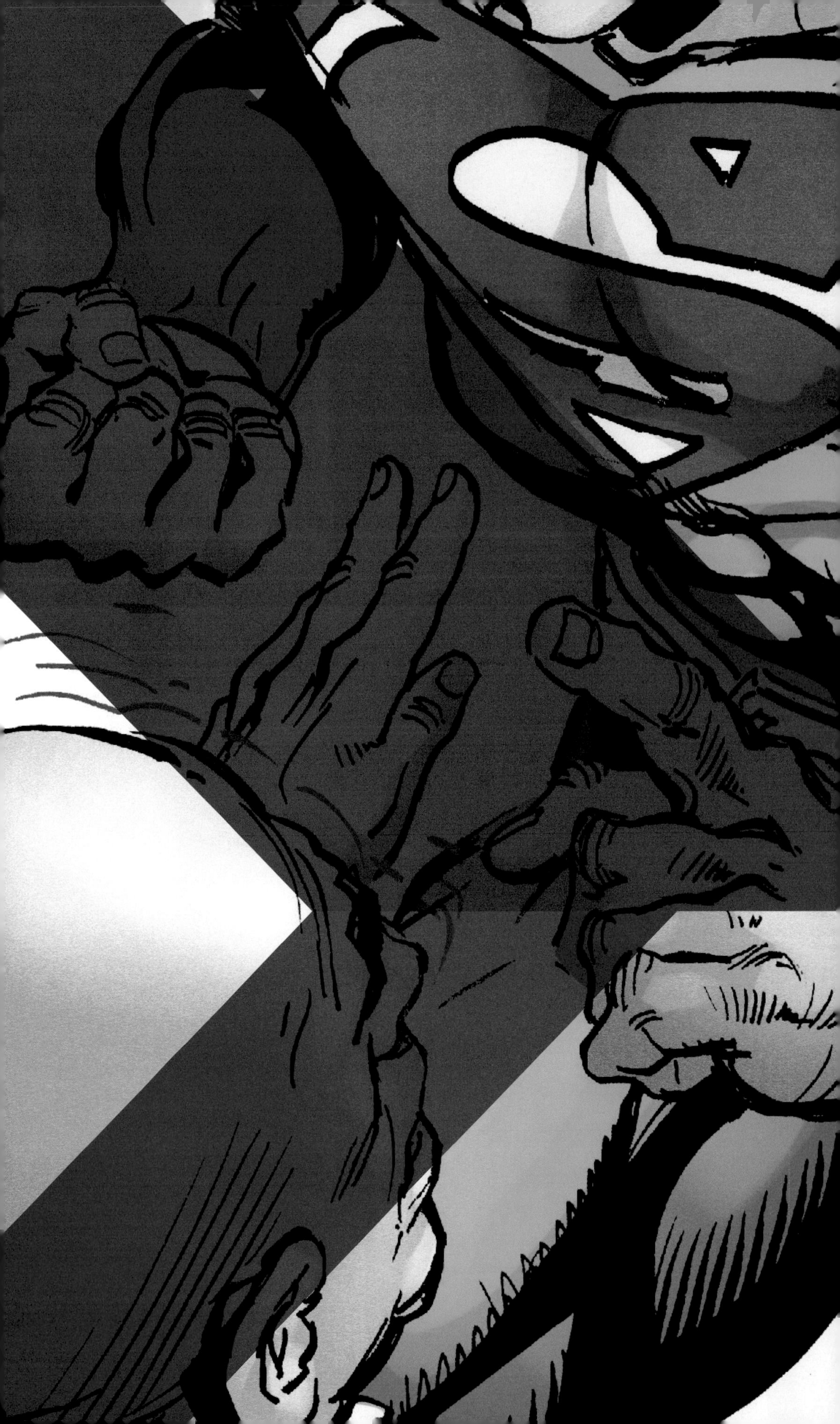

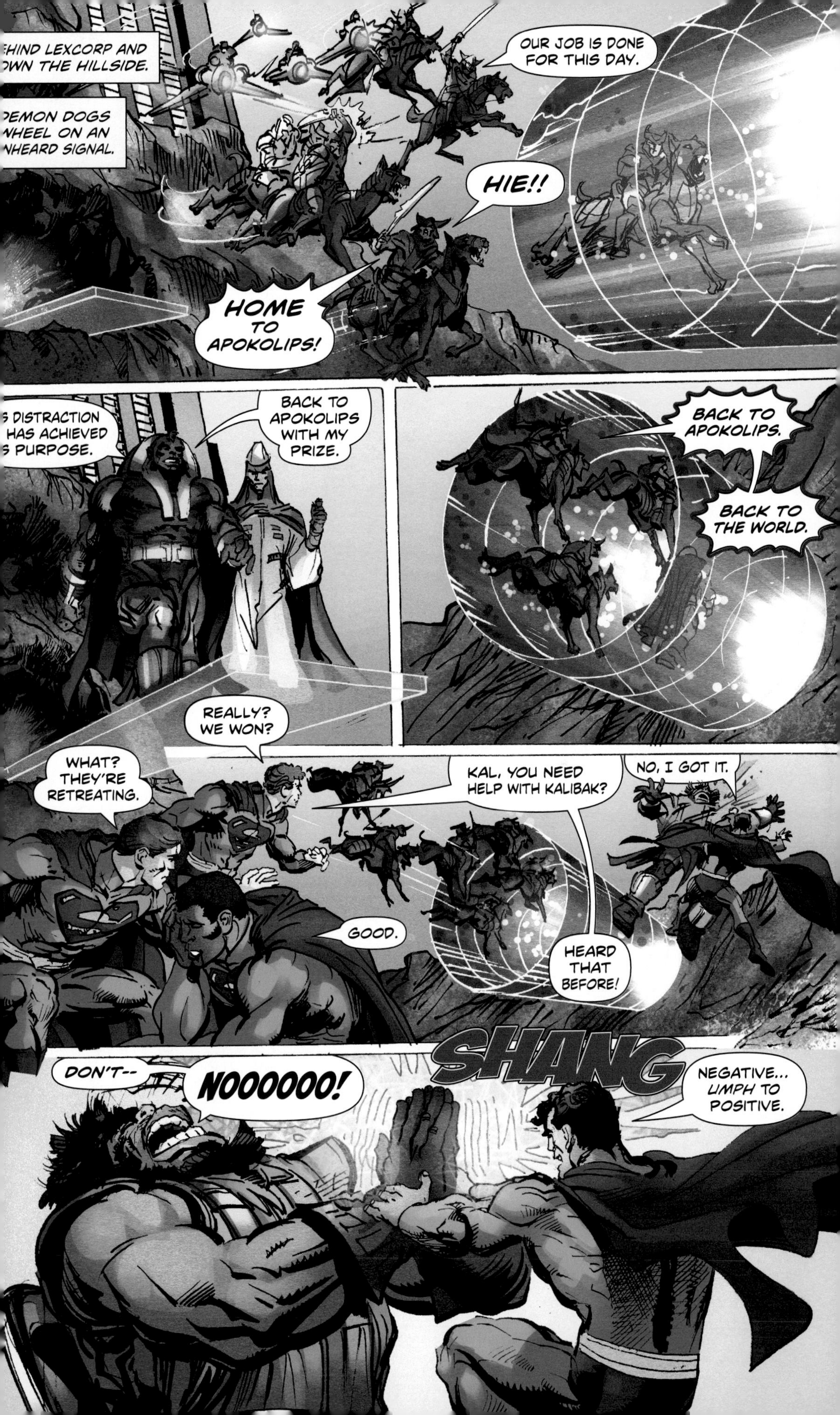
EHIND LEXCORP AND
OWN THE HILLSIDE.
DEMON DOGS
WHEEL ON AN
NHEARD SIGNAL.
OUR JOB IS DONE FOR THIS DAY.
HIE!!
HOME TO APOKOLIPS!
S DISTRACTION HAS ACHIEVED S PURPOSE.
BACK TO APOKOLIPS WITH MY PRIZE.
BACK TO APOKOLIPS.
BACK TO THE WORLD.
REALLY? WE WON?
WHAT? THEY'RE RETREATING.
KAL, YOU NEED HELP WITH KALIBAK?
NO, I GOT IT.
GOOD.
HEARD THAT BEFORE!
SHANG
DON'T--
NOOOOOO!
NEGATIVE... UMPH TO POSITIVE.

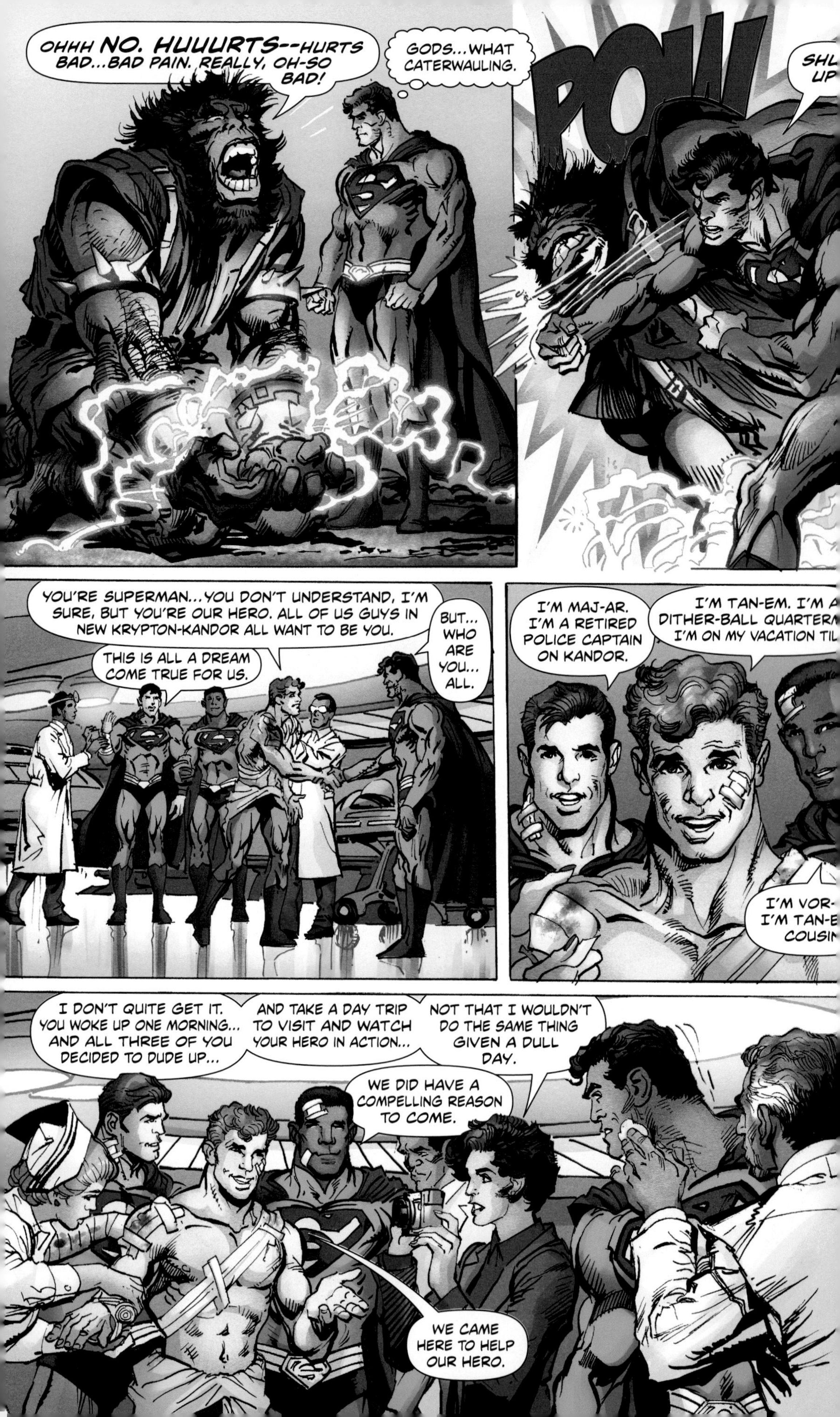
OHHH NO. HUUURTS--HURTS BAD...BAD PAIN. REALLY, OH-SO BAD!
GODS...WHAT CATERWAULING.
POW
SHL UP
YOU'RE SUPERMAN...YOU DON'T UNDERSTAND, I'M SURE, BUT YOU'RE OUR HERO. ALL OF US GUYS IN NEW KRYPTON-KANDOR ALL WANT TO BE YOU.
THIS IS ALL A DREAM COME TRUE FOR US.
BUT... WHO ARE YOU... ALL.
I'M MAJ-AR. I'M A RETIRED POLICE CAPTAIN ON KANDOR.
I'M TAN-EM. I'M A DITHER-BALL QUARTERM I'M ON MY VACATION TIL
I'M VOR- I'M TAN-E COUSIN
I DON'T QUITE GET IT. YOU WOKE UP ONE MORNING... AND ALL THREE OF YOU DECIDED TO DUDE UP...
AND TAKE A DAY TRIP TO VISIT AND WATCH YOUR HERO IN ACTION...
NOT THAT I WOULDN'T DO THE SAME THING GIVEN A DULL DAY.
WE DID HAVE A COMPELLING REASON TO COME.
WE CAME HERE TO HELP OUR HERO.

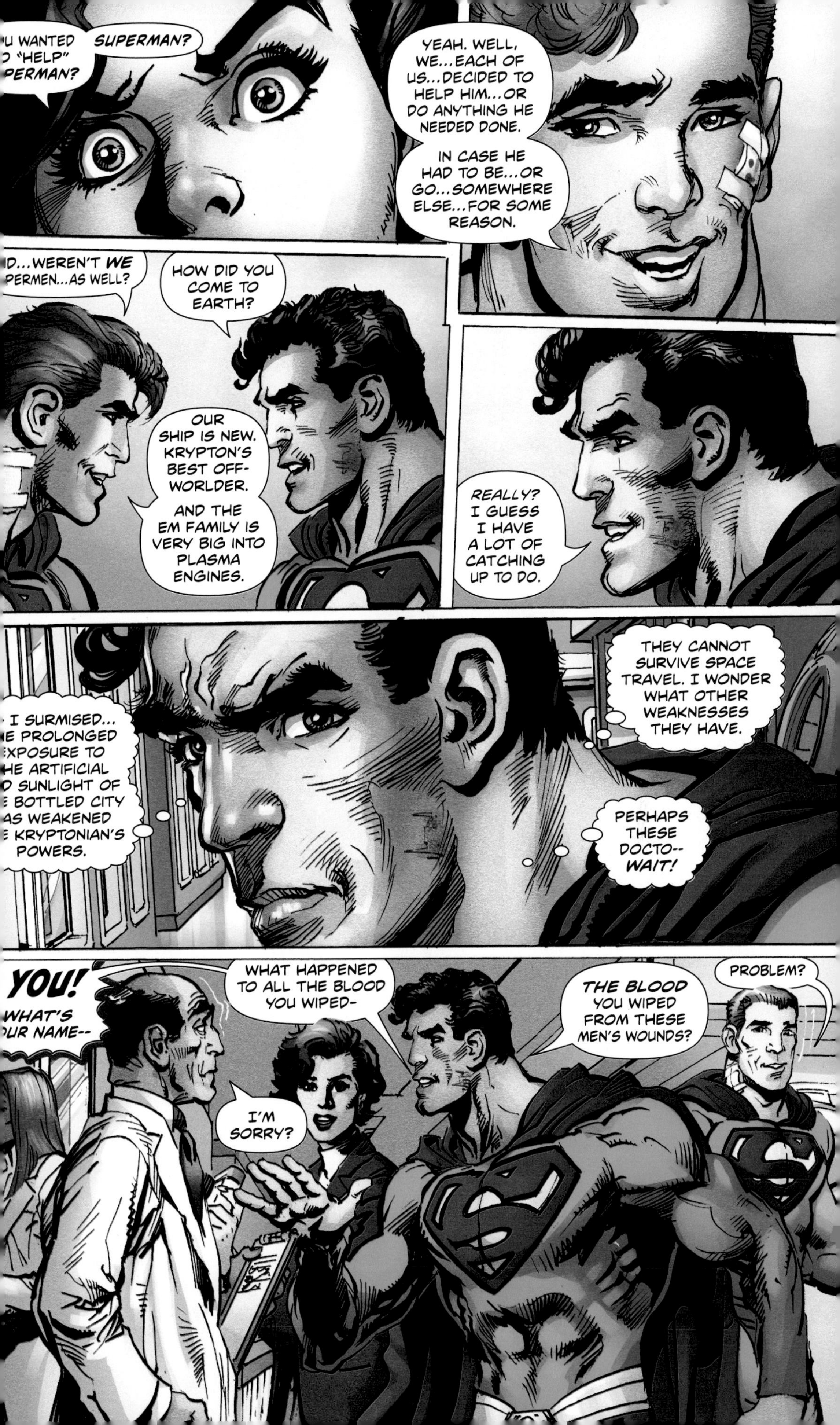

U WANTED
O "HELP"
PERMAN?
SUPERMAN?
YEAH. WELL, WE...EACH OF US...DECIDED TO HELP HIM...OR DO ANYTHING HE NEEDED DONE.
IN CASE HE HAD TO BE...OR GO...SOMEWHERE ELSE...FOR SOME REASON.
D...WEREN'T WE
PERMEN...AS WELL?
HOW DID YOU COME TO EARTH?
OUR SHIP IS NEW. KRYPTON'S BEST OFF-WORLDER.
AND THE EM FAMILY IS VERY BIG INTO PLASMA ENGINES.
REALLY? I GUESS I HAVE A LOT OF CATCHING UP TO DO.
I SURMISED...
E PROLONGED
EXPOSURE TO
HE ARTIFICIAL
D SUNLIGHT OF
E BOTTLED CITY
AS WEAKENED
E KRYPTONIAN'S
POWERS.
THEY CANNOT SURVIVE SPACE TRAVEL. I WONDER WHAT OTHER WEAKNESSES THEY HAVE.
PERHAPS THESE DOCTO-- WAIT!
YOU!
WHAT'S
OUR NAME--
WHAT HAPPENED TO ALL THE BLOOD YOU WIPED-
I'M SORRY?
THE BLOOD YOU WIPED FROM THESE MEN'S WOUNDS?
PROBLEM?

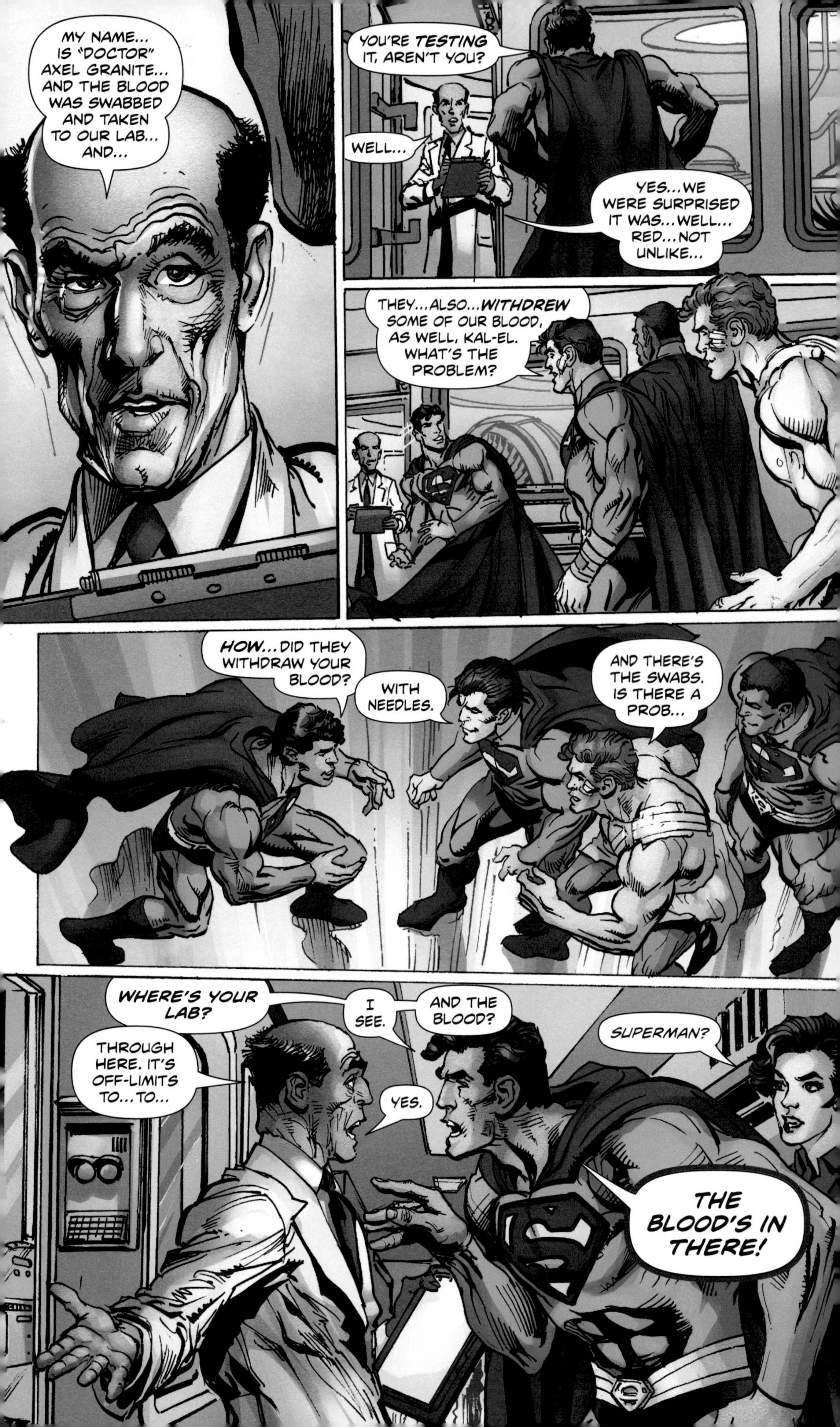
MY NAME... IS "DOCTOR" AXEL GRANITE... AND THE BLOOD WAS SWABBED AND TAKEN TO OUR LAB... AND...
YOU'RE *TESTING* IT, AREN'T YOU?
WELL...
YES...WE WERE SURPRISED IT WAS...WELL... RED...NOT UNLIKE...
THEY...ALSO...*WITHDREW* SOME OF OUR BLOOD, AS WELL, KAL-EL. WHAT'S THE PROBLEM?
HOW...DID THEY WITHDRAW YOUR BLOOD?
WITH NEEDLES.
AND THERE'S THE SWABS. IS THERE A PROB...
WHERE'S YOUR LAB?
THROUGH HERE. IT'S OFF-LIMITS TO...TO...
I SEE.
AND THE BLOOD?
YES.
SUPERMAN?
THE BLOOD'S IN THERE!

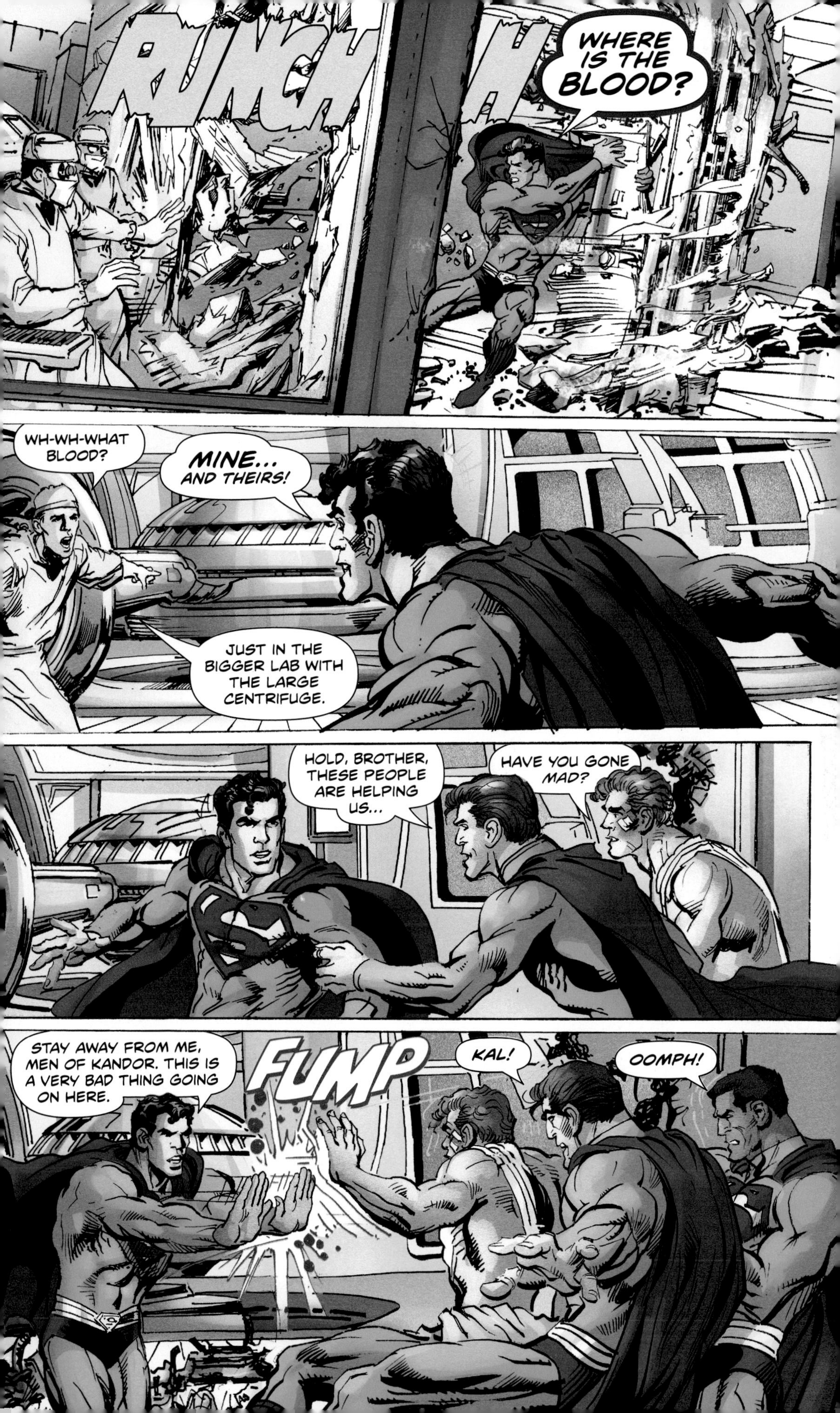
RUNCH
WHERE IS THE BLOOD?
WH-WH-WHAT BLOOD?
MINE... AND THEIRS!
JUST IN THE BIGGER LAB WITH THE LARGE CENTRIFUGE.
HOLD, BROTHER, THESE PEOPLE ARE HELPING US...
HAVE YOU GONE MAD?
STAY AWAY FROM ME, MEN OF KANDOR. THIS IS A VERY BAD THING GOING ON HERE.
FUMP
KAL!
OOMPH!

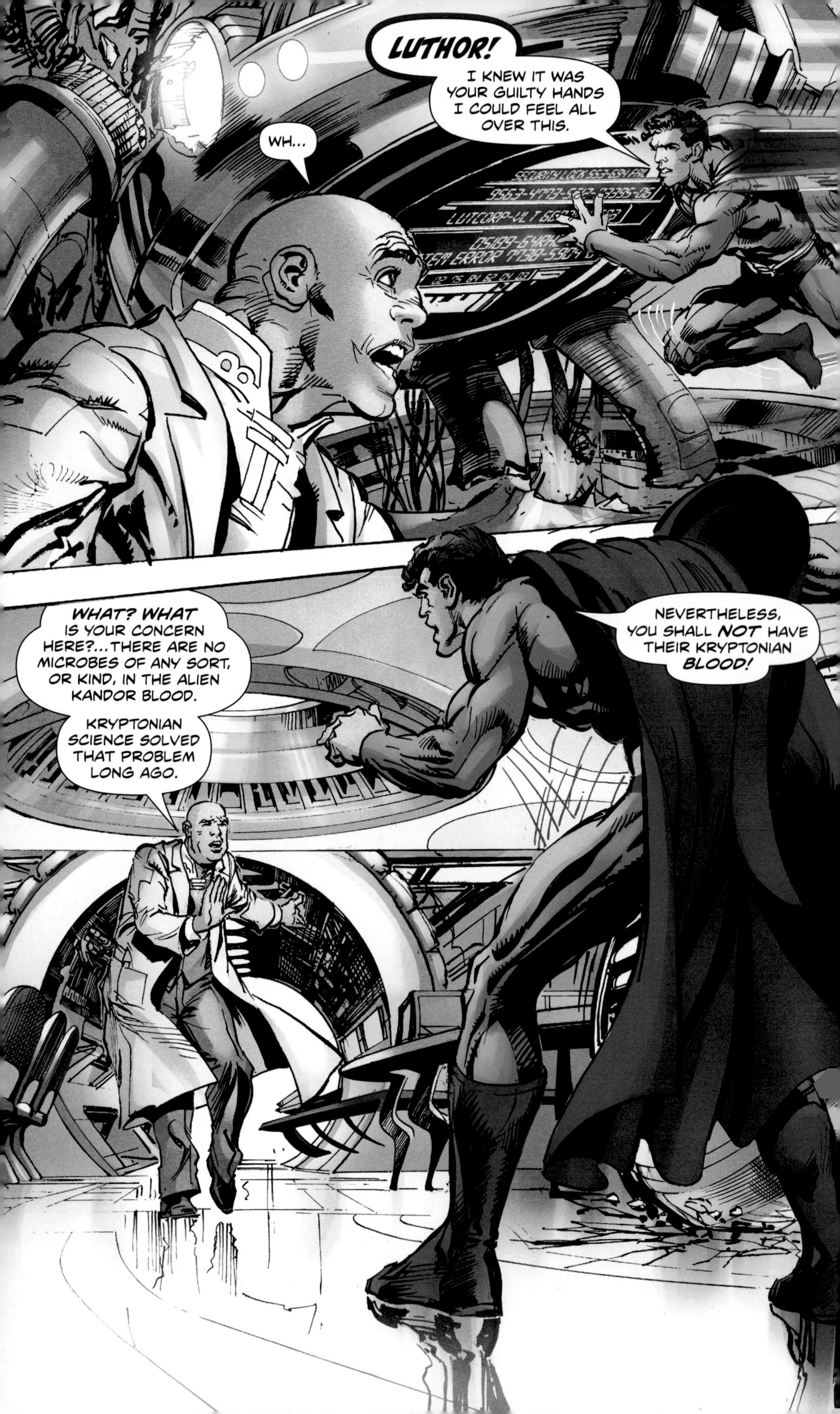

LUTHOR! I KNEW IT WAS YOUR GUILTY HANDS I COULD FEEL ALL OVER THIS.
WH...
WHAT? WHAT IS YOUR CONCERN HERE?...THERE ARE NO MICROBES OF ANY SORT, OR KIND, IN THE ALIEN KANDOR BLOOD.
KRYPTONIAN SCIENCE SOLVED THAT PROBLEM LONG AGO.
NEVERTHELESS, YOU SHALL NOT HAVE THEIR KRYPTONIAN BLOOD!

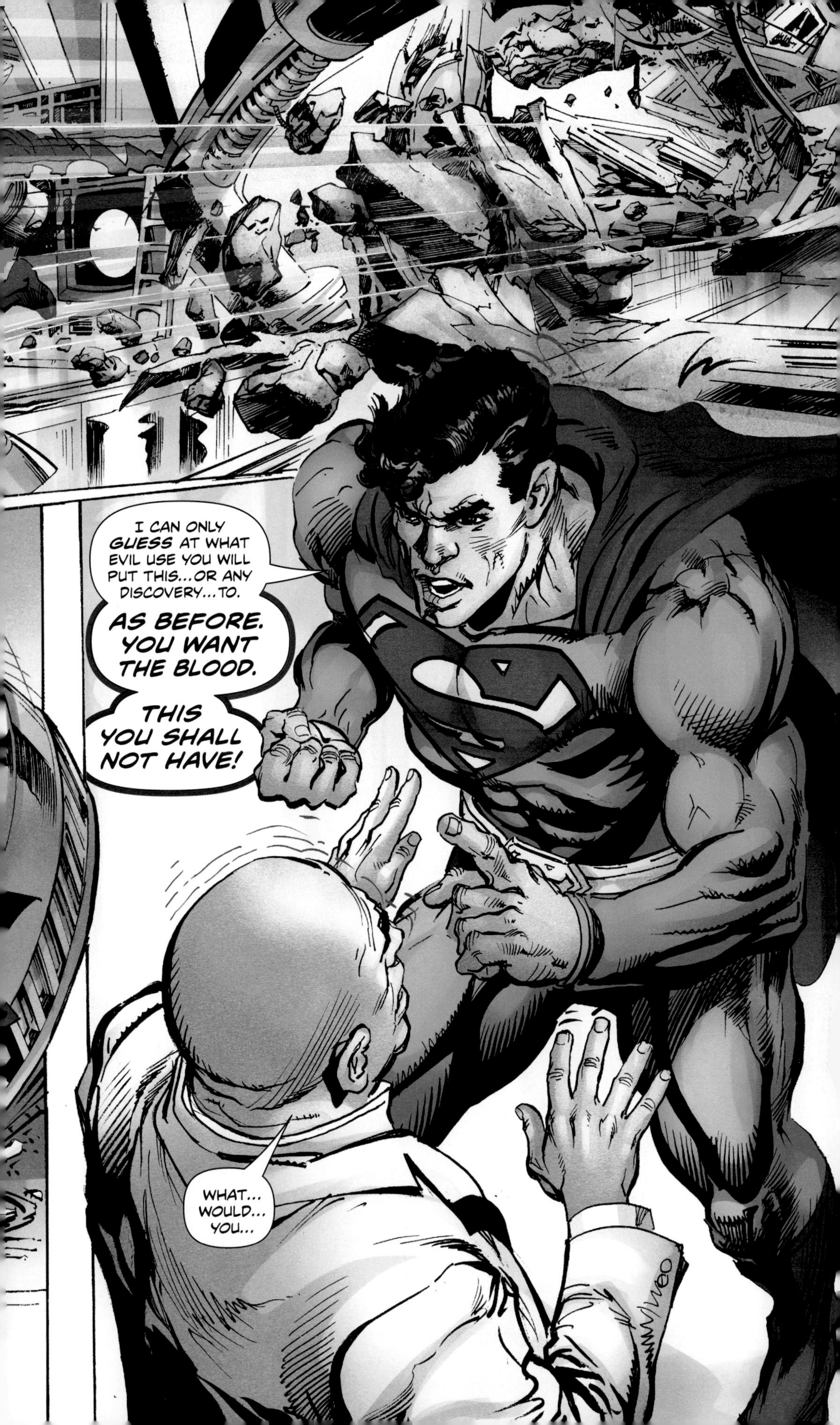
I CAN ONLY GUESS AT WHAT EVIL USE YOU WILL PUT THIS...OR ANY DISCOVERY...TO.
AS BEFORE. YOU WANT THE BLOOD.
THIS YOU SHALL NOT HAVE!
WHAT... WOULD... YOU...

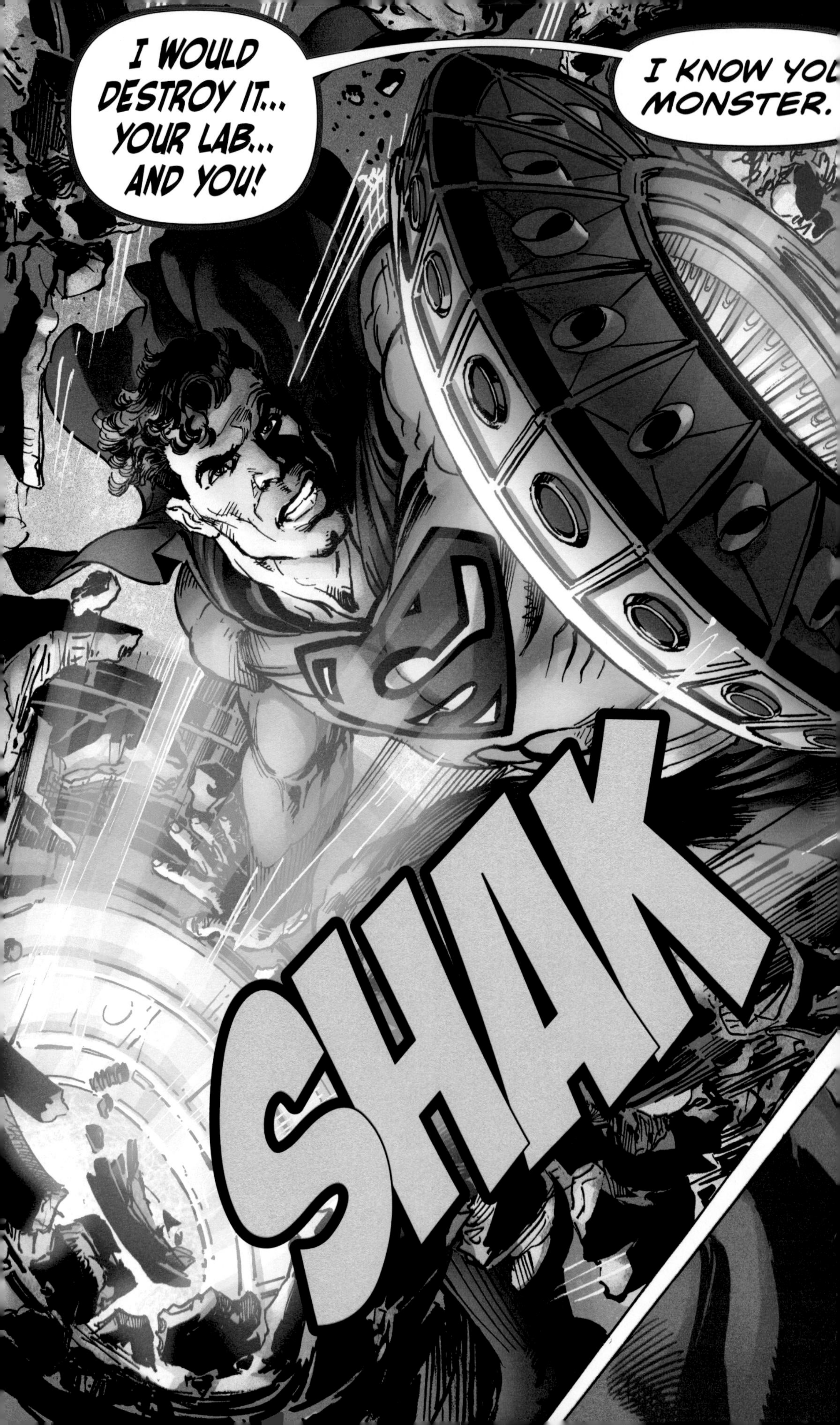
I WOULD DESTROY IT... YOUR LAB... AND YOU!
I KNOW YOU MONSTER.
SHAK

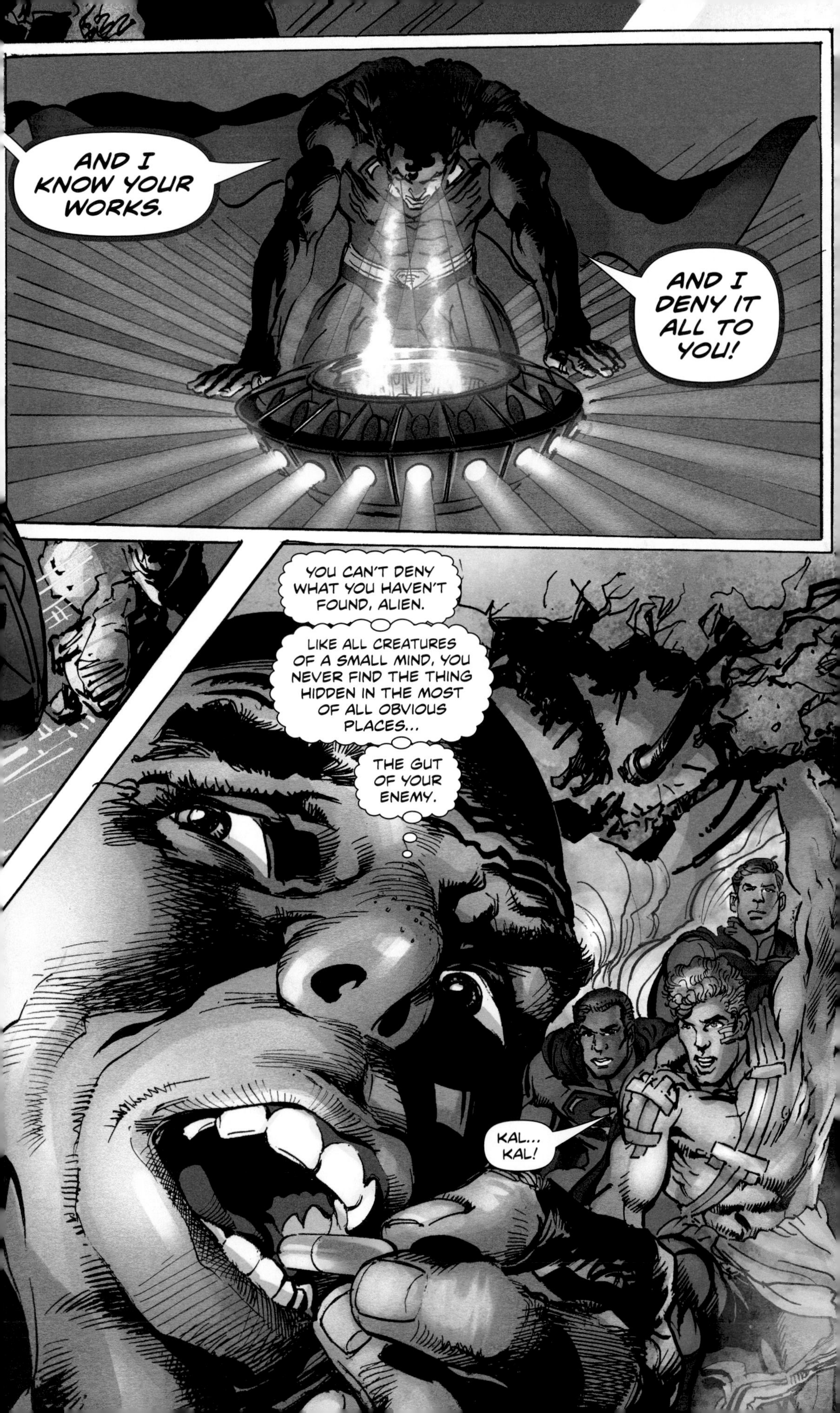
AND I KNOW YOUR WORKS.
AND I DENY IT ALL TO YOU!
YOU CAN'T DENY WHAT YOU HAVEN'T FOUND, ALIEN.
LIKE ALL CREATURES OF A SMALL MIND, YOU NEVER FIND THE THING HIDDEN IN THE MOST OF ALL OBVIOUS PLACES...
THE GUT OF YOUR ENEMY.
KAL... KAL!

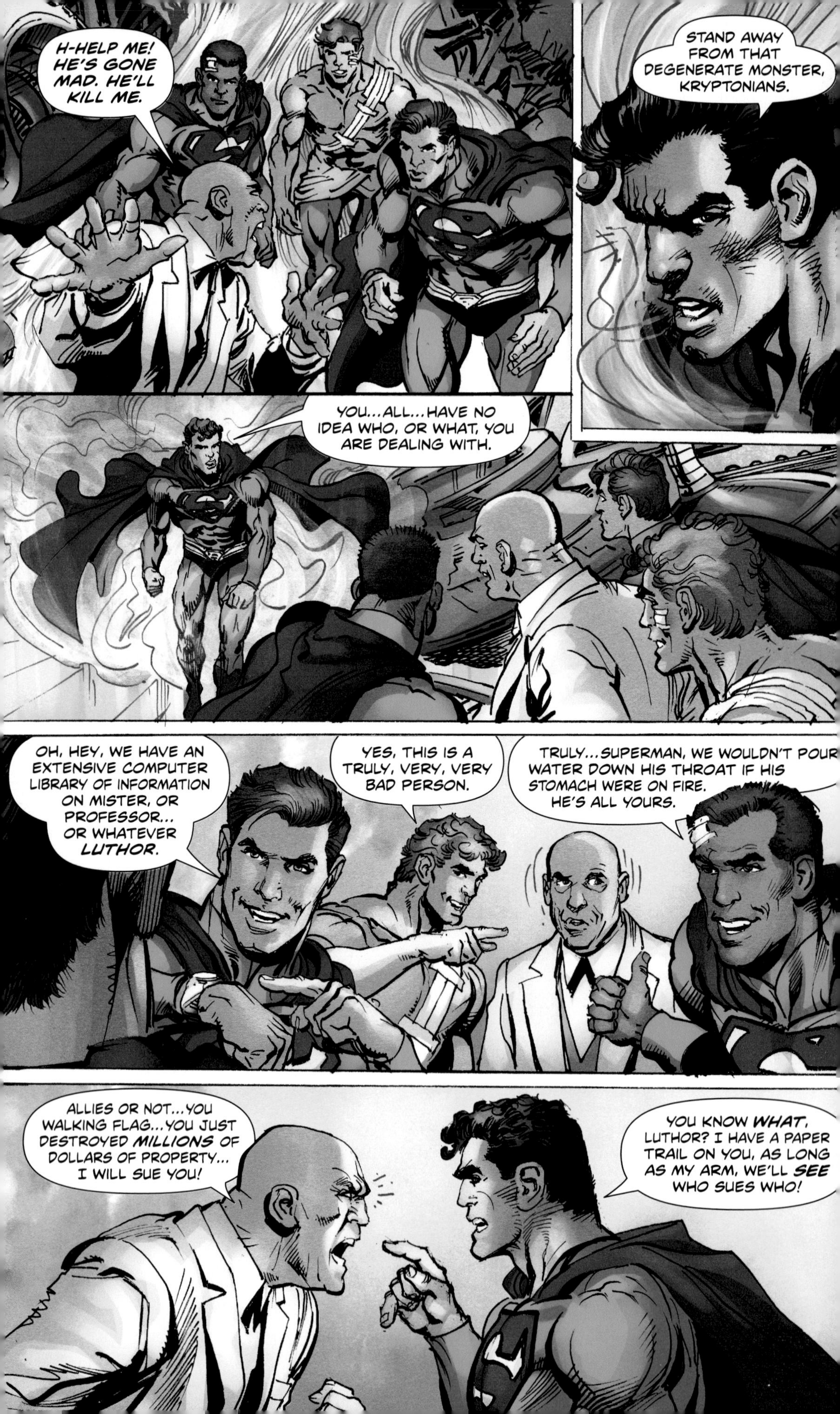
H-HELP ME! HE'S GONE MAD. HE'LL KILL ME.
STAND AWAY FROM THAT DEGENERATE MONSTER, KRYPTONIANS.
YOU...ALL...HAVE NO IDEA WHO, OR WHAT, YOU ARE DEALING WITH.
OH, HEY, WE HAVE AN EXTENSIVE COMPUTER LIBRARY OF INFORMATION ON MISTER, OR PROFESSOR... OR WHATEVER *LUTHOR*.
YES, THIS IS A TRULY, VERY, VERY BAD PERSON.
TRULY...SUPERMAN, WE WOULDN'T POUR WATER DOWN HIS THROAT IF HIS STOMACH WERE ON FIRE. HE'S ALL YOURS.
ALLIES OR NOT...YOU WALKING FLAG...YOU JUST DESTROYED *MILLIONS* OF DOLLARS OF PROPERTY... I WILL SUE YOU!
YOU KNOW *WHAT*, LUTHOR? I HAVE A PAPER TRAIL ON YOU, AS LONG AS MY ARM. WE'LL *SEE* WHO SUES WHO!

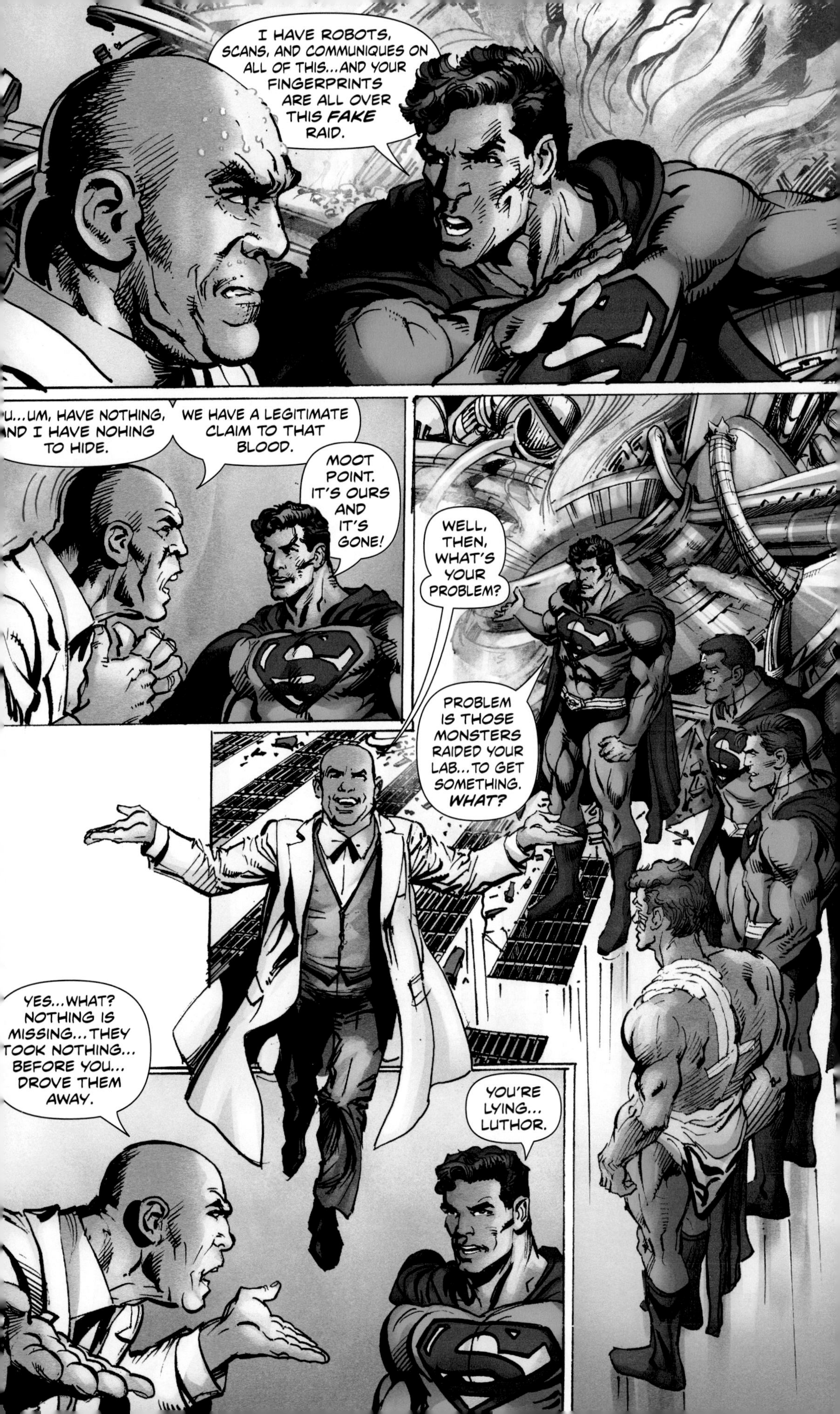
I HAVE ROBOTS, SCANS, AND COMMUNIQUES ON ALL OF THIS...AND YOUR FINGERPRINTS ARE ALL OVER THIS *FAKE* RAID.
U...UM, HAVE NOTHING, AND I HAVE NOHING TO HIDE.
WE HAVE A LEGITIMATE CLAIM TO THAT BLOOD.
MOOT POINT. IT'S OURS AND IT'S GONE!
WELL, THEN, WHAT'S YOUR PROBLEM?
PROBLEM IS THOSE MONSTERS RAIDED YOUR LAB...TO GET SOMETHING. *WHAT?*
YES...WHAT? NOTHING IS MISSING...THEY TOOK NOTHING... BEFORE YOU... DROVE THEM AWAY.
YOU'RE LYING... LUTHOR.

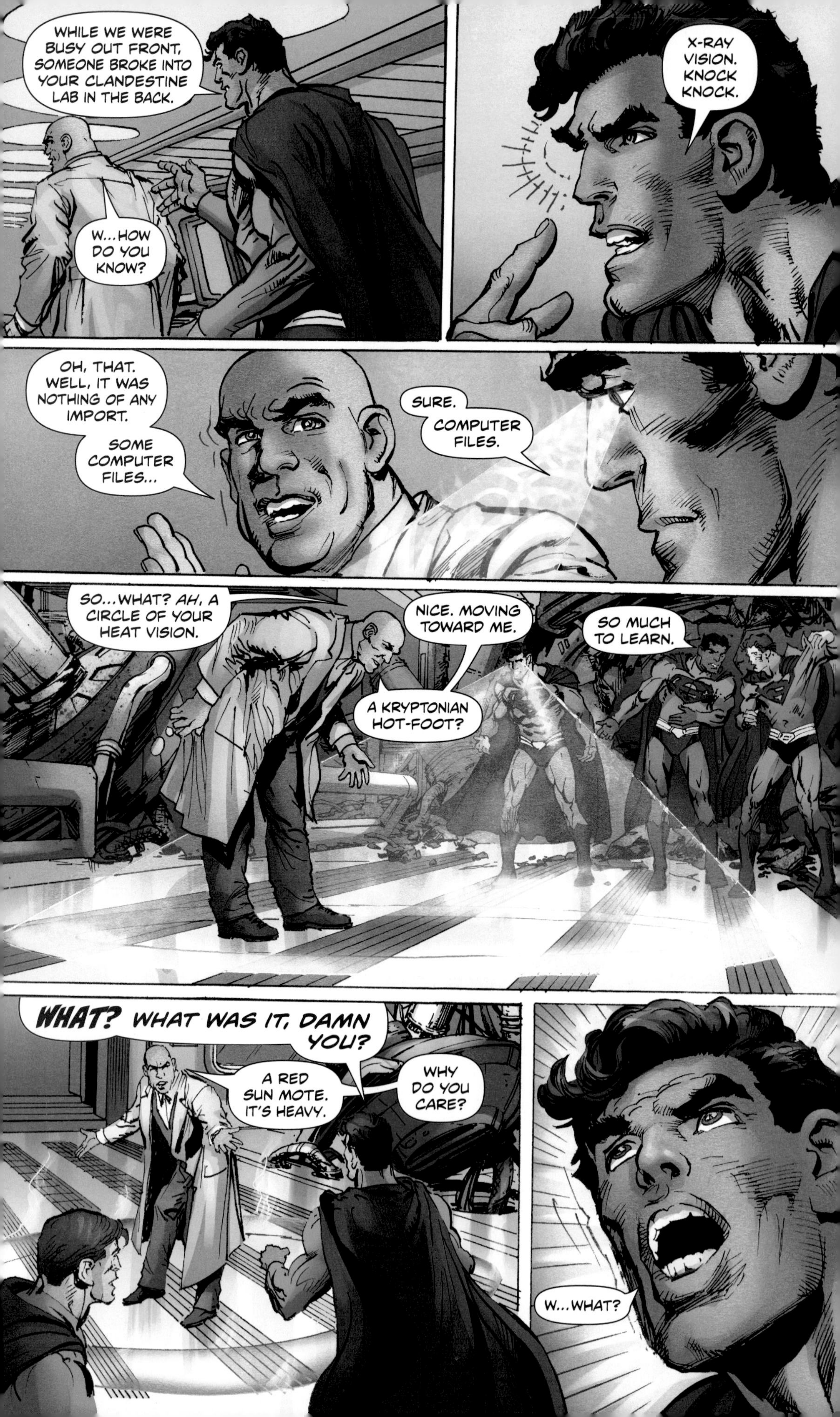
WHILE WE WERE BUSY OUT FRONT, SOMEONE BROKE INTO YOUR CLANDESTINE LAB IN THE BACK.
W...HOW DO YOU KNOW?
X-RAY VISION. KNOCK KNOCK.
OH, THAT. WELL, IT WAS NOTHING OF ANY IMPORT.
SOME COMPUTER FILES...
SURE. COMPUTER FILES.
SO...WHAT? AH, A CIRCLE OF YOUR HEAT VISION.
NICE. MOVING TOWARD ME.
A KRYPTONIAN HOT-FOOT?
SO MUCH TO LEARN.
WHAT? WHAT WAS IT, DAMN YOU?
A RED SUN MOTE. IT'S HEAVY.
WHY DO YOU CARE?
W...WHAT?

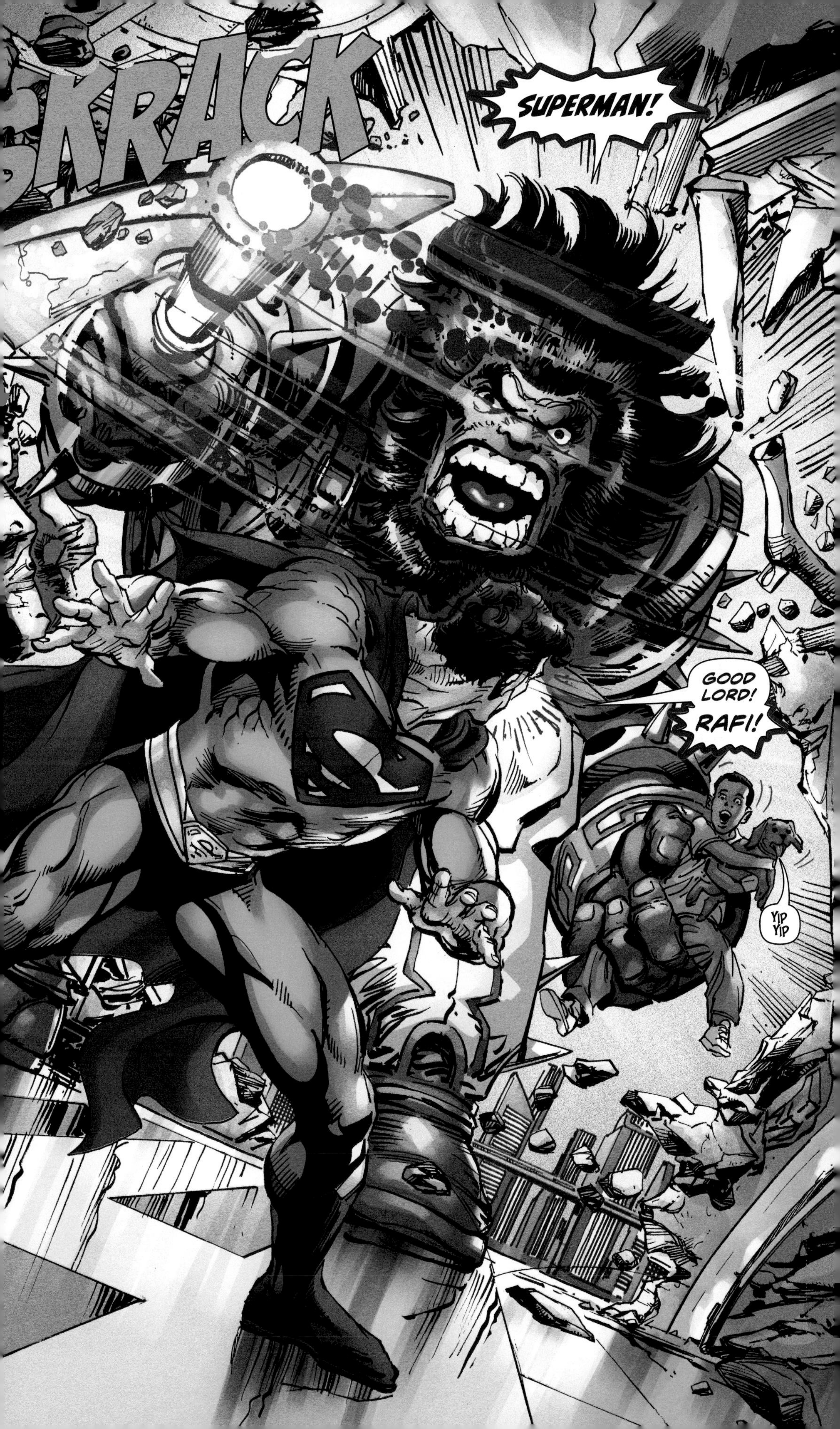
KRACK
SUPERMAN!
GOOD LORD!
RAFI!
YIP YIP

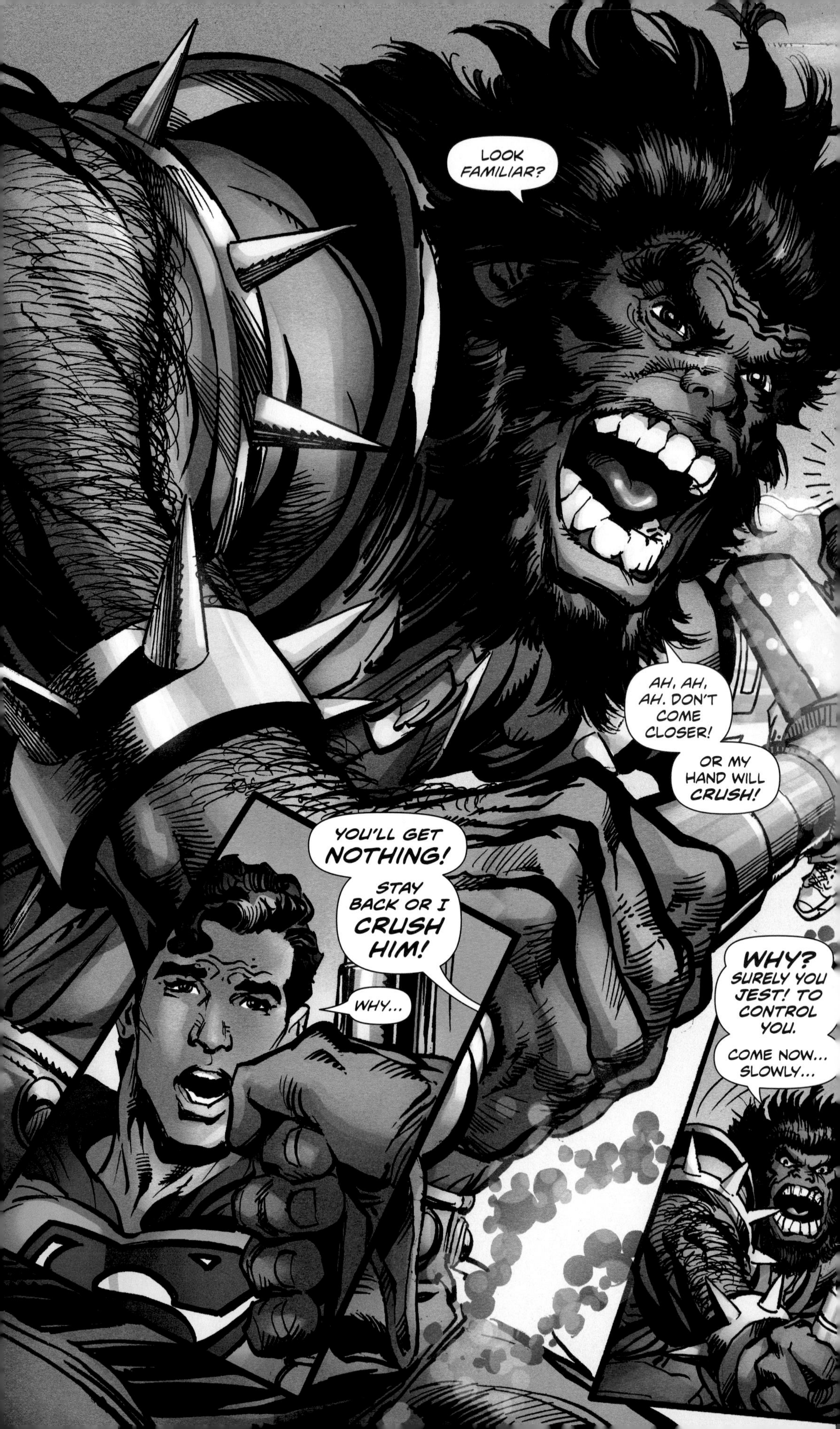
LOOK FAMILIAR?
AH, AH, AH. DON'T COME CLOSER!
OR MY HAND WILL CRUSH!
YOU'LL GET NOTHING!
STAY BACK OR I CRUSH HIM!
WHY...
WHY? SURELY YOU JEST! TO CONTROL YOU.
COME NOW... SLOWLY...

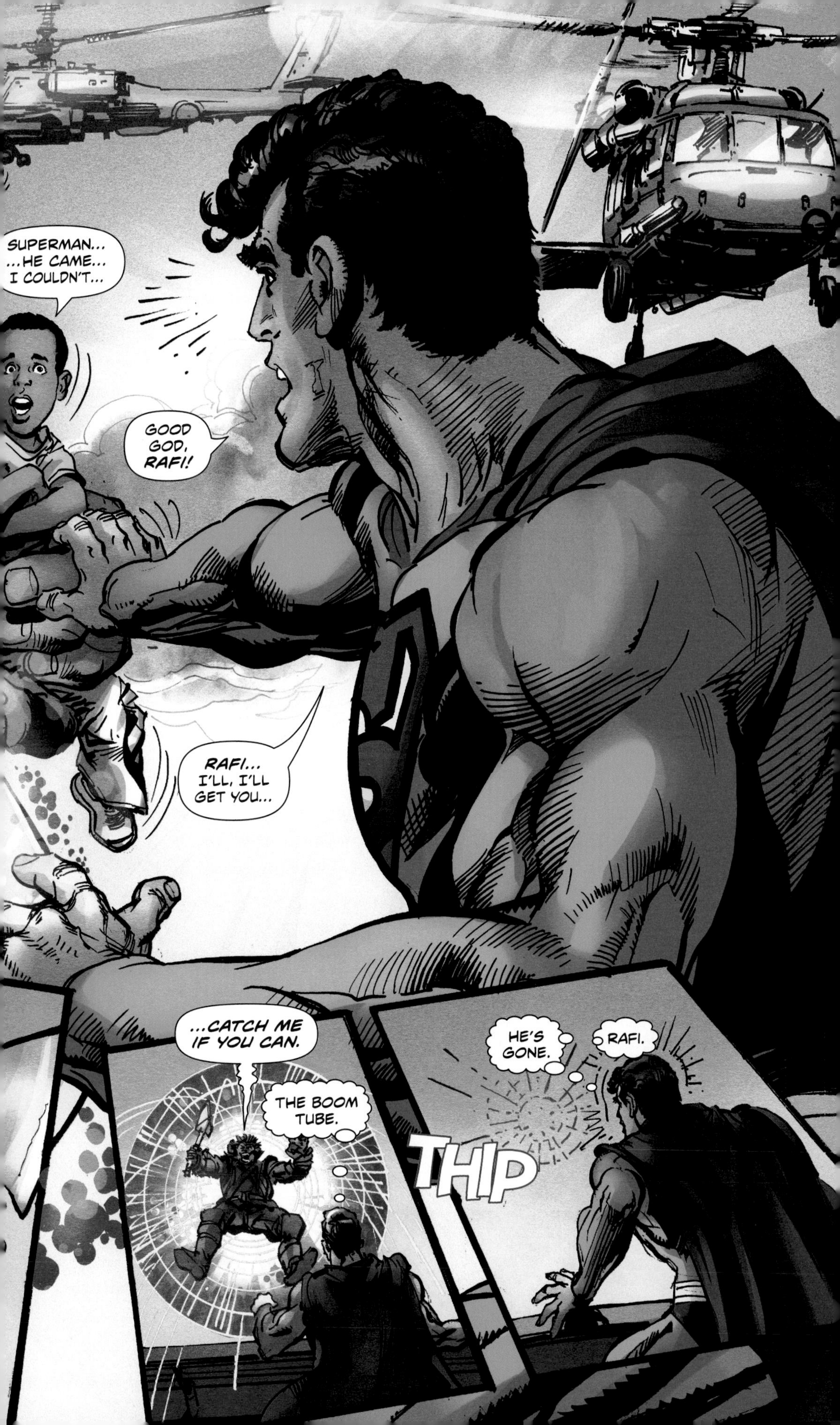
SUPERMAN... ...HE CAME... I COULDN'T...
GOOD GOD, RAFI!
RAFI... I'LL, I'LL GET YOU...
...CATCH ME IF YOU CAN.
THE BOOM TUBE.
THIP
HE'S GONE.
RAFI.

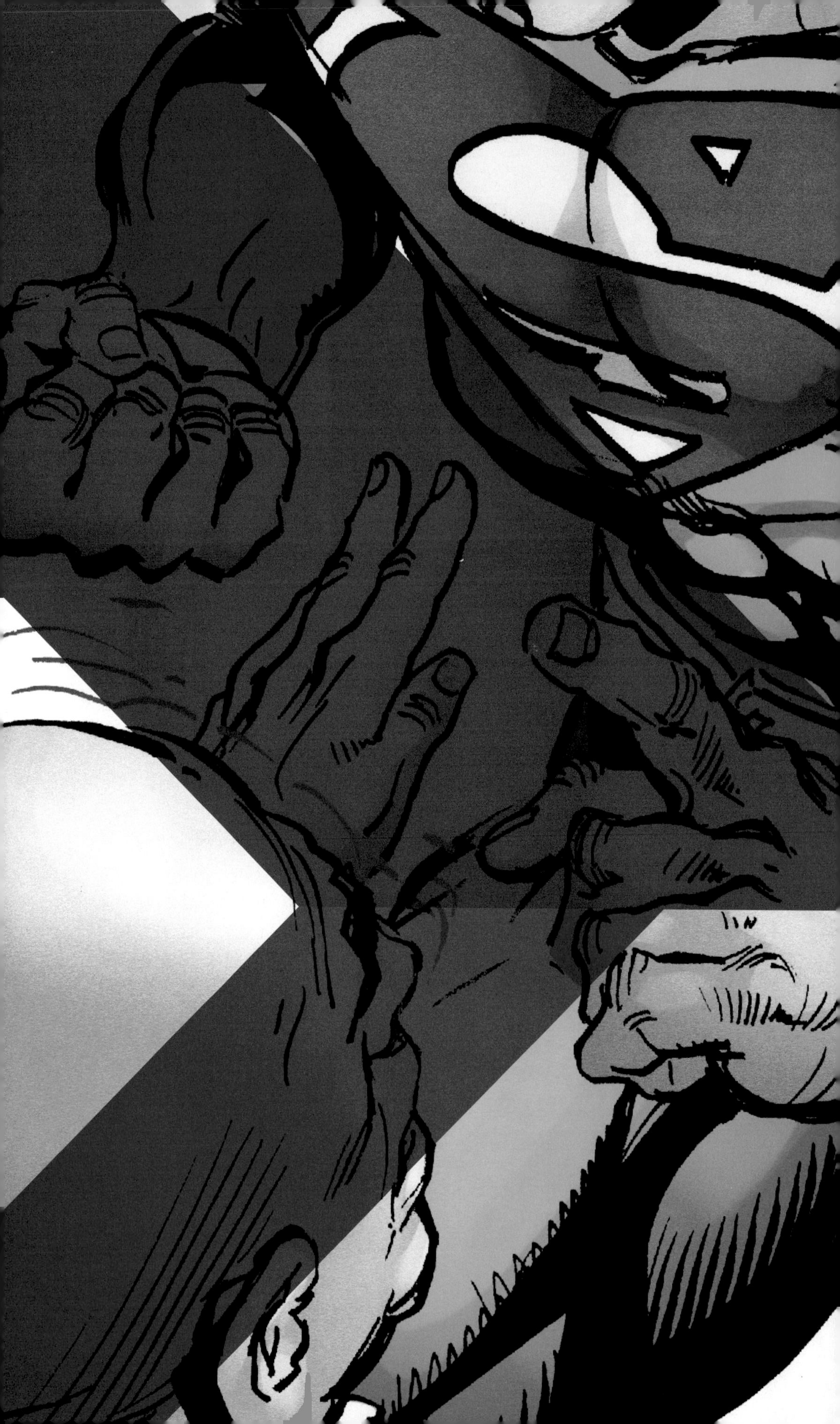

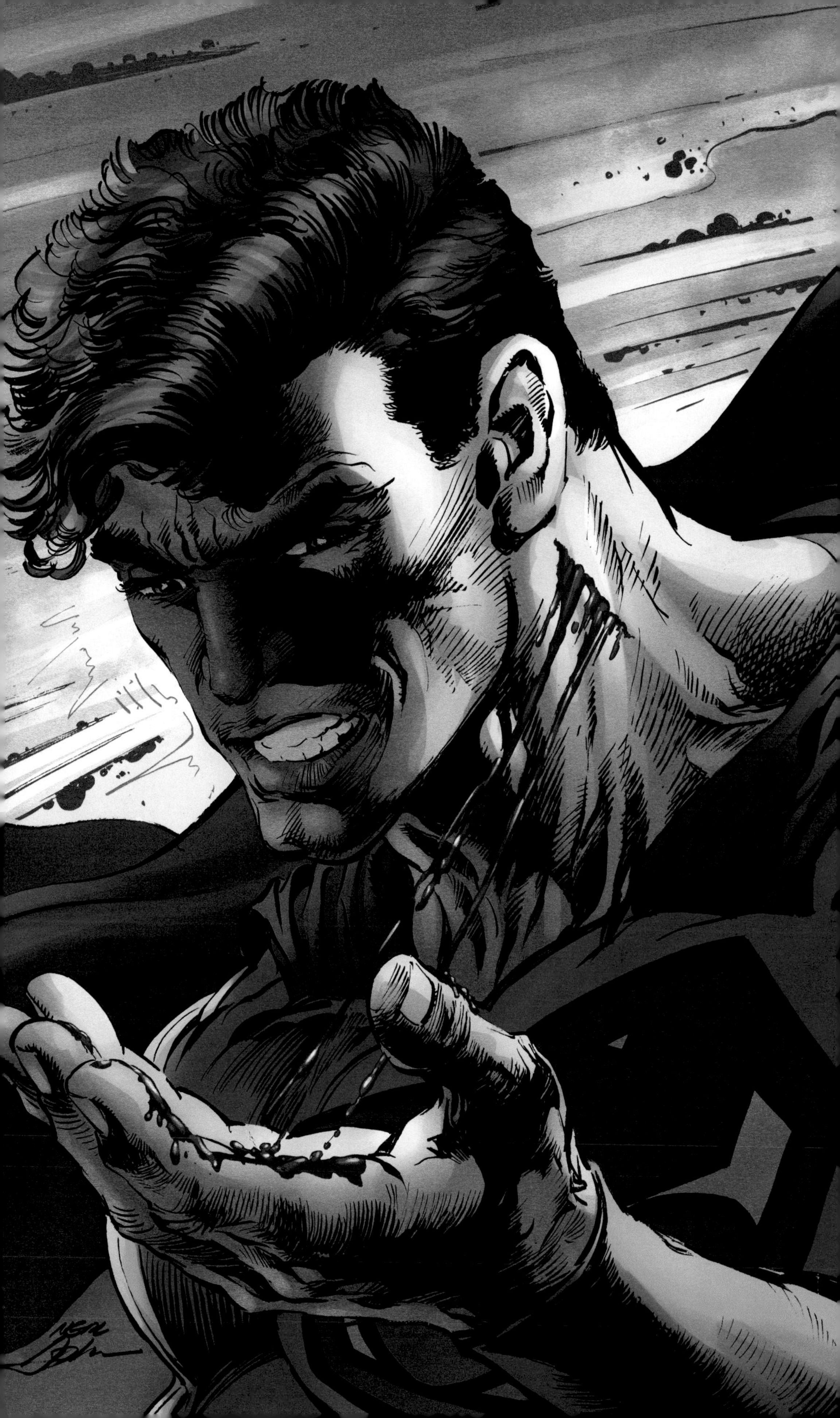

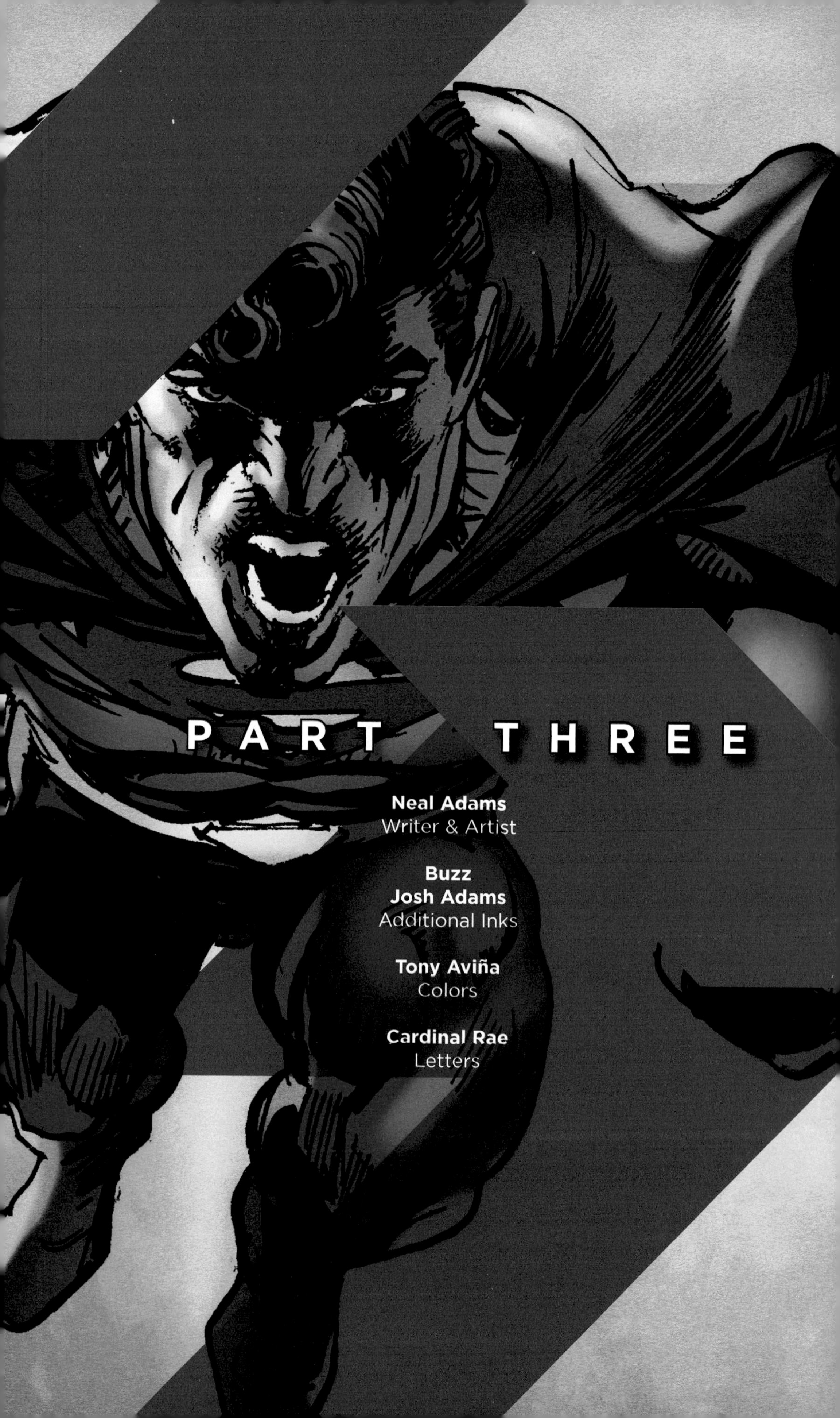

PART THREE

Neal Adams
Writer & Artist

Buzz
Josh Adams
Additional Inks

Tony Aviña
Colors

Cardinal Rae
Letters

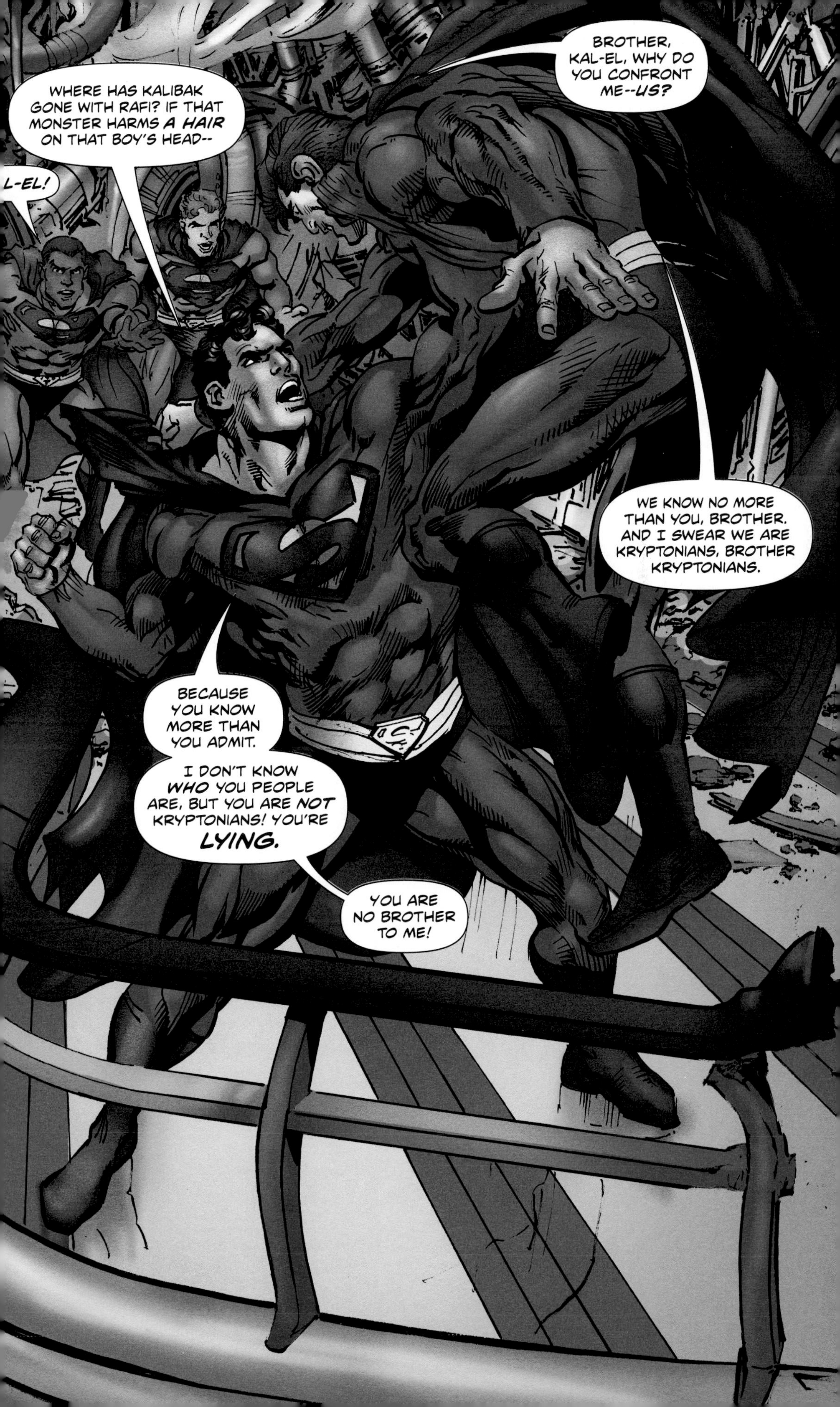

L-EL!
WHERE HAS KALIBAK GONE WITH RAFI? IF THAT MONSTER HARMS A HAIR ON THAT BOY'S HEAD--
BROTHER, KAL-EL, WHY DO YOU CONFRONT ME--US?
BECAUSE YOU KNOW MORE THAN YOU ADMIT.
I DON'T KNOW WHO YOU PEOPLE ARE, BUT YOU ARE NOT KRYPTONIANS! YOU'RE LYING.
WE KNOW NO MORE THAN YOU, BROTHER. AND I SWEAR WE ARE KRYPTONIANS, BROTHER KRYPTONIANS.
YOU ARE NO BROTHER TO ME!

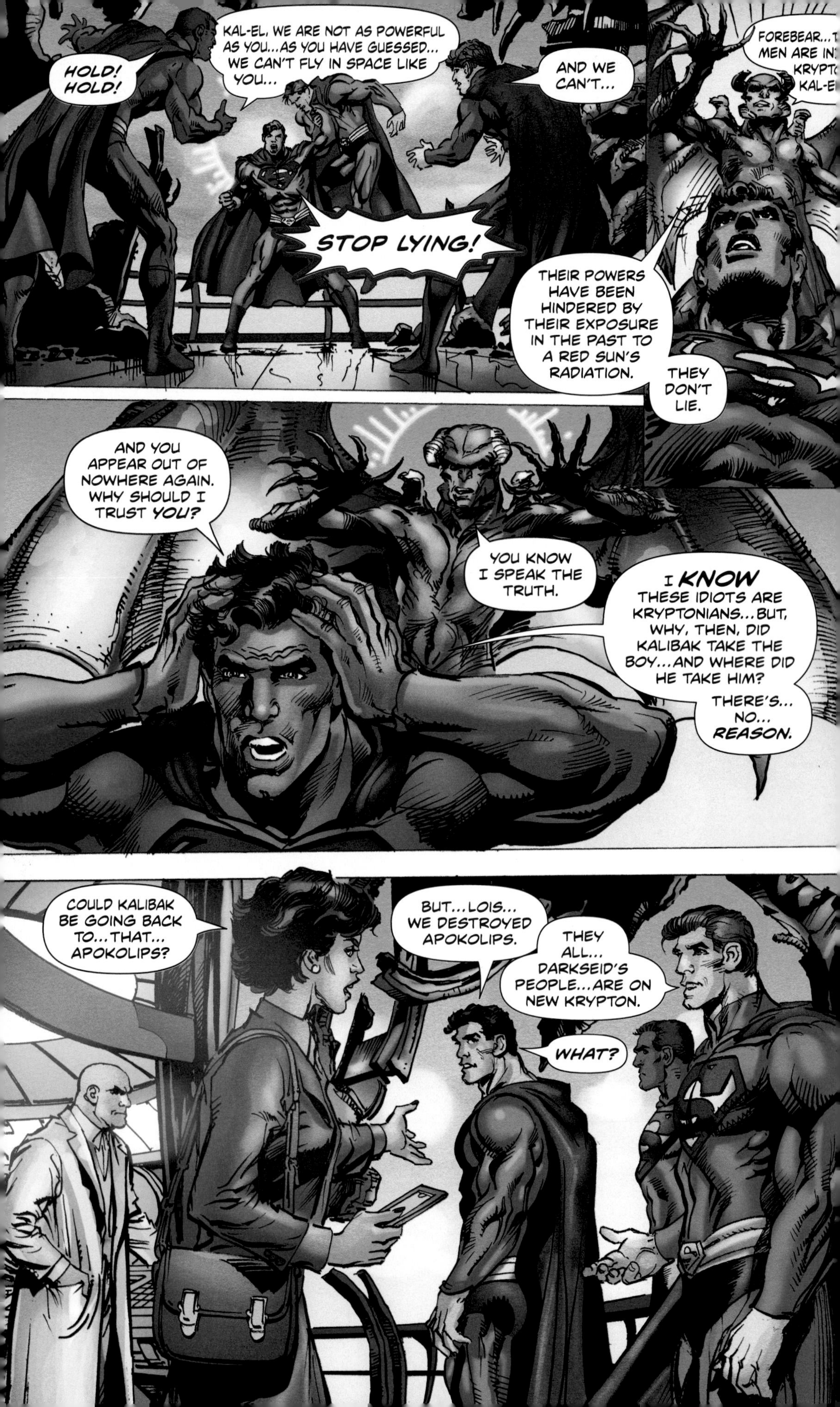

HOLD! HOLD!
KAL-EL, WE ARE NOT AS POWERFUL AS YOU...AS YOU HAVE GUESSED... WE CAN'T FLY IN SPACE LIKE YOU...
AND WE CAN'T...
STOP LYING!
FOREBEAR... MEN ARE IN
THEIR POWERS HAVE BEEN HINDERED BY THEIR EXPOSURE IN THE PAST TO A RED SUN'S RADIATION.
THEY DON'T LIE.
AND YOU APPEAR OUT OF NOWHERE AGAIN. WHY SHOULD I TRUST *YOU*?
YOU KNOW I SPEAK THE TRUTH.
I ***KNOW*** THESE IDIOTS ARE KRYPTONIANS...BUT, WHY, THEN, DID KALIBAK TAKE THE BOY...AND WHERE DID HE TAKE HIM?
THERE'S... NO... ***REASON.***
COULD KALIBAK BE GOING BACK TO...THAT... APOKOLIPS?
BUT...LOIS... WE DESTROYED APOKOLIPS.
THEY ALL... DARKSEID'S PEOPLE...ARE ON NEW KRYPTON.
WHAT?

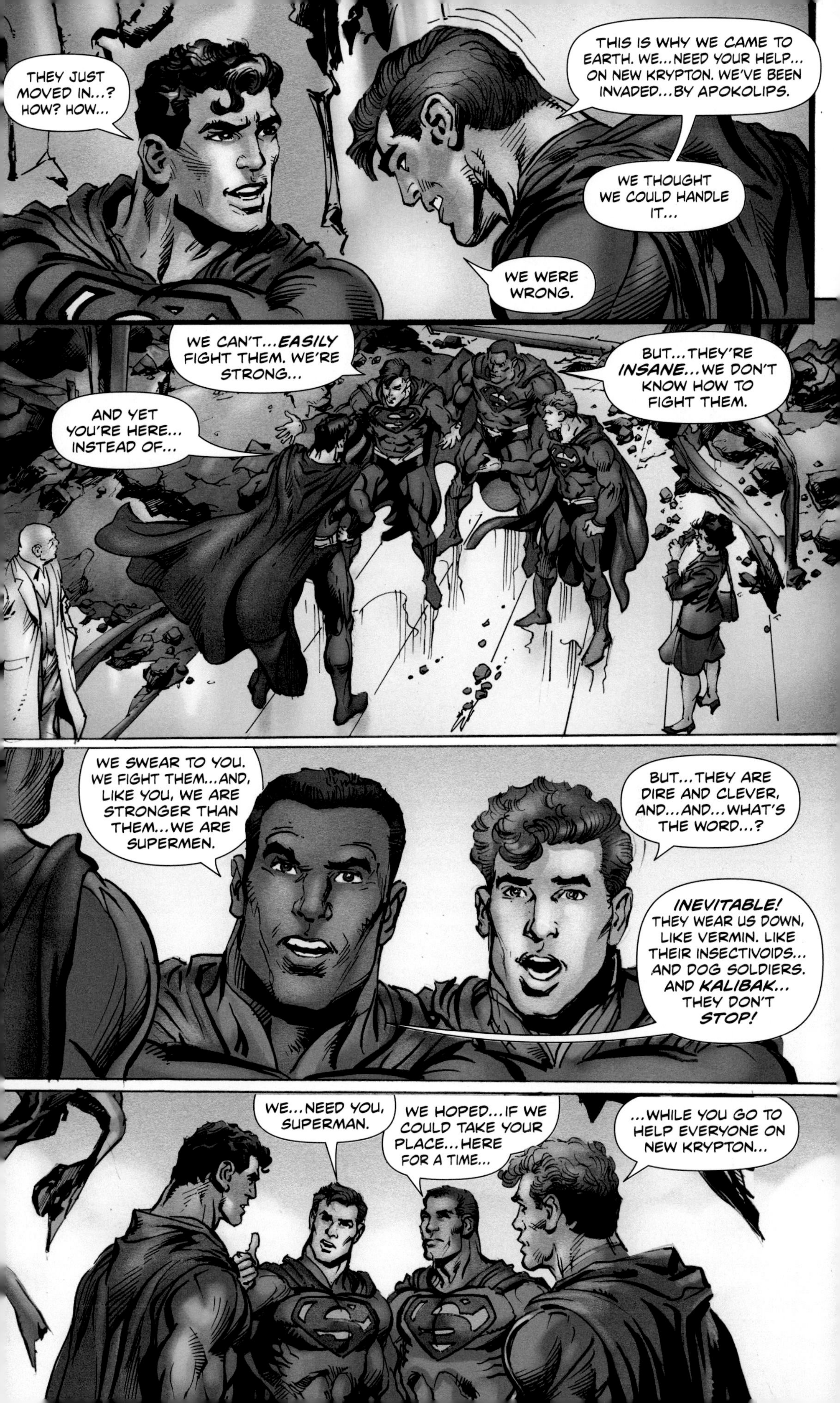
THEY JUST MOVED IN...? HOW? HOW...
THIS IS WHY WE CAME TO EARTH. WE...NEED YOUR HELP... ON NEW KRYPTON. WE'VE BEEN INVADED...BY APOKOLIPS.
WE THOUGHT WE COULD HANDLE IT...
WE WERE WRONG.
WE CAN'T...EASILY FIGHT THEM. WE'RE STRONG...
BUT...THEY'RE INSANE...WE DON'T KNOW HOW TO FIGHT THEM.
AND YET YOU'RE HERE... INSTEAD OF...
WE SWEAR TO YOU. WE FIGHT THEM...AND, LIKE YOU, WE ARE STRONGER THAN THEM...WE ARE SUPERMEN.
BUT...THEY ARE DIRE AND CLEVER, AND...AND...WHAT'S THE WORD...?
INEVITABLE! THEY WEAR US DOWN, LIKE VERMIN. LIKE THEIR INSECTIVOIDS... AND DOG SOLDIERS. AND KALIBAK... THEY DON'T STOP!
WE...NEED YOU, SUPERMAN.
WE HOPED...IF WE COULD TAKE YOUR PLACE...HERE FOR A TIME...
...WHILE YOU GO TO HELP EVERYONE ON NEW KRYPTON...

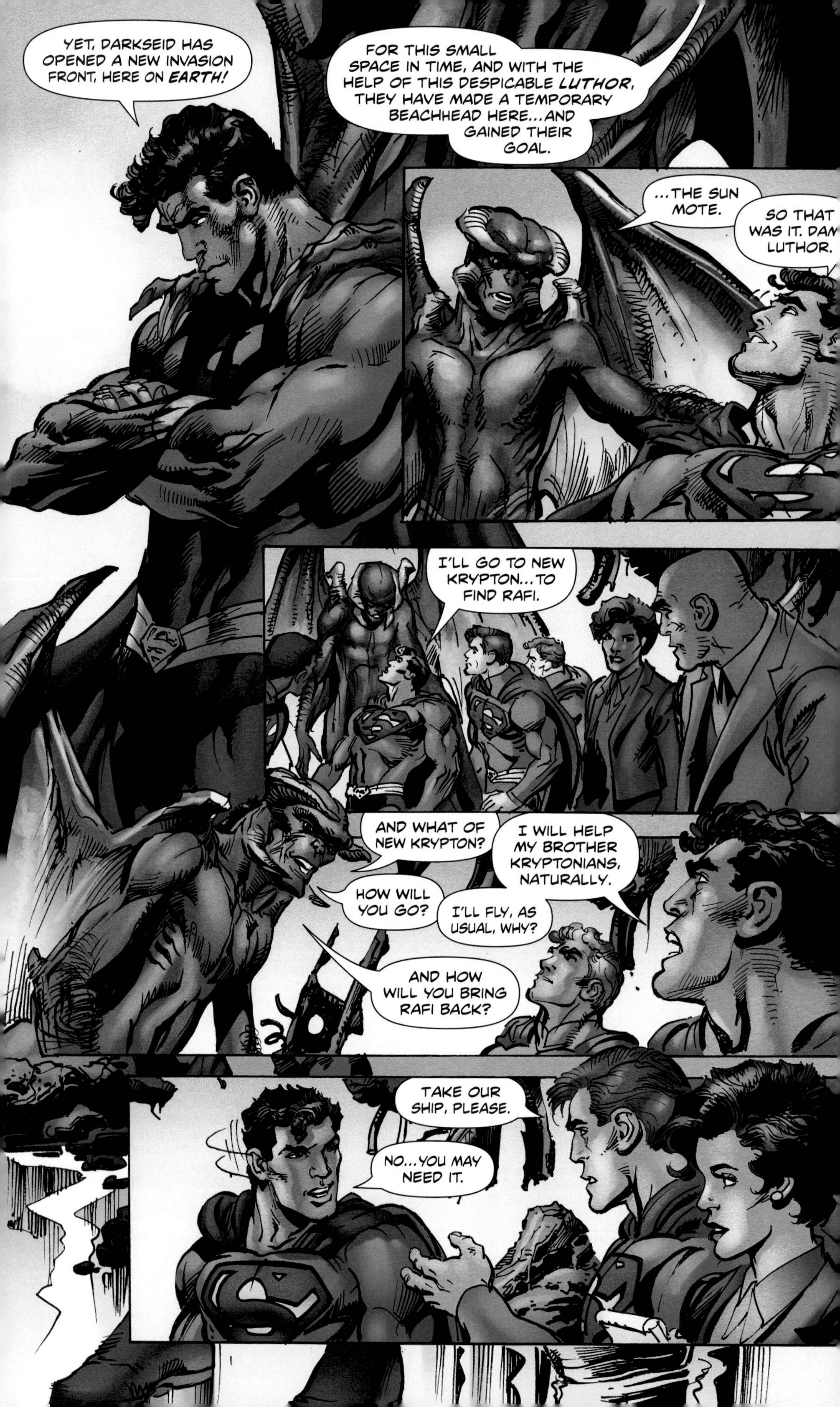

YET, DARKSEID HAS OPENED A NEW INVASION FRONT, HERE ON *EARTH!*
FOR THIS SMALL SPACE IN TIME, AND WITH THE HELP OF THIS DESPICABLE *LUTHOR*, THEY HAVE MADE A TEMPORARY BEACHHEAD HERE...AND GAINED THEIR GOAL.
...THE SUN MOTE.
SO THAT WAS IT. DAM LUTHOR.
I'LL GO TO NEW KRYPTON...TO FIND RAFI.
AND WHAT OF NEW KRYPTON?
I WILL HELP MY BROTHER KRYPTONIANS, NATURALLY.
HOW WILL YOU GO?
I'LL FLY, AS USUAL, WHY?
AND HOW WILL YOU BRING RAFI BACK?
TAKE OUR SHIP, PLEASE.
NO...YOU MAY NEED IT.

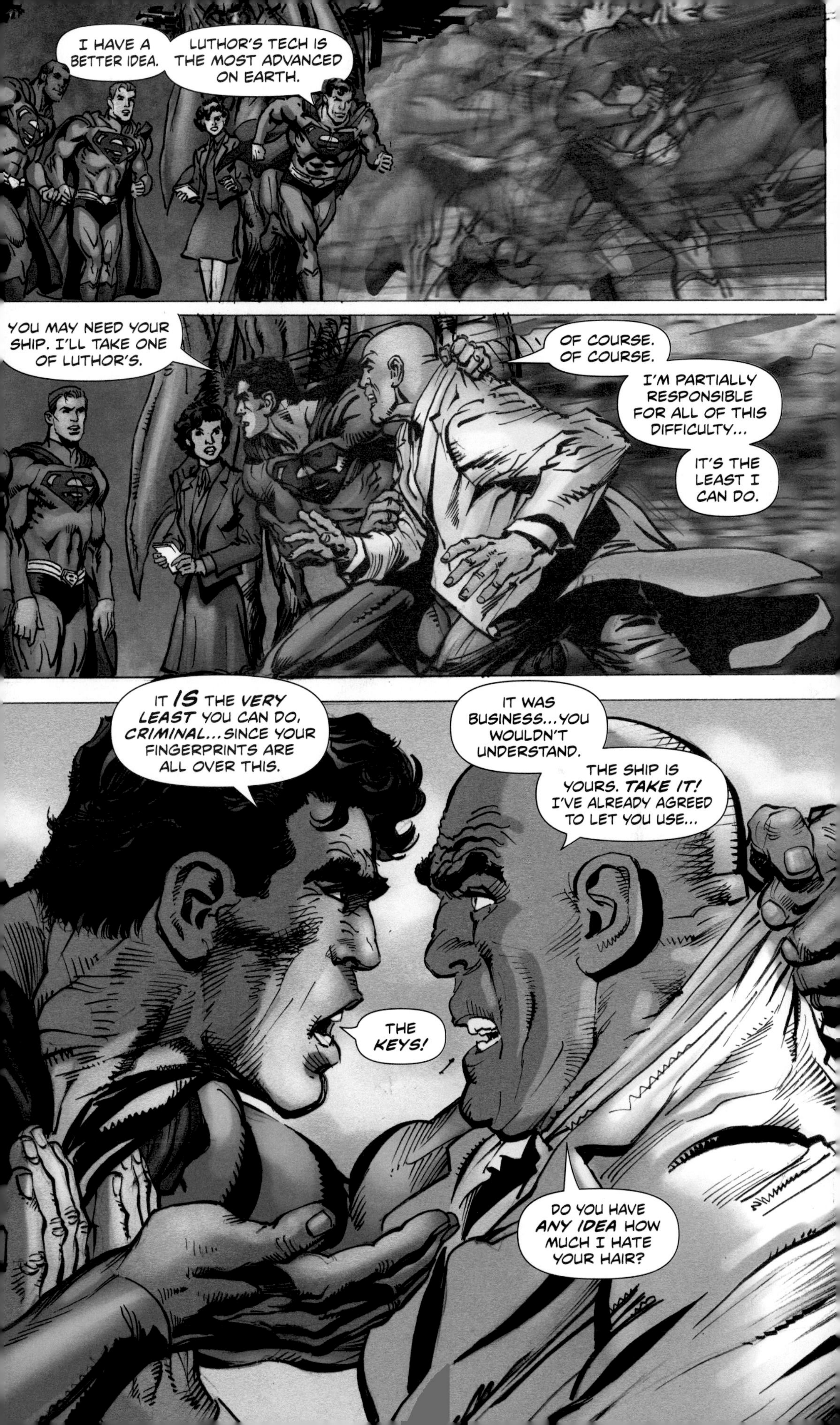

I HAVE A BETTER IDEA.
LUTHOR'S TECH IS THE MOST ADVANCED ON EARTH.
YOU MAY NEED YOUR SHIP. I'LL TAKE ONE OF LUTHOR'S.
OF COURSE. OF COURSE.
I'M PARTIALLY RESPONSIBLE FOR ALL OF THIS DIFFICULTY...
IT'S THE LEAST I CAN DO.
IT *IS* THE *VERY LEAST* YOU CAN DO, *CRIMINAL*...SINCE YOUR FINGERPRINTS ARE ALL OVER THIS.
IT WAS BUSINESS...YOU WOULDN'T UNDERSTAND.
THE SHIP IS YOURS. *TAKE IT!* I'VE ALREADY AGREED TO LET YOU USE...
THE *KEYS!*
DO YOU HAVE *ANY IDEA* HOW MUCH I HATE YOUR HAIR?

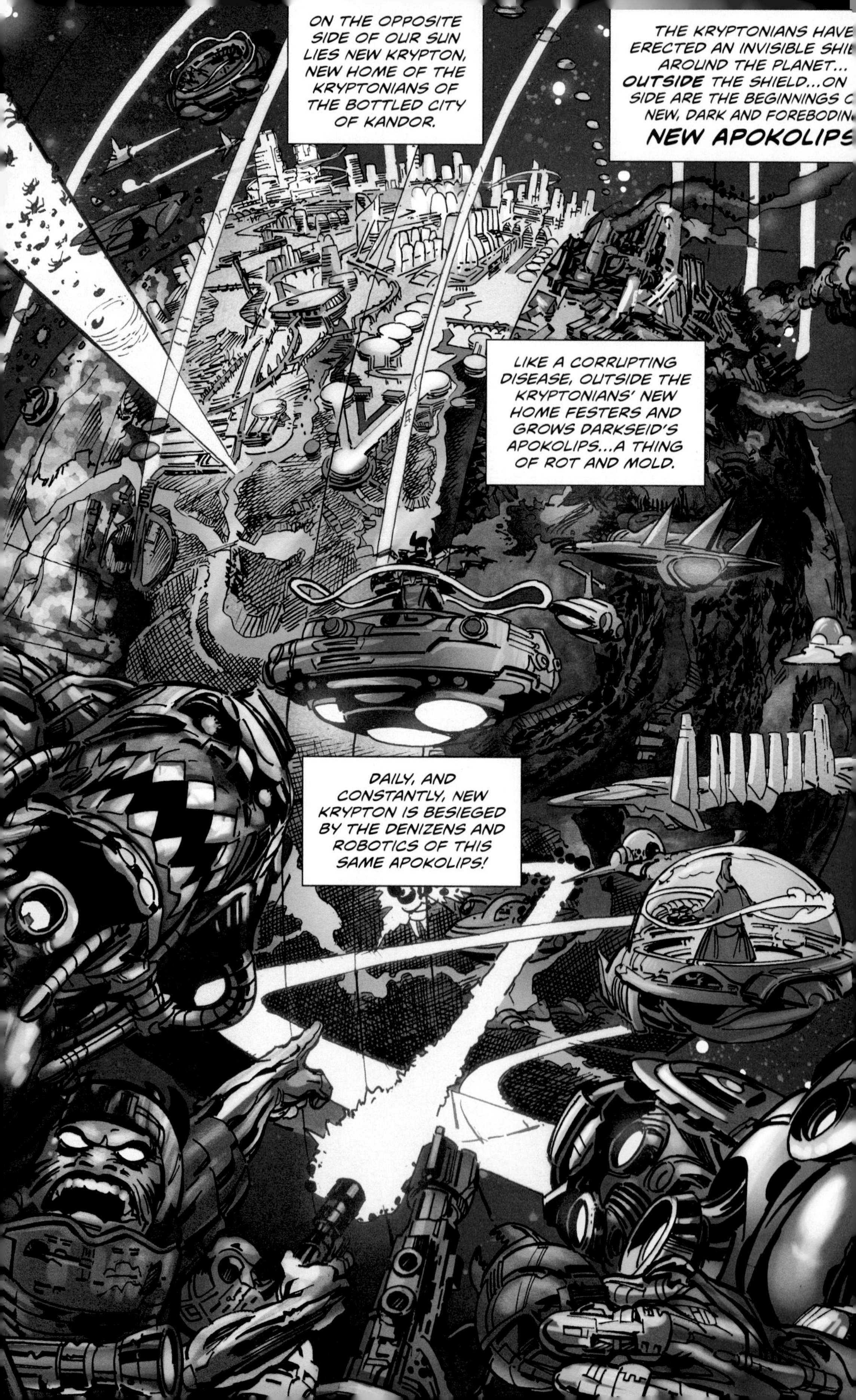

ON THE OPPOSITE SIDE OF OUR SUN LIES NEW KRYPTON, NEW HOME OF THE KRYPTONIANS OF THE BOTTLED CITY OF KANDOR.
THE KRYPTONIANS HAVE ERECTED AN INVISIBLE SHIE AROUND THE PLANET... OUTSIDE THE SHIELD...ON SIDE ARE THE BEGINNINGS C NEW, DARK AND FOREBODIN NEW APOKOLIPS
LIKE A CORRUPTING DISEASE, OUTSIDE THE KRYPTONIANS' NEW HOME FESTERS AND GROWS DARKSEID'S APOKOLIPS...A THING OF ROT AND MOLD.
DAILY, AND CONSTANTLY, NEW KRYPTON IS BESIEGED BY THE DENIZENS AND ROBOTICS OF THIS SAME APOKOLIPS!

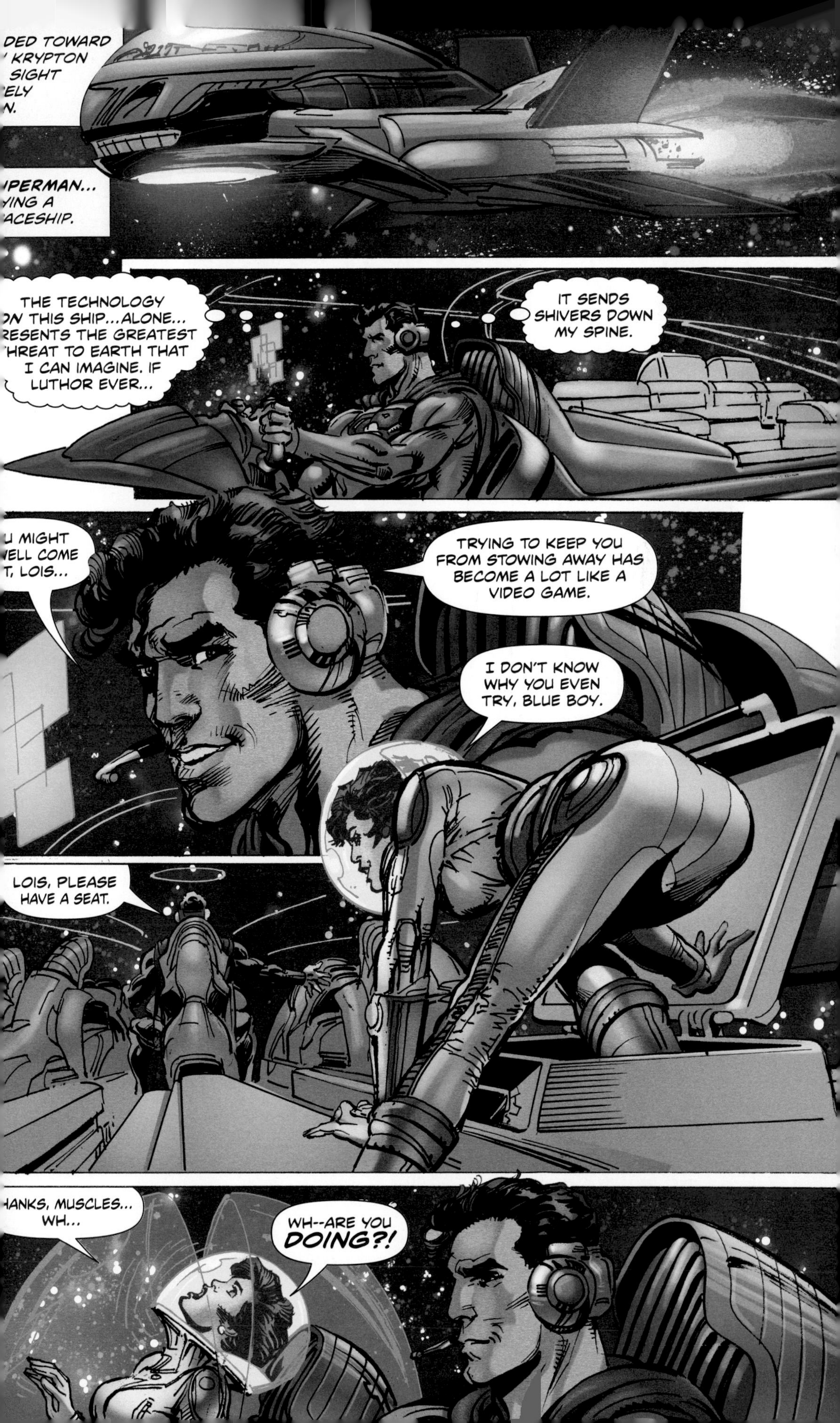

DED TOWARD
' KRYPTON
SIGHT
'ELY
N.
IPERMAN...
YING A
ACESHIP.
THE TECHNOLOGY
ON THIS SHIP...ALONE...
RESENTS THE GREATEST
THREAT TO EARTH THAT
I CAN IMAGINE. IF
LUTHOR EVER...
IT SENDS SHIVERS DOWN MY SPINE.
U MIGHT
VELL COME
T, LOIS...
TRYING TO KEEP YOU FROM STOWING AWAY HAS BECOME A LOT LIKE A VIDEO GAME.
I DON'T KNOW WHY YOU EVEN TRY, BLUE BOY.
LOIS, PLEASE HAVE A SEAT.
HANKS, MUSCLES...
WH...
WH--ARE YOU DOING?!

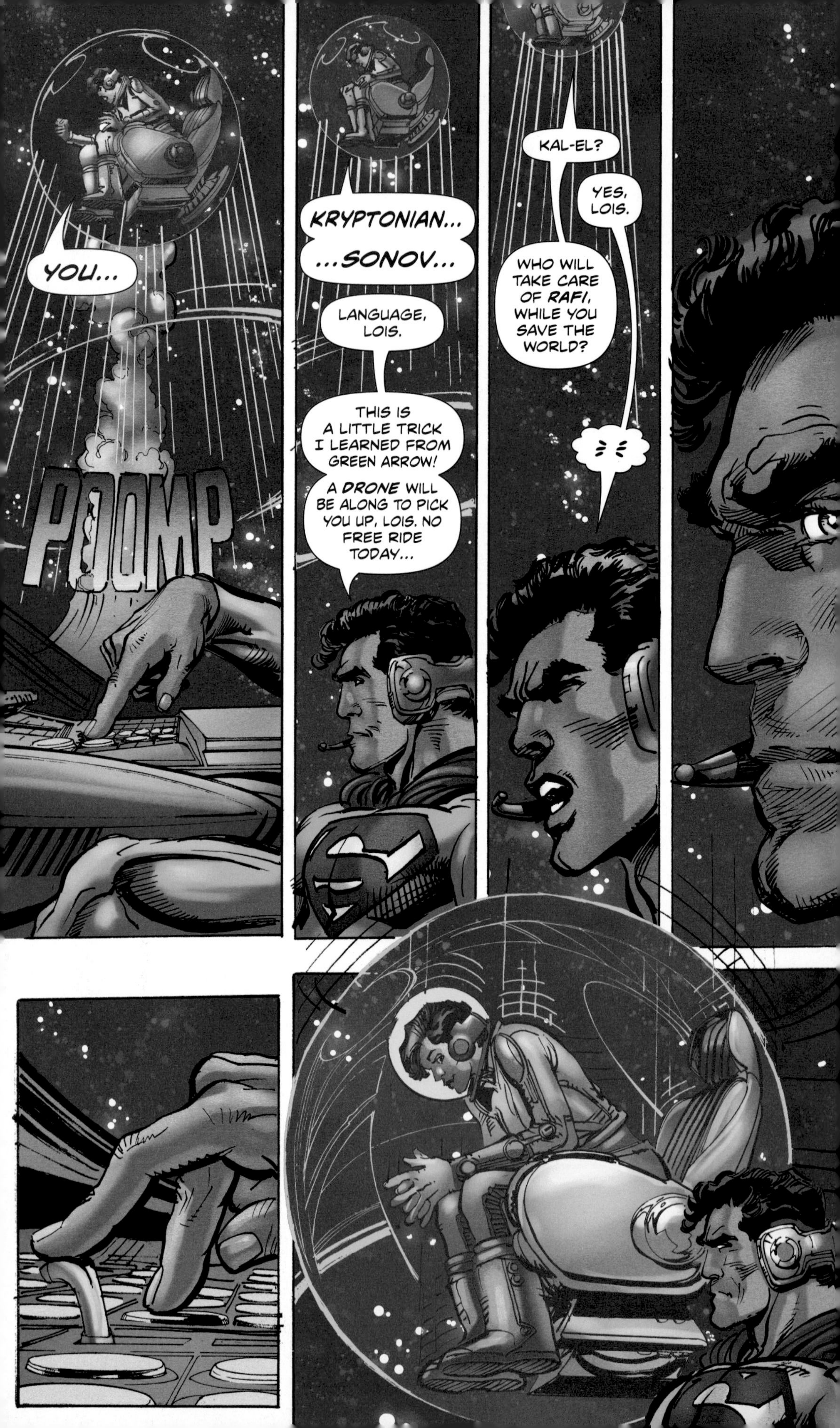
YOU...
POOMP
KRYPTONIAN...
...SONOV...
LANGUAGE, LOIS.
THIS IS A LITTLE TRICK I LEARNED FROM GREEN ARROW!
A DRONE WILL BE ALONG TO PICK YOU UP, LOIS. NO FREE RIDE TODAY...
KAL-EL?
YES, LOIS.
WHO WILL TAKE CARE OF RAFI, WHILE YOU SAVE THE WORLD?

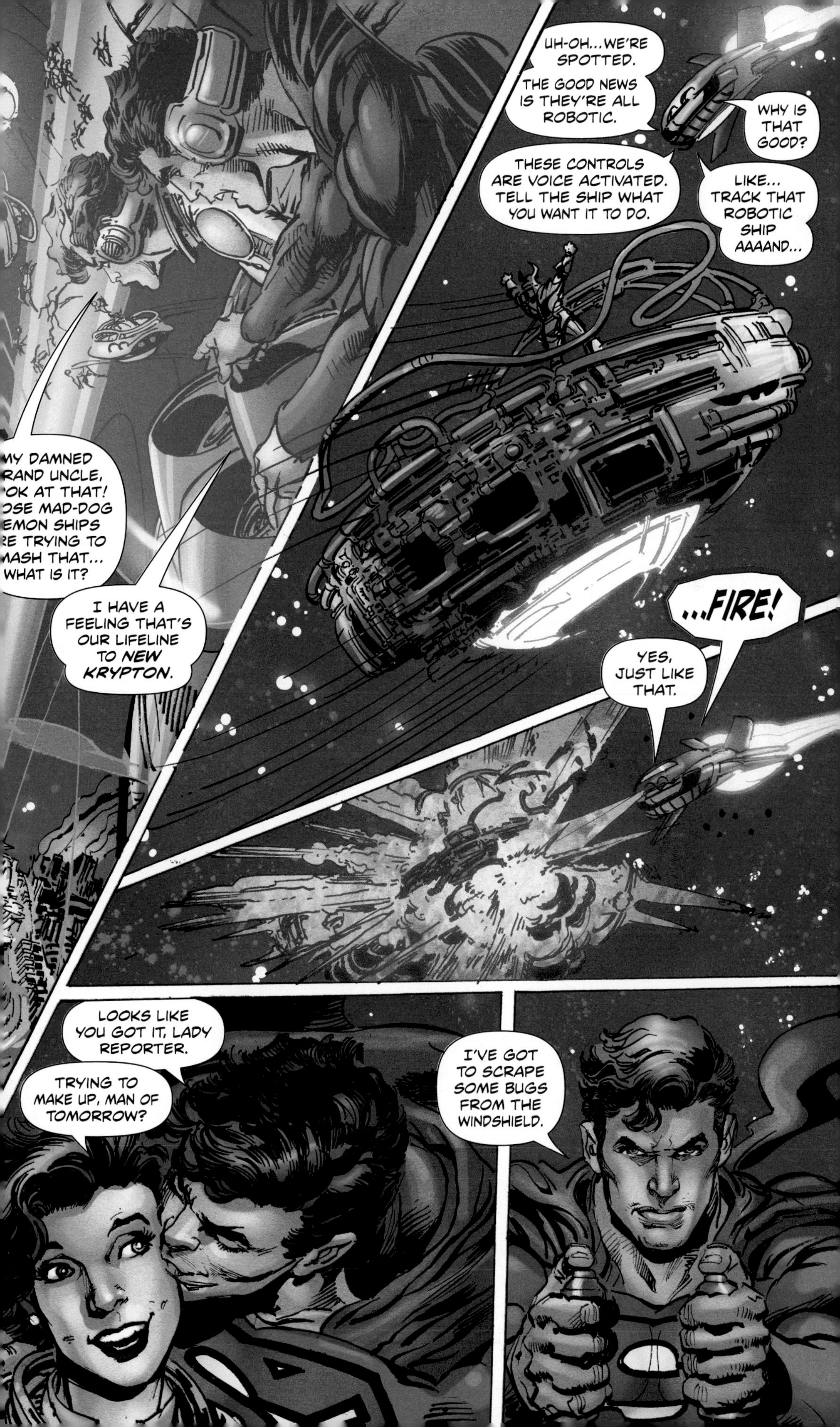

MY DAMNED
RAND UNCLE,
OK AT THAT!
OSE MAD-DOG
EMON SHIPS
E TRYING TO
MASH THAT...
WHAT IS IT?
I HAVE A FEELING THAT'S OUR LIFELINE TO NEW KRYPTON.
UH-OH...WE'RE SPOTTED.
THE GOOD NEWS IS THEY'RE ALL ROBOTIC.
WHY IS THAT GOOD?
THESE CONTROLS ARE VOICE ACTIVATED. TELL THE SHIP WHAT YOU WANT IT TO DO.
LIKE... TRACK THAT ROBOTIC SHIP AAAAND...
...FIRE!
YES, JUST LIKE THAT.
LOOKS LIKE YOU GOT IT, LADY REPORTER.
TRYING TO MAKE UP, MAN OF TOMORROW?
I'VE GOT TO SCRAPE SOME BUGS FROM THE WINDSHIELD.

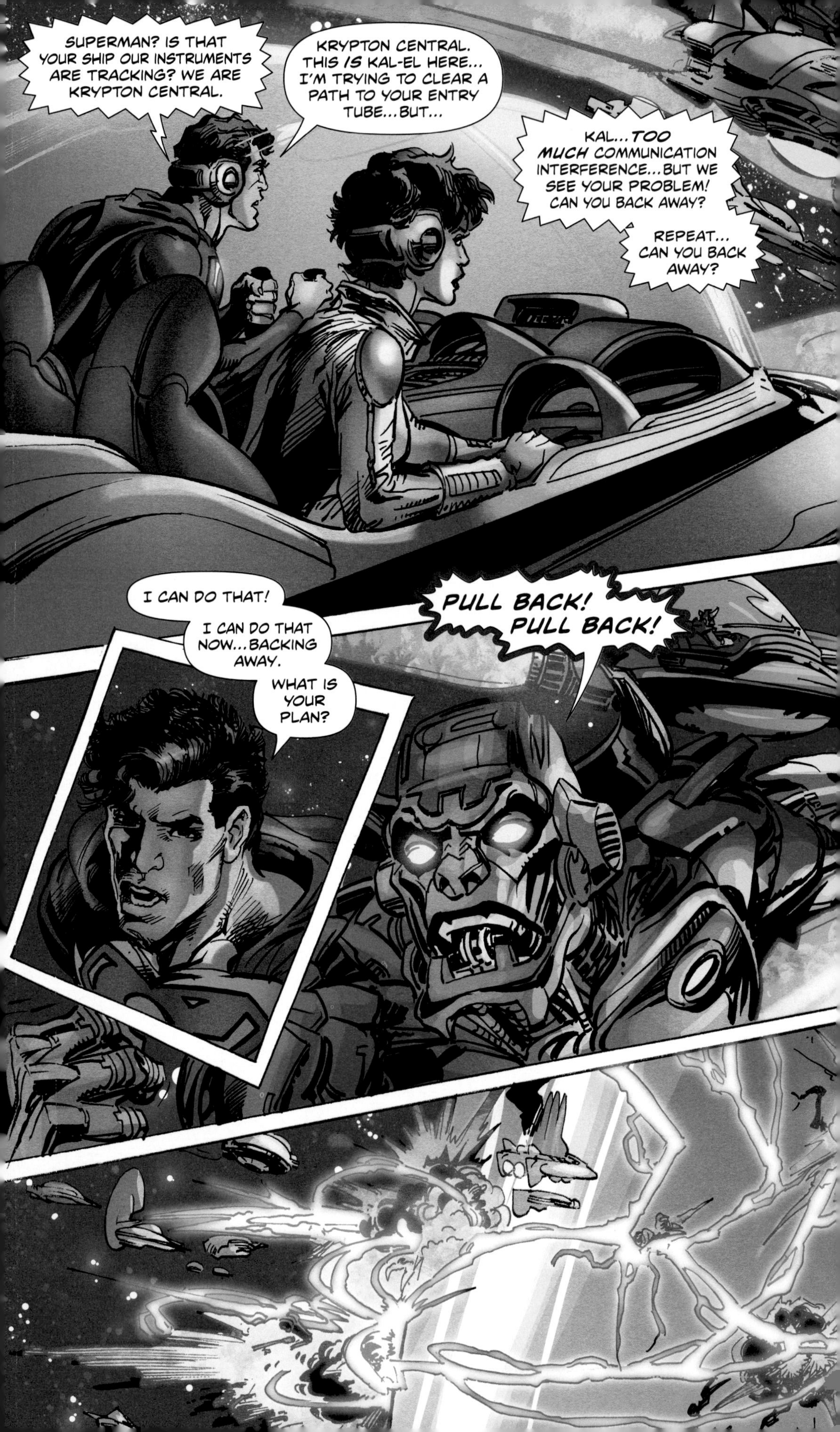
SUPERMAN? IS THAT YOUR SHIP OUR INSTRUMENTS ARE TRACKING? WE ARE KRYPTON CENTRAL.
KRYPTON CENTRAL. THIS *IS* KAL-EL HERE... I'M TRYING TO CLEAR A PATH TO YOUR ENTRY TUBE...BUT...
KAL...**TOO MUCH** COMMUNICATION INTERFERENCE...BUT WE SEE YOUR PROBLEM! CAN YOU BACK AWAY?
REPEAT... CAN YOU BACK AWAY?
I CAN DO THAT!
I CAN DO THAT NOW...BACKING AWAY.
WHAT IS YOUR PLAN?
PULL BACK! PULL BACK!

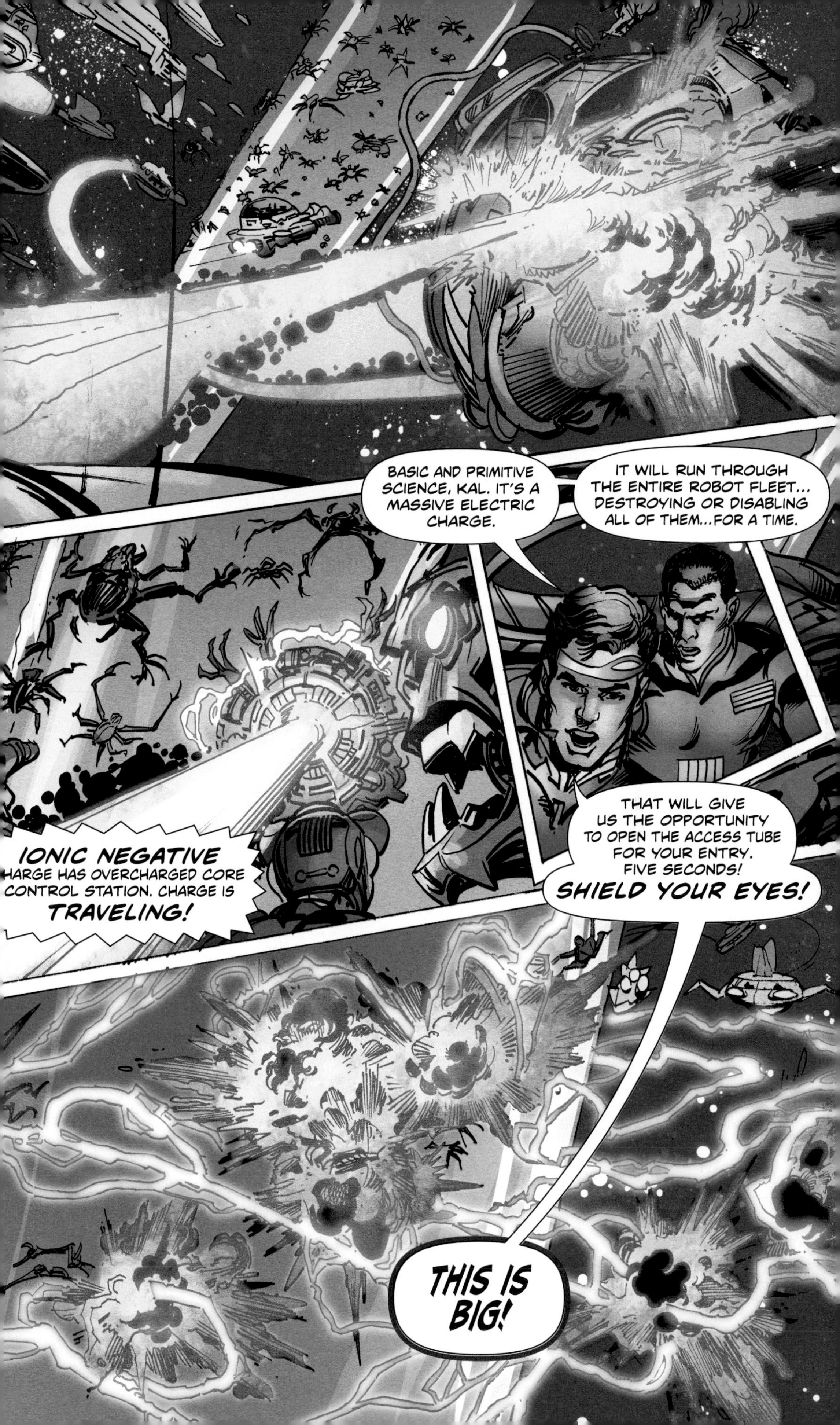
BASIC AND PRIMITIVE SCIENCE, KAL. IT'S A MASSIVE ELECTRIC CHARGE.
IT WILL RUN THROUGH THE ENTIRE ROBOT FLEET... DESTROYING OR DISABLING ALL OF THEM...FOR A TIME.
IONIC NEGATIVE HARGE HAS OVERCHARGED CORE CONTROL STATION. CHARGE IS TRAVELING!
THAT WILL GIVE US THE OPPORTUNITY TO OPEN THE ACCESS TUBE FOR YOUR ENTRY. FIVE SECONDS! SHIELD YOUR EYES!
THIS IS BIG!

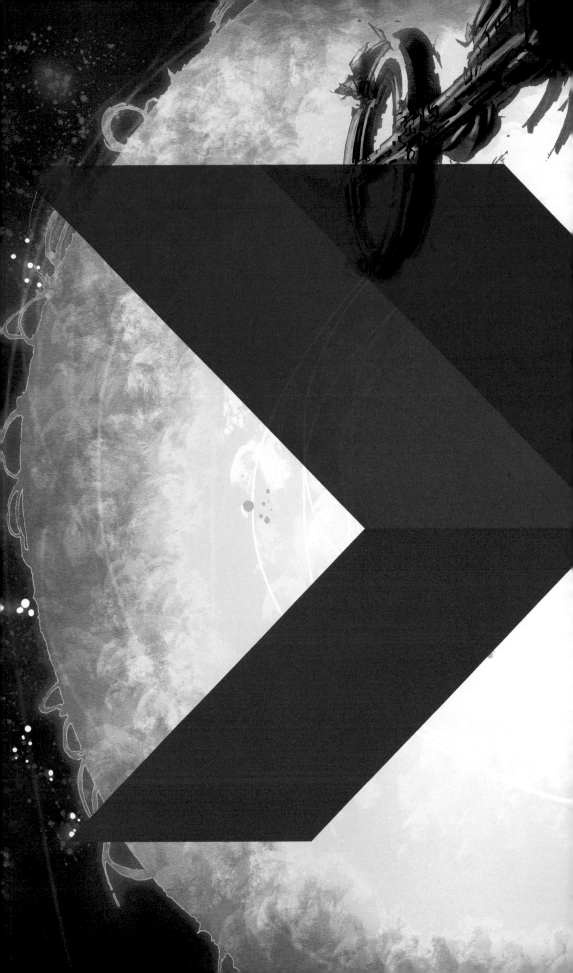

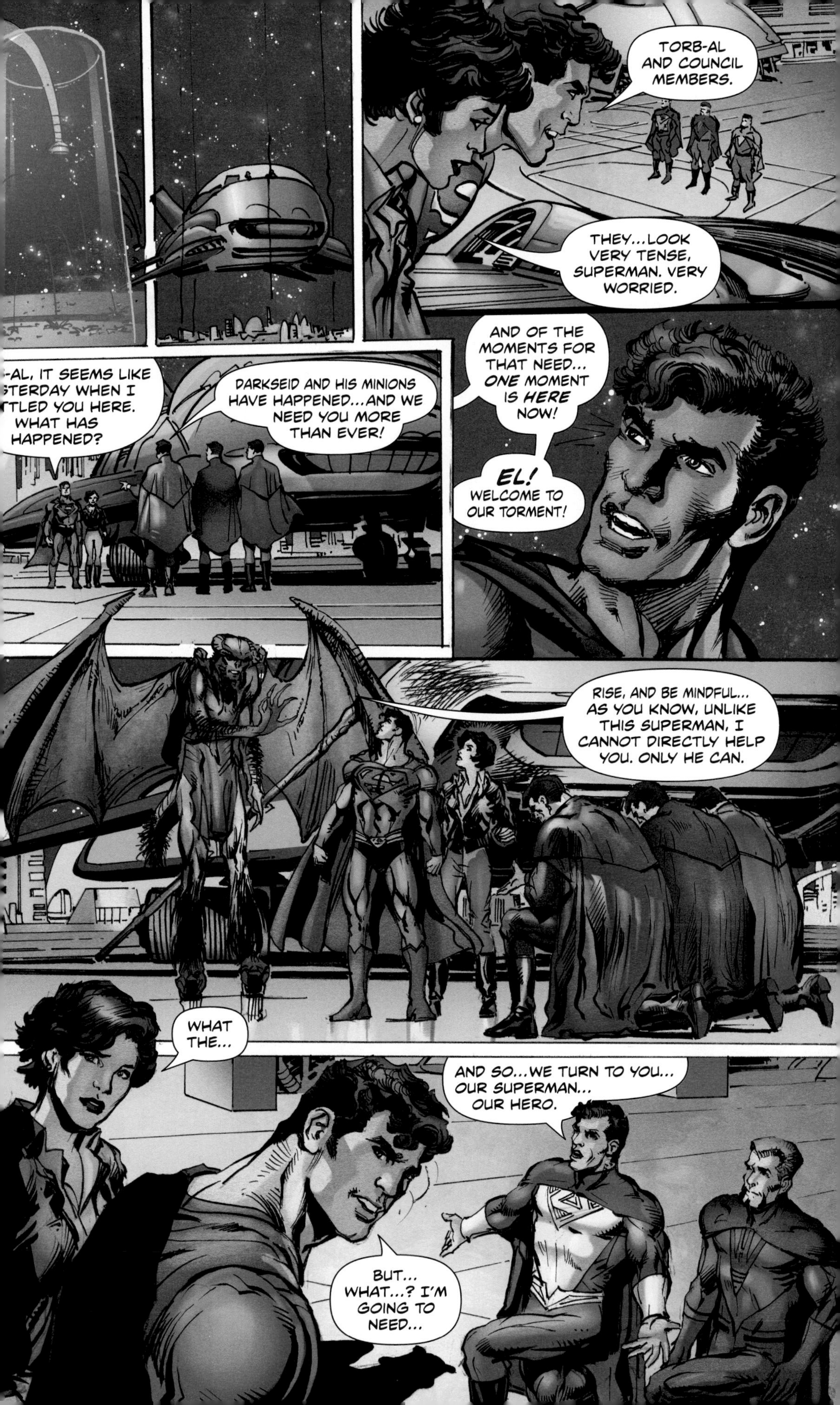
TORB-AL AND COUNCIL MEMBERS.
THEY...LOOK VERY TENSE, SUPERMAN. VERY WORRIED.
-AL, IT SEEMS LIKE STERDAY WHEN I TTLED YOU HERE. WHAT HAS HAPPENED?
DARKSEID AND HIS MINIONS HAVE HAPPENED...AND WE NEED YOU MORE THAN EVER!
AND OF THE MOMENTS FOR THAT NEED... ONE MOMENT IS HERE NOW!
EL! WELCOME TO OUR TORMENT!
RISE, AND BE MINDFUL... AS YOU KNOW, UNLIKE THIS SUPERMAN, I CANNOT DIRECTLY HELP YOU. ONLY HE CAN.
WHAT THE...
AND SO...WE TURN TO YOU... OUR SUPERMAN... OUR HERO.
BUT... WHAT...? I'M GOING TO NEED...

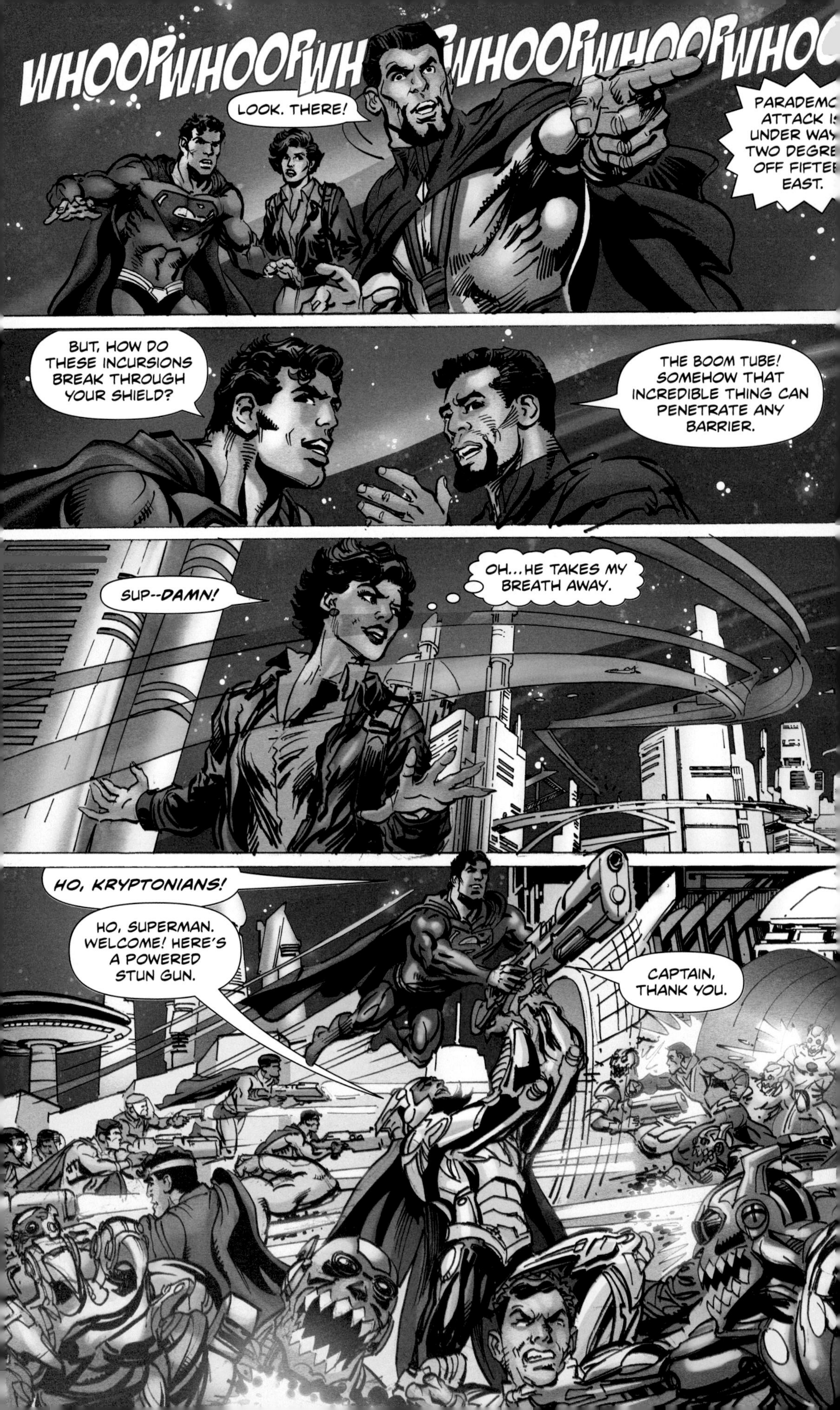
WHOOPWHOOPWH WHOOPWHOOPWHOO
LOOK. THERE!
PARADEMO ATTACK IS UNDER WAY TWO DEGRE OFF FIFTE EAST.
BUT, HOW DO THESE INCURSIONS BREAK THROUGH YOUR SHIELD?
THE BOOM TUBE! SOMEHOW THAT INCREDIBLE THING CAN PENETRATE ANY BARRIER.
SUP--DAMN!
OH...HE TAKES MY BREATH AWAY.
HO, KRYPTONIANS!
HO, SUPERMAN. WELCOME! HERE'S A POWERED STUN GUN.
CAPTAIN, THANK YOU.

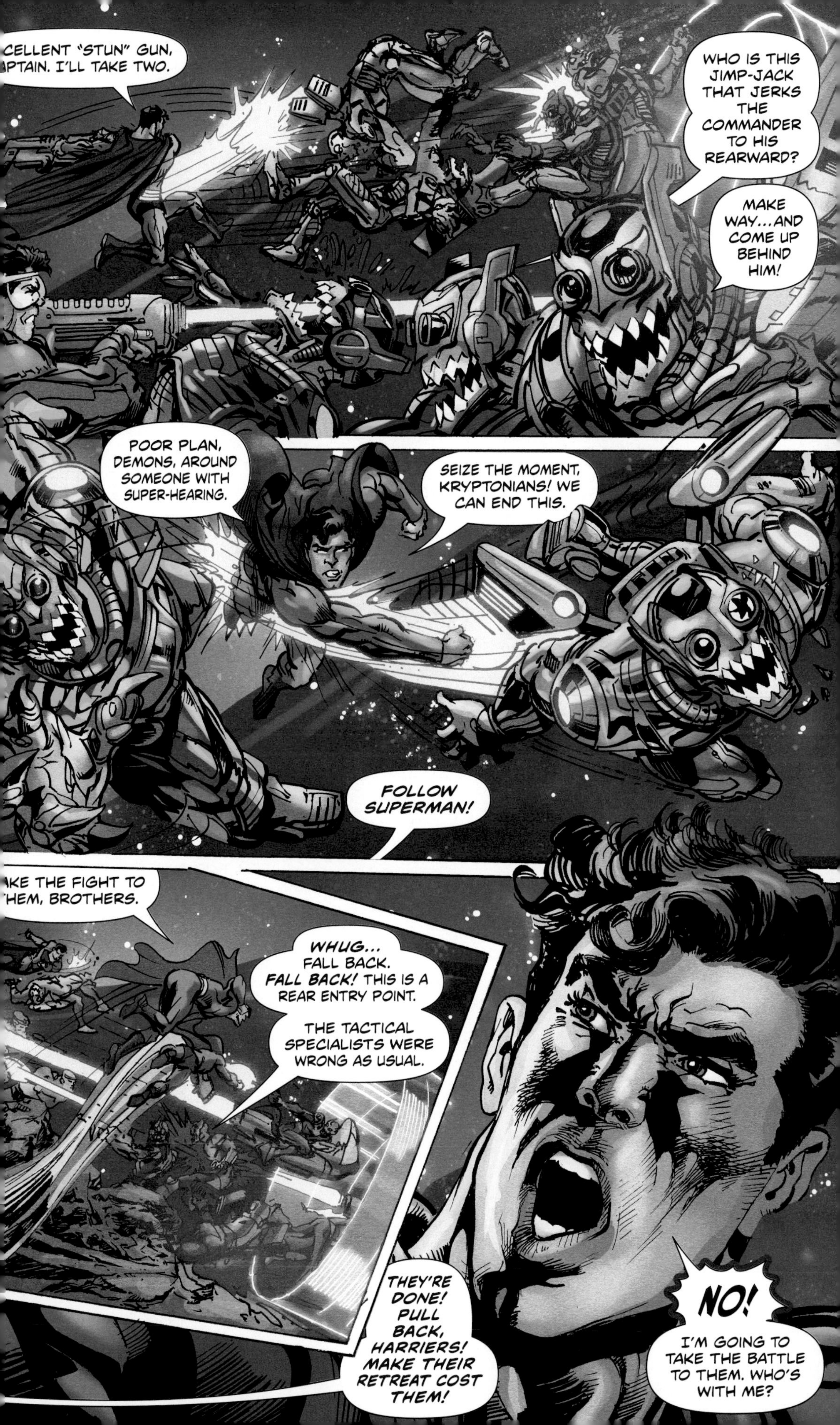
CELLENT "STUN" GUN, PTAIN. I'LL TAKE TWO.
WHO IS THIS JIMP-JACK THAT JERKS THE COMMANDER TO HIS REARWARD?
MAKE WAY...AND COME UP BEHIND HIM!
POOR PLAN, DEMONS, AROUND SOMEONE WITH SUPER-HEARING.
SEIZE THE MOMENT, KRYPTONIANS! WE CAN END THIS.
FOLLOW SUPERMAN!
AKE THE FIGHT TO THEM, BROTHERS.
WHUG... FALL BACK. FALL BACK! THIS IS A REAR ENTRY POINT.
THE TACTICAL SPECIALISTS WERE WRONG AS USUAL.
THEY'RE DONE! PULL BACK, HARRIERS! MAKE THEIR RETREAT COST THEM!
NO!
I'M GOING TO TAKE THE BATTLE TO THEM. WHO'S WITH ME?

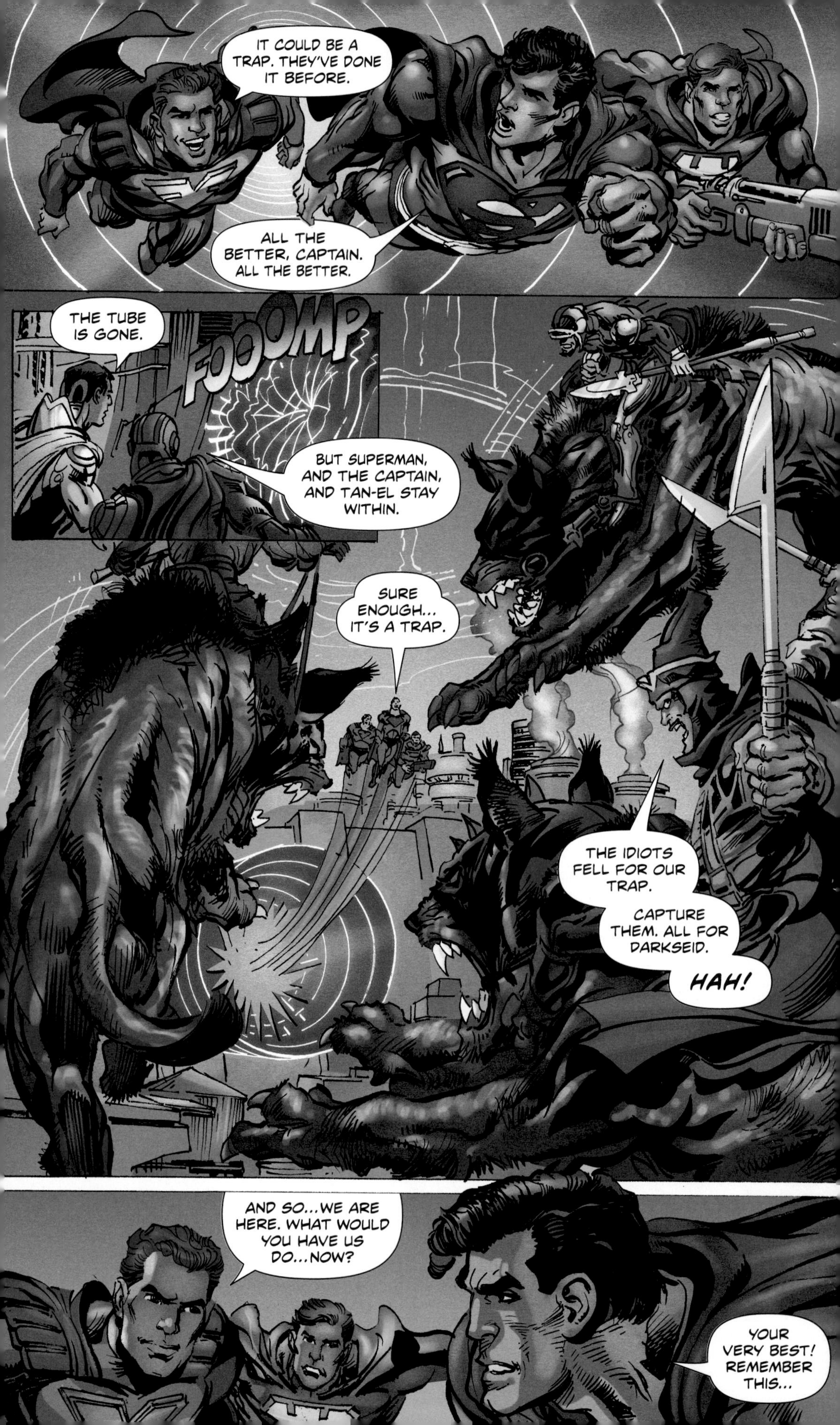
IT COULD BE A TRAP. THEY'VE DONE IT BEFORE.
ALL THE BETTER, CAPTAIN. ALL THE BETTER.
THE TUBE IS GONE.
FOOOMP
BUT SUPERMAN, AND THE CAPTAIN, AND TAN-EL STAY WITHIN.
SURE ENOUGH... IT'S A TRAP.
THE IDIOTS FELL FOR OUR TRAP.
CAPTURE THEM. ALL FOR DARKSEID.
HAH!
AND SO...WE ARE HERE. WHAT WOULD YOU HAVE US DO...NOW?
YOUR VERY BEST! REMEMBER THIS...

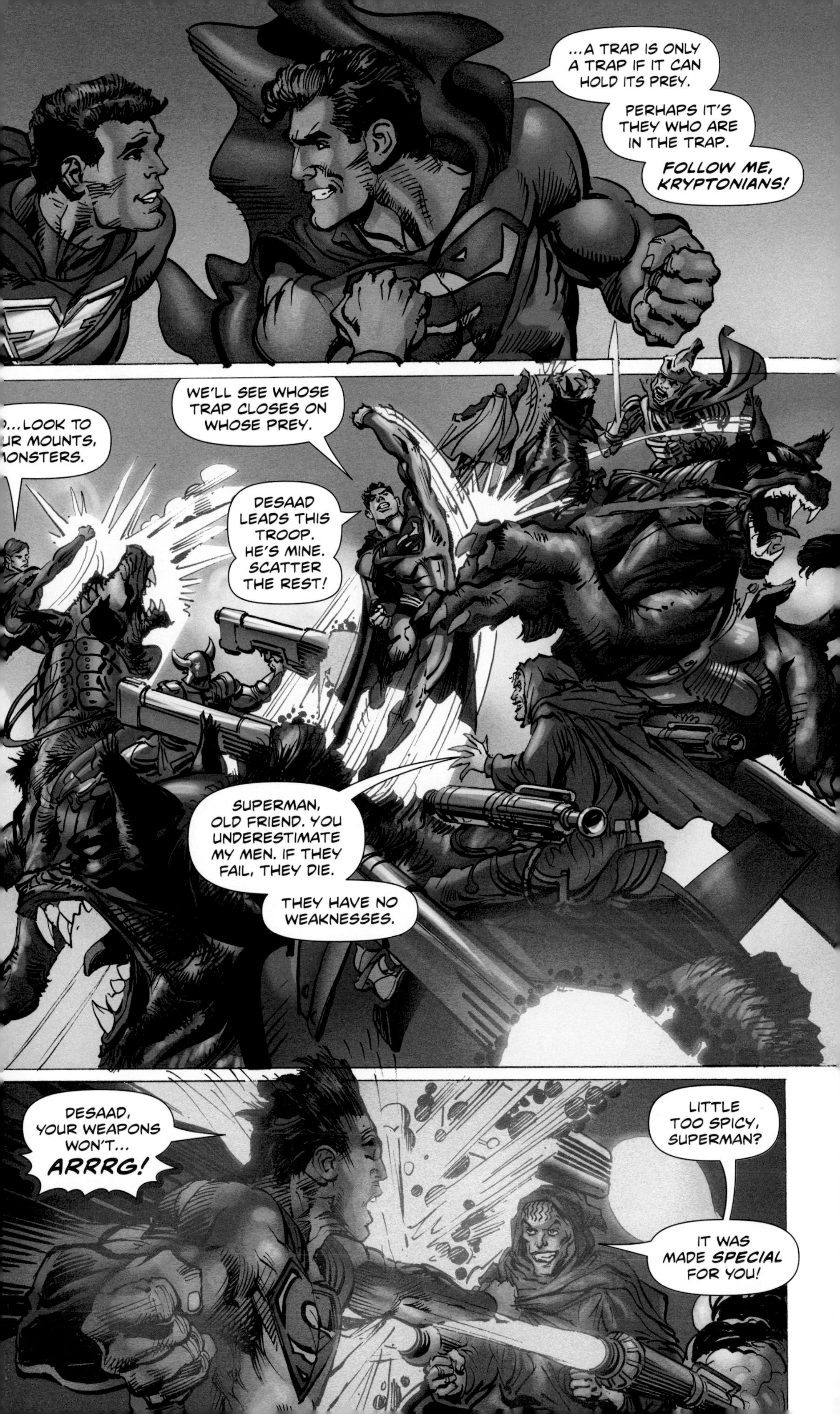
...A TRAP IS ONLY A TRAP IF IT CAN HOLD ITS PREY.
PERHAPS IT'S THEY WHO ARE IN THE TRAP.
FOLLOW ME, KRYPTONIANS!
...LOOK TO UR MOUNTS, ONSTERS.
WE'LL SEE WHOSE TRAP CLOSES ON WHOSE PREY.
DESAAD LEADS THIS TROOP. HE'S MINE. SCATTER THE REST!
SUPERMAN, OLD FRIEND. YOU UNDERESTIMATE MY MEN. IF THEY FAIL, THEY DIE.
THEY HAVE NO WEAKNESSES.
DESAAD, YOUR WEAPONS WON'T...
ARRRG!
LITTLE TOO SPICY, SUPERMAN?
IT WAS MADE SPECIAL FOR YOU!

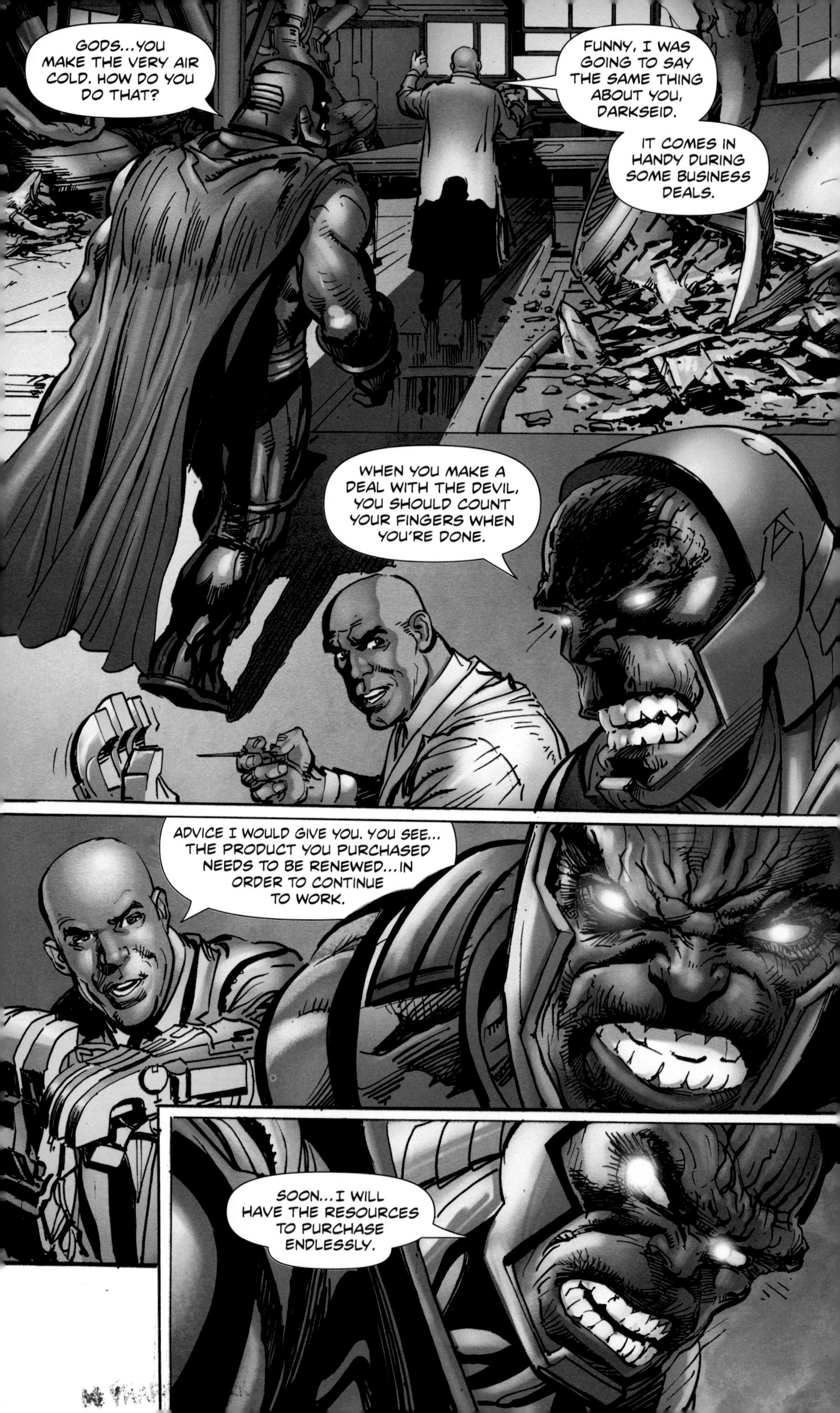
GODS...YOU MAKE THE VERY AIR COLD. HOW DO YOU DO THAT?
FUNNY, I WAS GOING TO SAY THE SAME THING ABOUT YOU, DARKSEID.
IT COMES IN HANDY DURING SOME BUSINESS DEALS.
WHEN YOU MAKE A DEAL WITH THE DEVIL, YOU SHOULD COUNT YOUR FINGERS WHEN YOU'RE DONE.
ADVICE I WOULD GIVE YOU. YOU SEE... THE PRODUCT YOU PURCHASED NEEDS TO BE RENEWED...IN ORDER TO CONTINUE TO WORK.
SOON...I WILL HAVE THE RESOURCES TO PURCHASE ENDLESSLY.

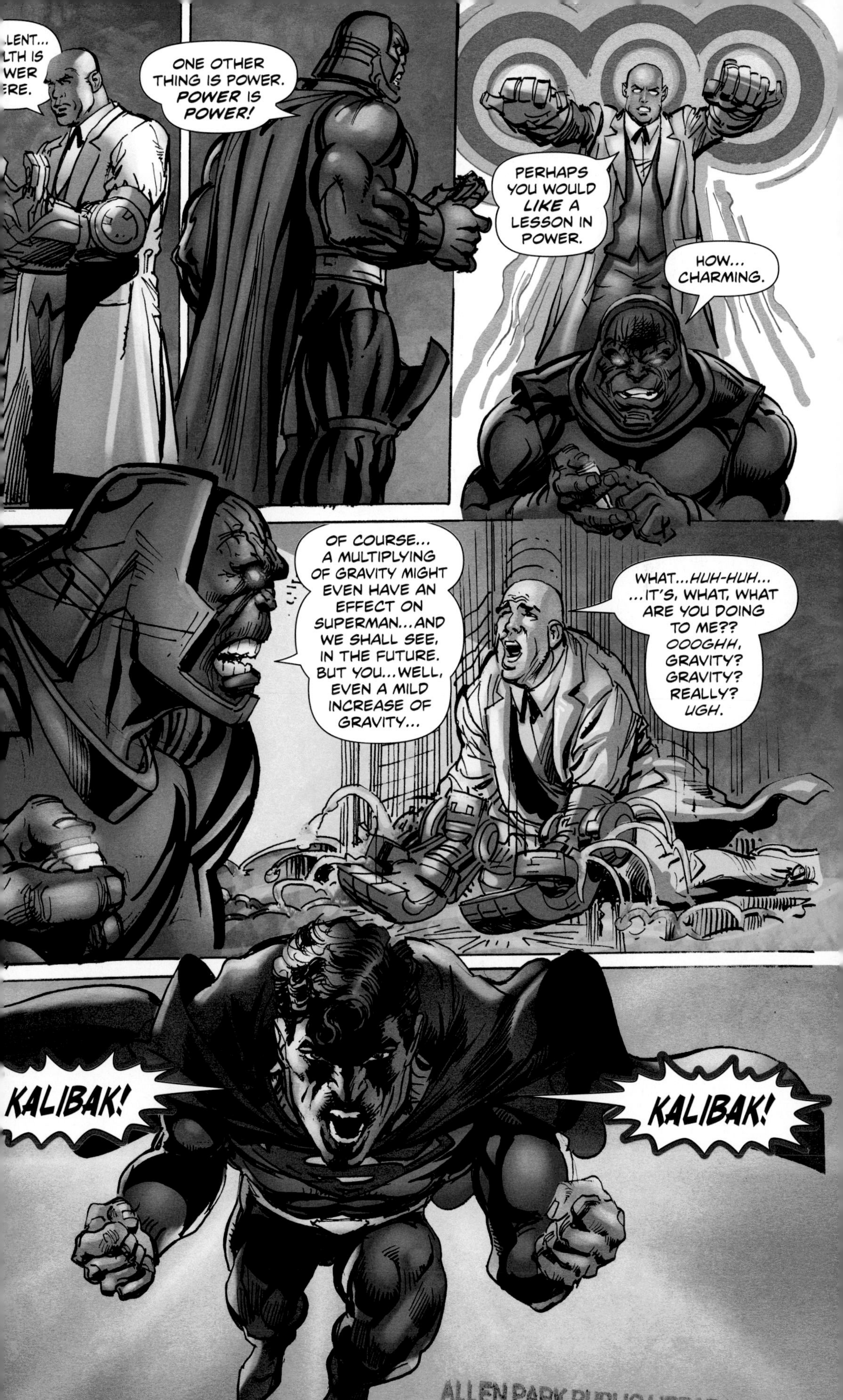
...LENT... ...LTH IS ...WER ...ERE.
ONE OTHER THING IS POWER. POWER IS POWER!
PERHAPS YOU WOULD LIKE A LESSON IN POWER.
HOW... CHARMING.
OF COURSE... A MULTIPLYING OF GRAVITY MIGHT EVEN HAVE AN EFFECT ON SUPERMAN...AND WE SHALL SEE, IN THE FUTURE. BUT YOU...WELL, EVEN A MILD INCREASE OF GRAVITY...
WHAT...HUH-HUH... ...IT'S, WHAT, WHAT ARE YOU DOING TO ME?? OOOGHH, GRAVITY? GRAVITY? REALLY? UGH.
KALIBAK!
KALIBAK!

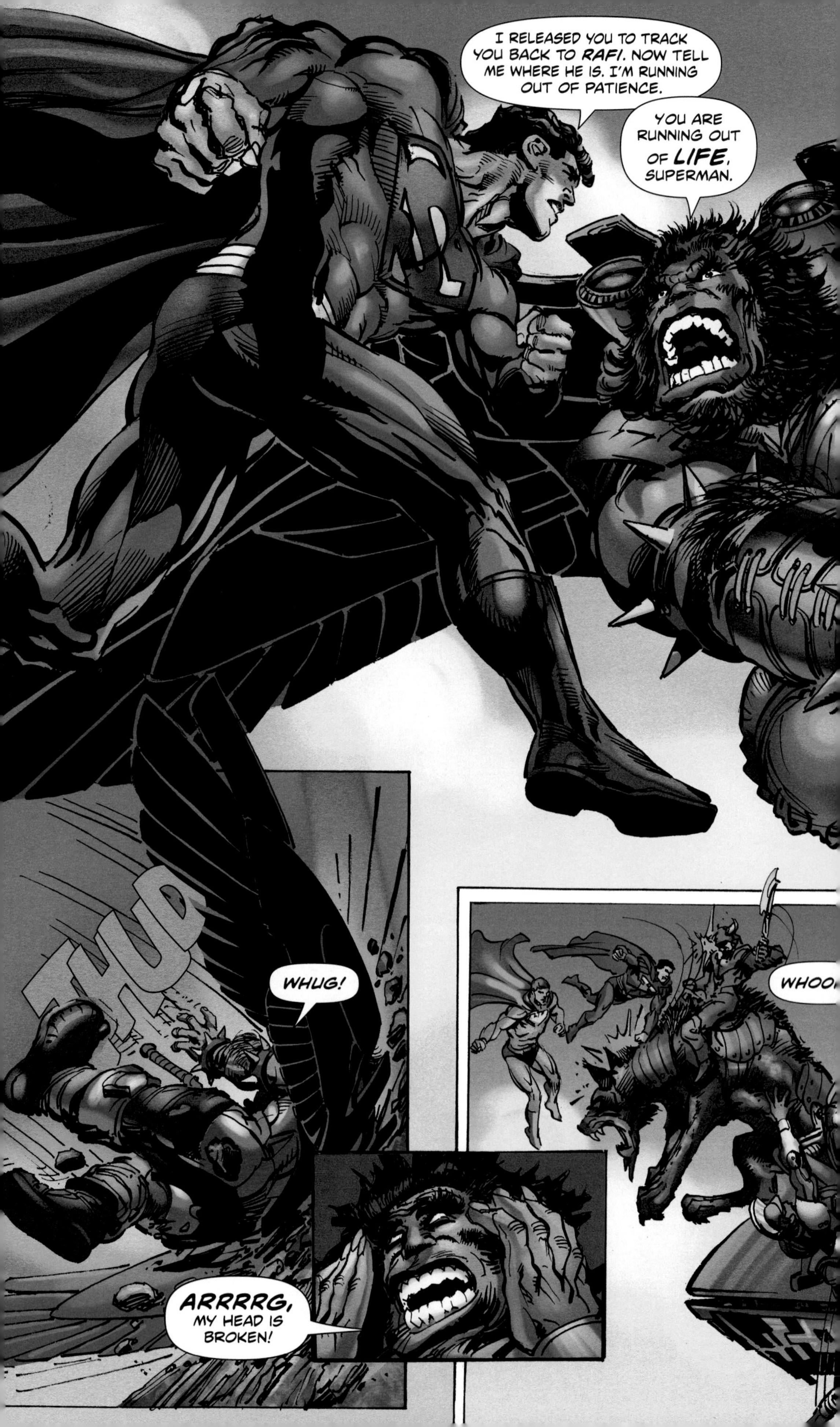

I RELEASED YOU TO TRACK YOU BACK TO RAFI. NOW TELL ME WHERE HE IS. I'M RUNNING OUT OF PATIENCE.
YOU ARE RUNNING OUT OF LIFE, SUPERMAN.
THUD
WHUG!
ARRRRG, MY HEAD IS BROKEN!
WHOO

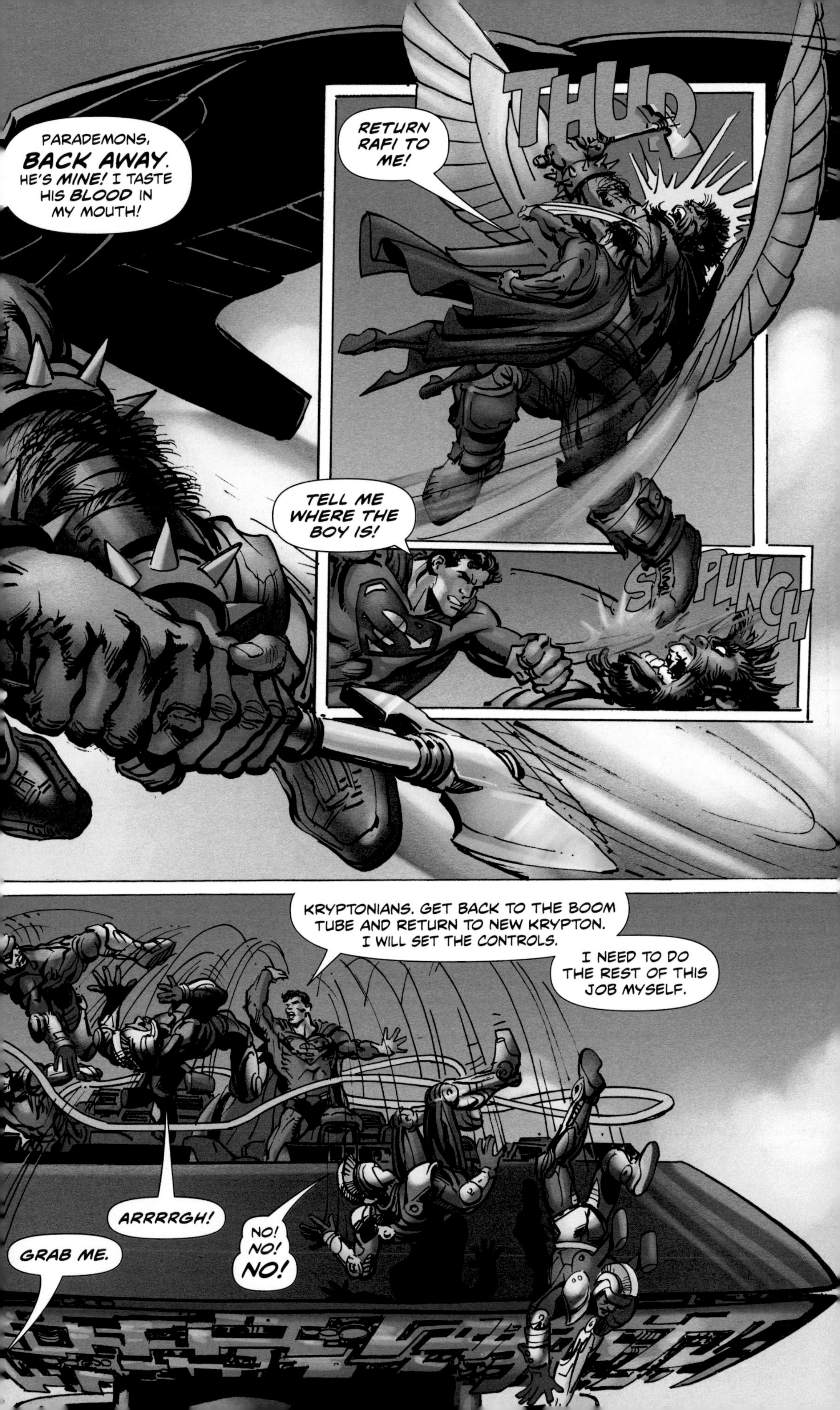

PARADEMONS, BACK AWAY. HE'S MINE! I TASTE HIS BLOOD IN MY MOUTH!
RETURN RAFI TO ME!
THUD
TELL ME WHERE THE BOY IS!
SPLUNCH
KRYPTONIANS. GET BACK TO THE BOOM TUBE AND RETURN TO NEW KRYPTON. I WILL SET THE CONTROLS.
I NEED TO DO THE REST OF THIS JOB MYSELF.
ARRRRGH!
GRAB ME.
NO! NO! NO!

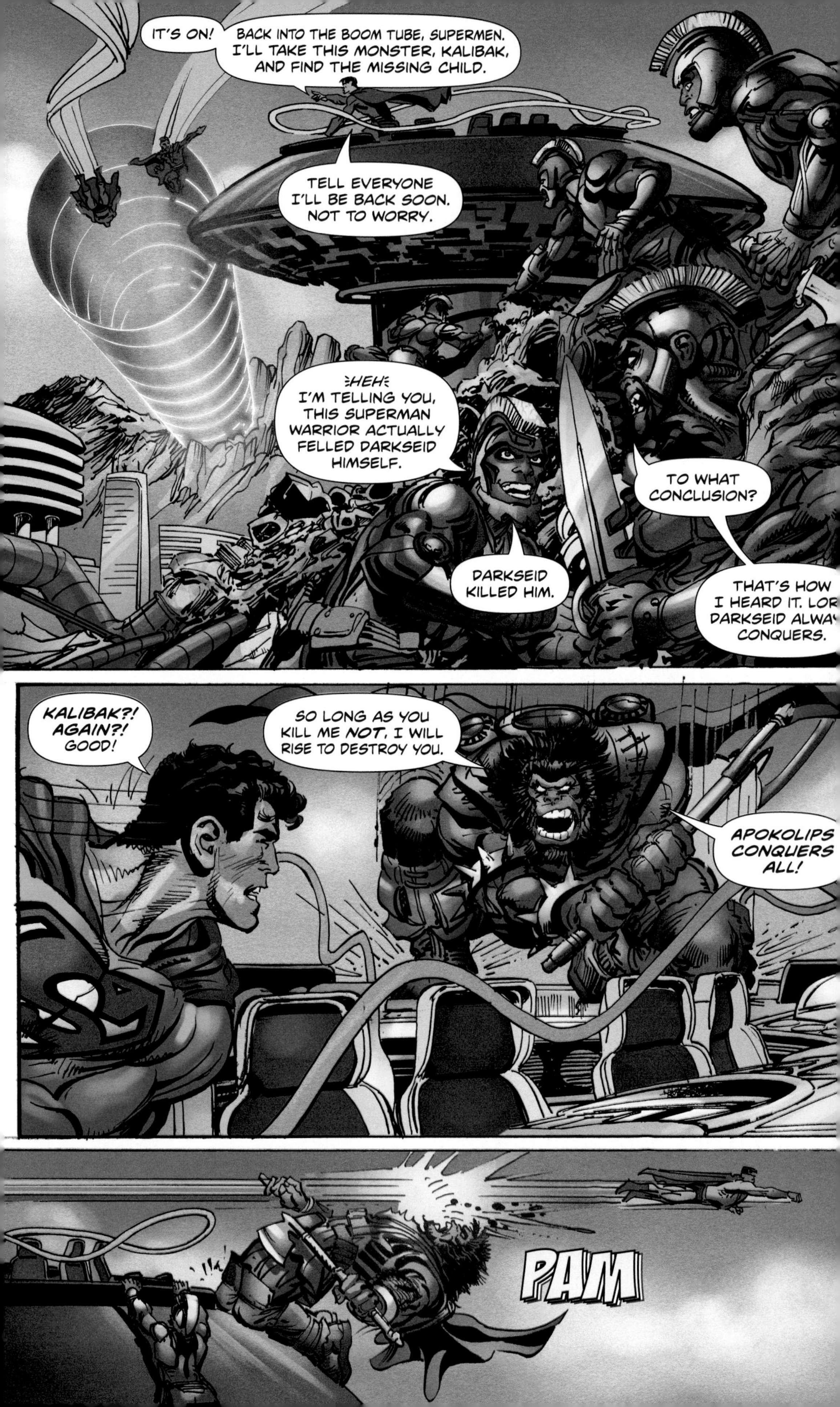
IT'S ON!
BACK INTO THE BOOM TUBE, SUPERMEN. I'LL TAKE THIS MONSTER, KALIBAK, AND FIND THE MISSING CHILD.
TELL EVERYONE I'LL BE BACK SOON. NOT TO WORRY.
HEH
I'M TELLING YOU, THIS SUPERMAN WARRIOR ACTUALLY FELLED DARKSEID HIMSELF.
TO WHAT CONCLUSION?
DARKSEID KILLED HIM.
THAT'S HOW I HEARD IT. LOR DARKSEID ALWA CONQUERS.
KALIBAK?! AGAIN?! GOOD!
SO LONG AS YOU KILL ME NOT, I WILL RISE TO DESTROY YOU.
APOKOLIPS CONQUERS ALL!
PAM

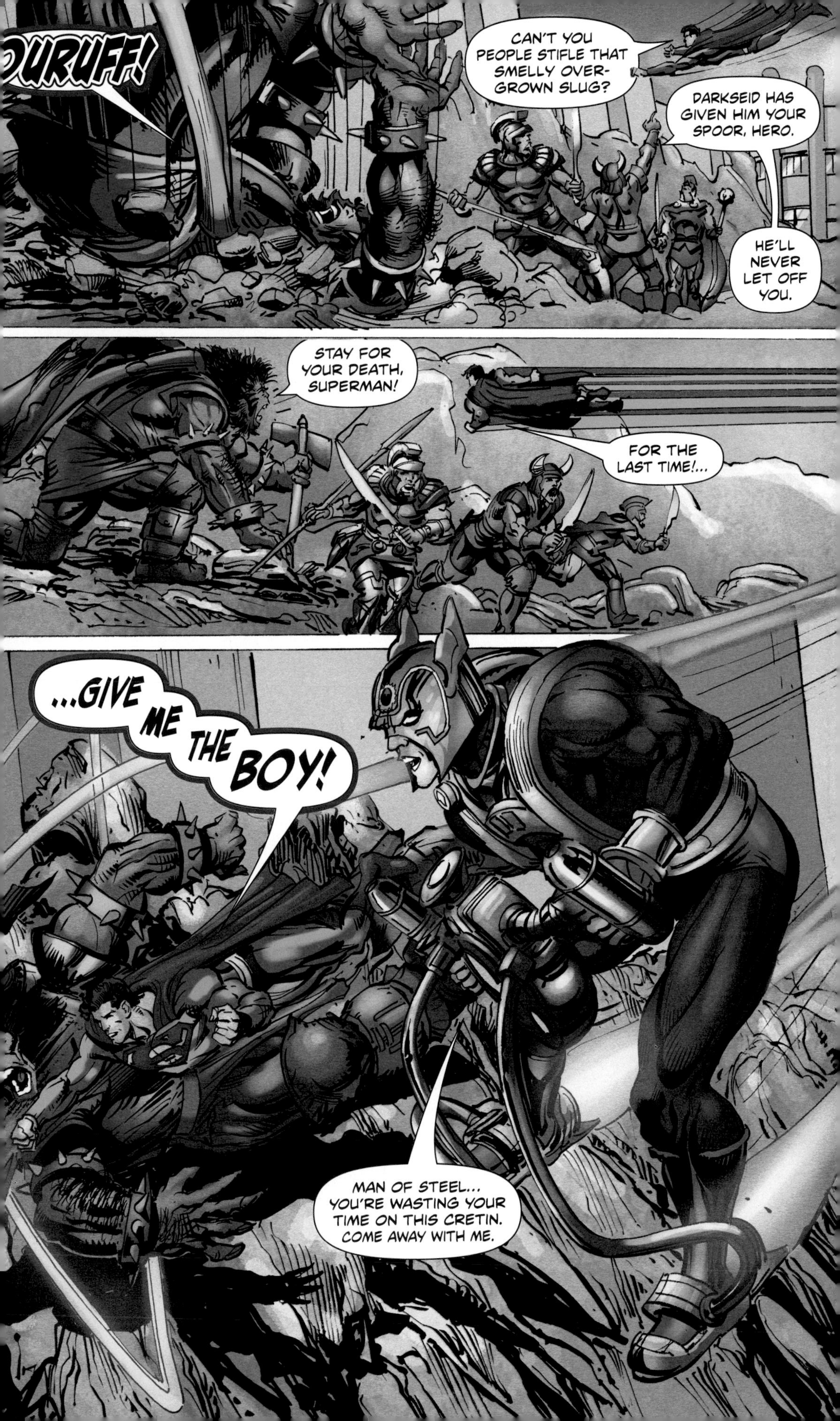
OURUFF!
CAN'T YOU PEOPLE STIFLE THAT SMELLY OVER-GROWN SLUG?
DARKSEID HAS GIVEN HIM YOUR SPOOR, HERO.
HE'LL NEVER LET OFF YOU.
STAY FOR YOUR DEATH, SUPERMAN!
FOR THE LAST TIME!...
...GIVE ME THE BOY!
MAN OF STEEL... YOU'RE WASTING YOUR TIME ON THIS CRETIN. COME AWAY WITH ME.

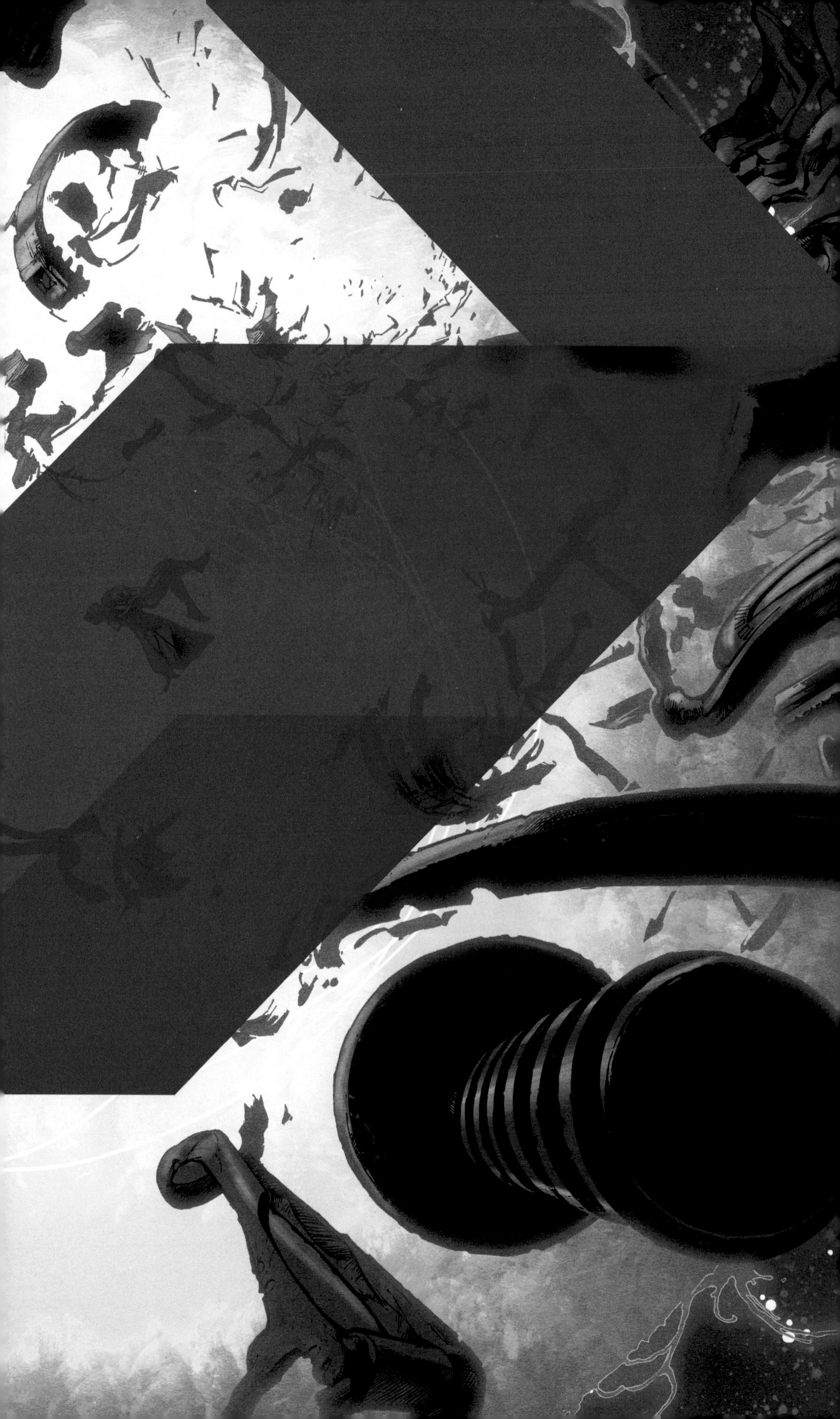

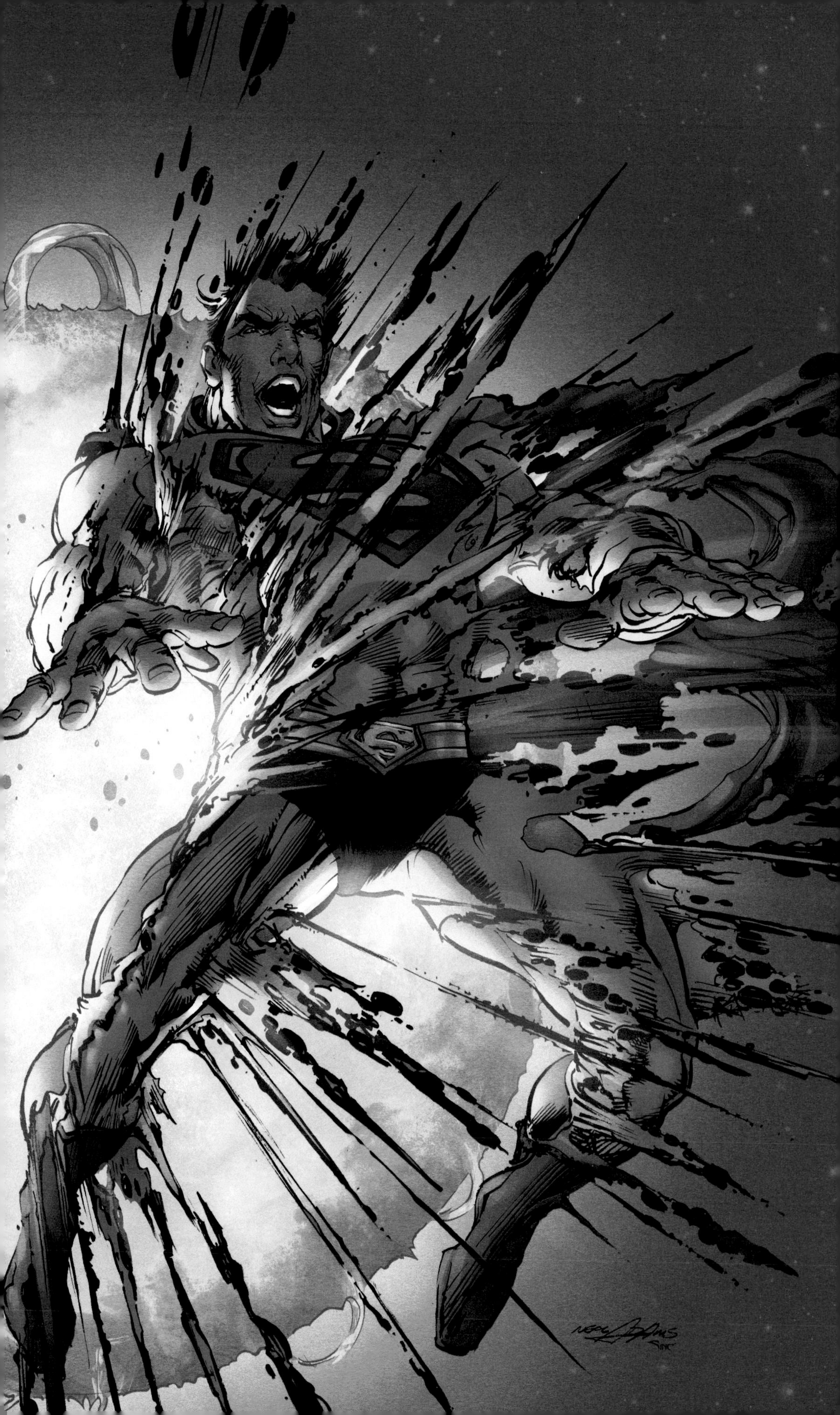

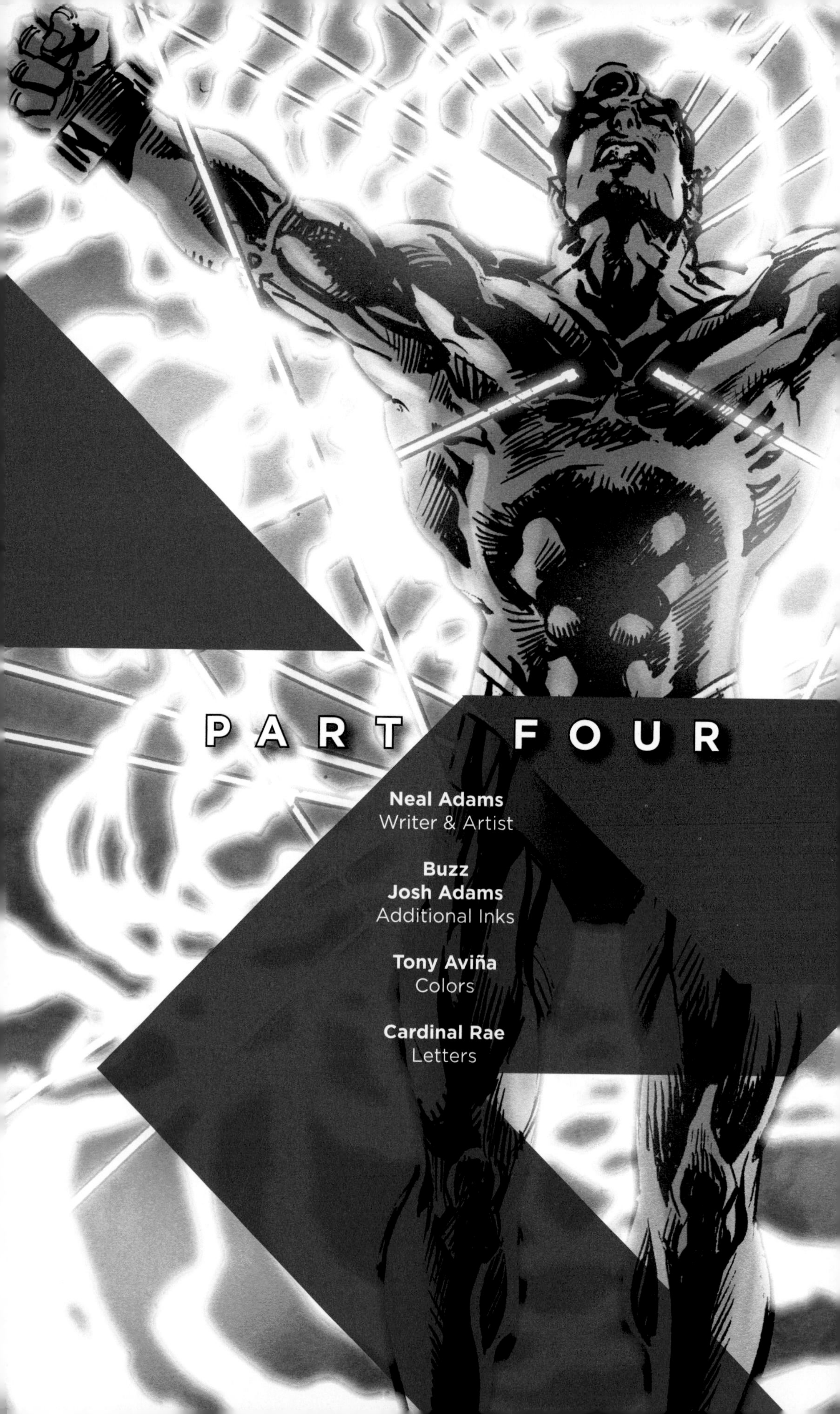

PART FOUR

Neal Adams
Writer & Artist

Buzz
Josh Adams
Additional Inks

Tony Aviña
Colors

Cardinal Rae
Letters

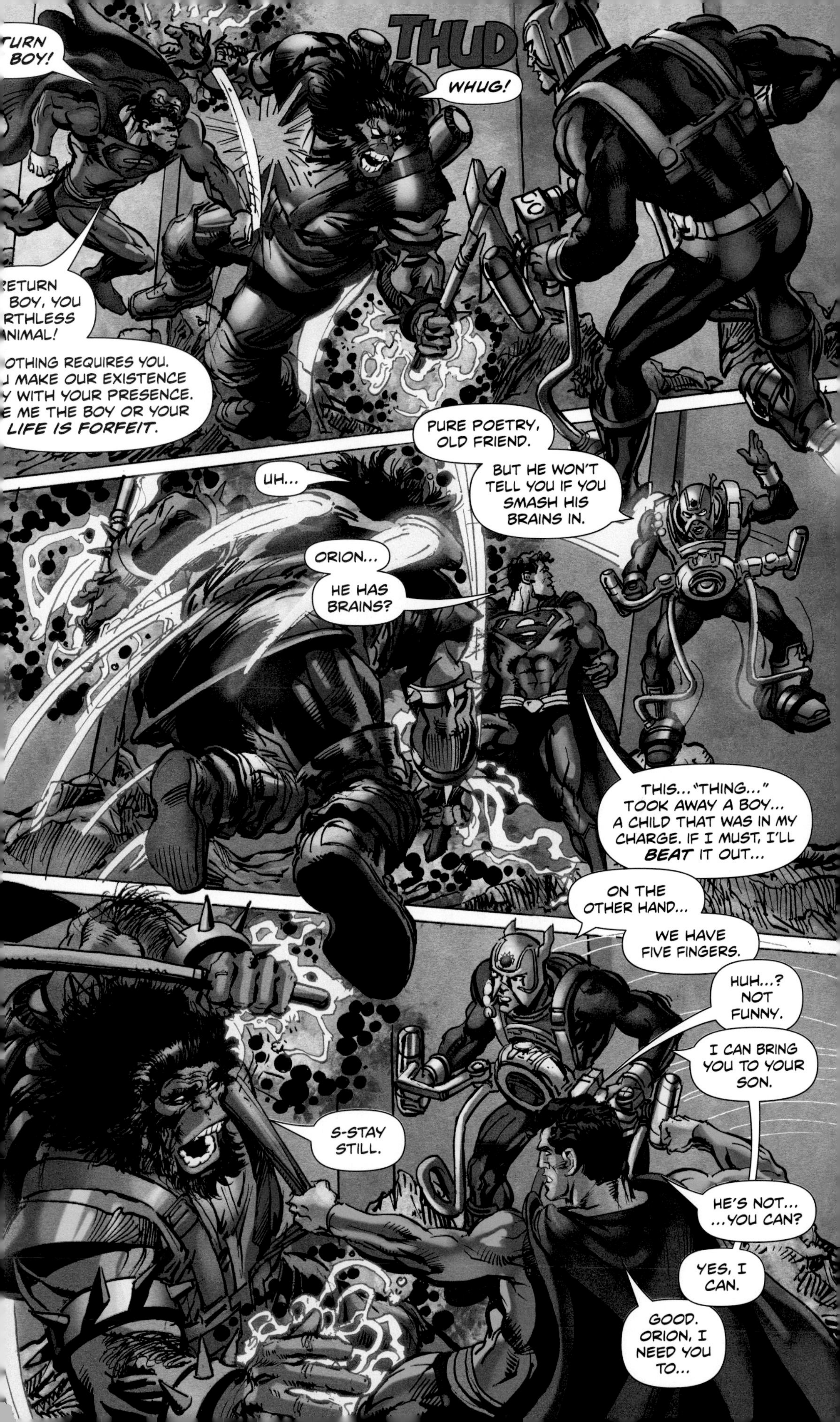

THUD
TURN
BOY!
WHUG!
RETURN
BOY, YOU
RTHLESS
NIMAL!
OTHING REQUIRES YOU.
J MAKE OUR EXISTENCE
Y WITH YOUR PRESENCE.
E ME THE BOY OR YOUR
LIFE IS FORFEIT.
PURE POETRY, OLD FRIEND.
BUT HE WON'T TELL YOU IF YOU SMASH HIS BRAINS IN.
UH...
ORION...
HE HAS BRAINS?
THIS... "THING..." TOOK AWAY A BOY... A CHILD THAT WAS IN MY CHARGE. IF I MUST, I'LL BEAT IT OUT...
ON THE OTHER HAND...
WE HAVE FIVE FINGERS.
HUH...? NOT FUNNY.
I CAN BRING YOU TO YOUR SON.
S-STAY STILL.
HE'S NOT... ...YOU CAN?
YES, I CAN.
GOOD. ORION, I NEED YOU TO...

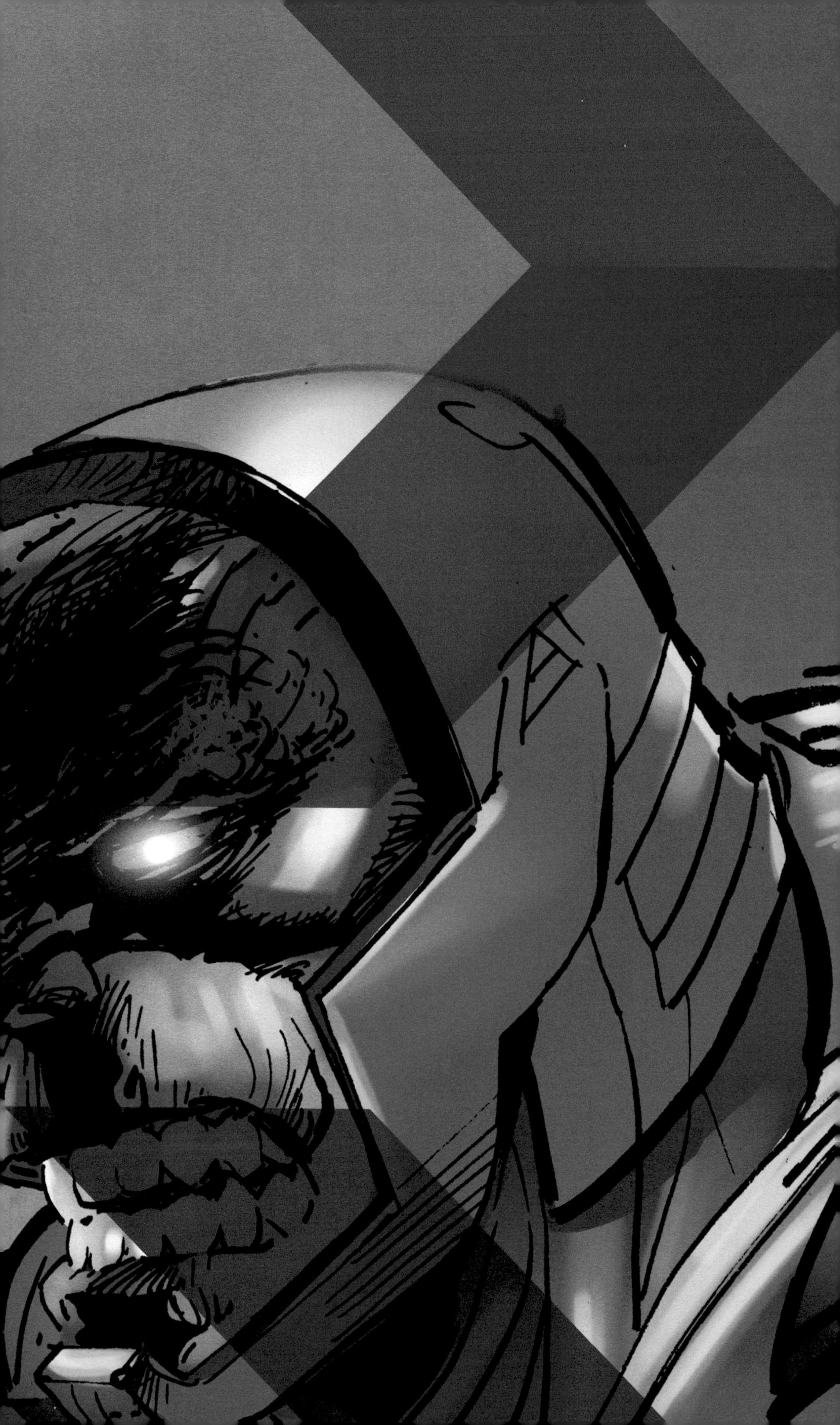

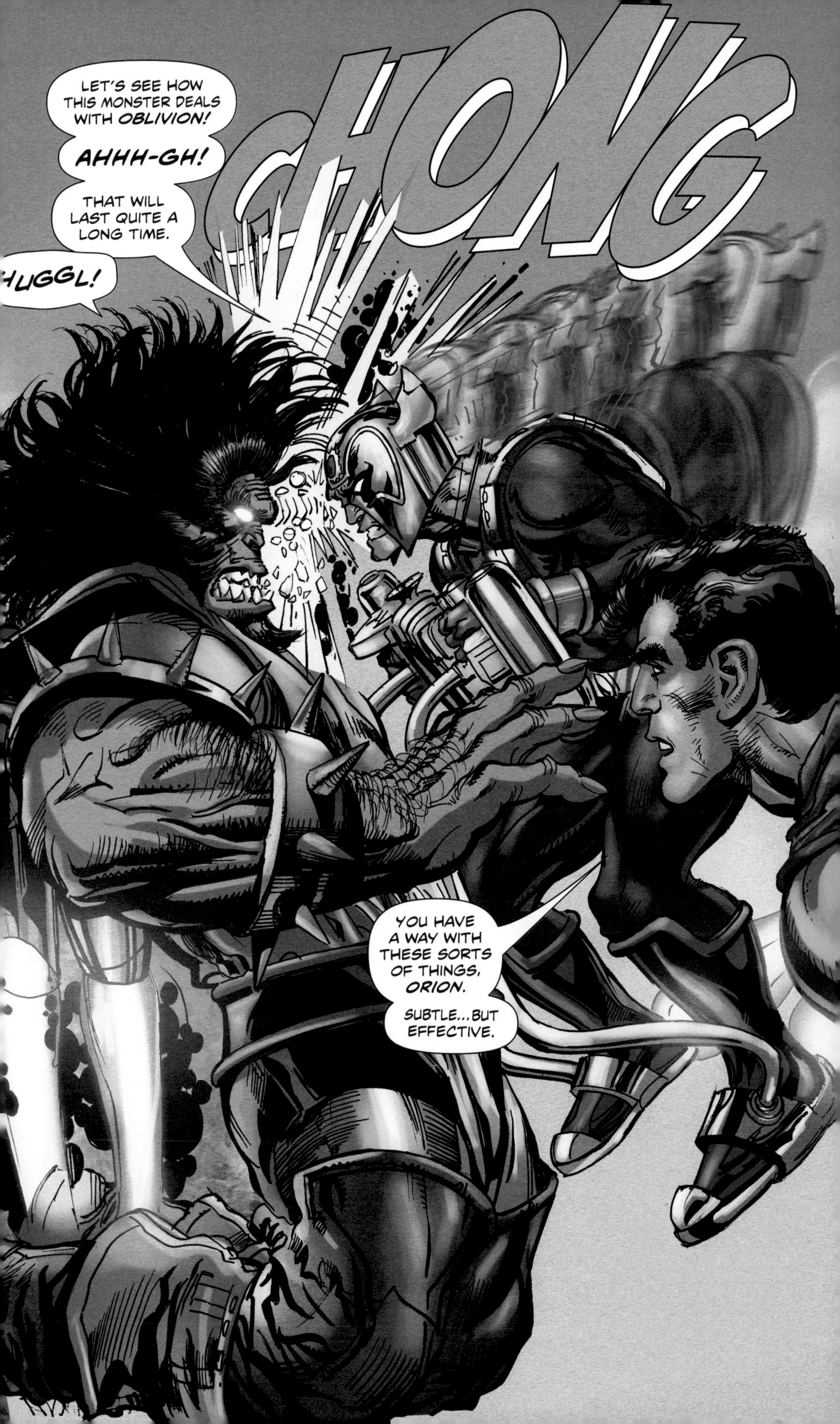
LET'S SEE HOW THIS MONSTER DEALS WITH OBLIVION!
AHHH-GH!
THAT WILL LAST QUITE A LONG TIME.
HUGGL!
CHONG
YOU HAVE A WAY WITH THESE SORTS OF THINGS, ORION.
SUBTLE...BUT EFFECTIVE.

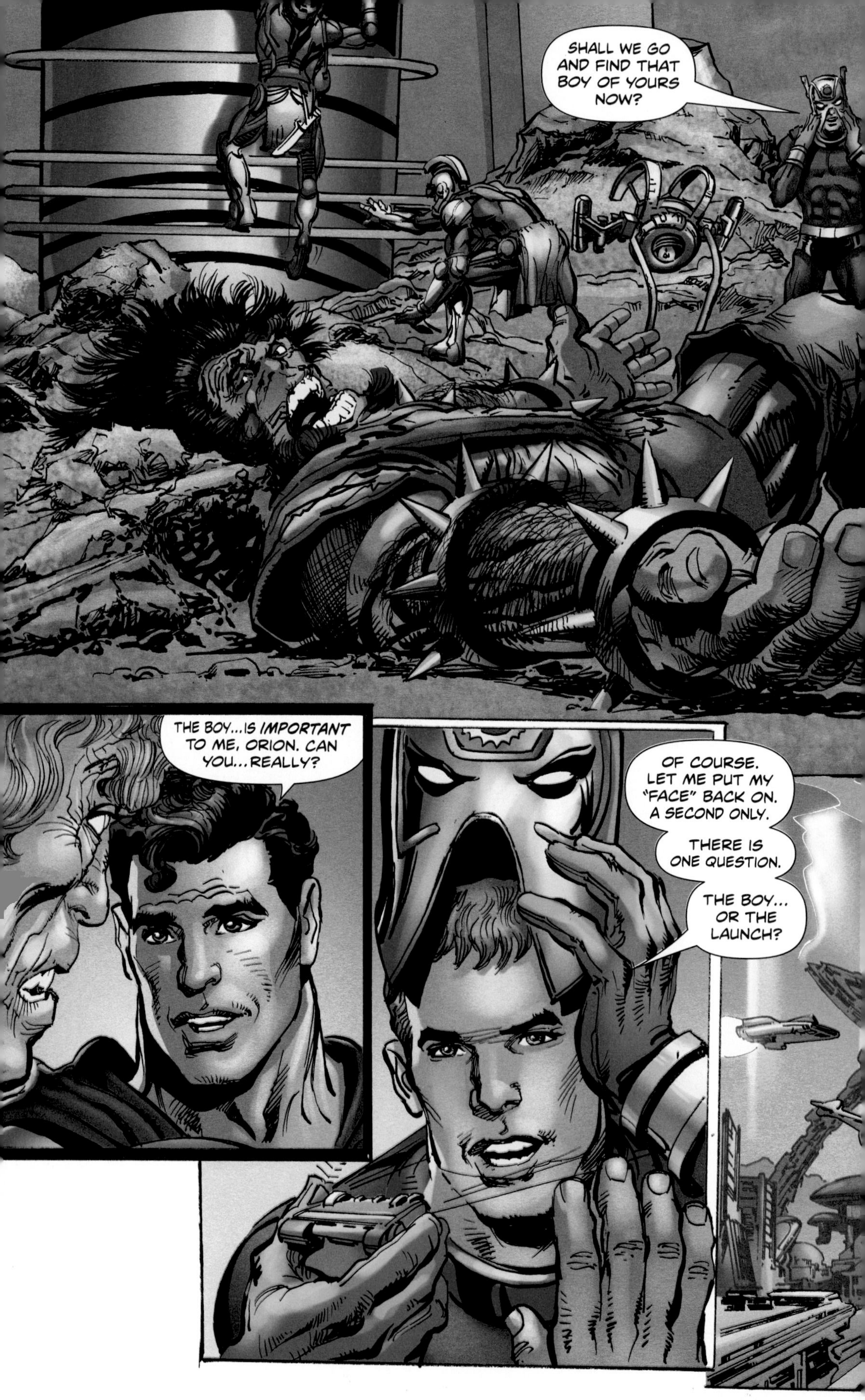
SHALL WE GO AND FIND THAT BOY OF YOURS NOW?
THE BOY...IS *IMPORTANT* TO ME, ORION. CAN YOU...REALLY?
OF COURSE. LET ME PUT MY "FACE" BACK ON. A SECOND ONLY.
THERE IS ONE QUESTION.
THE BOY... OR THE LAUNCH?

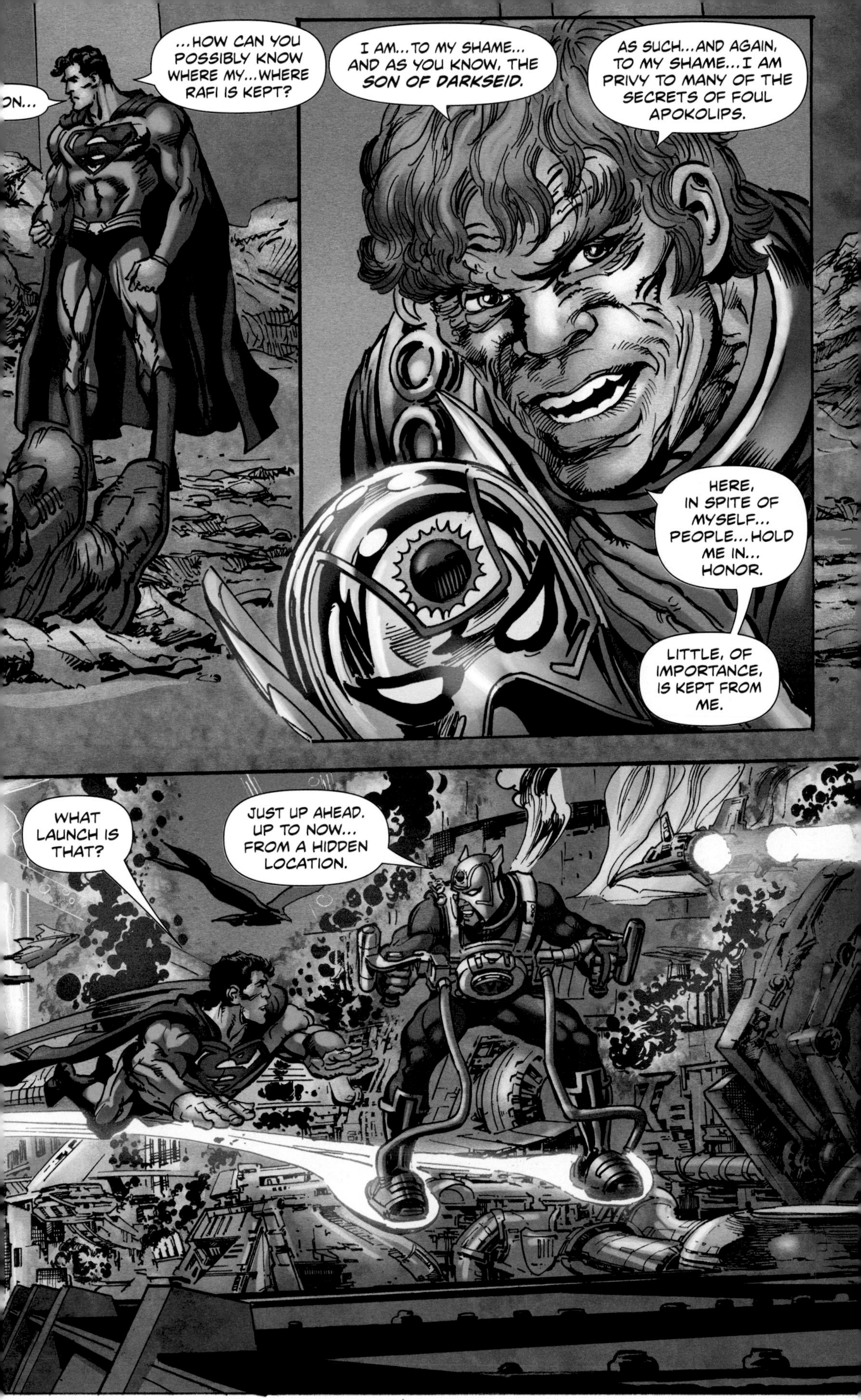
...ON...
...HOW CAN YOU POSSIBLY KNOW WHERE MY...WHERE RAFI IS KEPT?
I AM...TO MY SHAME... AND AS YOU KNOW, THE SON OF DARKSEID.
AS SUCH...AND AGAIN, TO MY SHAME...I AM PRIVY TO MANY OF THE SECRETS OF FOUL APOKOLIPS.
HERE, IN SPITE OF MYSELF... PEOPLE...HOLD ME IN... HONOR.
LITTLE, OF IMPORTANCE, IS KEPT FROM ME.
WHAT LAUNCH IS THAT?
JUST UP AHEAD. UP TO NOW... FROM A HIDDEN LOCATION.

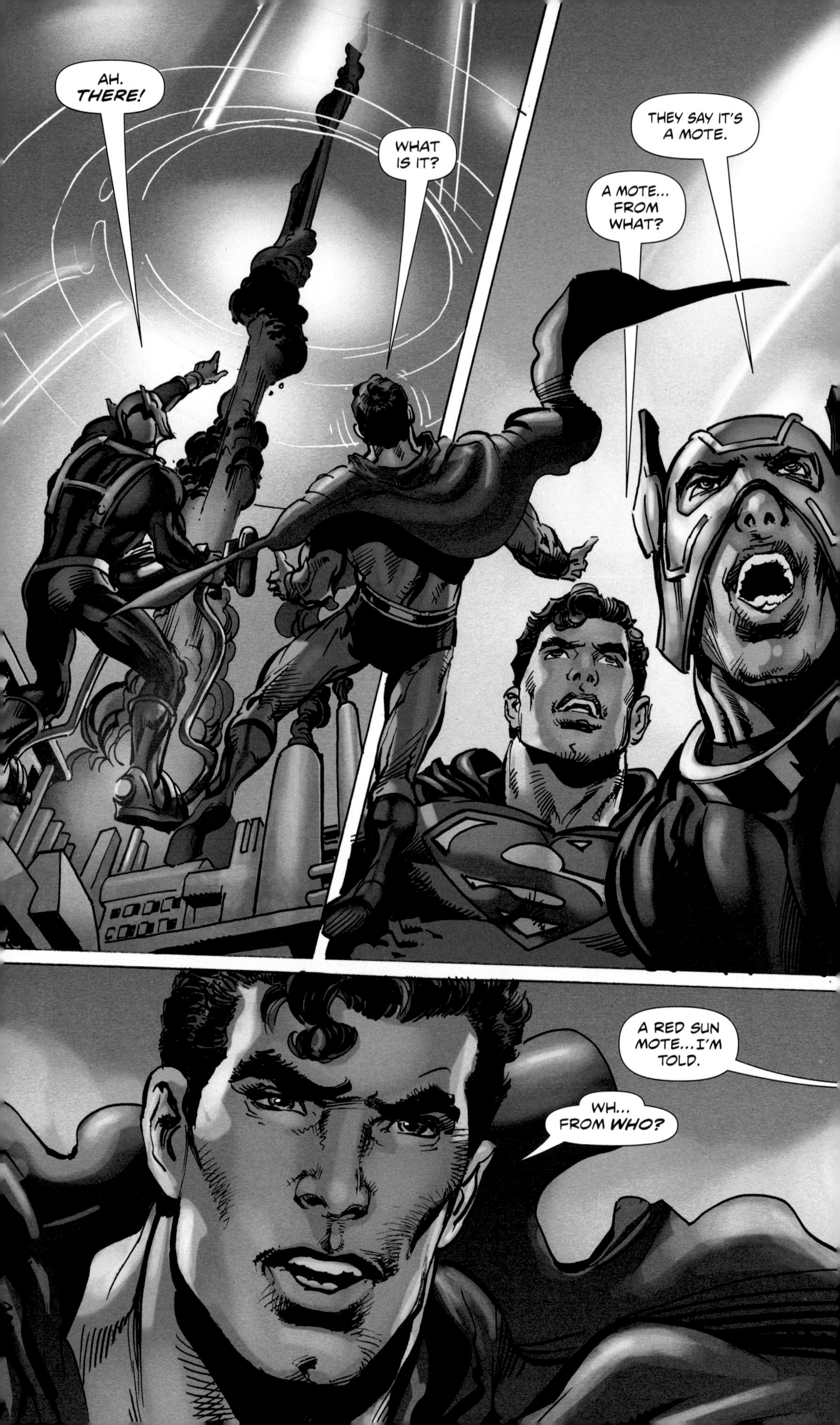
AH. *THERE!*
WHAT IS IT?
THEY SAY IT'S A MOTE.
A MOTE... FROM WHAT?
A RED SUN MOTE...I'M TOLD.
WH... FROM *WHO?*

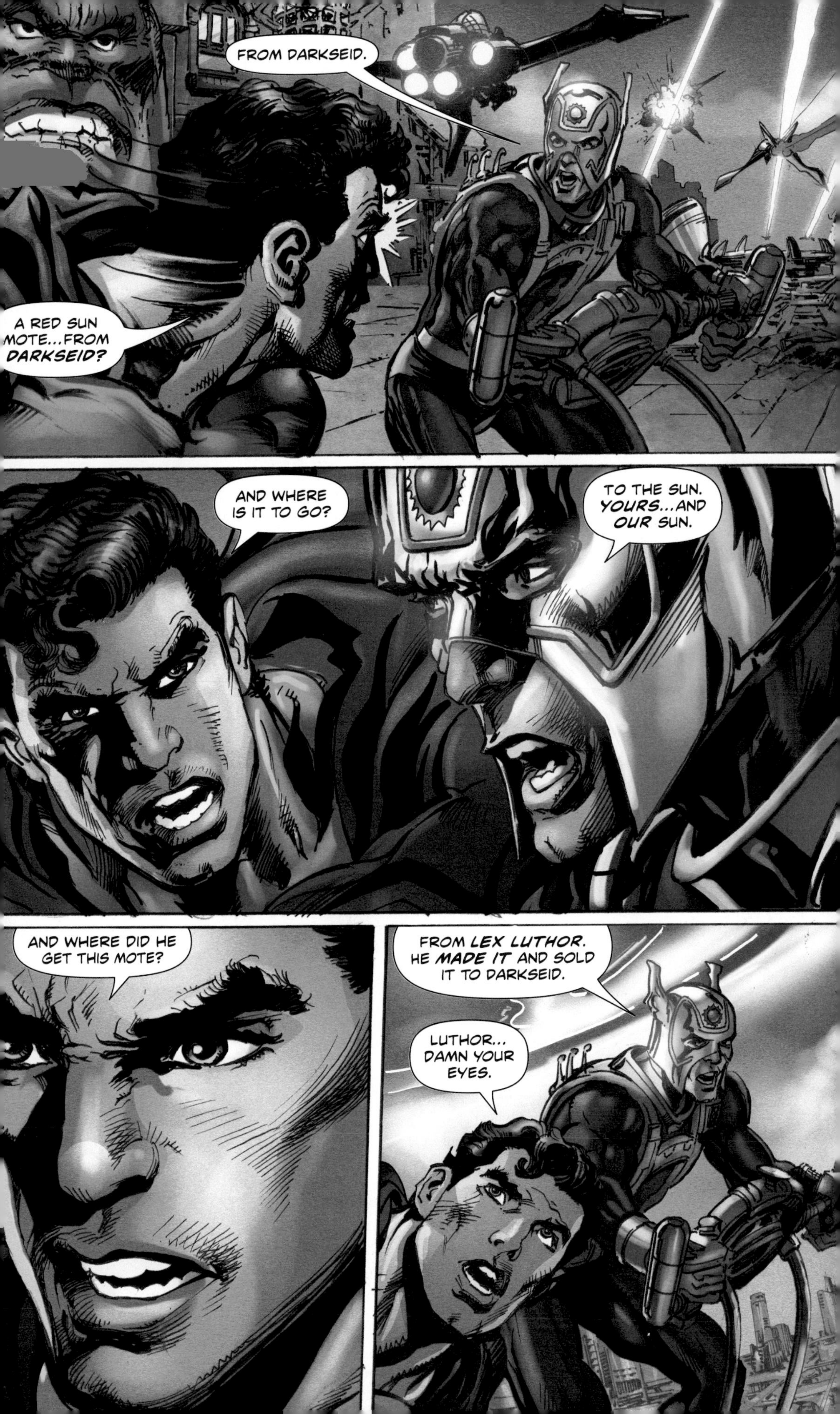
FROM DARKSEID.
A RED SUN MOTE...FROM *DARKSEID?*
AND WHERE IS IT TO GO?
TO THE SUN. *YOURS*...AND *OUR* SUN.
AND WHERE DID HE GET THIS MOTE?
FROM *LEX LUTHOR*. HE *MADE IT* AND SOLD IT TO DARKSEID.
LUTHOR... DAMN YOUR EYES.

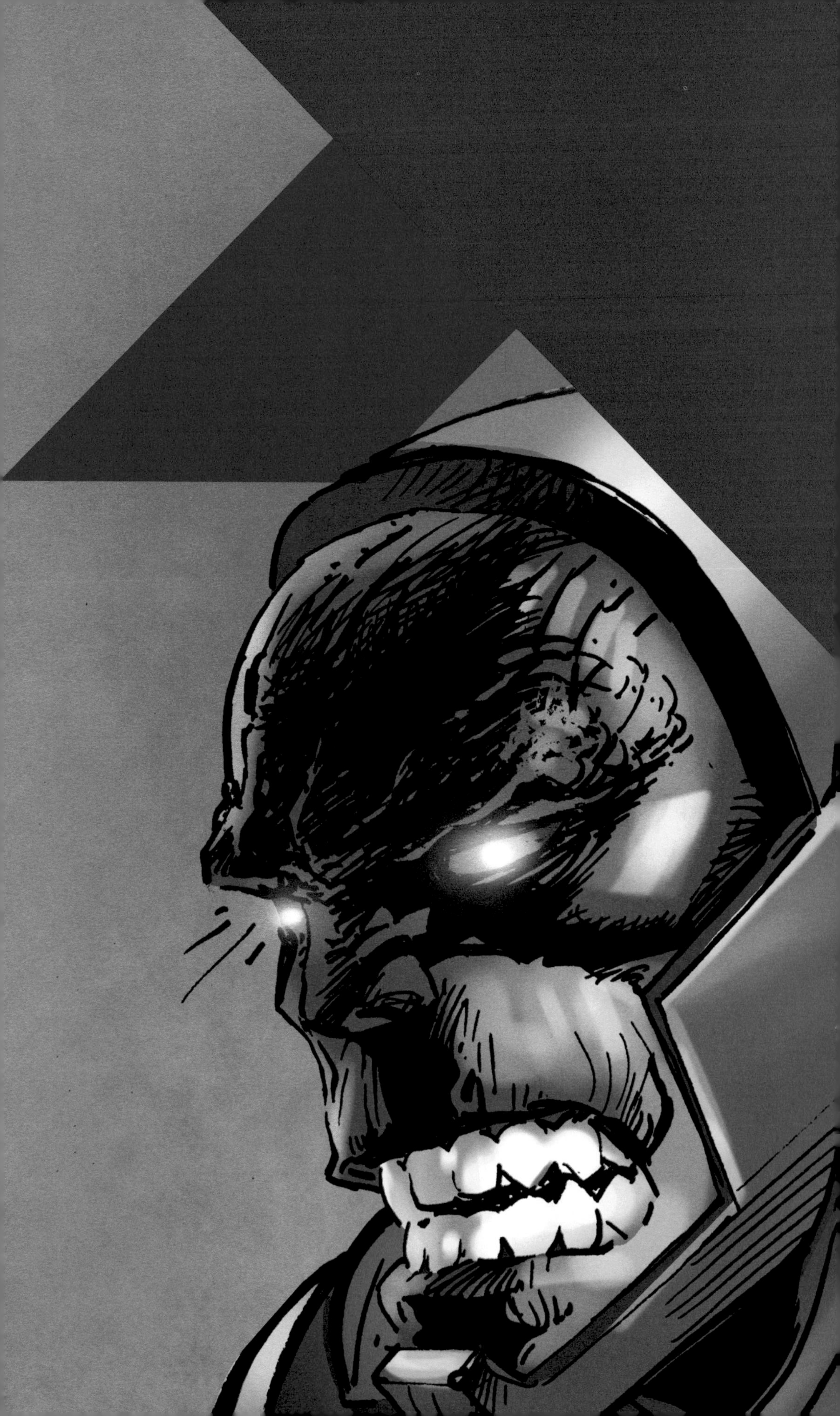

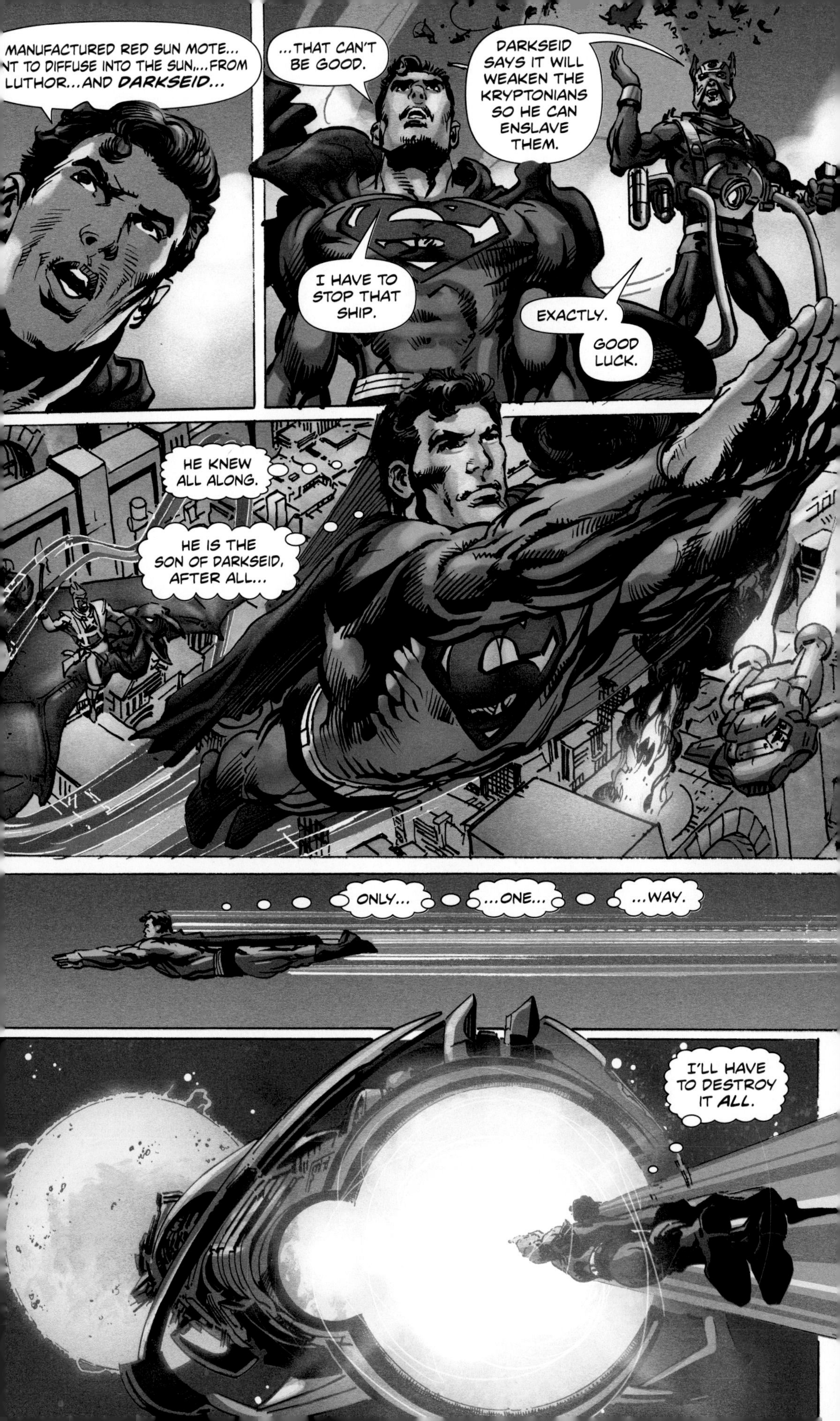

MANUFACTURED RED SUN MOTE... NT TO DIFFUSE INTO THE SUN,...FROM LUTHOR...AND DARKSEID...
...THAT CAN'T BE GOOD.
DARKSEID SAYS IT WILL WEAKEN THE KRYPTONIANS SO HE CAN ENSLAVE THEM.
I HAVE TO STOP THAT SHIP.
EXACTLY.
GOOD LUCK.
HE KNEW ALL ALONG.
HE IS THE SON OF DARKSEID, AFTER ALL...
ONLY...
...ONE...
...WAY.
I'LL HAVE TO DESTROY IT ALL.

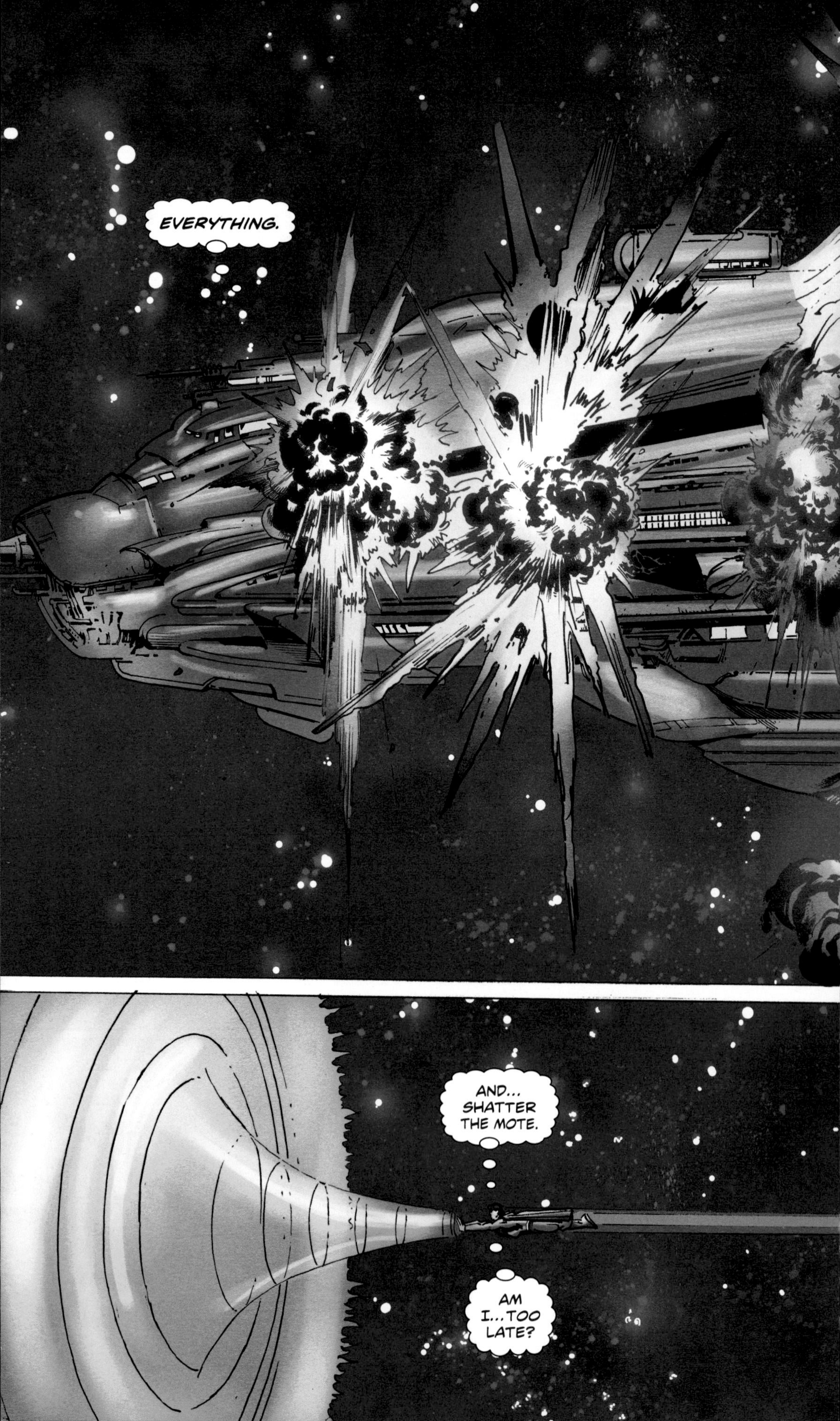
EVERYTHING.
AND... SHATTER THE MOTE.
AM I...TOO LATE?

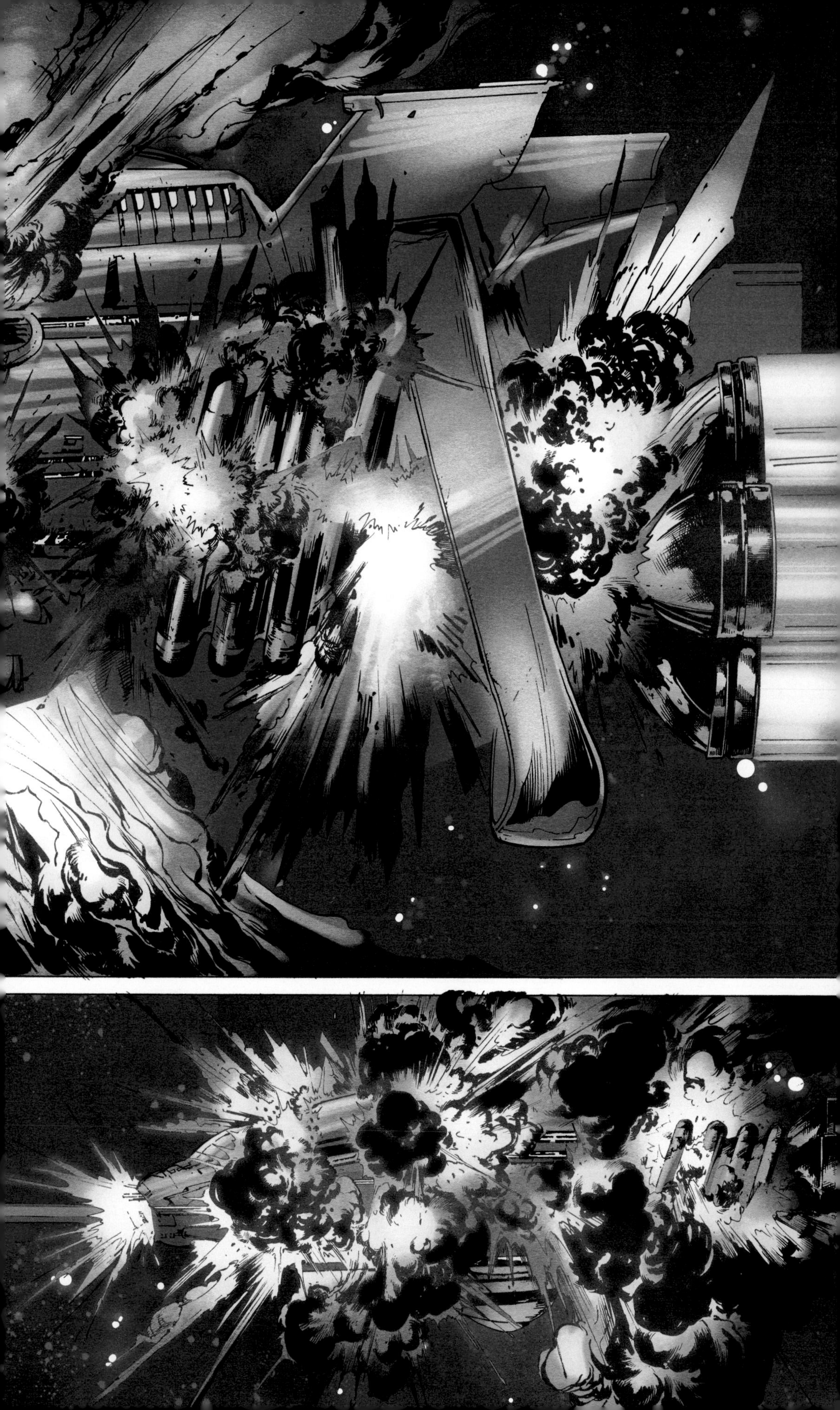

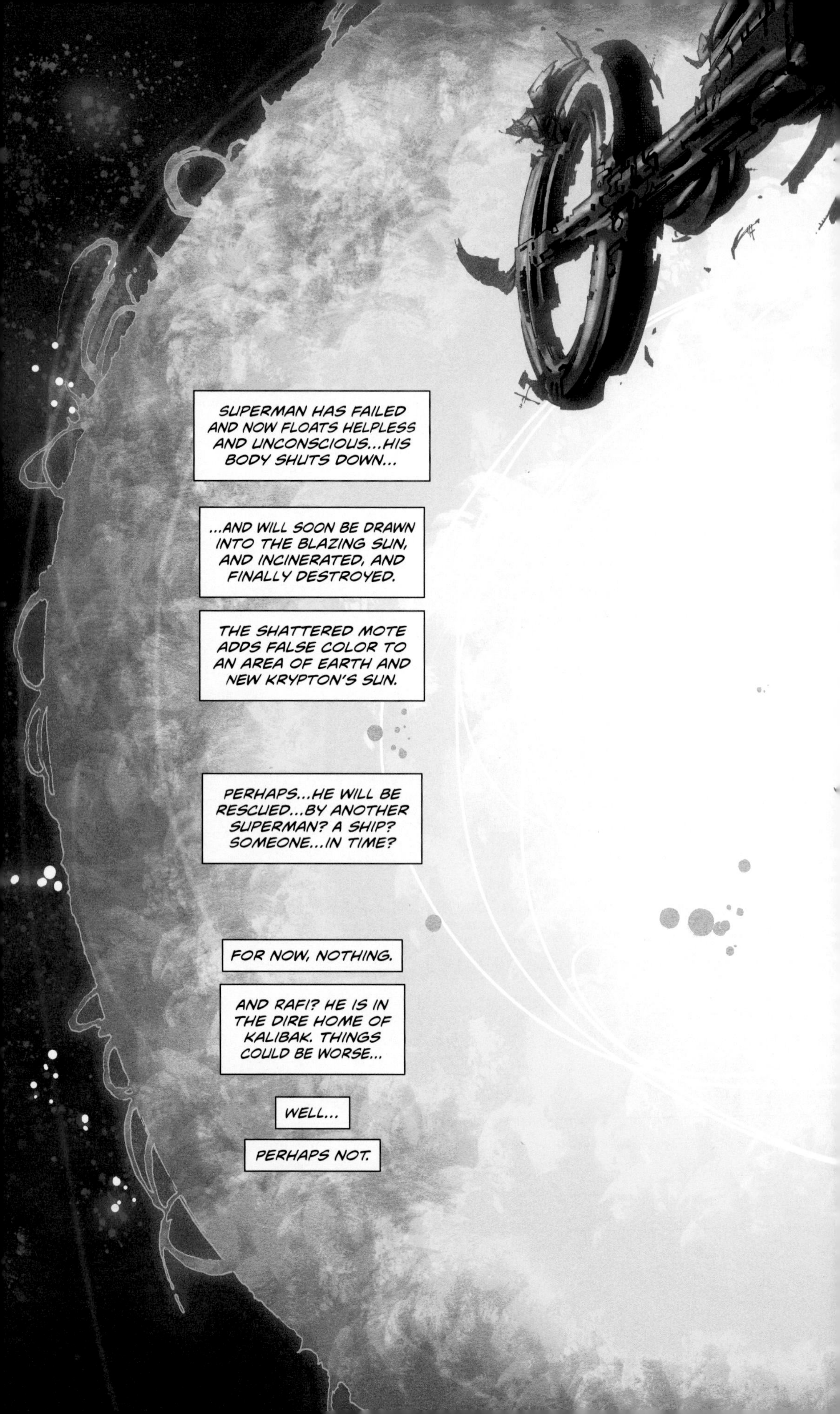
SUPERMAN HAS FAILED AND NOW FLOATS HELPLESS AND UNCONSCIOUS...HIS BODY SHUTS DOWN...
...AND WILL SOON BE DRAWN INTO THE BLAZING SUN, AND INCINERATED, AND FINALLY DESTROYED.
THE SHATTERED MOTE ADDS FALSE COLOR TO AN AREA OF EARTH AND NEW KRYPTON'S SUN.
PERHAPS...HE WILL BE RESCUED...BY ANOTHER SUPERMAN? A SHIP? SOMEONE...IN TIME?
FOR NOW, NOTHING.
AND RAFI? HE IS IN THE DIRE HOME OF KALIBAK. THINGS COULD BE WORSE...
WELL...
PERHAPS NOT.

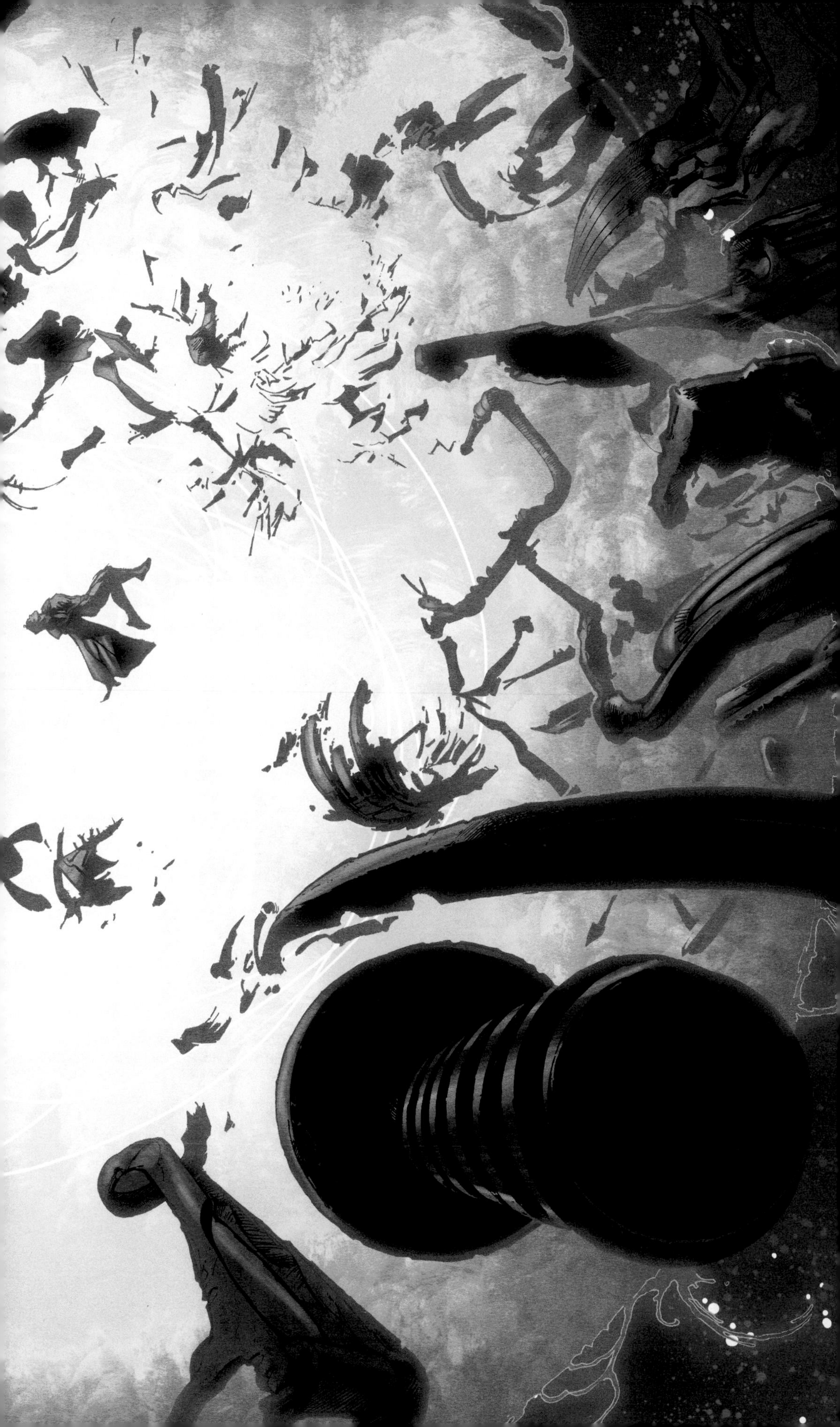

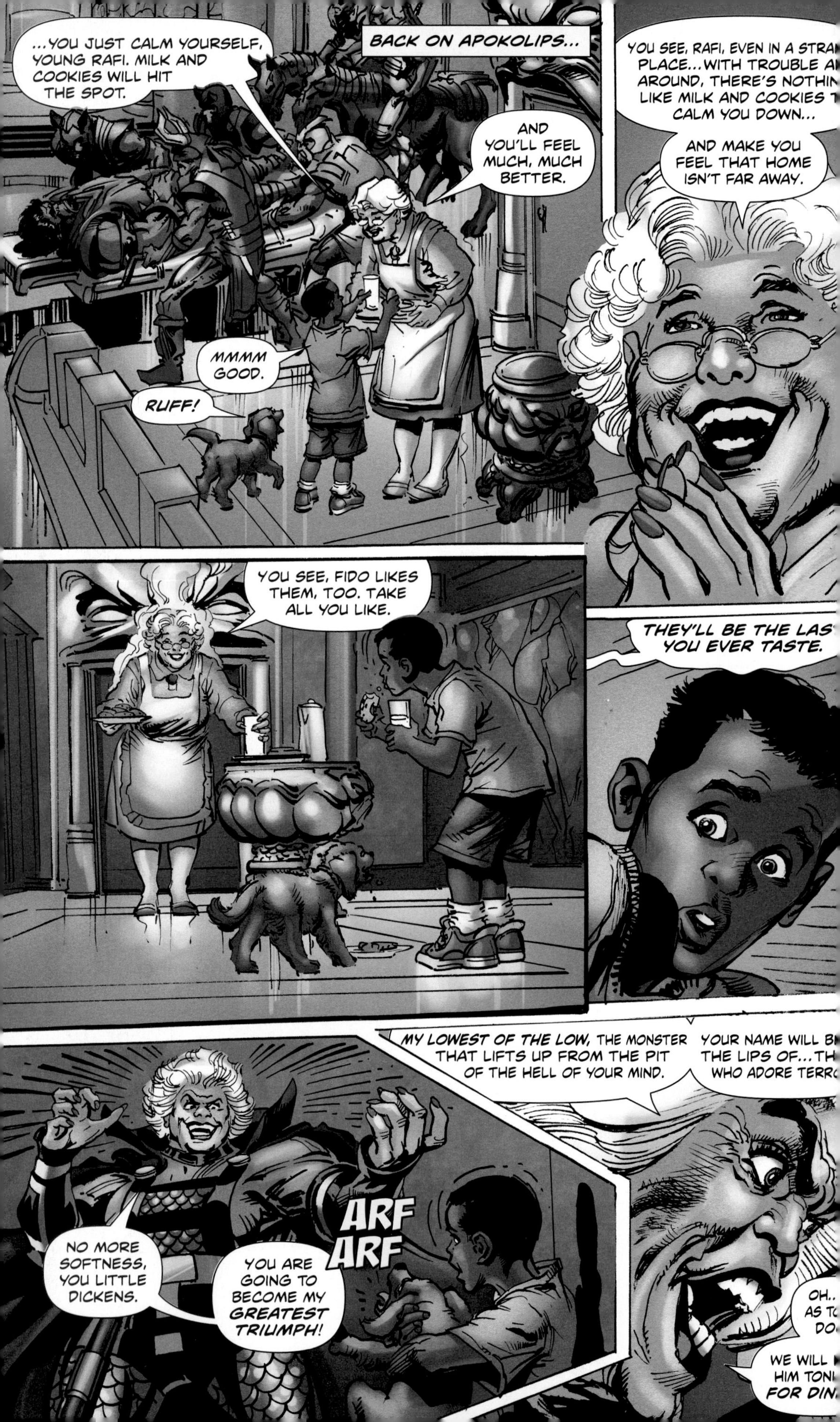
...YOU JUST CALM YOURSELF, YOUNG RAFI. MILK AND COOKIES WILL HIT THE SPOT.
BACK ON APOKOLIPS...
AND YOU'LL FEEL MUCH, MUCH BETTER.
MMMM GOOD.
RUFF!
YOU SEE, RAFI, EVEN IN A STRA
PLACE...WITH TROUBLE A
AROUND, THERE'S NOTHIN
LIKE MILK AND COOKIES T
CALM YOU DOWN...
AND MAKE YOU FEEL THAT HOME ISN'T FAR AWAY.
YOU SEE, FIDO LIKES THEM, TOO. TAKE ALL YOU LIKE.
THEY'LL BE THE LAS
YOU EVER TASTE.
NO MORE SOFTNESS, YOU LITTLE DICKENS.
YOU ARE GOING TO BECOME MY GREATEST TRIUMPH!
ARF ARF
MY LOWEST OF THE LOW, THE MONSTER THAT LIFTS UP FROM THE PIT OF THE HELL OF YOUR MIND.
YOUR NAME WILL B
THE LIPS OF...TH
WHO ADORE TERR
OH..
AS T
DO
WE WILL
HIM TON
FOR DIN

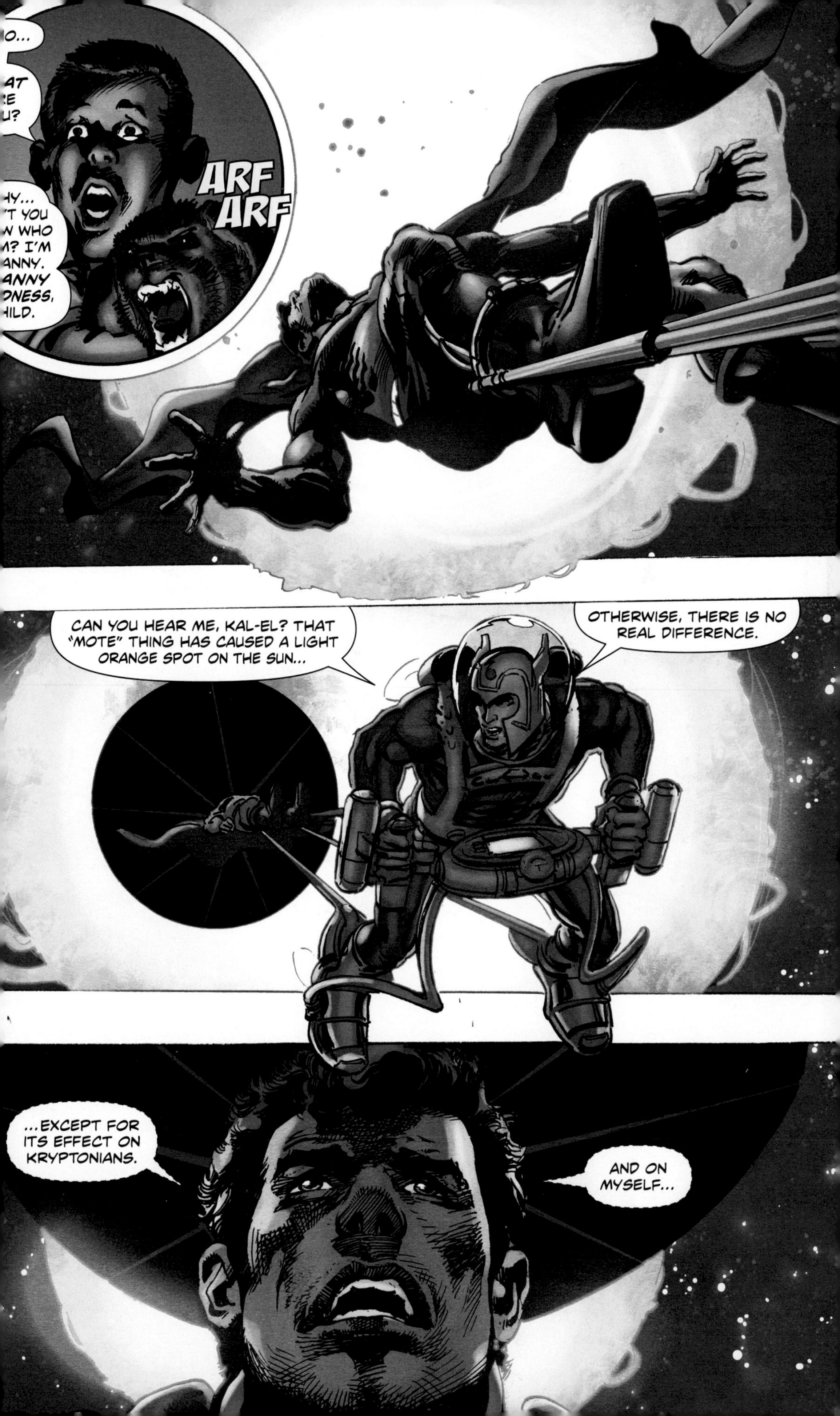
O...
AT
E
U?
ARF ARF
HY...
'T YOU
V WHO
M? I'M
ANNY.
ANNY
ONESS,
HILD.
CAN YOU HEAR ME, KAL-EL? THAT "MOTE" THING HAS CAUSED A LIGHT ORANGE SPOT ON THE SUN...
OTHERWISE, THERE IS NO REAL DIFFERENCE.
...EXCEPT FOR ITS EFFECT ON KRYPTONIANS.
AND ON MYSELF...

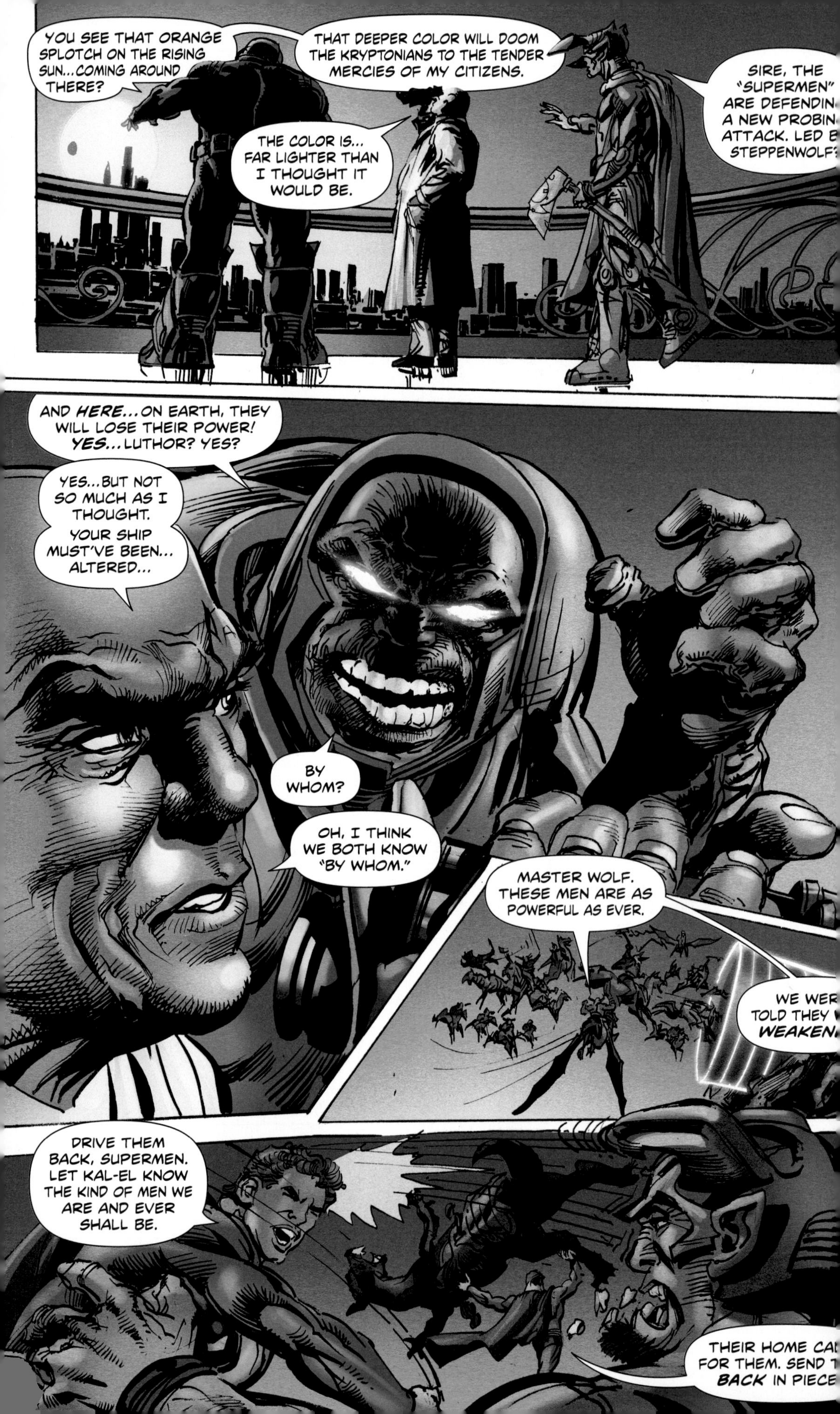

YOU SEE THAT ORANGE SPLOTCH ON THE RISING SUN...COMING AROUND THERE?
THAT DEEPER COLOR WILL DOOM THE KRYPTONIANS TO THE TENDER MERCIES OF MY CITIZENS.
THE COLOR IS... FAR LIGHTER THAN I THOUGHT IT WOULD BE.
SIRE, THE "SUPERMEN" ARE DEFENDIN A NEW PROBIN ATTACK. LED B STEPPENWOLF?
AND *HERE...* ON EARTH, THEY WILL LOSE THEIR POWER! *YES...* LUTHOR? YES?
YES...BUT NOT SO MUCH AS I THOUGHT.
YOUR SHIP MUST'VE BEEN... ALTERED...
BY WHOM?
OH, I THINK WE BOTH KNOW "BY WHOM."
MASTER WOLF. THESE MEN ARE AS POWERFUL AS EVER.
WE WER TOLD THEY *WEAKEN*
DRIVE THEM BACK, SUPERMEN. LET KAL-EL KNOW THE KIND OF MEN WE ARE AND EVER SHALL BE.
THEIR HOME CA FOR THEM. SEND *BACK* IN PIECE

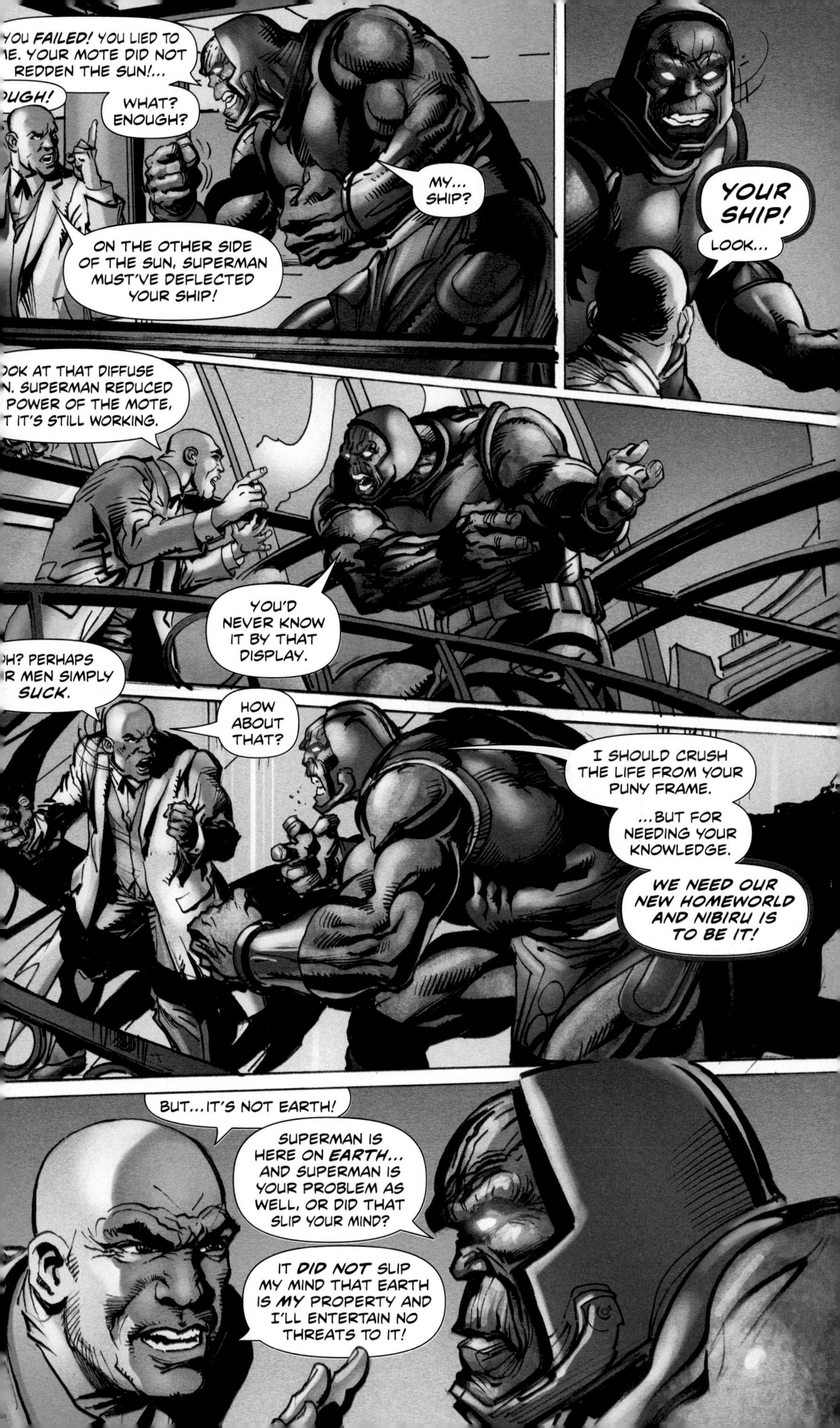

YOU FAILED! YOU LIED TO ME. YOUR MOTE DID NOT REDDEN THE SUN!...
UGH!
WHAT? ENOUGH?
MY... SHIP?
ON THE OTHER SIDE OF THE SUN, SUPERMAN MUST'VE DEFLECTED YOUR SHIP!
YOUR SHIP!
LOOK...
OOK AT THAT DIFFUSE N. SUPERMAN REDUCED POWER OF THE MOTE, T IT'S STILL WORKING.
YOU'D NEVER KNOW IT BY THAT DISPLAY.
OH? PERHAPS R MEN SIMPLY SUCK.
HOW ABOUT THAT?
I SHOULD CRUSH THE LIFE FROM YOUR PUNY FRAME.
...BUT FOR NEEDING YOUR KNOWLEDGE.
WE NEED OUR NEW HOMEWORLD AND NIBIRU IS TO BE IT!
BUT... IT'S NOT EARTH!
SUPERMAN IS HERE ON EARTH... AND SUPERMAN IS YOUR PROBLEM AS WELL, OR DID THAT SLIP YOUR MIND?
IT DID NOT SLIP MY MIND THAT EARTH IS MY PROPERTY AND I'LL ENTERTAIN NO THREATS TO IT!

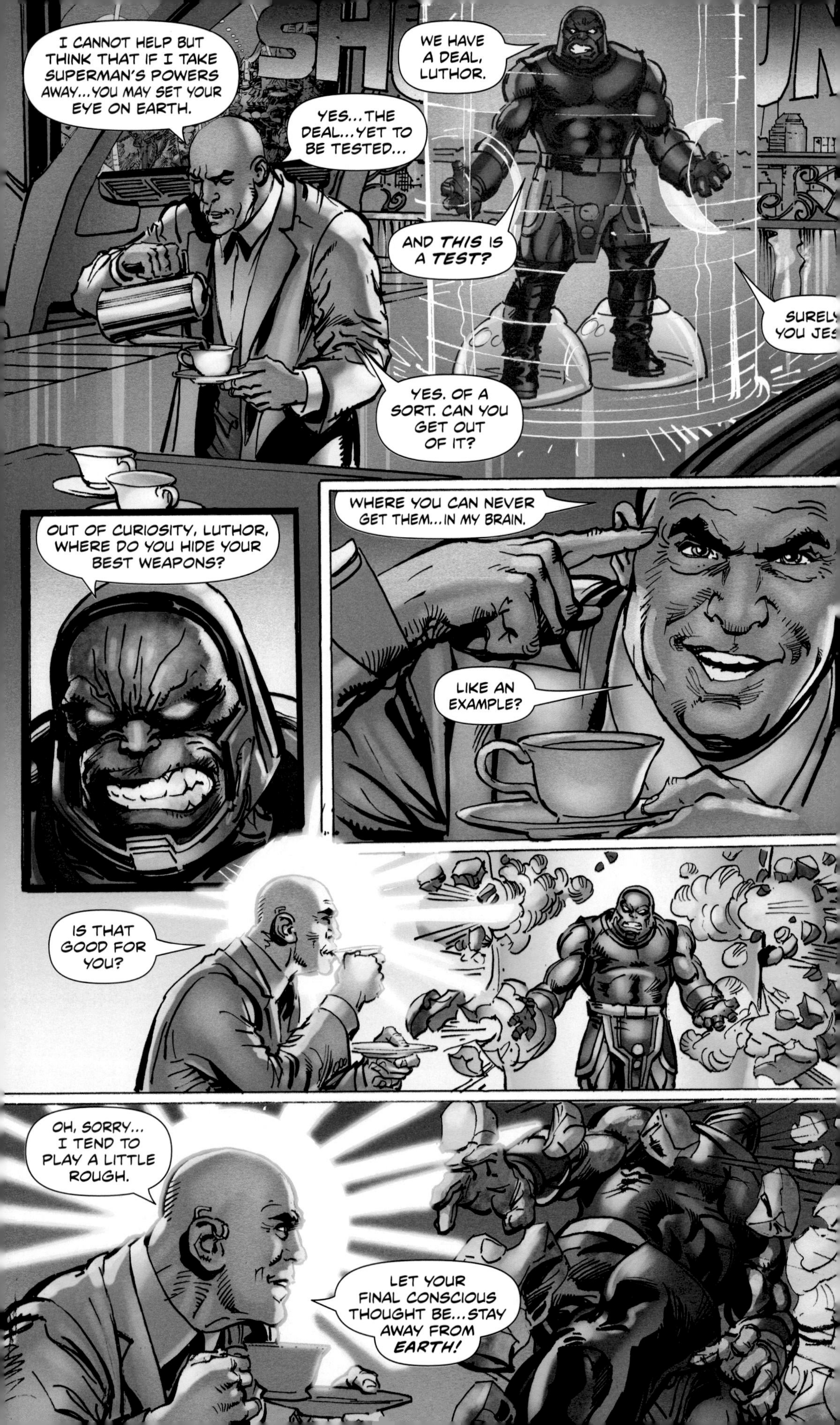
I CANNOT HELP BUT THINK THAT IF I TAKE SUPERMAN'S POWERS AWAY...YOU MAY SET YOUR EYE ON EARTH.
WE HAVE A DEAL, LUTHOR.
YES...THE DEAL...YET TO BE TESTED...
AND THIS IS A TEST?
SURELY YOU JES
YES. OF A SORT. CAN YOU GET OUT OF IT?
OUT OF CURIOSITY, LUTHOR, WHERE DO YOU HIDE YOUR BEST WEAPONS?
WHERE YOU CAN NEVER GET THEM...IN MY BRAIN.
LIKE AN EXAMPLE?
IS THAT GOOD FOR YOU?
OH, SORRY... I TEND TO PLAY A LITTLE ROUGH.
LET YOUR FINAL CONSCIOUS THOUGHT BE...STAY AWAY FROM EARTH!

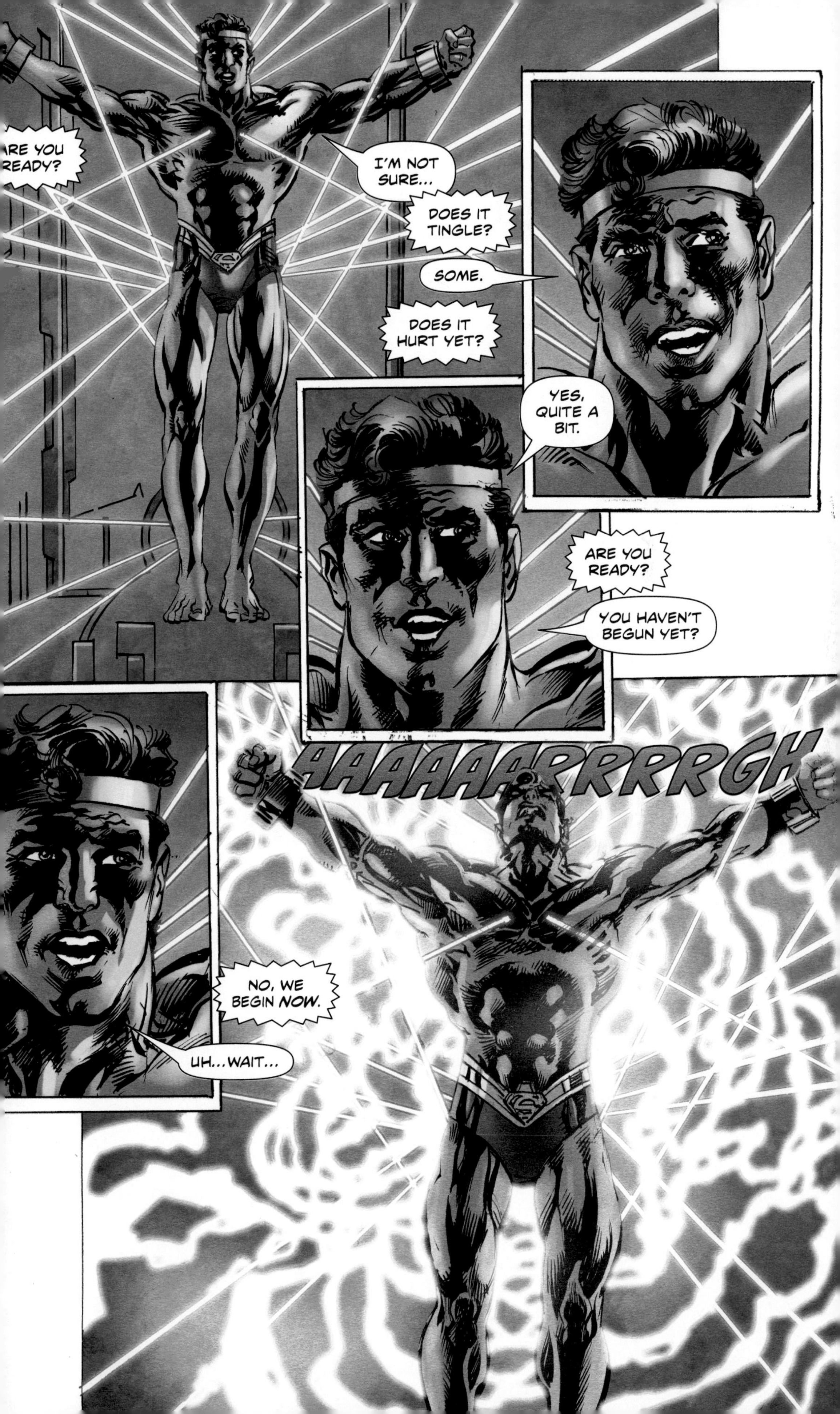
ARE YOU READY?
I'M NOT SURE...
DOES IT TINGLE?
SOME.
DOES IT HURT YET?
YES, QUITE A BIT.
ARE YOU READY?
YOU HAVEN'T BEGUN YET?
NO, WE BEGIN NOW.
UH...WAIT...
AAAAAARRRRGH

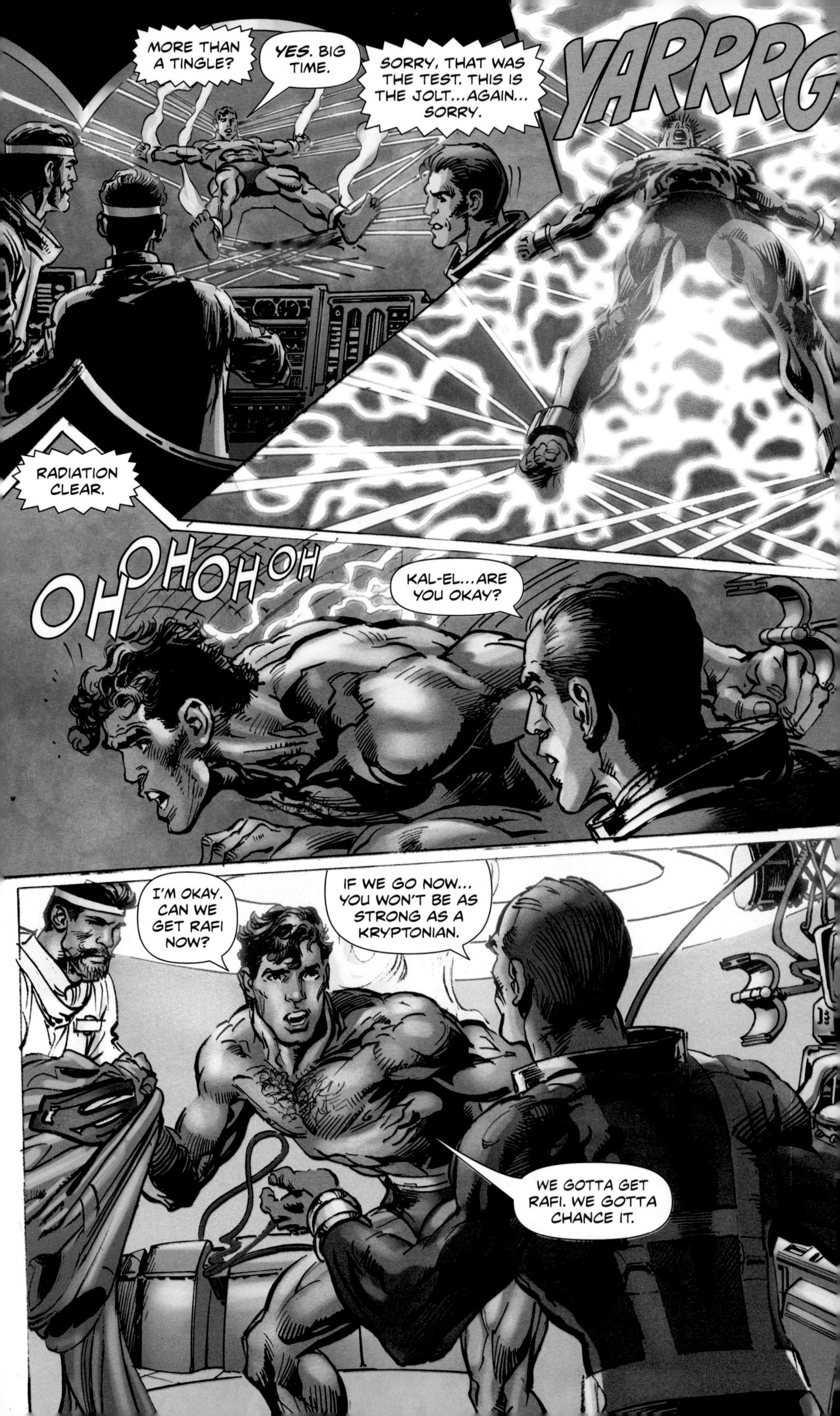
MORE THAN A TINGLE?
YES. BIG TIME.
SORRY, THAT WAS THE TEST. THIS IS THE JOLT...AGAIN... SORRY.
YARRRG
RADIATION CLEAR.
OHOHOHOH
KAL-EL...ARE YOU OKAY?
I'M OKAY. CAN WE GET RAFI NOW?
IF WE GO NOW... YOU WON'T BE AS STRONG AS A KRYPTONIAN.
WE GOTTA GET RAFI. WE GOTTA CHANCE IT.

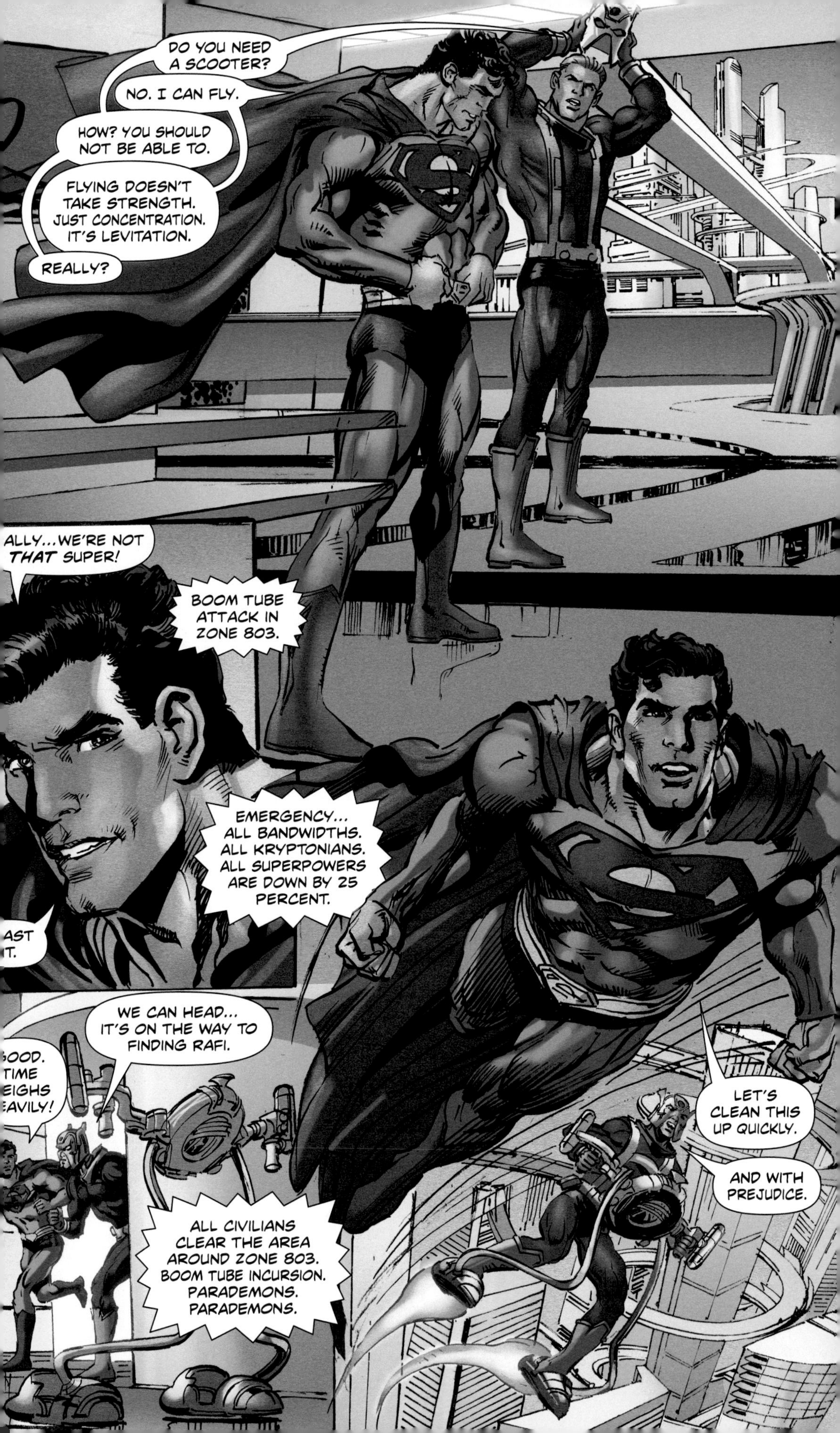

DO YOU NEED A SCOOTER?
NO. I CAN FLY.
HOW? YOU SHOULD NOT BE ABLE TO.
FLYING DOESN'T TAKE STRENGTH. JUST CONCENTRATION. IT'S LEVITATION.
REALLY?
ALLY...WE'RE NOT THAT SUPER!
BOOM TUBE ATTACK IN ZONE 803.
EMERGENCY... ALL BANDWIDTHS. ALL KRYPTONIANS. ALL SUPERPOWERS ARE DOWN BY 25 PERCENT.
AST
T.
WE CAN HEAD... IT'S ON THE WAY TO FINDING RAFI.
OOD. TIME EIGHS EAVILY!
LET'S CLEAN THIS UP QUICKLY.
AND WITH PREJUDICE.
ALL CIVILIANS CLEAR THE AREA AROUND ZONE 803. BOOM TUBE INCURSION. PARADEMONS. PARADEMONS.

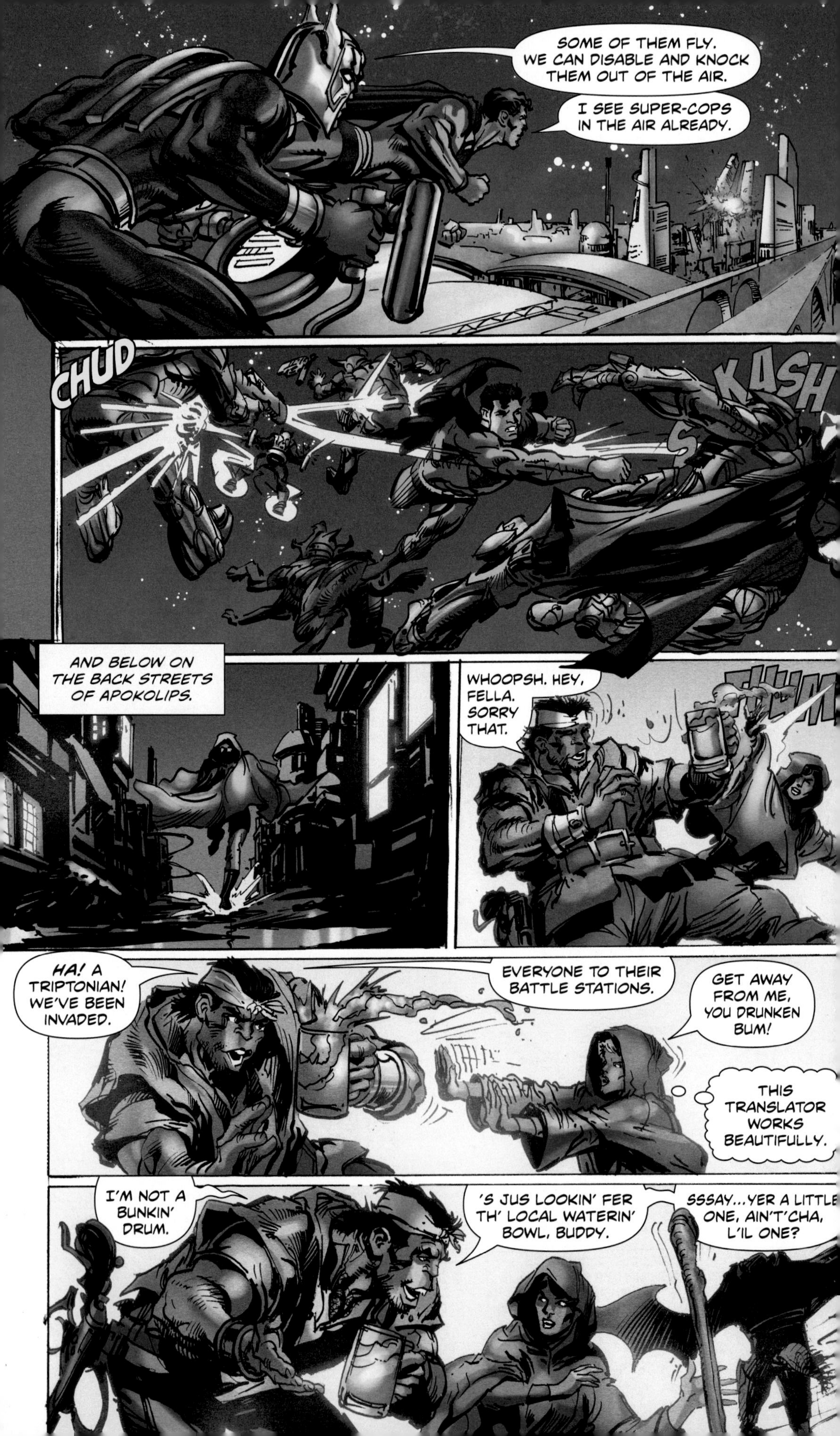
SOME OF THEM FLY. WE CAN DISABLE AND KNOCK THEM OUT OF THE AIR.
I SEE SUPER-COPS IN THE AIR ALREADY.
CHUD
KASH
AND BELOW ON THE BACK STREETS OF APOKOLIPS.
WHOOPSH. HEY, FELLA. SORRY THAT.
HA! A TRIPTONIAN! WE'VE BEEN INVADED.
EVERYONE TO THEIR BATTLE STATIONS.
GET AWAY FROM ME, YOU DRUNKEN BUM!
THIS TRANSLATOR WORKS BEAUTIFULLY.
I'M NOT A BUNKIN' DRUM.
'S JUS LOOKIN' FER TH' LOCAL WATERIN' BOWL, BUDDY.
SSSAY...YER A LITTLE ONE, AIN'T'CHA, L'IL ONE?

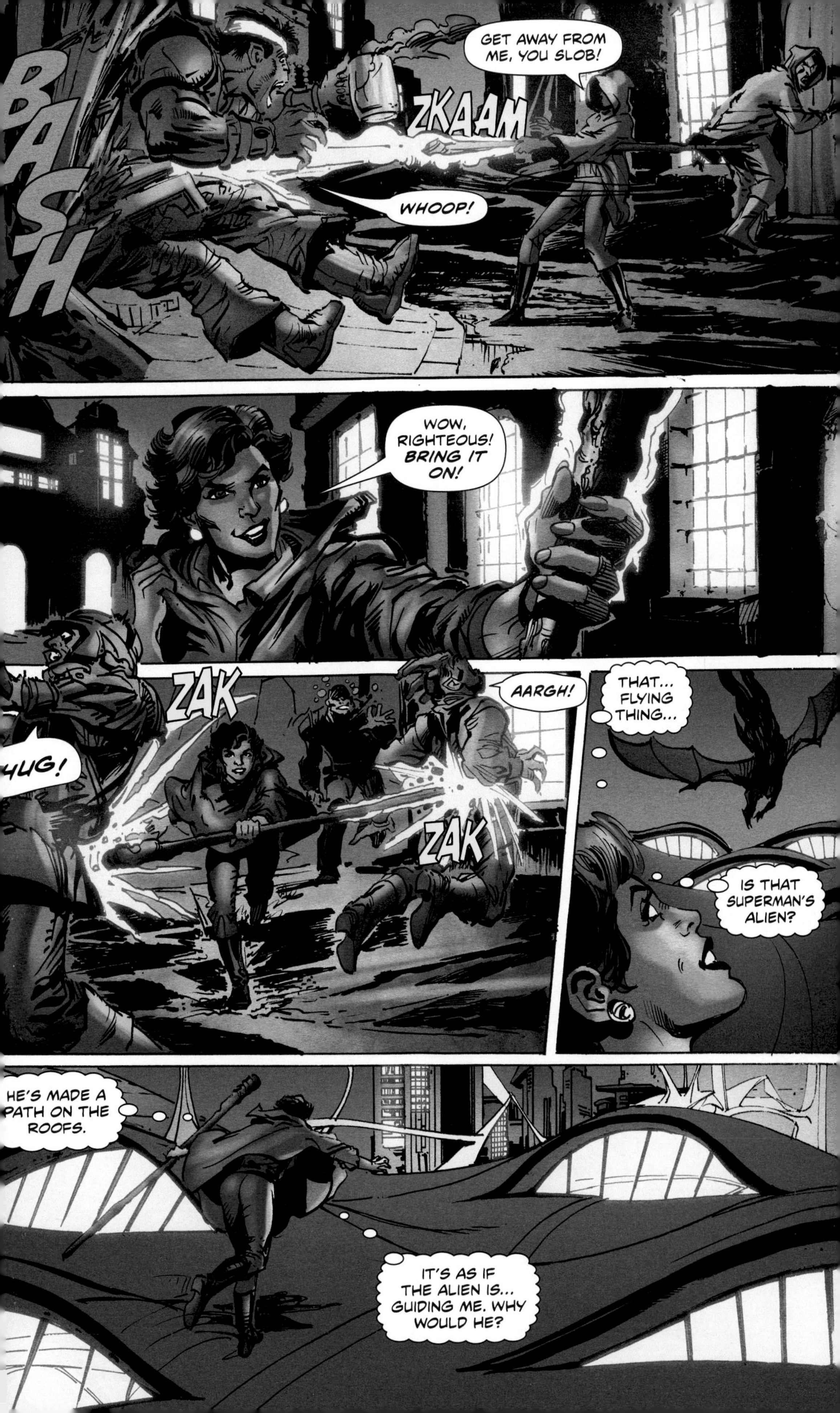
BASH
GET AWAY FROM ME, YOU SLOB!
ZKAAM
WHOOP!
WOW, RIGHTEOUS! BRING IT ON!
ZAK
UG!
AARGH!
ZAK
THAT... FLYING THING...
IS THAT SUPERMAN'S ALIEN?
HE'S MADE A PATH ON THE ROOFS.
IT'S AS IF THE ALIEN IS... GUIDING ME. WHY WOULD HE?

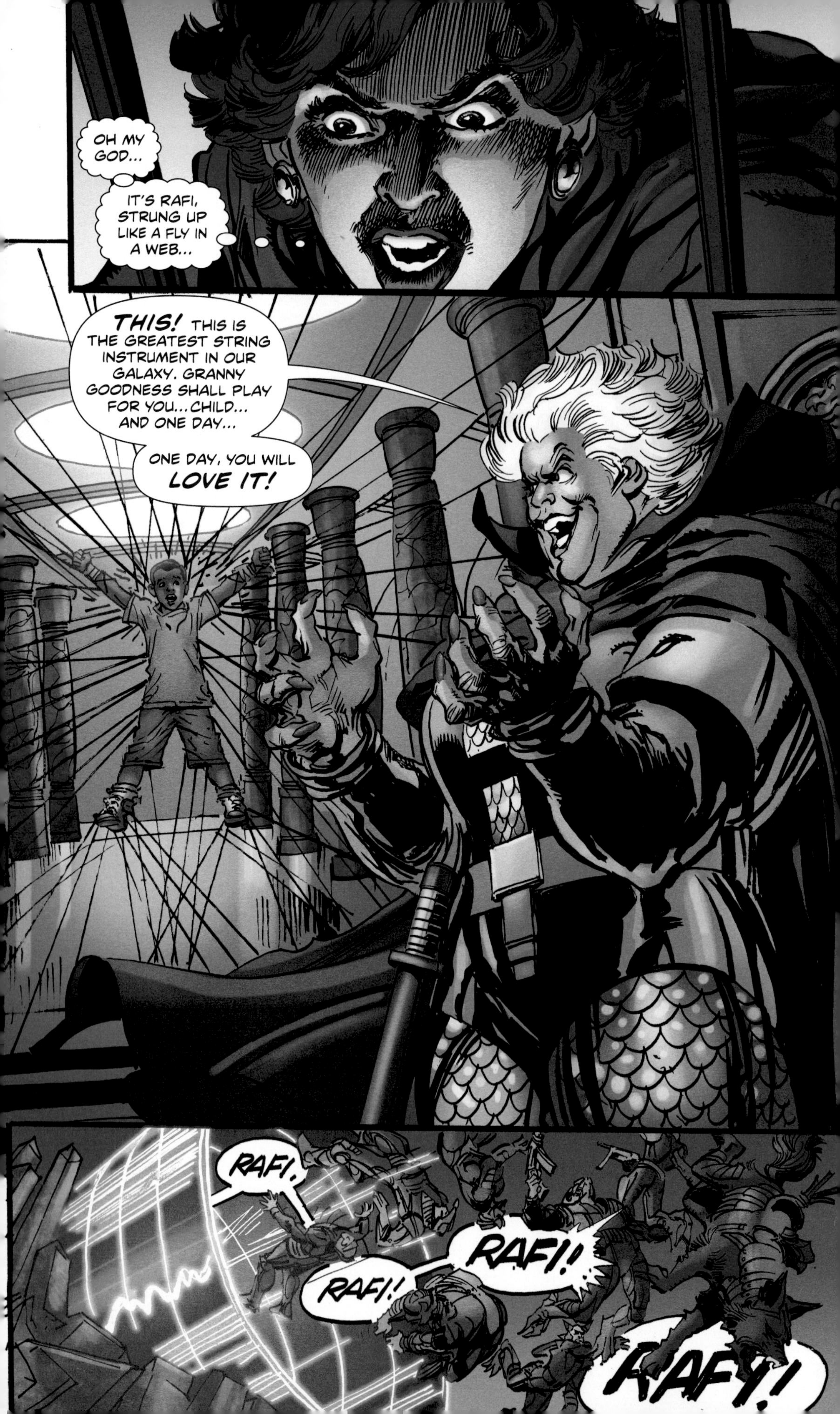
OH MY GOD...
IT'S RAFI, STRUNG UP LIKE A FLY IN A WEB...
THIS! THIS IS THE GREATEST STRING INSTRUMENT IN OUR GALAXY. GRANNY GOODNESS SHALL PLAY FOR YOU...CHILD... AND ONE DAY...
ONE DAY, YOU WILL LOVE IT!
RAFI.
RAFI!
RAFI!
RAFY!

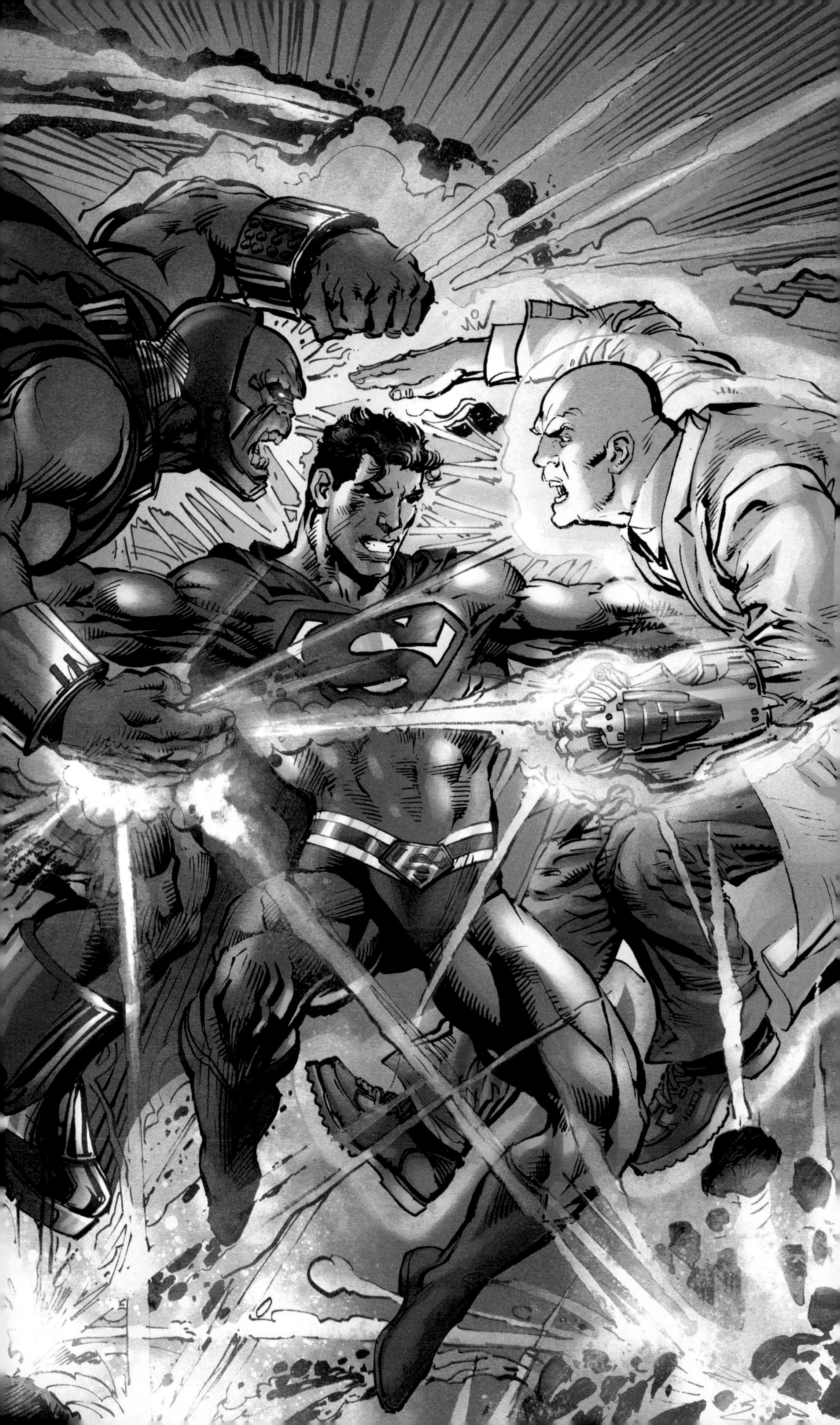

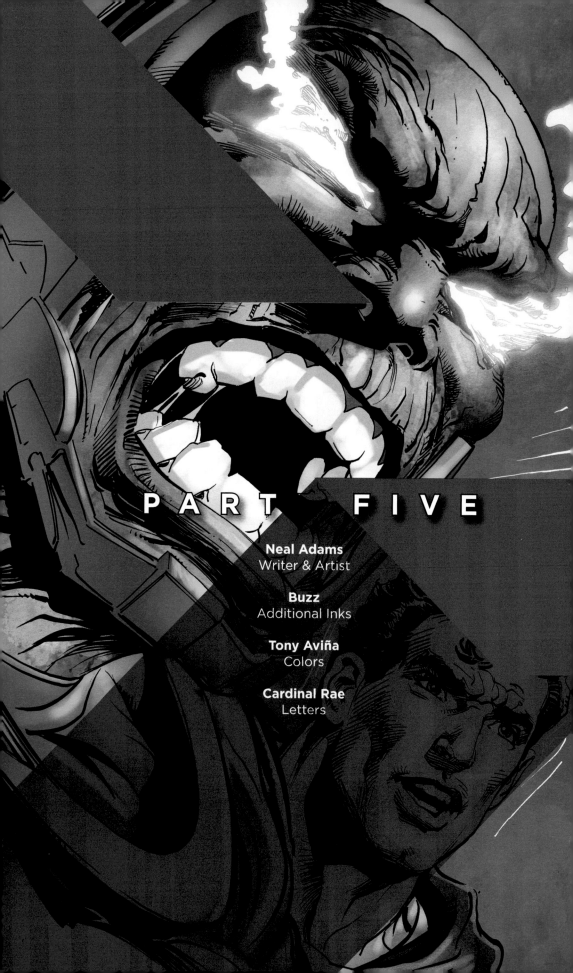

PART FIVE

Neal Adams
Writer & Artist

Buzz
Additional Inks

Tony Aviña
Colors

Cardinal Rae
Letters

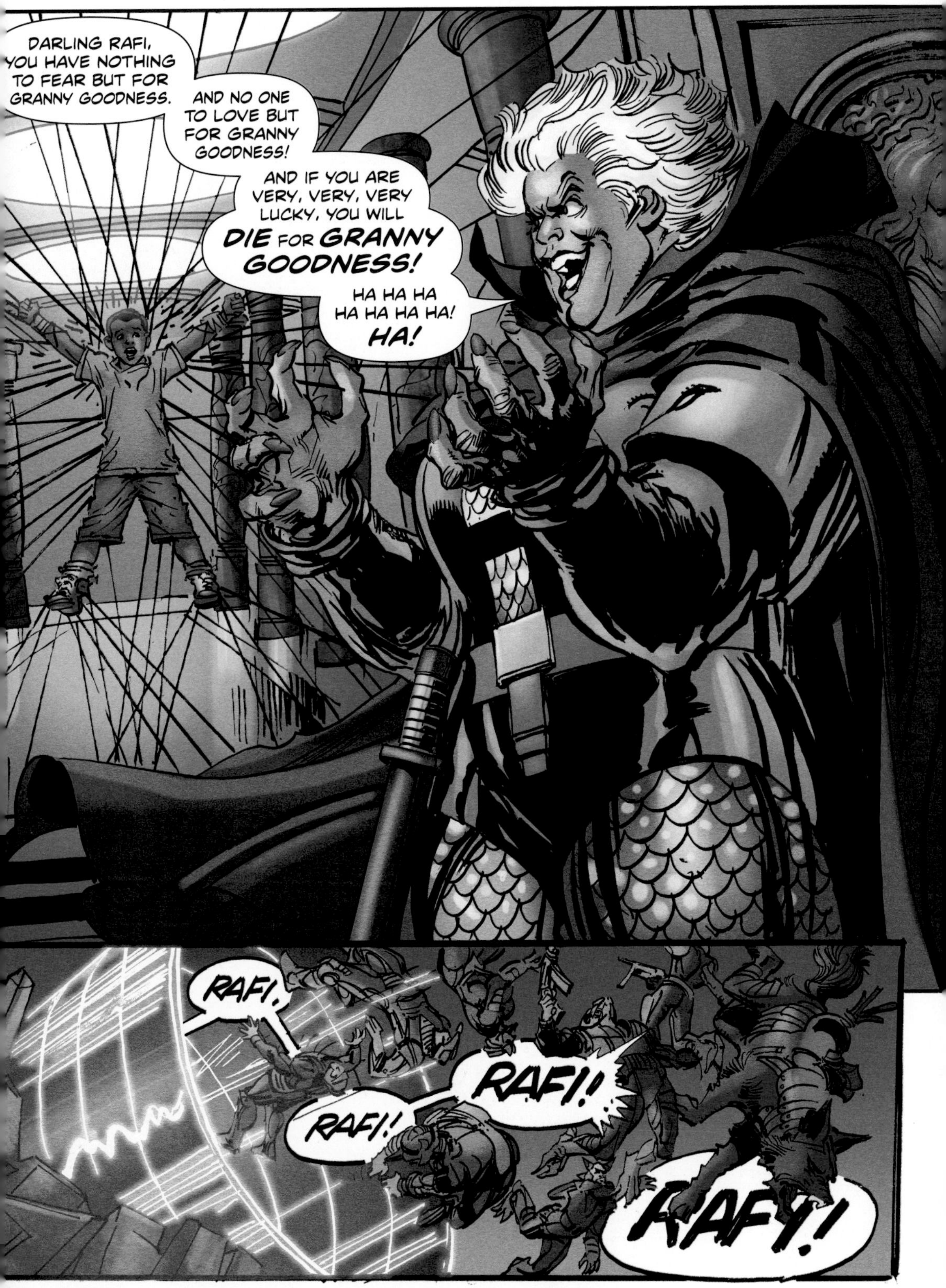
DARLING RAFI, YOU HAVE NOTHING TO FEAR BUT FOR GRANNY GOODNESS.
AND NO ONE TO LOVE BUT FOR GRANNY GOODNESS!
AND IF YOU ARE VERY, VERY, VERY LUCKY, YOU WILL DIE FOR GRANNY GOODNESS!
HA HA HA HA HA HA HA! HA!
RAFI.
RAFI!
RAFI!
RAFY!

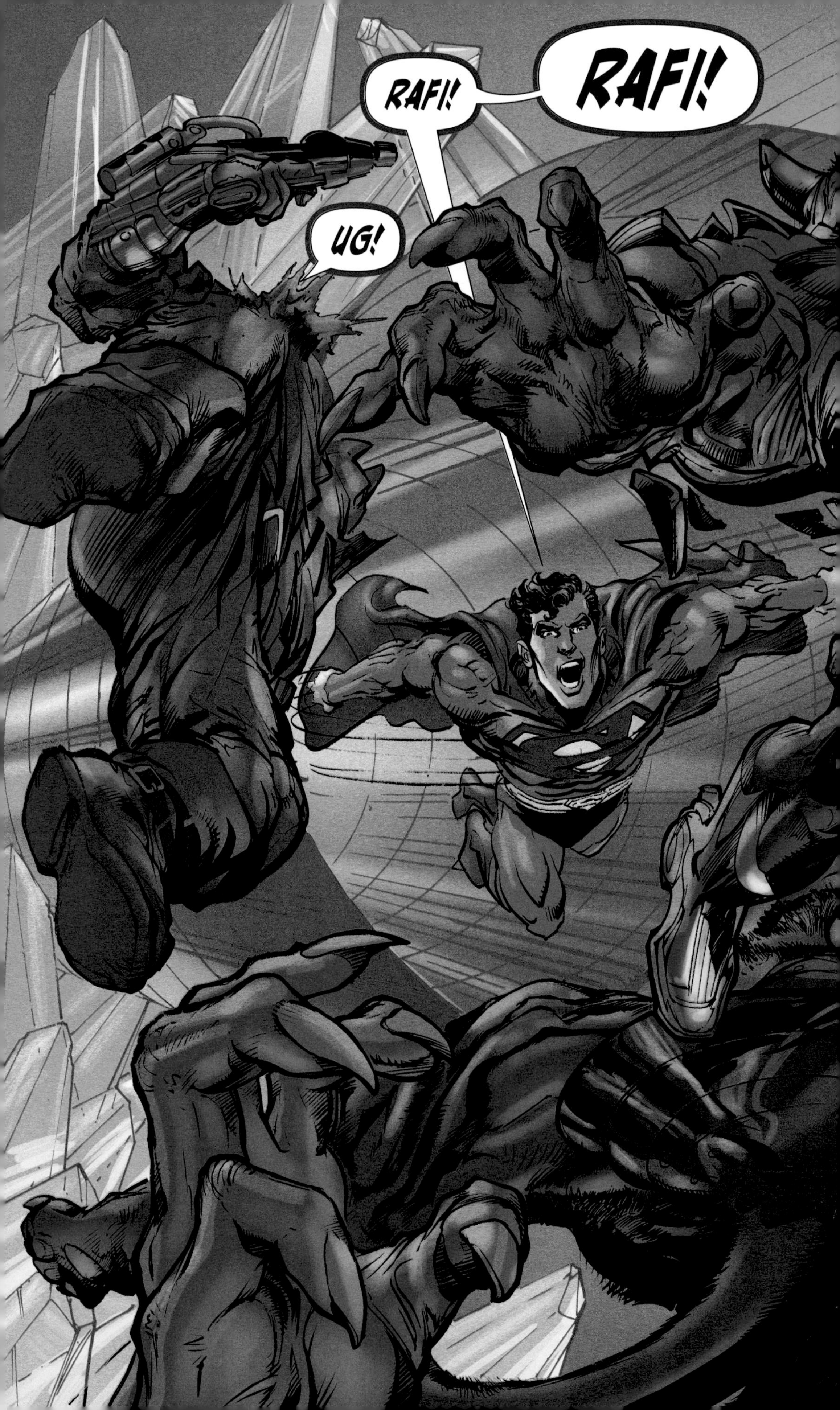
UG!
RAFI!
RAFI!

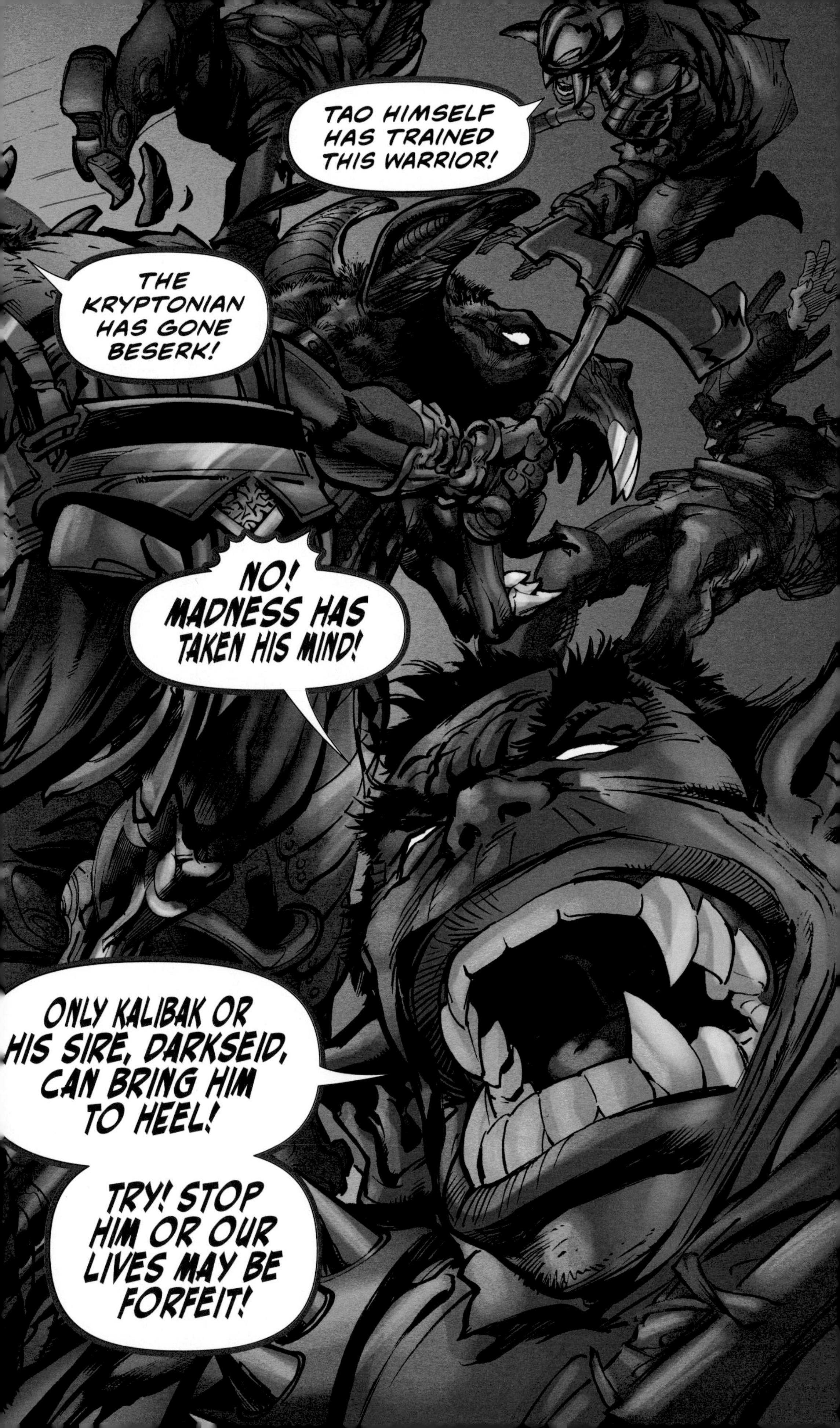
TAO HIMSELF HAS TRAINED THIS WARRIOR!
THE KRYPTONIAN HAS GONE BESERK!
NO! MADNESS HAS TAKEN HIS MIND!
ONLY KALIBAK OR HIS SIRE, DARKSEID, CAN BRING HIM TO HEEL!
TRY! STOP HIM OR OUR LIVES MAY BE FORFEIT!

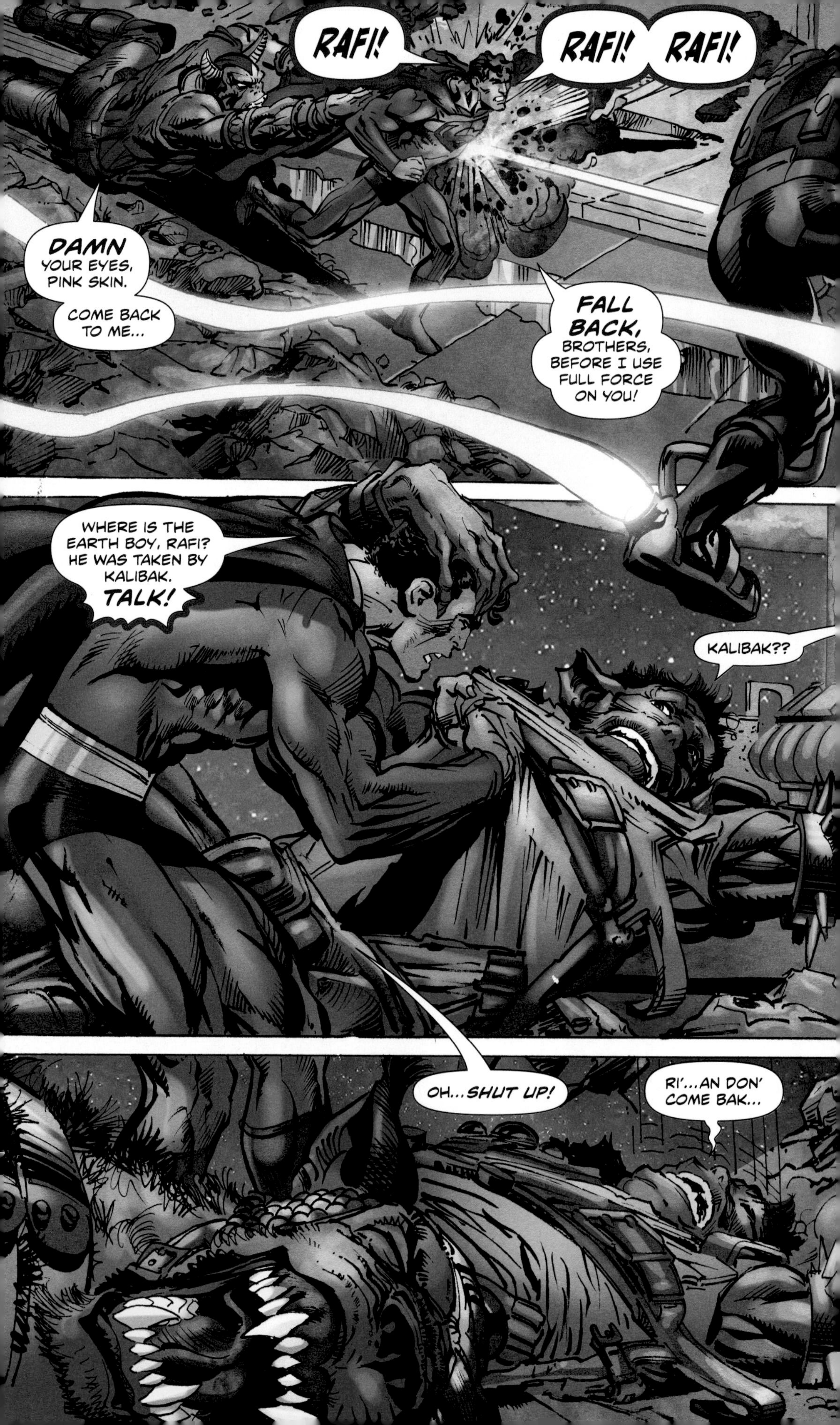
RAFI!
RAFI! RAFI!
DAMN YOUR EYES, PINK SKIN.
COME BACK TO ME...
FALL BACK, BROTHERS, BEFORE I USE FULL FORCE ON YOU!
WHERE IS THE EARTH BOY, RAFI? HE WAS TAKEN BY KALIBAK. TALK!
KALIBAK??
OH...SHUT UP!
RI'...AN DON' COME BAK...

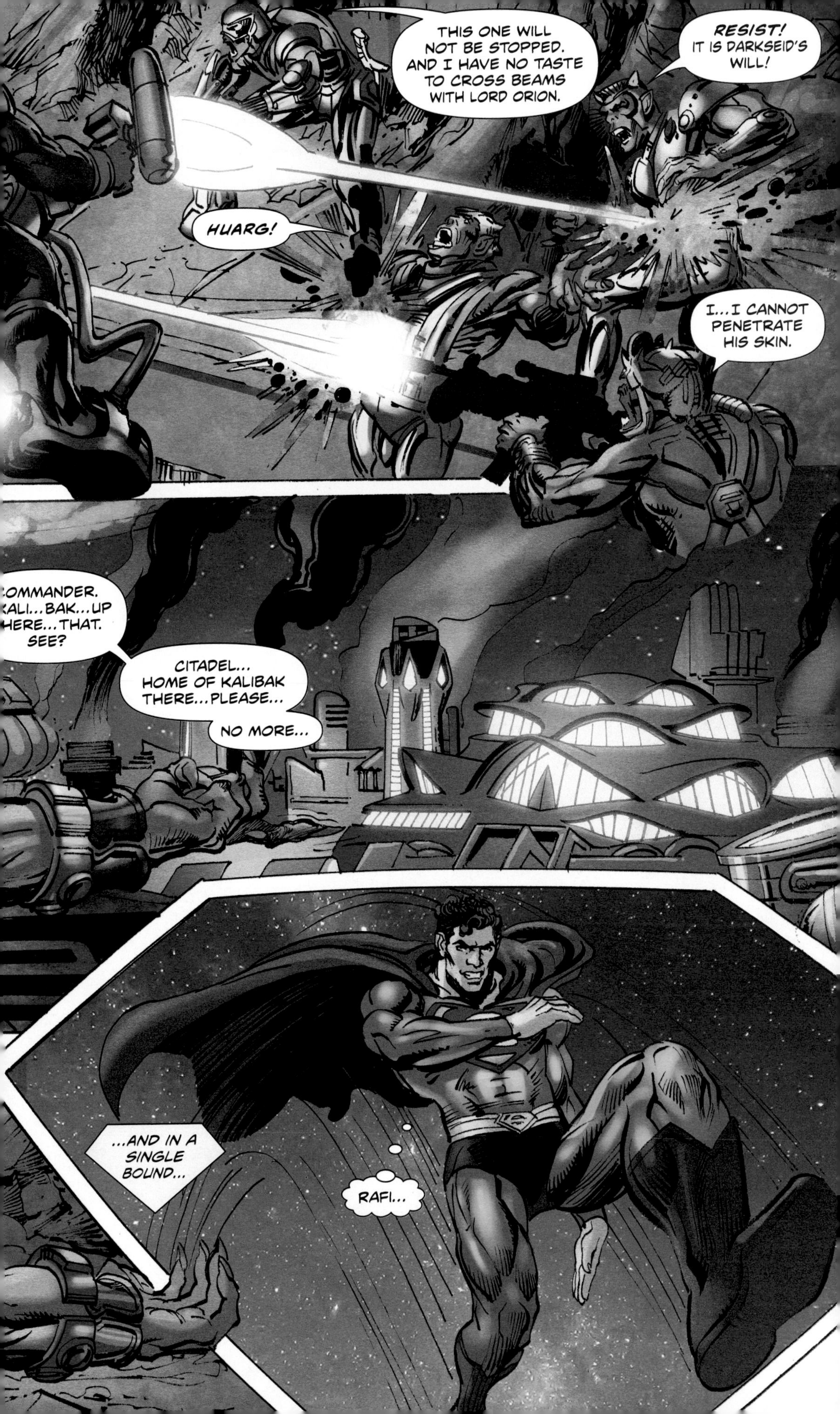
THIS ONE WILL NOT BE STOPPED. AND I HAVE NO TASTE TO CROSS BEAMS WITH LORD ORION.
RESIST! IT IS DARKSEID'S WILL!
HUARG!
I... I CANNOT PENETRATE HIS SKIN.
OMMANDER. ALI...BAK...UP HERE...THAT. SEE?
CITADEL... HOME OF KALIBAK THERE...PLEASE...
NO MORE...
...AND IN A SINGLE BOUND...
RAFI...

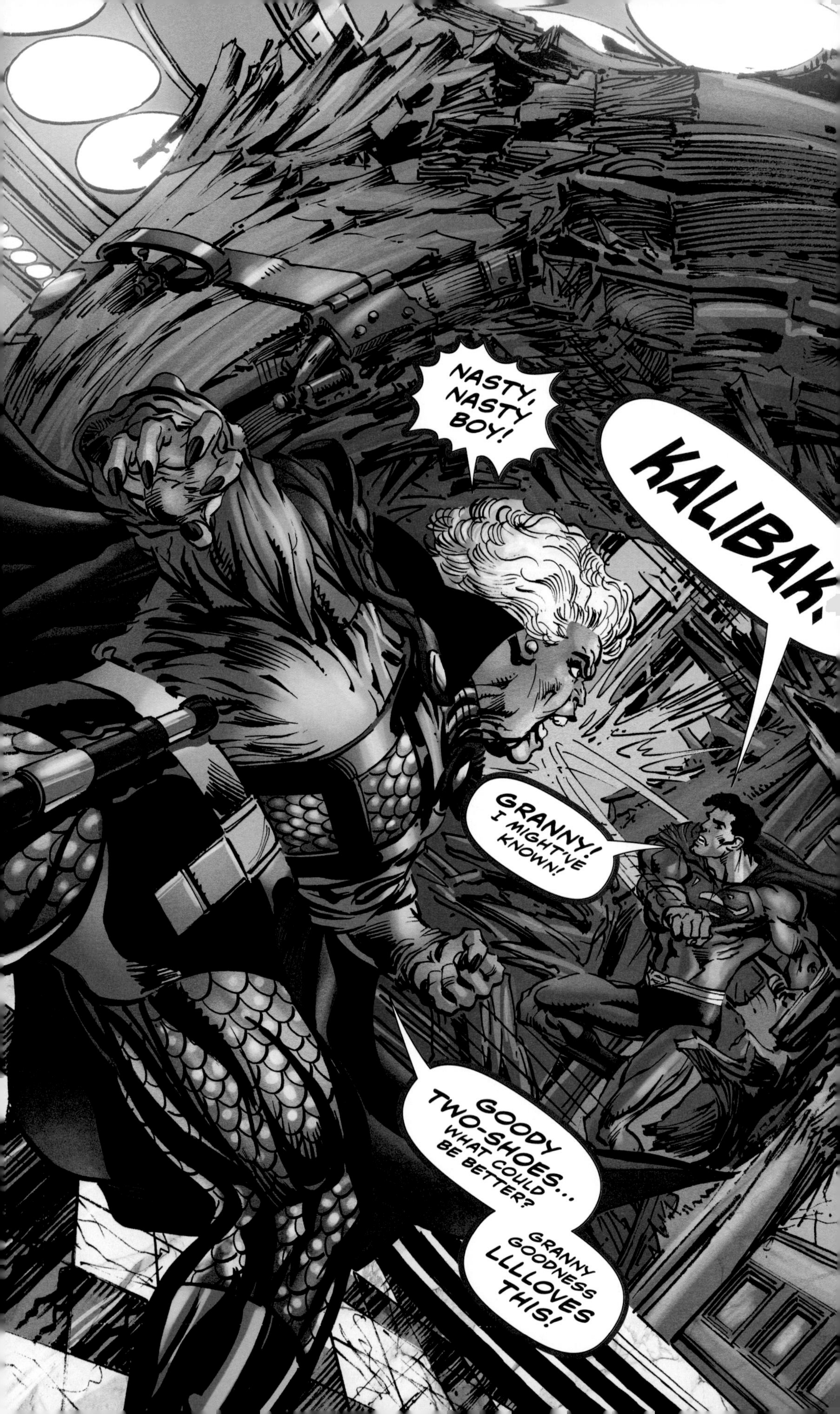
NASTY, NASTY BOY!
KALIBAK!
GRANNY! I MIGHT'VE KNOWN!
GOODY TWO-SHOES... WHAT COULD BE BETTER?
GRANNY GOODNESS LLLLOVES THIS!

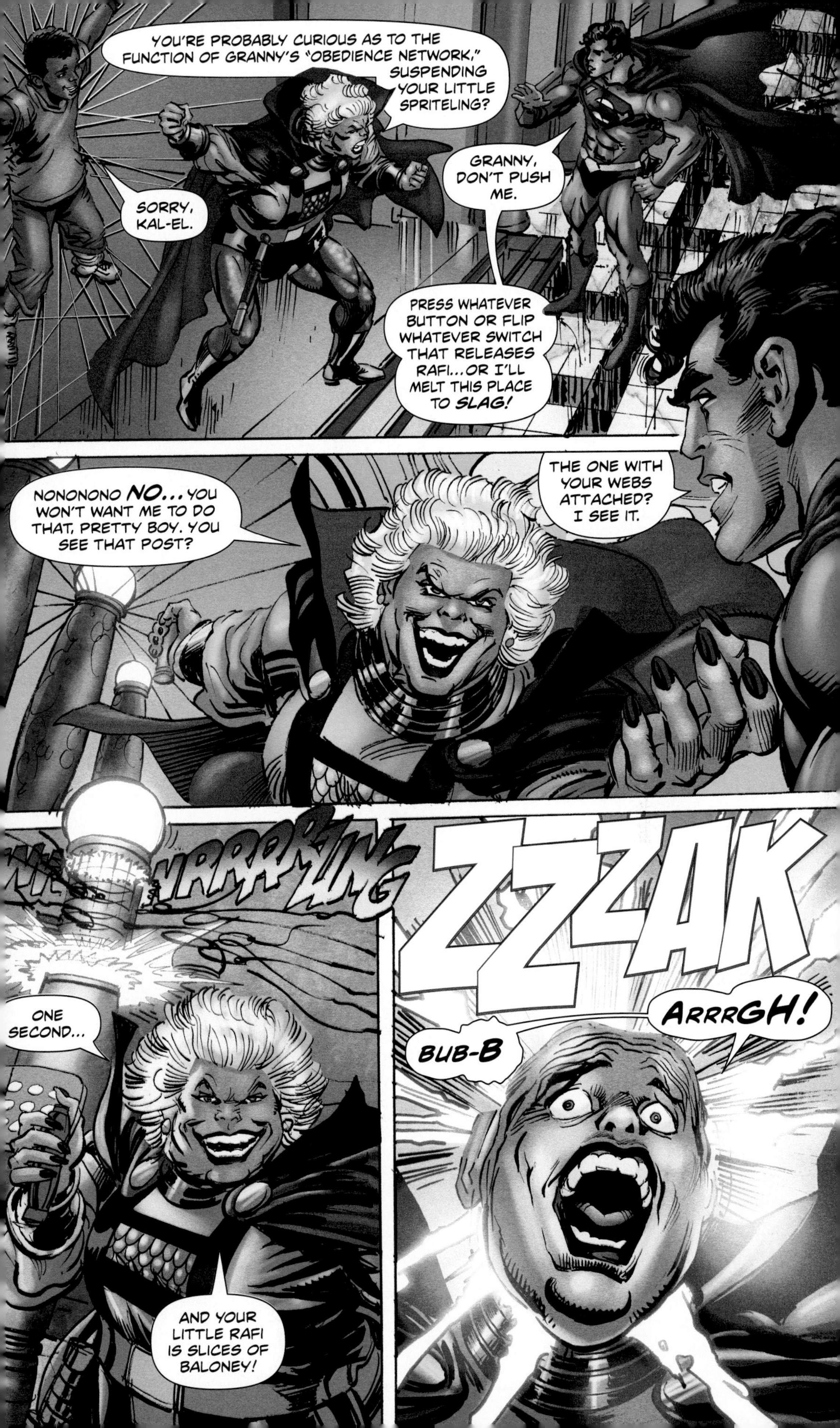
YOU'RE PROBABLY CURIOUS AS TO THE FUNCTION OF GRANNY'S "OBEDIENCE NETWORK," SUSPENDING YOUR LITTLE SPRITELING?
SORRY, KAL-EL.
GRANNY, DON'T PUSH ME.
PRESS WHATEVER BUTTON OR FLIP WHATEVER SWITCH THAT RELEASES RAFI...OR I'LL MELT THIS PLACE TO SLAG!
NONONONO NO... YOU WON'T WANT ME TO DO THAT, PRETTY BOY. YOU SEE THAT POST?
THE ONE WITH YOUR WEBS ATTACHED? I SEE IT.
ONE SECOND...
AND YOUR LITTLE RAFI IS SLICES OF BALONEY!
ZZZAK
BUB-B
ARRRGH!

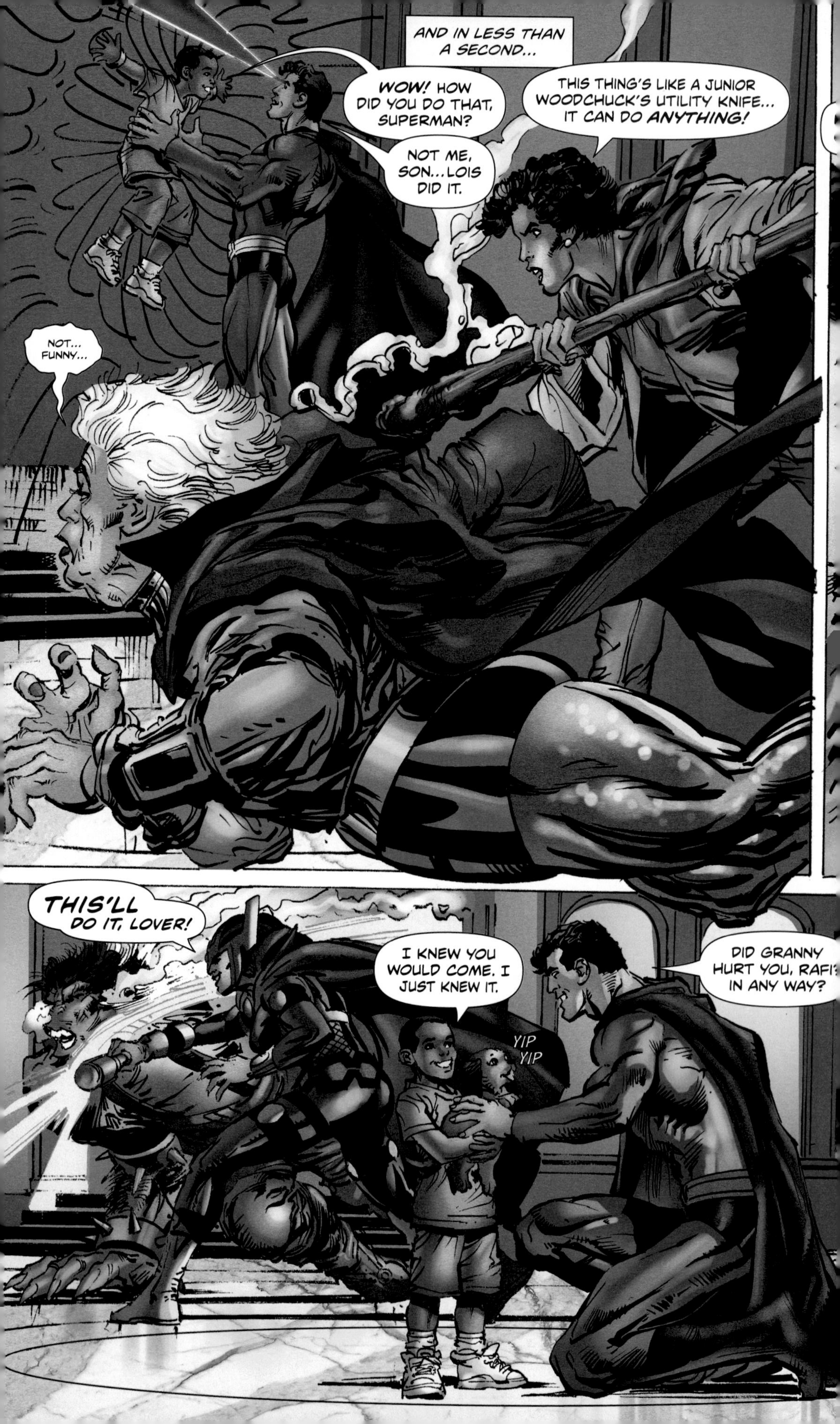
AND IN LESS THAN A SECOND...
WOW! HOW DID YOU DO THAT, SUPERMAN?
NOT ME, SON...LOIS DID IT.
THIS THING'S LIKE A JUNIOR WOODCHUCK'S UTILITY KNIFE... IT CAN DO ANYTHING!
NOT... FUNNY...
THIS'LL DO IT, LOVER!
I KNEW YOU WOULD COME. I JUST KNEW IT.
YIP YIP
DID GRANNY HURT YOU, RAFI IN ANY WAY?

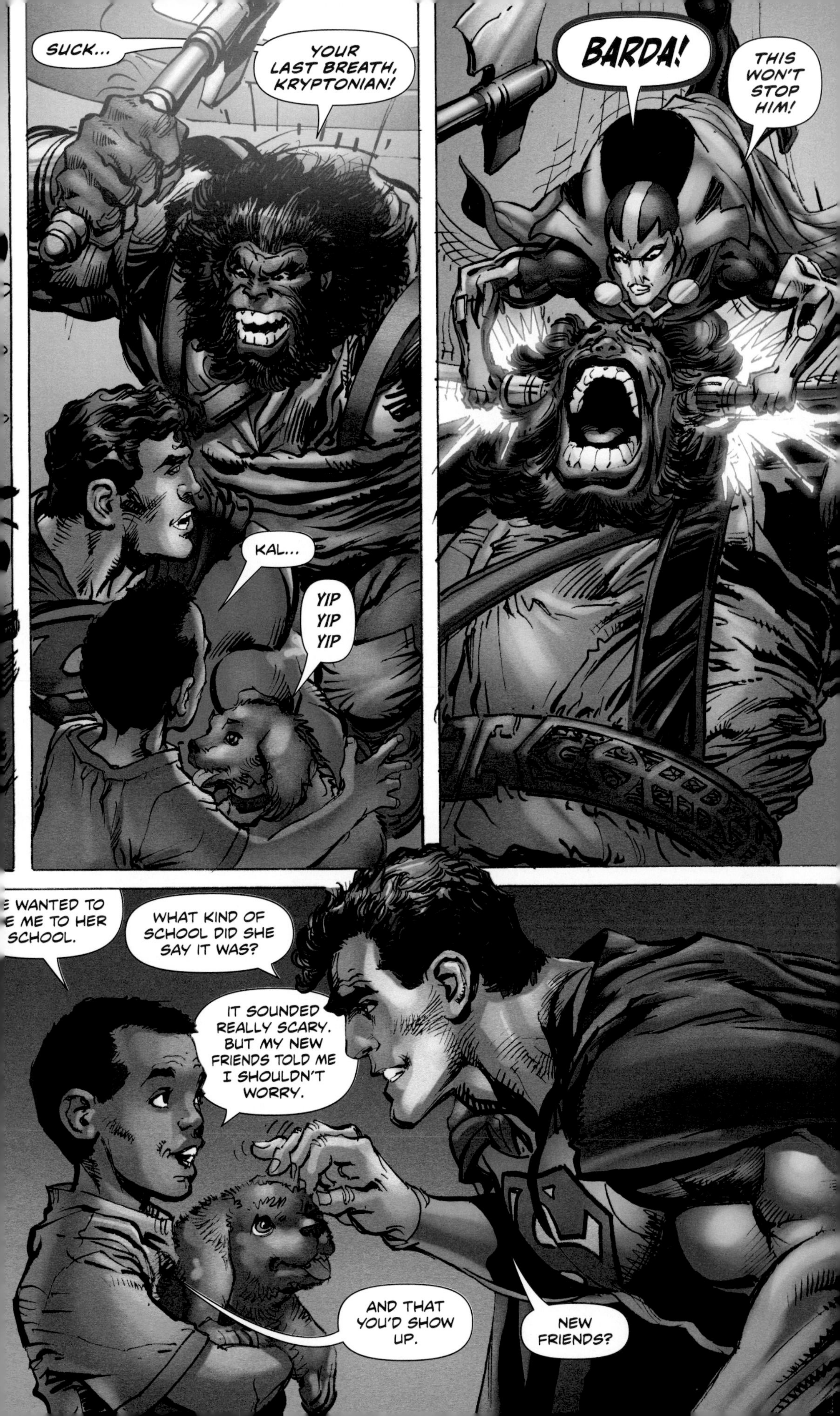
SUCK...
YOUR LAST BREATH, KRYPTONIAN!
KAL...
YIP YIP YIP
BARDA!
THIS WON'T STOP HIM!
E WANTED TO
E ME TO HER
SCHOOL.
WHAT KIND OF SCHOOL DID SHE SAY IT WAS?
IT SOUNDED REALLY SCARY. BUT MY NEW FRIENDS TOLD ME I SHOULDN'T WORRY.
AND THAT YOU'D SHOW UP.
NEW FRIENDS?

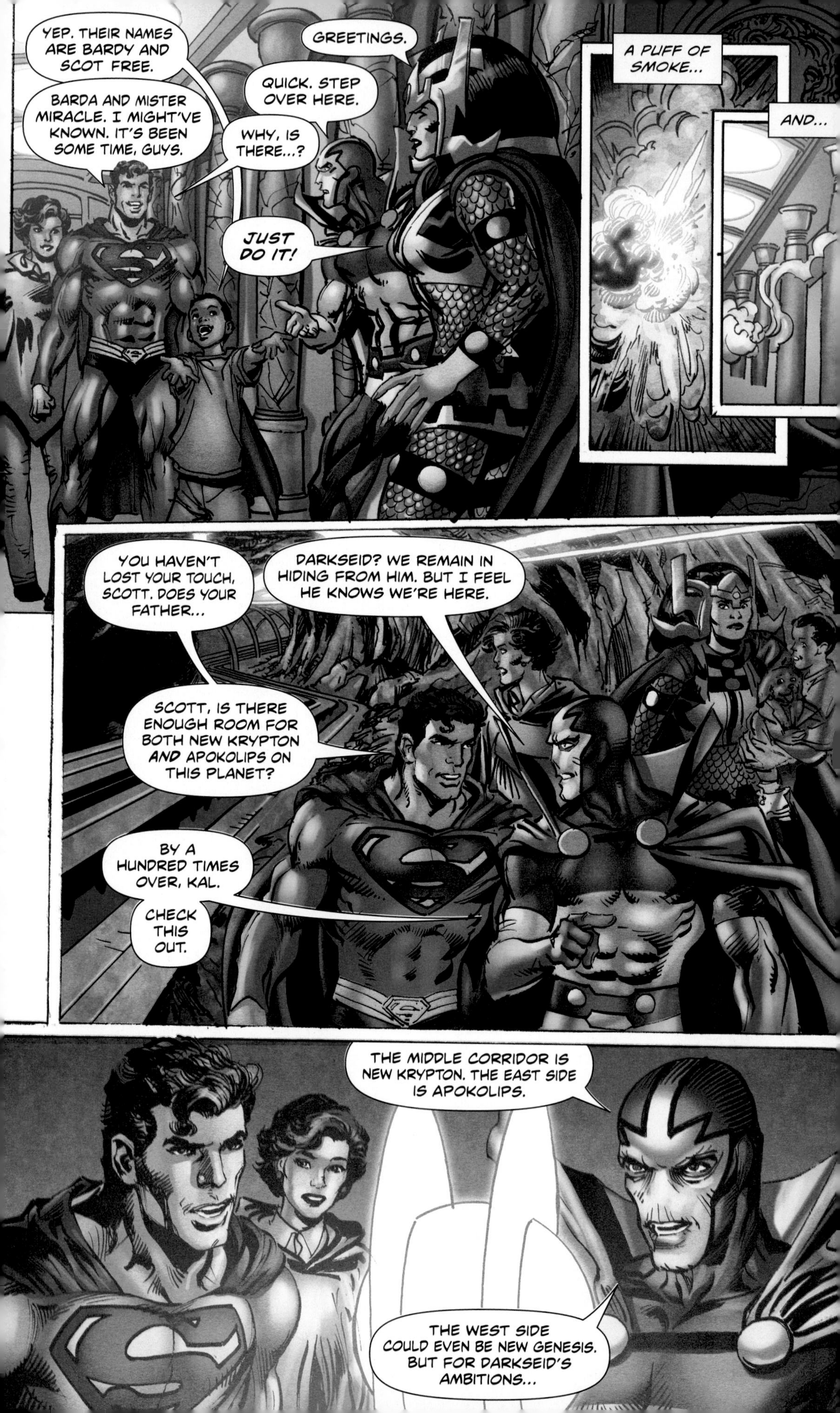

YEP. THEIR NAMES ARE BARDY AND SCOT FREE.
BARDA AND MISTER MIRACLE. I MIGHT'VE KNOWN. IT'S BEEN SOME TIME, GUYS.
GREETINGS.
QUICK. STEP OVER HERE.
WHY, IS THERE...?
JUST DO IT!
A PUFF OF SMOKE...
AND...
YOU HAVEN'T LOST YOUR TOUCH, SCOTT. DOES YOUR FATHER...
DARKSEID? WE REMAIN IN HIDING FROM HIM. BUT I FEEL HE KNOWS WE'RE HERE.
SCOTT, IS THERE ENOUGH ROOM FOR BOTH NEW KRYPTON AND APOKOLIPS ON THIS PLANET?
BY A HUNDRED TIMES OVER, KAL.
CHECK THIS OUT.
THE MIDDLE CORRIDOR IS NEW KRYPTON. THE EAST SIDE IS APOKOLIPS.
THE WEST SIDE COULD EVEN BE NEW GENESIS. BUT FOR DARKSEID'S AMBITIONS...

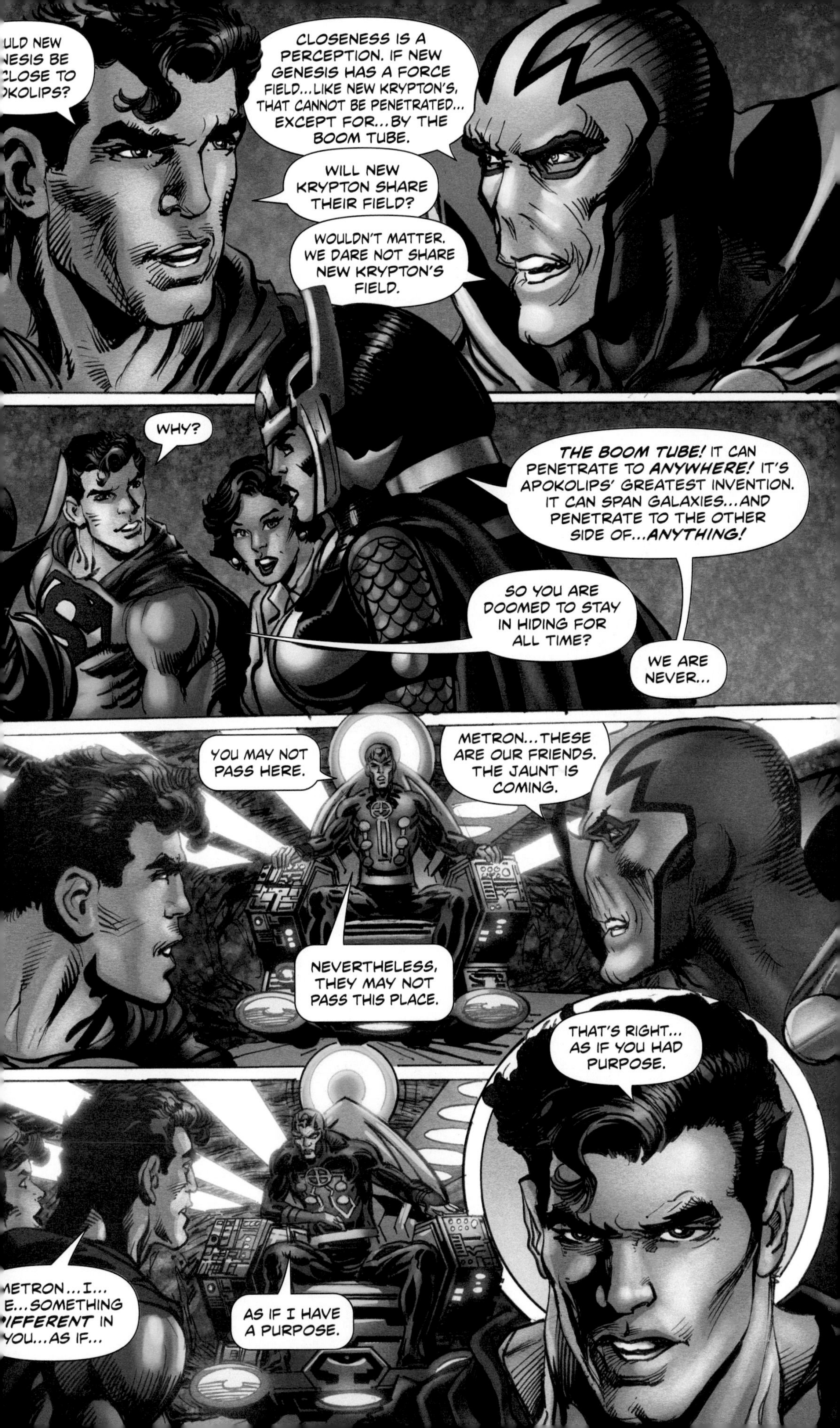

ULD NEW
NESIS BE
CLOSE TO
OKOLIPS?
CLOSENESS IS A PERCEPTION. IF NEW GENESIS HAS A FORCE FIELD...LIKE NEW KRYPTON'S, THAT CANNOT BE PENETRATED... EXCEPT FOR...BY THE BOOM TUBE.
WILL NEW KRYPTON SHARE THEIR FIELD?
WOULDN'T MATTER. WE DARE NOT SHARE NEW KRYPTON'S FIELD.
WHY?
THE BOOM TUBE! IT CAN PENETRATE TO ANYWHERE! IT'S APOKOLIPS' GREATEST INVENTION. IT CAN SPAN GALAXIES...AND PENETRATE TO THE OTHER SIDE OF...ANYTHING!
SO YOU ARE DOOMED TO STAY IN HIDING FOR ALL TIME?
WE ARE NEVER...
YOU MAY NOT PASS HERE.
METRON...THESE ARE OUR FRIENDS. THE JAUNT IS COMING.
NEVERTHELESS, THEY MAY NOT PASS THIS PLACE.
METRON...I...
E...SOMETHING
IFFERENT IN
YOU...AS IF...
AS IF I HAVE A PURPOSE.
THAT'S RIGHT... AS IF YOU HAD PURPOSE.

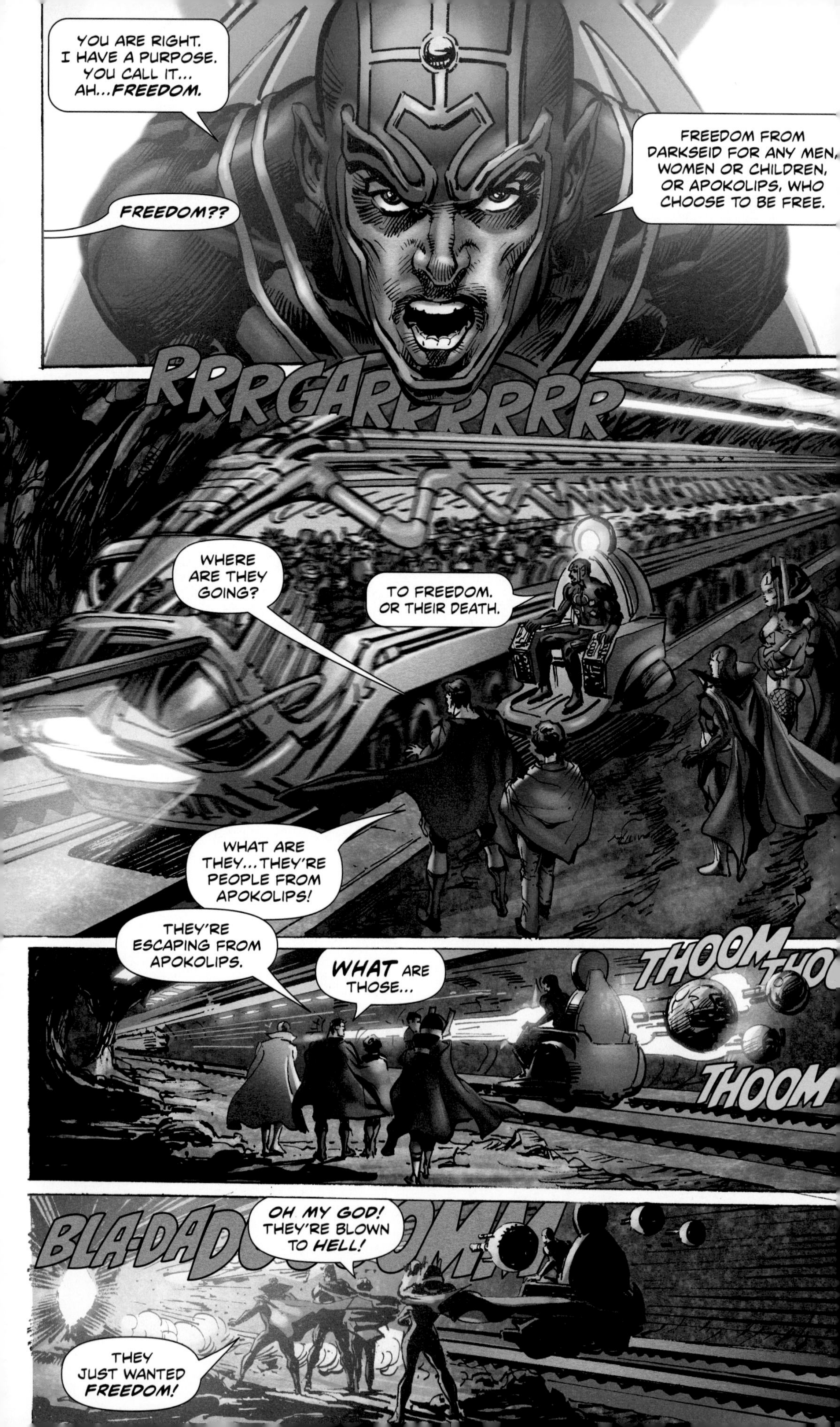
YOU ARE RIGHT. I HAVE A PURPOSE. YOU CALL IT... AH...FREEDOM.
FREEDOM??
FREEDOM FROM DARKSEID FOR ANY MEN, WOMEN OR CHILDREN, OR APOKOLIPS, WHO CHOOSE TO BE FREE.
RRRGARRRRRRR
WHERE ARE THEY GOING?
TO FREEDOM. OR THEIR DEATH.
WHAT ARE THEY...THEY'RE PEOPLE FROM APOKOLIPS!
THEY'RE ESCAPING FROM APOKOLIPS.
WHAT ARE THOSE...
THOOM
THOOM
OH MY GOD! THEY'RE BLOWN TO HELL!
THEY JUST WANTED FREEDOM!

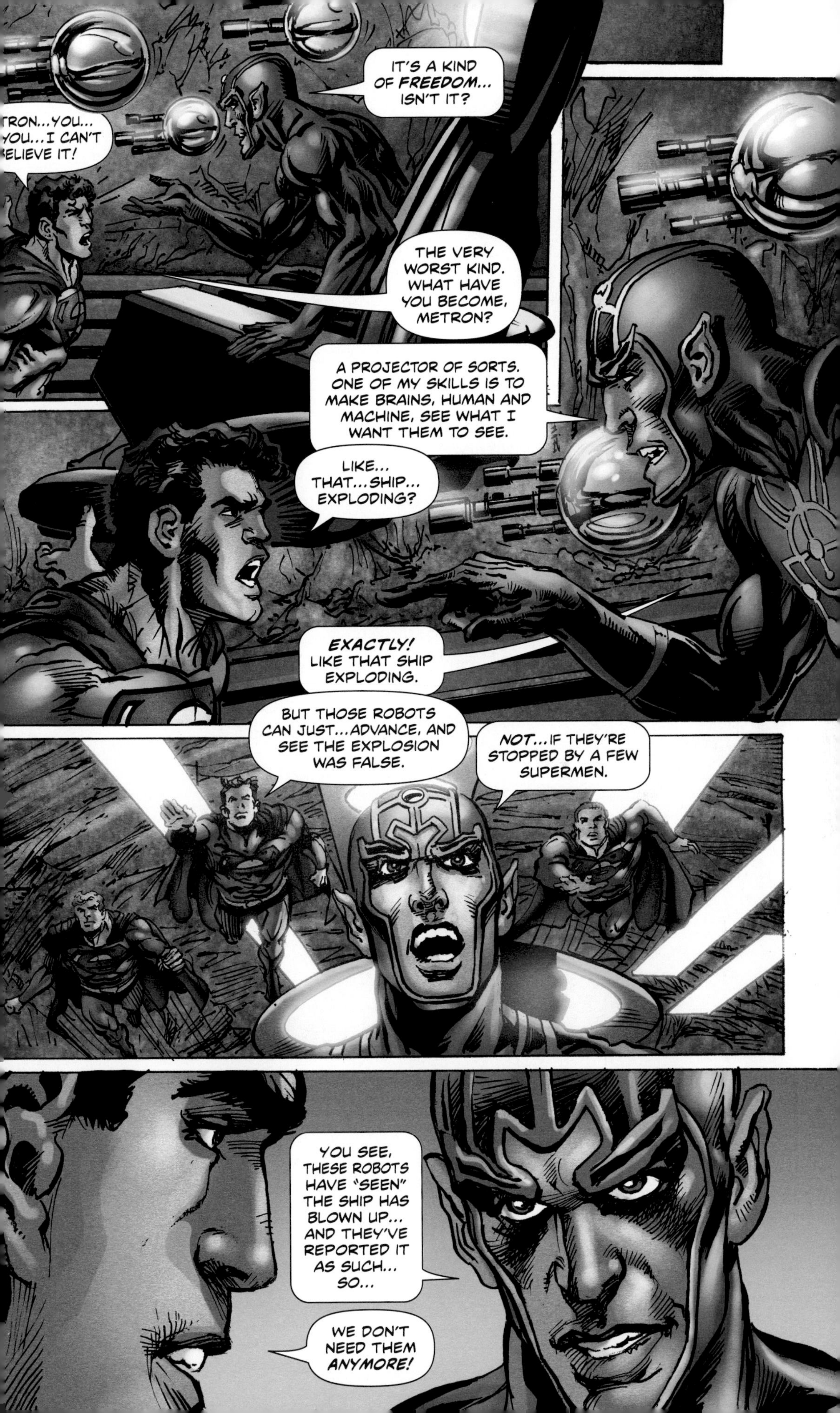
IT'S A KIND OF FREEDOM... ISN'T IT?
TRON...YOU... YOU...I CAN'T BELIEVE IT!
THE VERY WORST KIND. WHAT HAVE YOU BECOME, METRON?
A PROJECTOR OF SORTS. ONE OF MY SKILLS IS TO MAKE BRAINS, HUMAN AND MACHINE, SEE WHAT I WANT THEM TO SEE.
LIKE... THAT...SHIP... EXPLODING?
EXACTLY! LIKE THAT SHIP EXPLODING.
BUT THOSE ROBOTS CAN JUST...ADVANCE, AND SEE THE EXPLOSION WAS FALSE.
NOT...IF THEY'RE STOPPED BY A FEW SUPERMEN.
YOU SEE, THESE ROBOTS HAVE "SEEN" THE SHIP HAS BLOWN UP... AND THEY'VE REPORTED IT AS SUCH... SO...
WE DON'T NEED THEM ANYMORE!

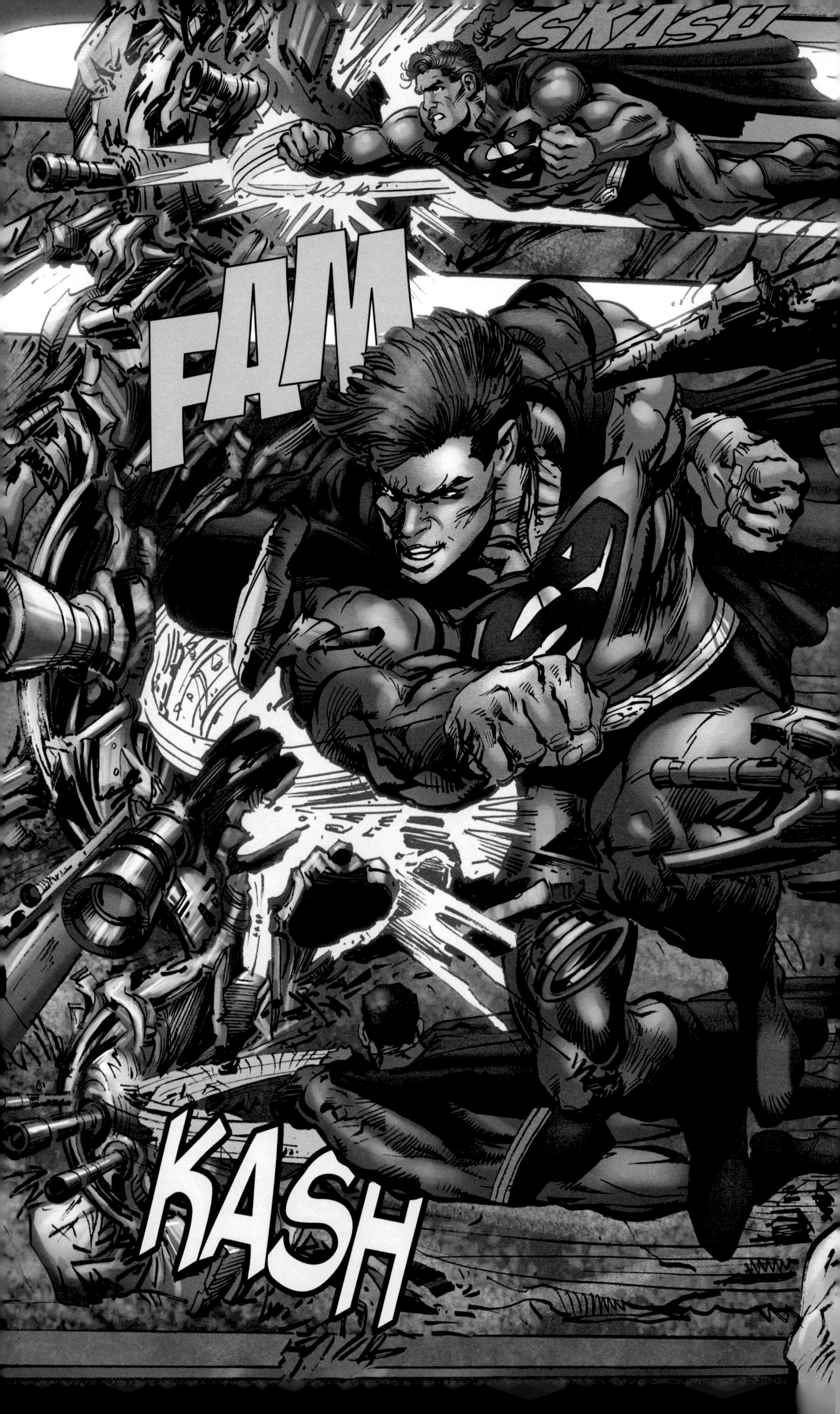
SKASH
FAM
KASH

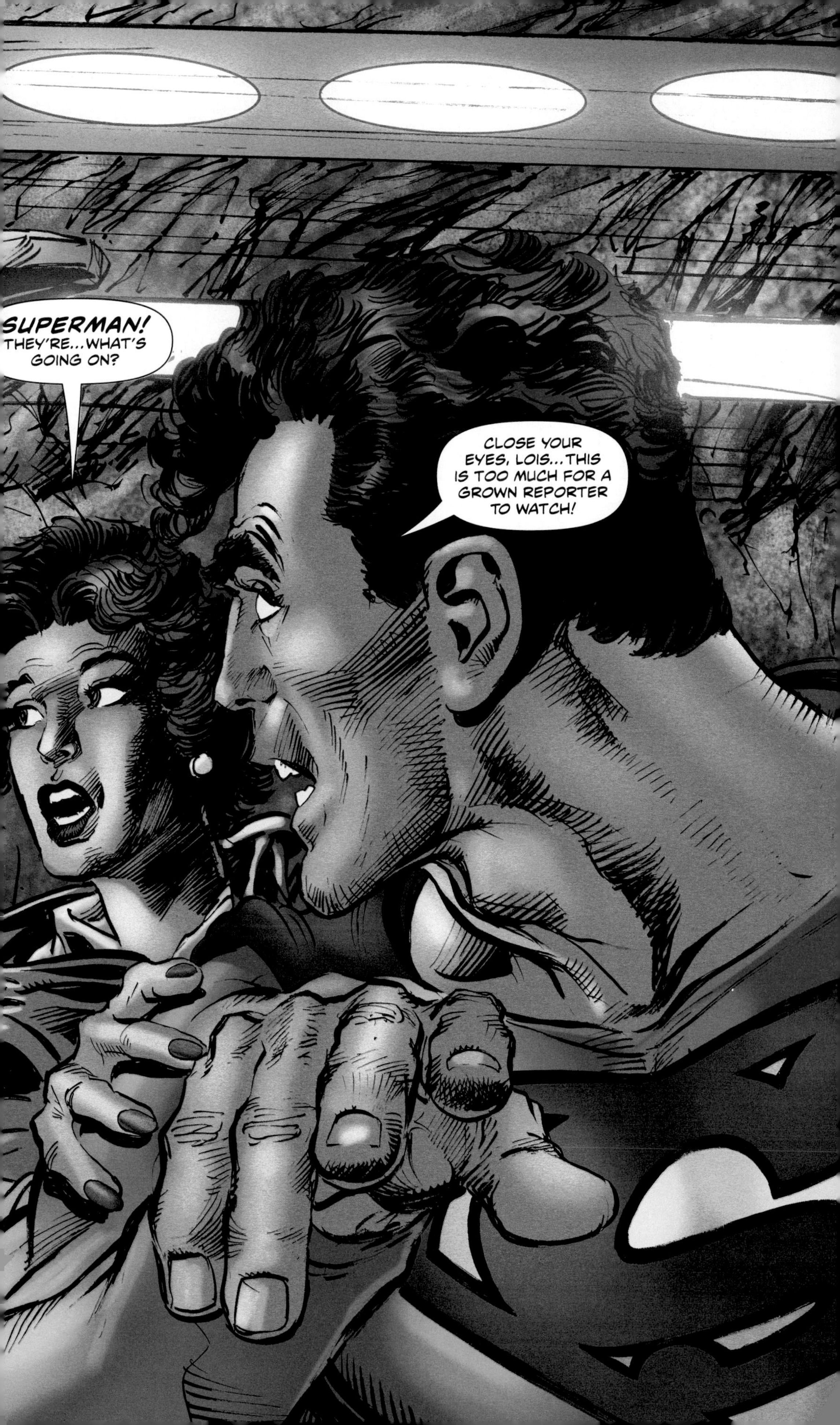
SUPERMAN! THEY'RE...WHAT'S GOING ON?
CLOSE YOUR EYES, LOIS...THIS IS TOO MUCH FOR A GROWN REPORTER TO WATCH!

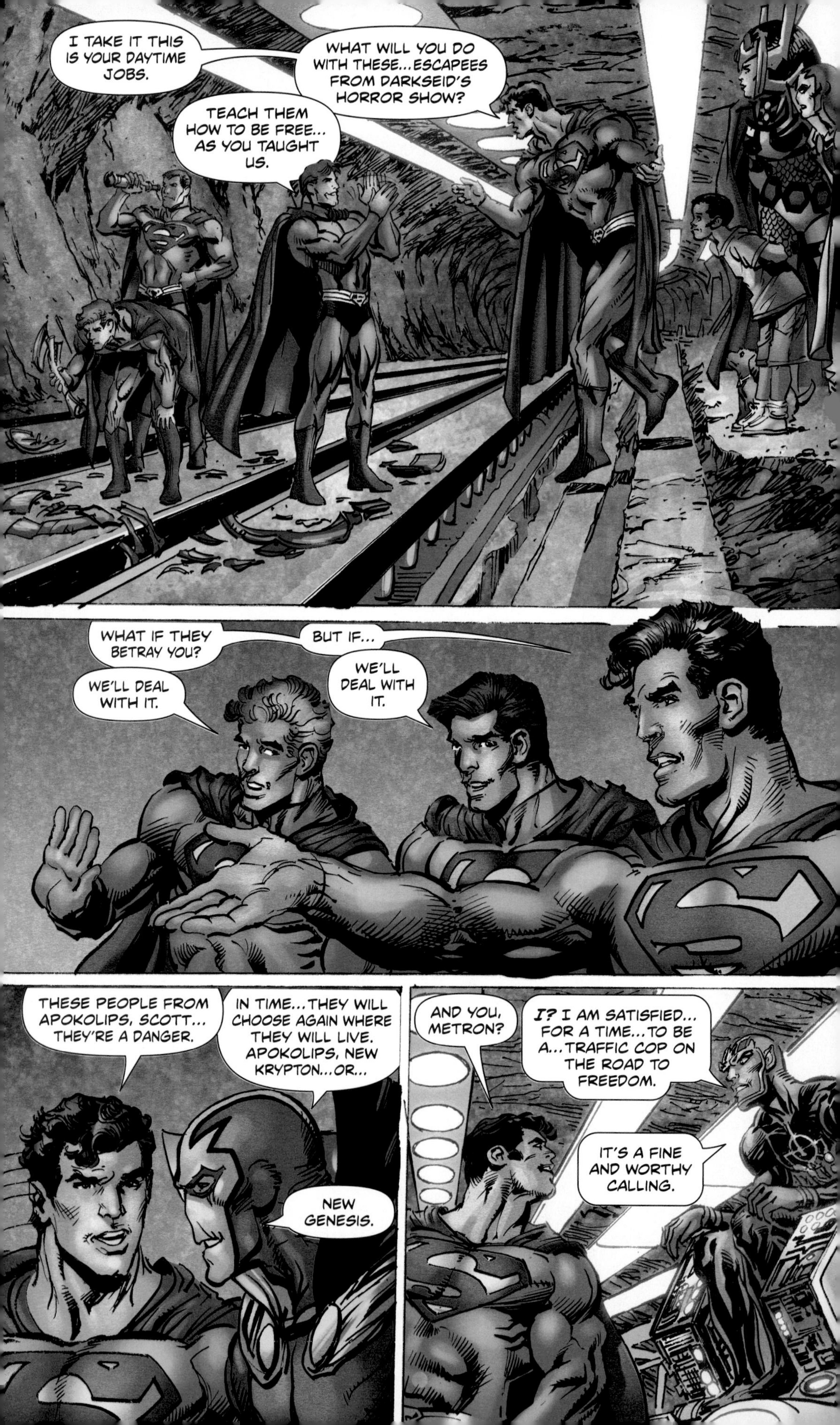
I TAKE IT THIS IS YOUR DAYTIME JOBS.
WHAT WILL YOU DO WITH THESE...ESCAPEES FROM DARKSEID'S HORROR SHOW?
TEACH THEM HOW TO BE FREE... AS YOU TAUGHT US.
WHAT IF THEY BETRAY YOU?
BUT IF...
WE'LL DEAL WITH IT.
WE'LL DEAL WITH IT.
THESE PEOPLE FROM APOKOLIPS, SCOTT... THEY'RE A DANGER.
IN TIME...THEY WILL CHOOSE AGAIN WHERE THEY WILL LIVE. APOKOLIPS, NEW KRYPTON...OR...
NEW GENESIS.
AND YOU, METRON?
I? I AM SATISFIED... FOR A TIME...TO BE A...TRAFFIC COP ON THE ROAD TO FREEDOM.
IT'S A FINE AND WORTHY CALLING.

THIS IS THE CROSSROADS, LOIS. I NEED TO GO WITH MY SUPERMEN AND TAKE *RAFI* TO NEW KRYPTON.

NOPE, I NEED TO STAY WITH YOU. *RAFI'S* SAFE WITH BARDA AND SCOTT.

TA-RUE.

I NEED YOU TO UNDERSTAND... LOIS.

I UNDERSTAND EVERYTHING.

NO... YOU DON'T.

LOIS, I HAVE FAILED IN ALL OF THIS.

NO!

YES, I HAVE! OH, I FOUGHT IN THE STREET... WITH PUNKS... WHILE DARKSEID AND LUTHOR MOVED THE CHESS PIECES UP IN THEIR TOWER.

NOW... THINGS HAVE TO CHANGE. EVIL HAS ADVANCED TOO FAR. AND ONLY I CAN FIX IT.

AND I SHOULD BE THERE.

ONLY AT THE SACRIFICE OF *RAFI*... AND YOU. YOU TWO ARE MY ACHILLES HEEL.

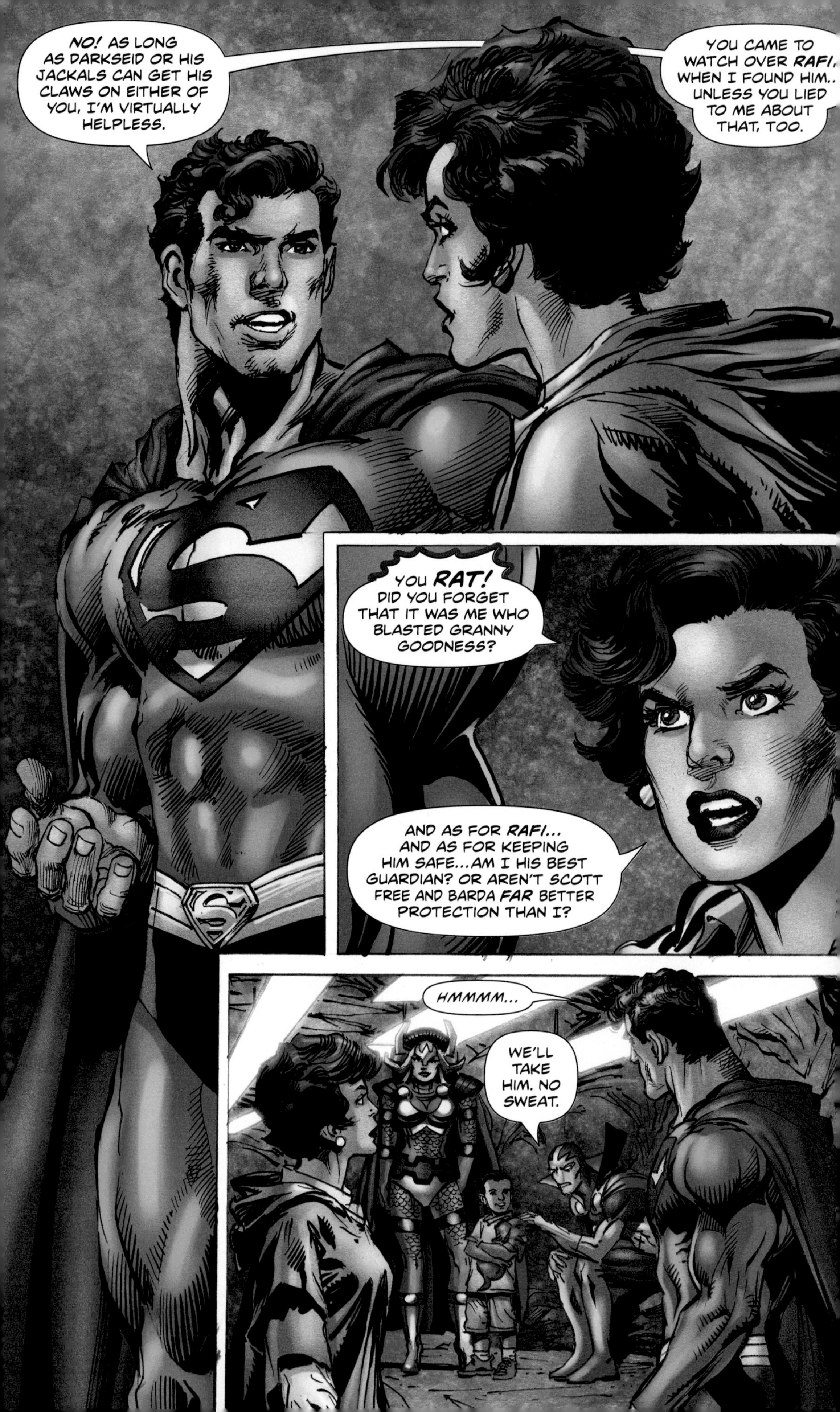
NO! AS LONG AS DARKSEID OR HIS JACKALS CAN GET HIS CLAWS ON EITHER OF YOU, I'M VIRTUALLY HELPLESS.
YOU CAME TO WATCH OVER RAFI, WHEN I FOUND HIM.. UNLESS YOU LIED TO ME ABOUT THAT, TOO.
YOU RAT! DID YOU FORGET THAT IT WAS ME WHO BLASTED GRANNY GOODNESS?
AND AS FOR RAFI... AND AS FOR KEEPING HIM SAFE...AM I HIS BEST GUARDIAN? OR AREN'T SCOTT FREE AND BARDA FAR BETTER PROTECTION THAN I?
HMMMM...
WE'LL TAKE HIM. NO SWEAT.

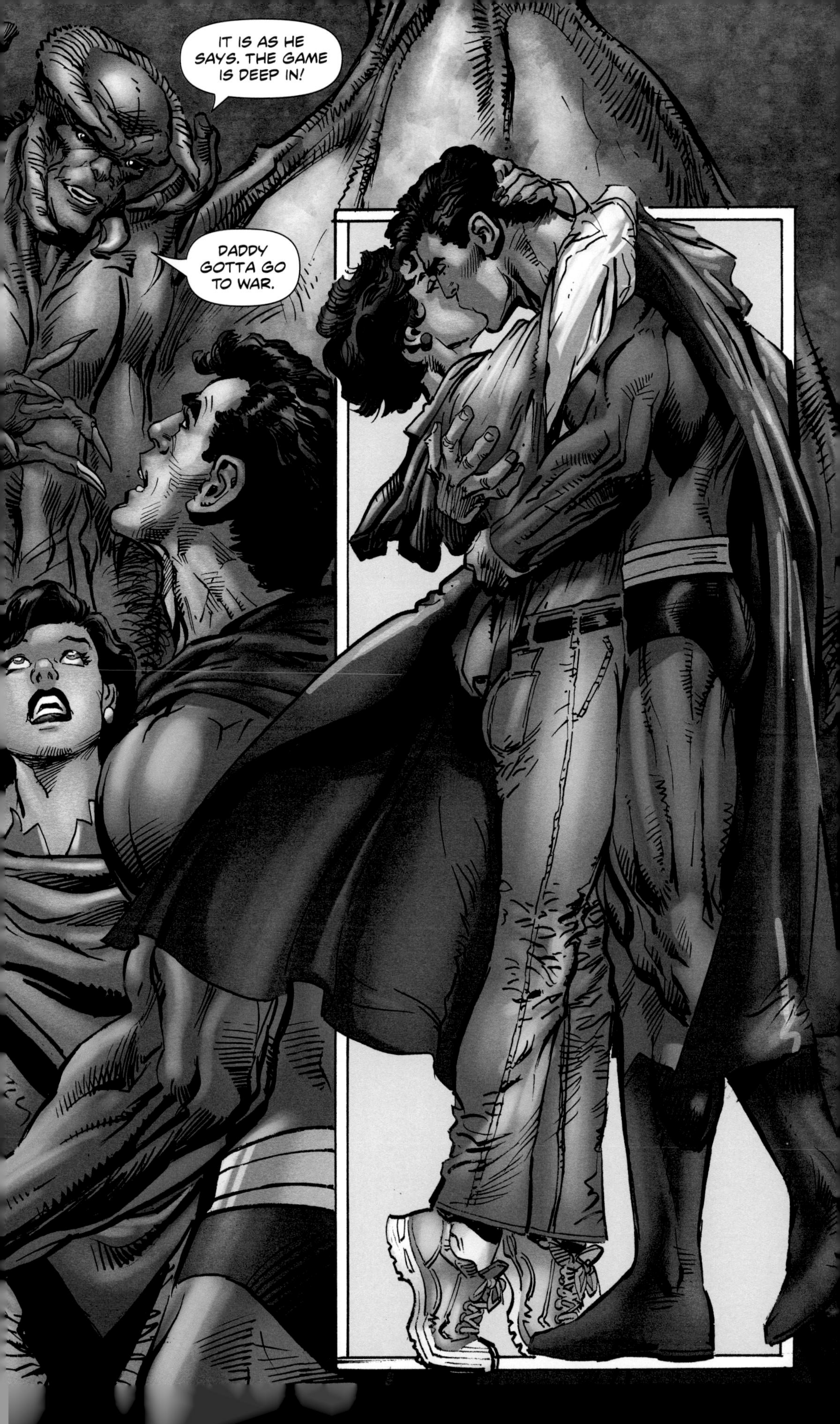
IT IS AS HE SAYS. THE GAME IS DEEP IN!
DADDY GOTTA GO TO WAR.

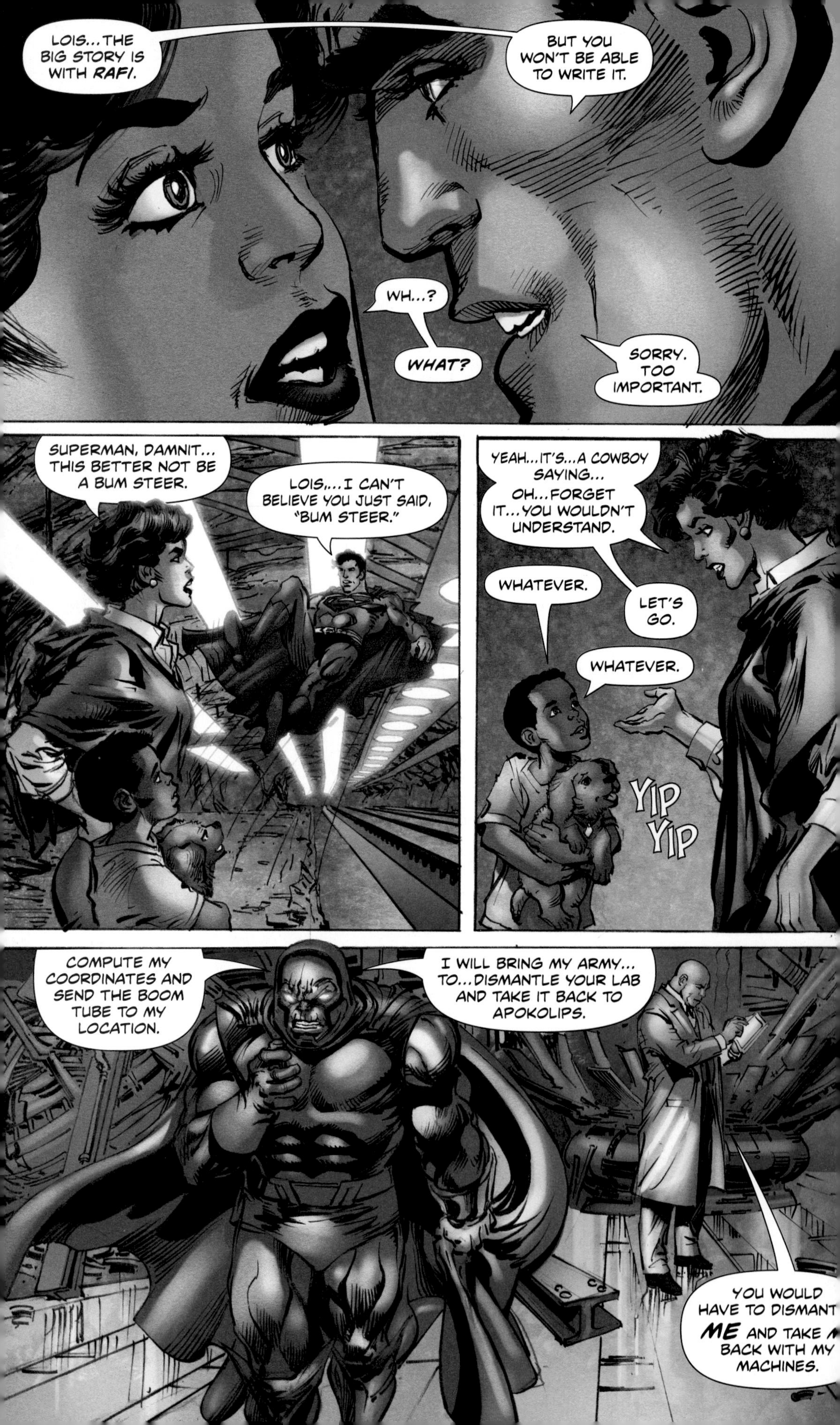
LOIS...THE BIG STORY IS WITH RAFI.
BUT YOU WON'T BE ABLE TO WRITE IT.
WH...?
WHAT?
SORRY. TOO IMPORTANT.
SUPERMAN, DAMNIT... THIS BETTER NOT BE A BUM STEER.
LOIS,...I CAN'T BELIEVE YOU JUST SAID, "BUM STEER."
YEAH...IT'S...A COWBOY SAYING...
OH...FORGET IT...YOU WOULDN'T UNDERSTAND.
WHATEVER.
LET'S GO.
WHATEVER.
YIP YIP
COMPUTE MY COORDINATES AND SEND THE BOOM TUBE TO MY LOCATION.
I WILL BRING MY ARMY... TO...DISMANTLE YOUR LAB AND TAKE IT BACK TO APOKOLIPS.
YOU WOULD HAVE TO DISMANT
ME AND TAKE
BACK WITH MY MACHINES.

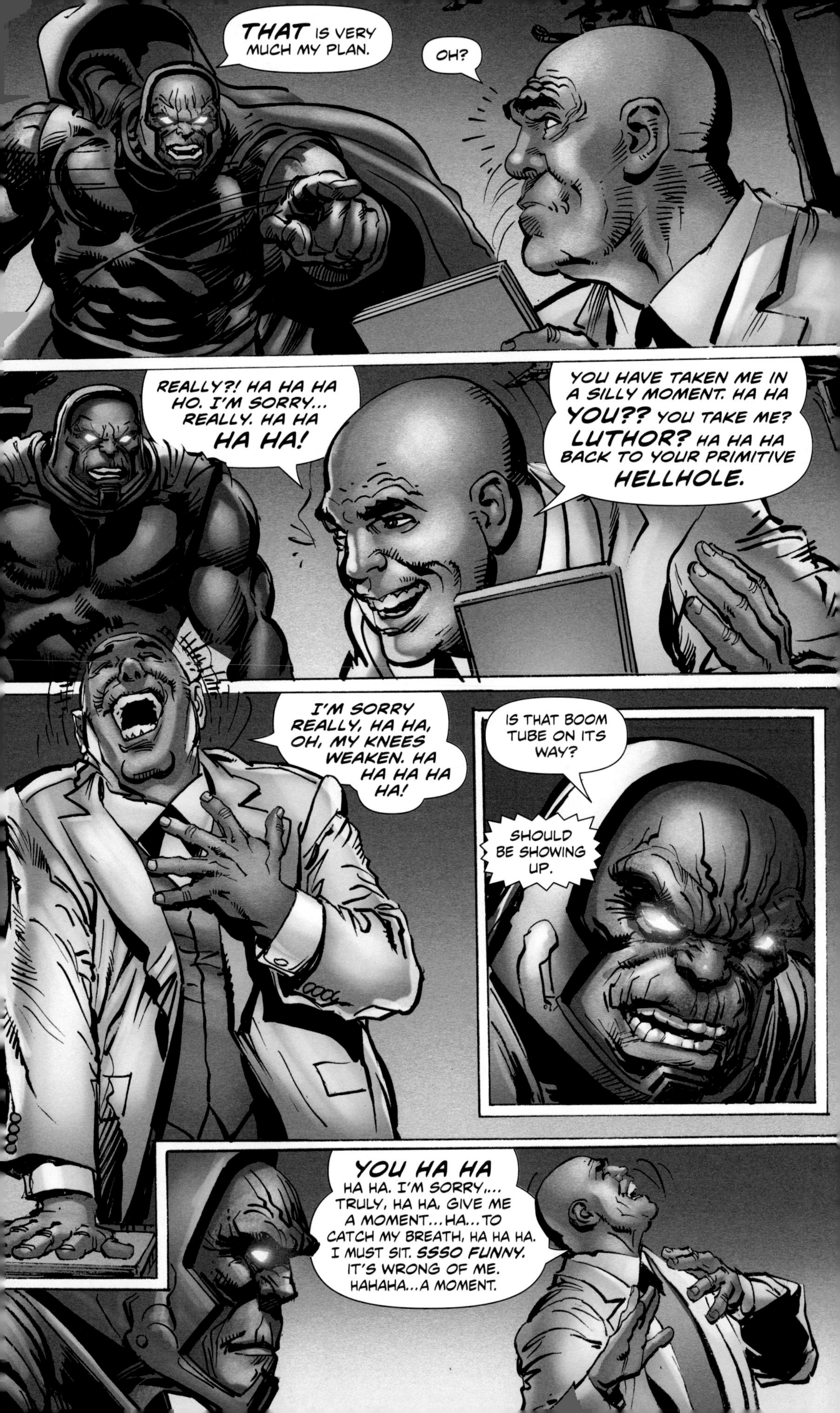
THAT IS VERY MUCH MY PLAN.
OH?
REALLY?! HA HA HA HO. I'M SORRY... REALLY. HA HA HA HA!
YOU HAVE TAKEN ME IN A SILLY MOMENT. HA HA YOU?? YOU TAKE ME? LUTHOR? HA HA HA BACK TO YOUR PRIMITIVE HELLHOLE.
I'M SORRY REALLY, HA HA, OH, MY KNEES WEAKEN. HA HA HA HA HA!
IS THAT BOOM TUBE ON ITS WAY?
SHOULD BE SHOWING UP.
YOU HA HA HA HA. I'M SORRY.... TRULY, HA HA, GIVE ME A MOMENT...HA...TO CATCH MY BREATH, HA HA HA. I MUST SIT. SSSO FUNNY. IT'S WRONG OF ME. HAHAHA...A MOMENT.

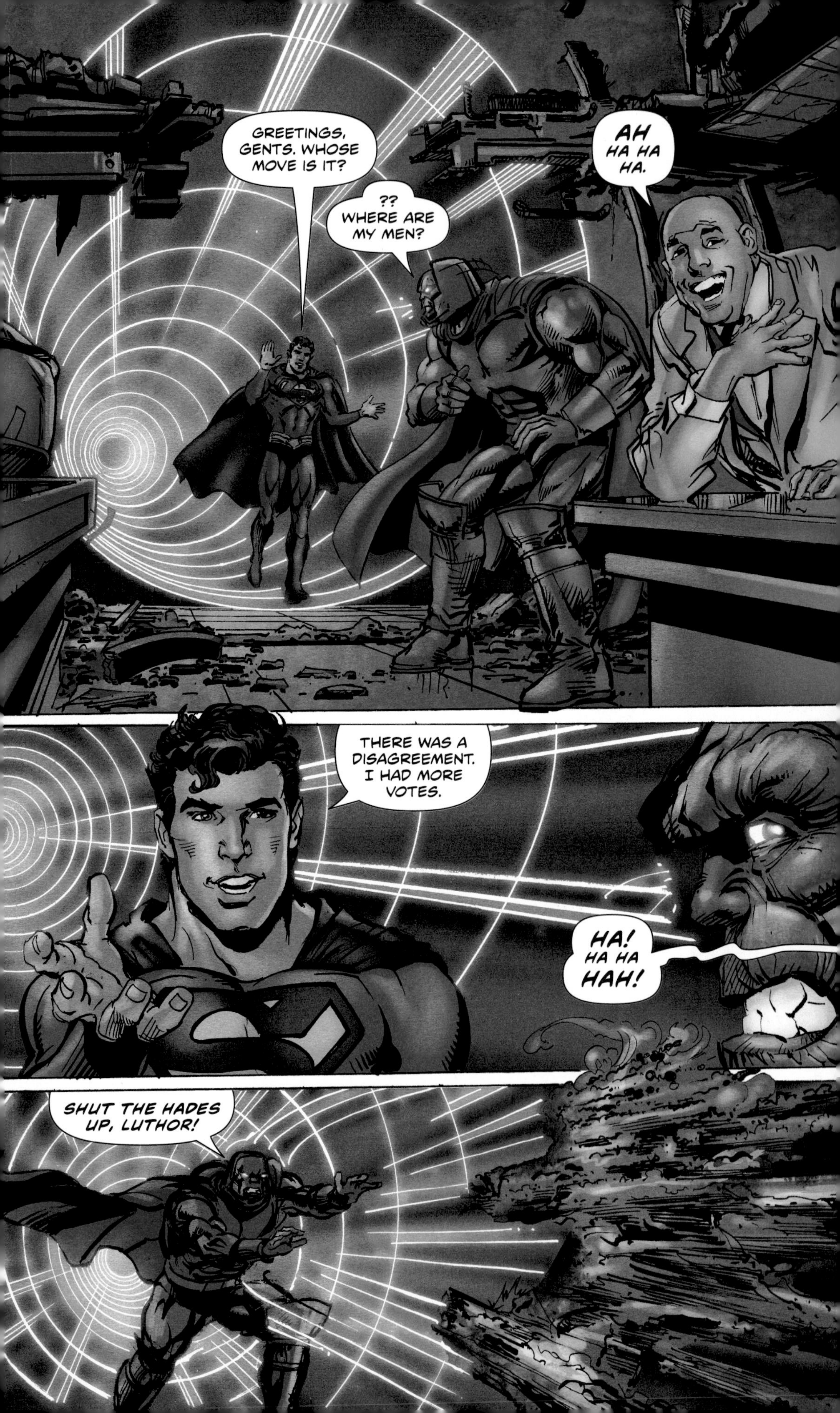
GREETINGS, GENTS. WHOSE MOVE IS IT?
?? WHERE ARE MY MEN?
AH HA HA HA.
THERE WAS A DISAGREEMENT. I HAD MORE VOTES.
HA! HA HA HAH!
SHUT THE HADES UP, LUTHOR!

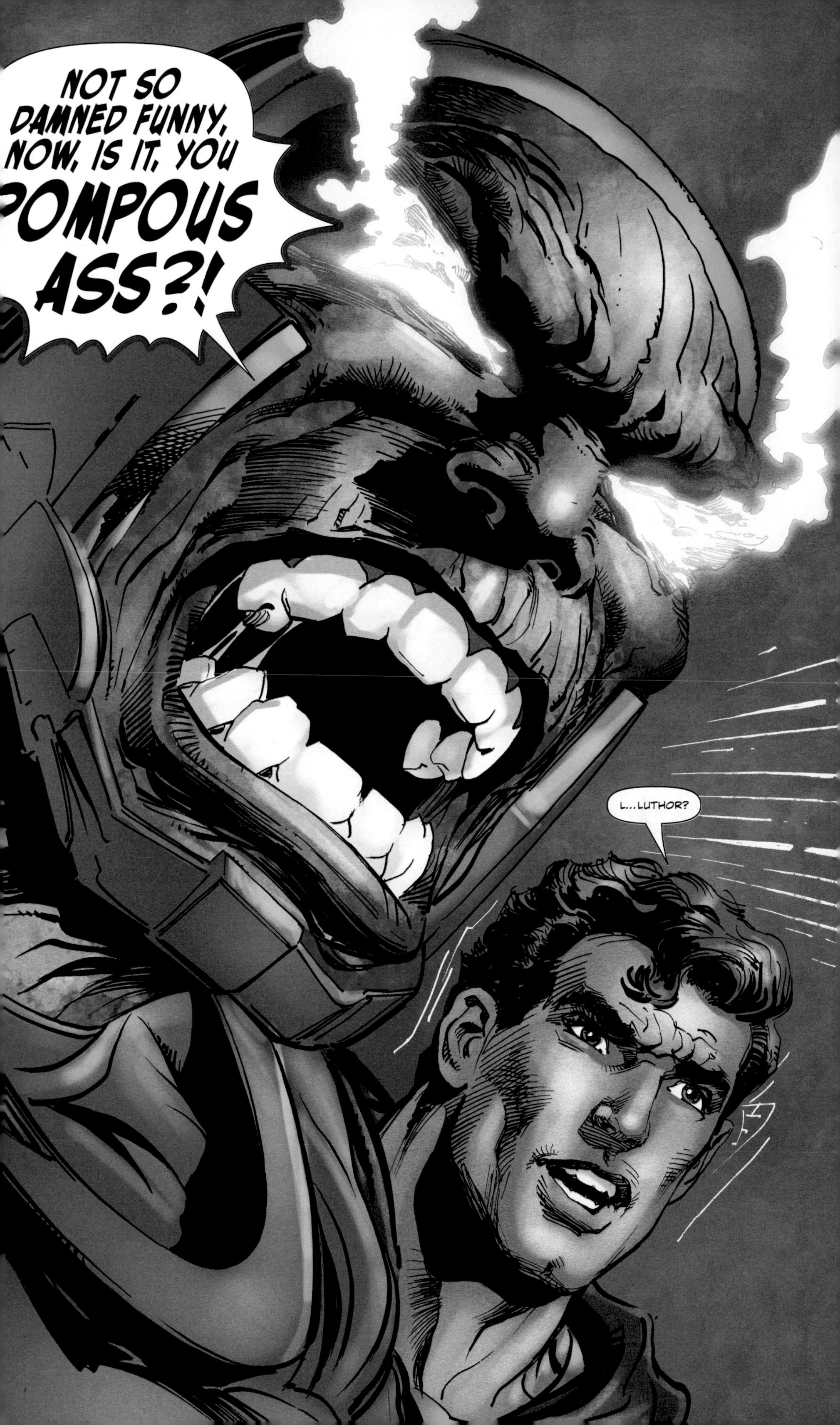
NOT SO DAMNED FUNNY, NOW, IS IT, YOU POMPOUS ASS?!
L...LUTHOR?

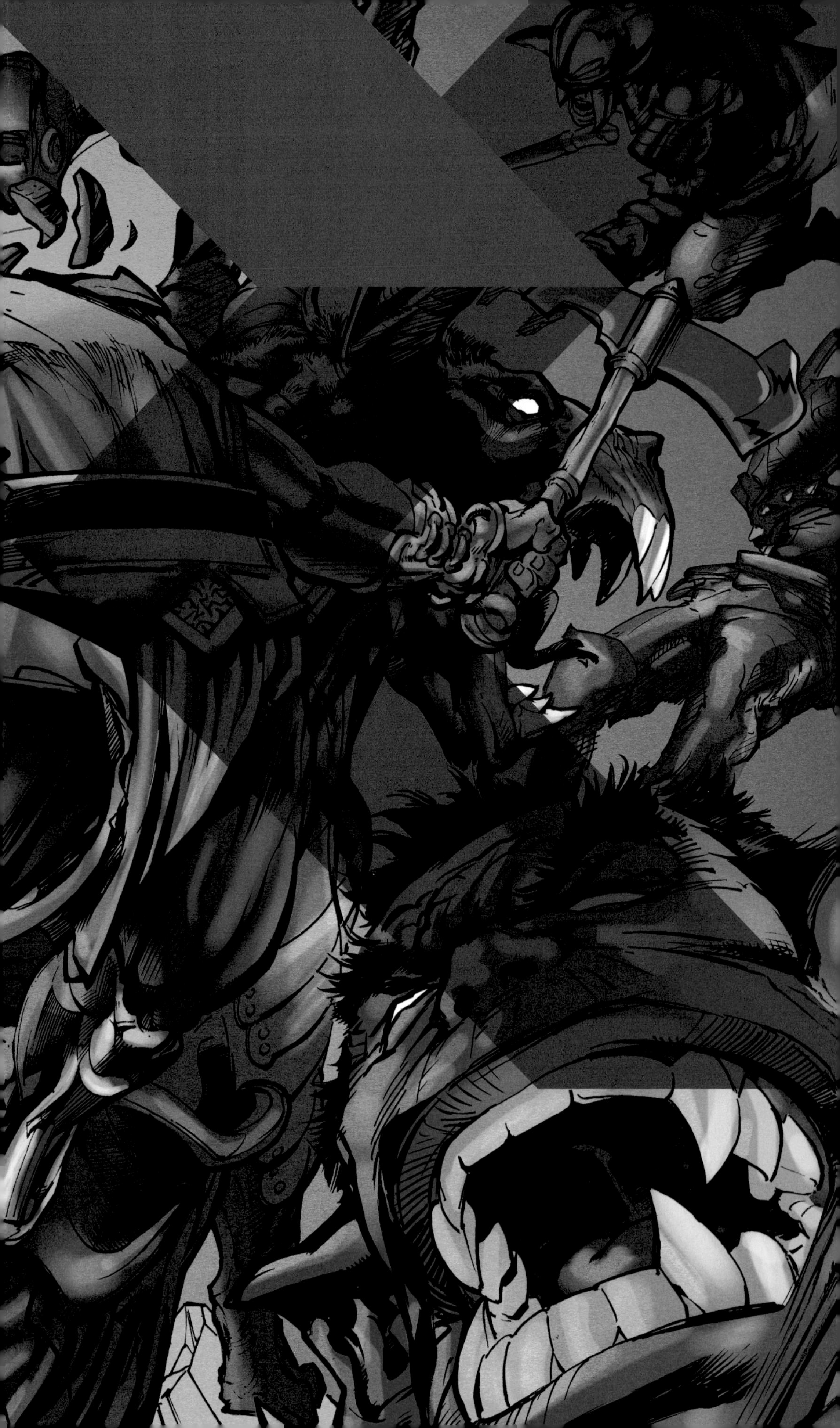

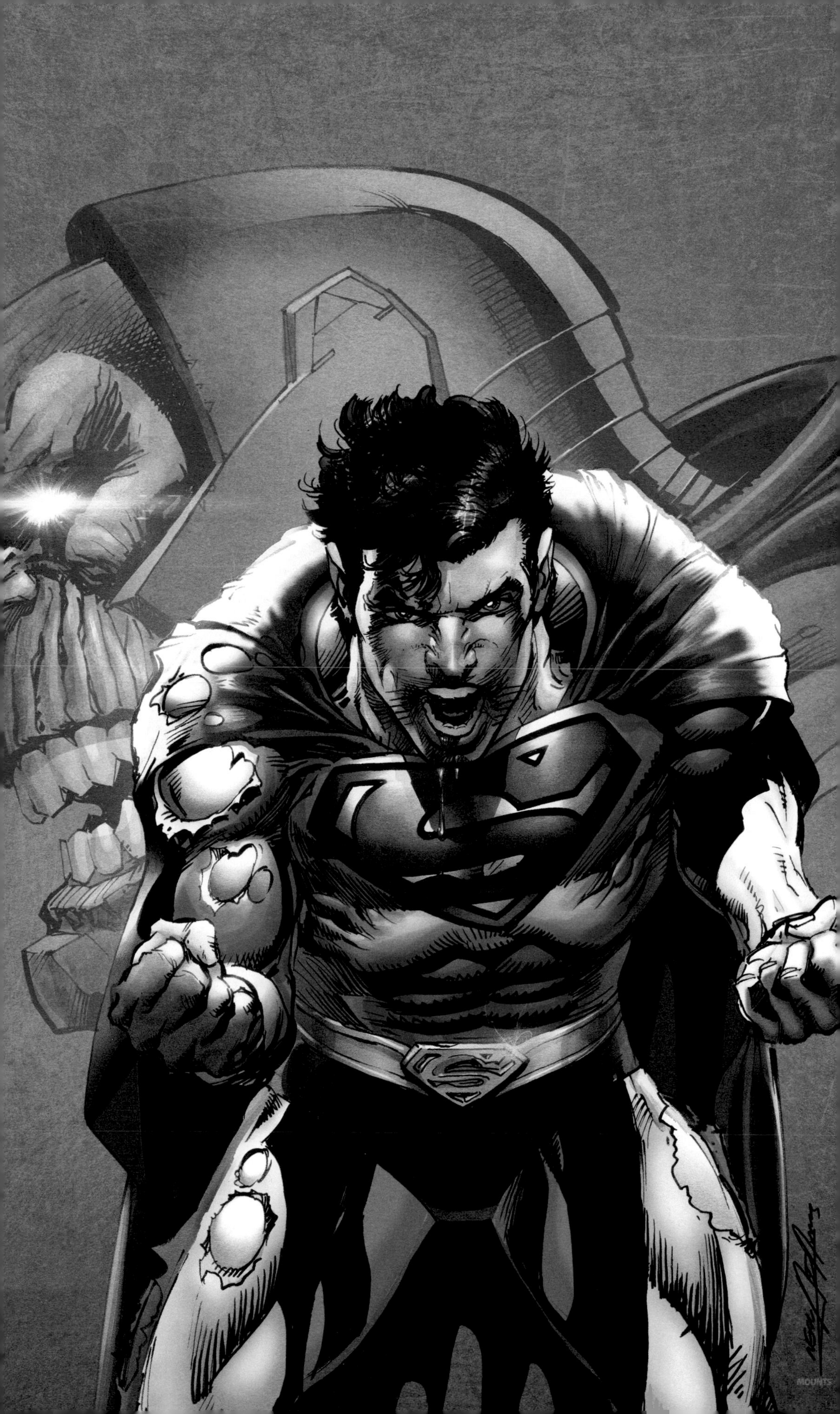

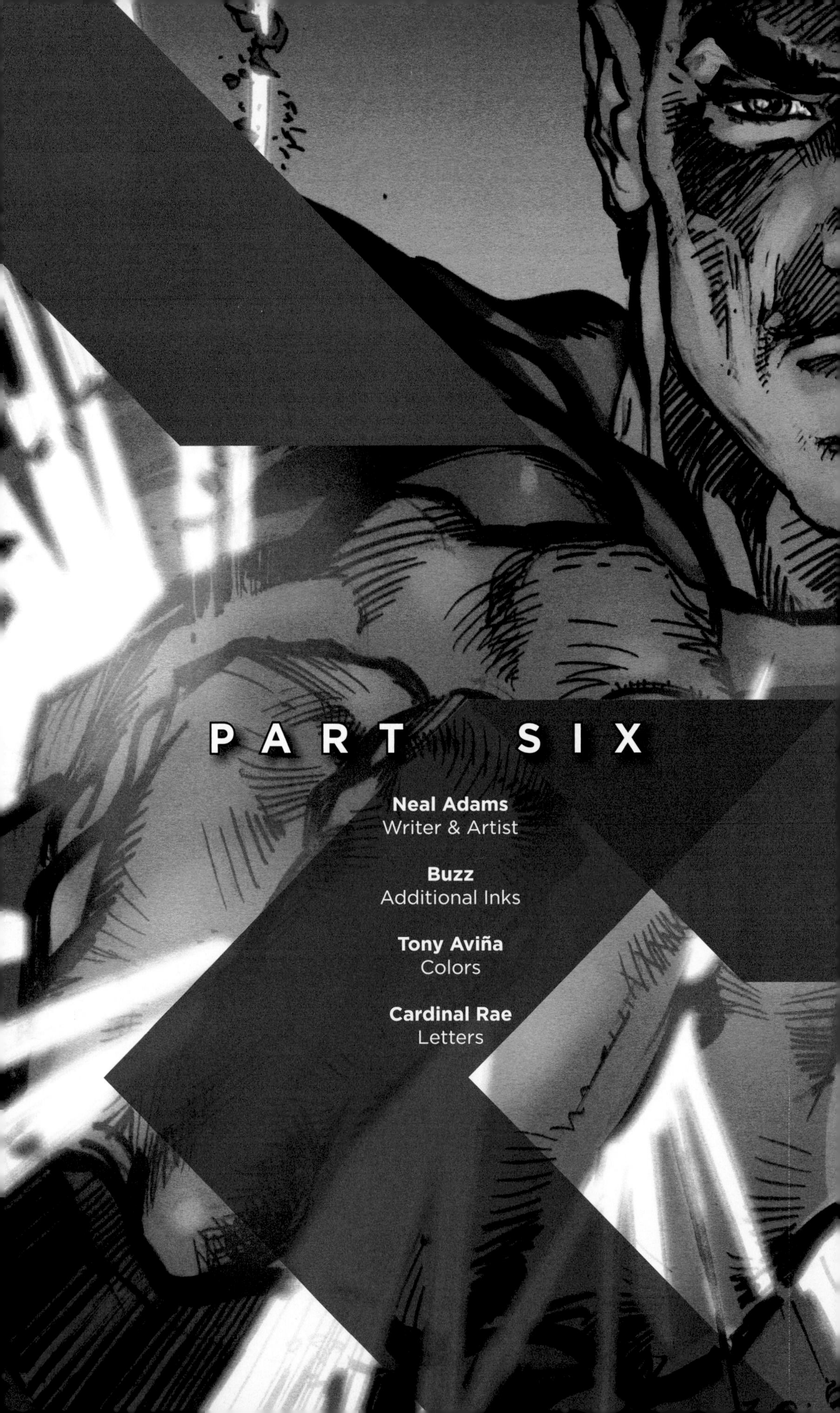

PART SIX

Neal Adams
Writer & Artist

Buzz
Additional Inks

Tony Aviña
Colors

Cardinal Rae
Letters

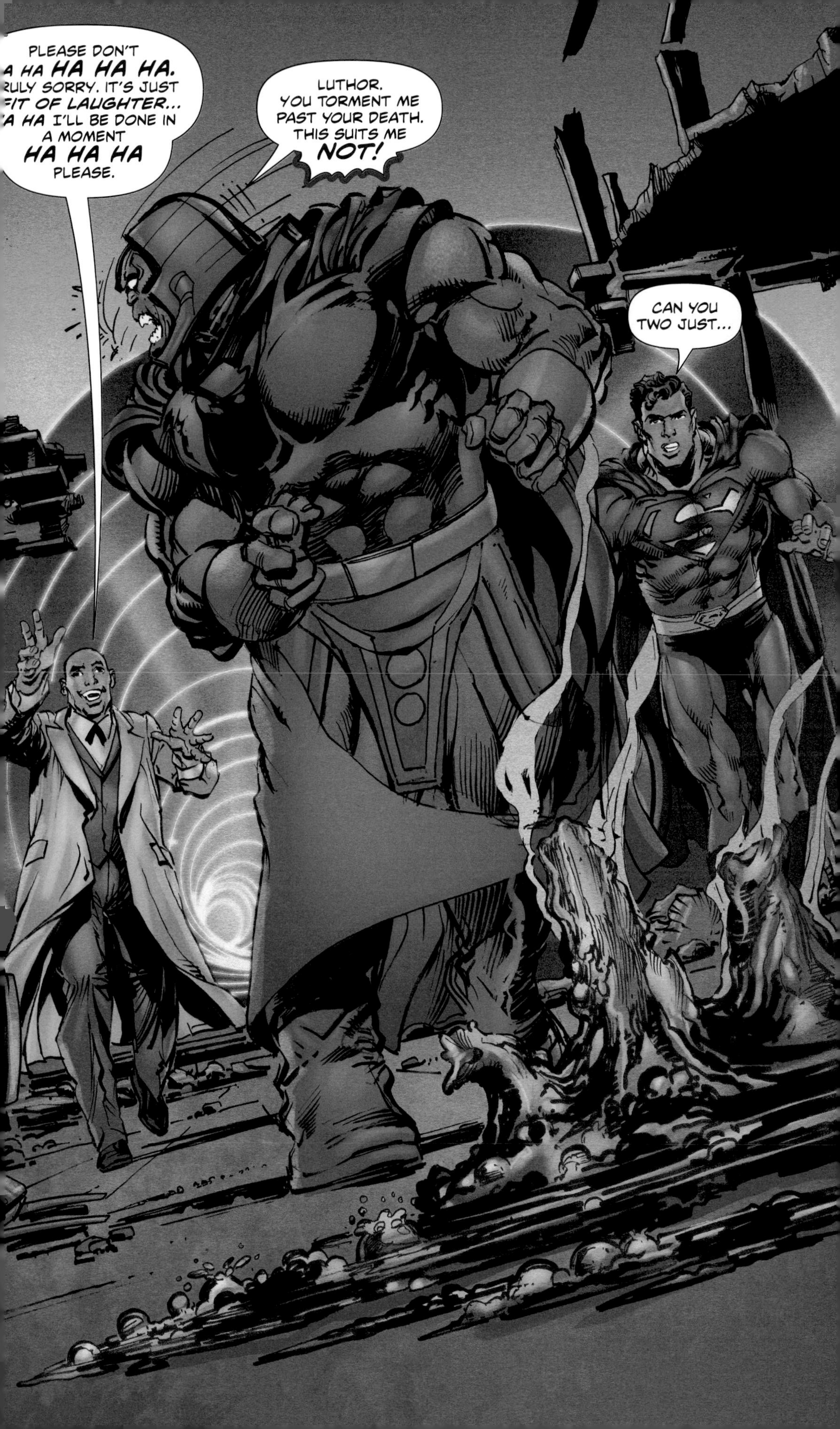
PLEASE DON'T A HA HA HA HA. RULY SORRY. IT'S JUST FIT OF LAUGHTER... A HA I'LL BE DONE IN A MOMENT HA HA HA PLEASE.
LUTHOR. YOU TORMENT ME PAST YOUR DEATH. THIS SUITS ME NOT!
CAN YOU TWO JUST...

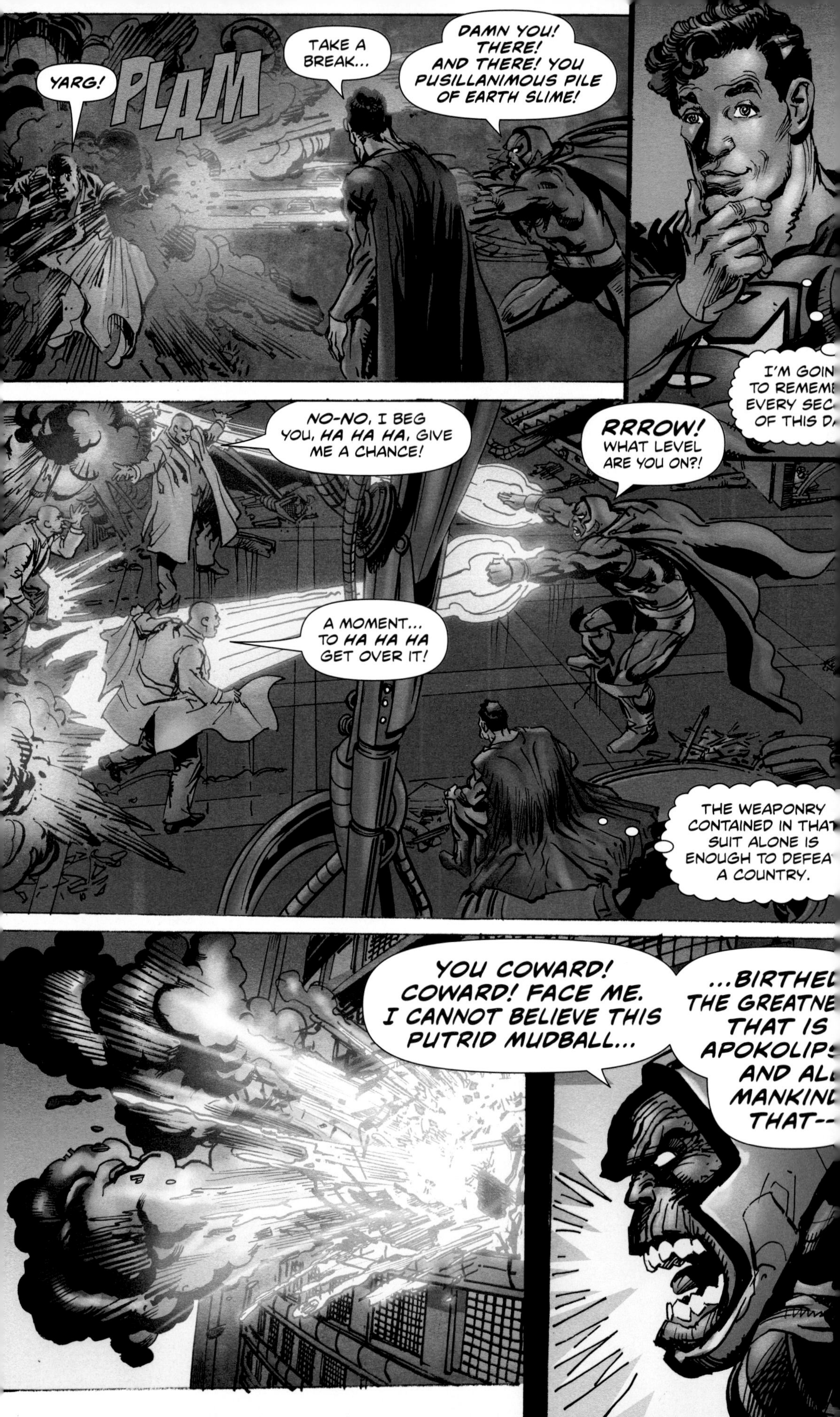
YARG!
PLAM
TAKE A BREAK...
DAMN YOU! THERE! AND THERE! YOU PUSILLANIMOUS PILE OF EARTH SLIME!
I'M GOIN TO REMEME EVERY SEC OF THIS DA
NO-NO, I BEG YOU, HA HA HA, GIVE ME A CHANCE!
RRROW! WHAT LEVEL ARE YOU ON?!
A MOMENT... TO HA HA HA GET OVER IT!
THE WEAPONRY CONTAINED IN THAT SUIT ALONE IS ENOUGH TO DEFEA A COUNTRY.
YOU COWARD! COWARD! FACE ME. I CANNOT BELIEVE THIS PUTRID MUDBALL...
...BIRTHE THE GREATNE THAT IS APOKOLIPS AND AL MANKIN THAT--

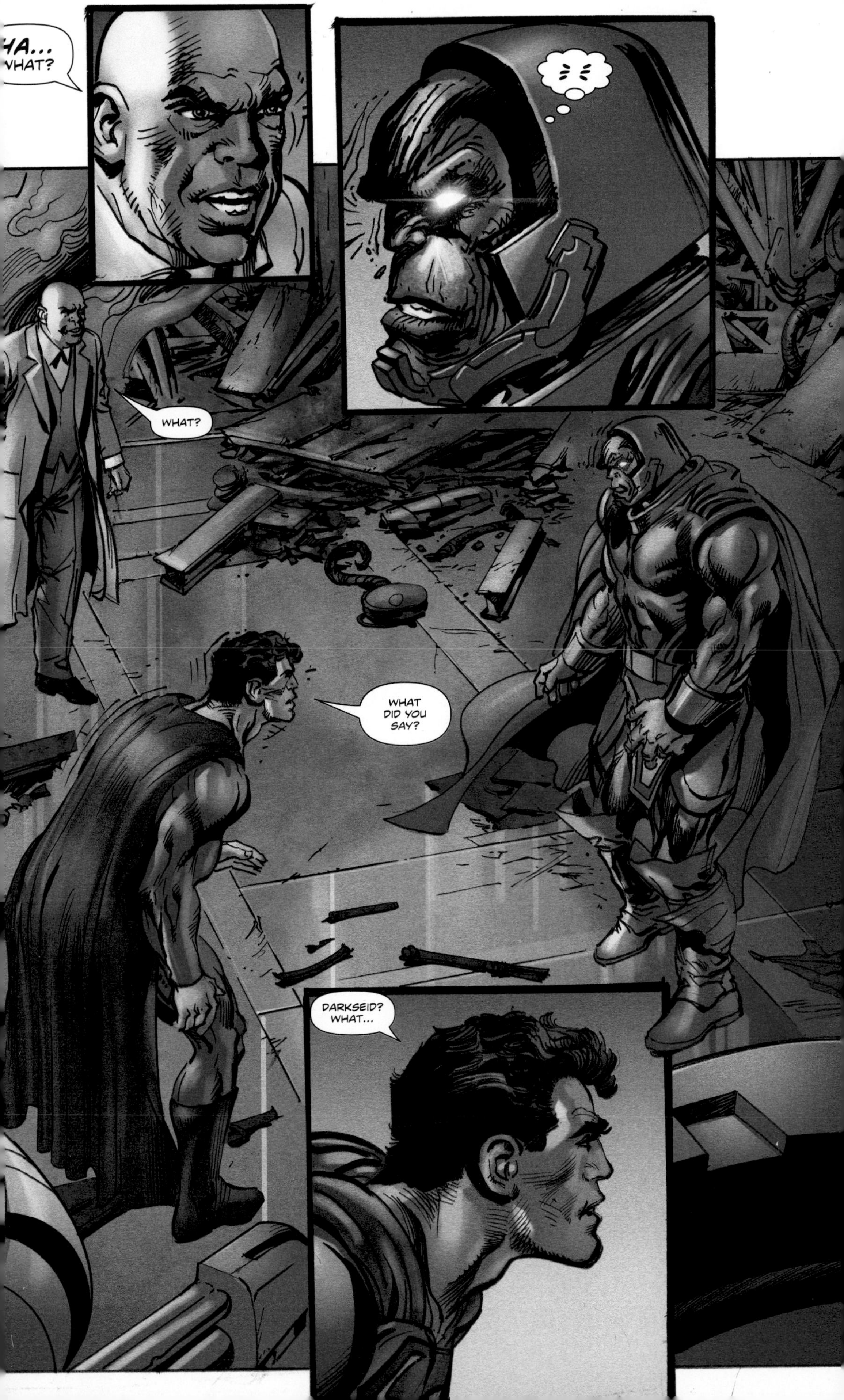
HA...
WHAT?
WHAT?
WHAT DID YOU SAY?
DARKSEID? WHAT...

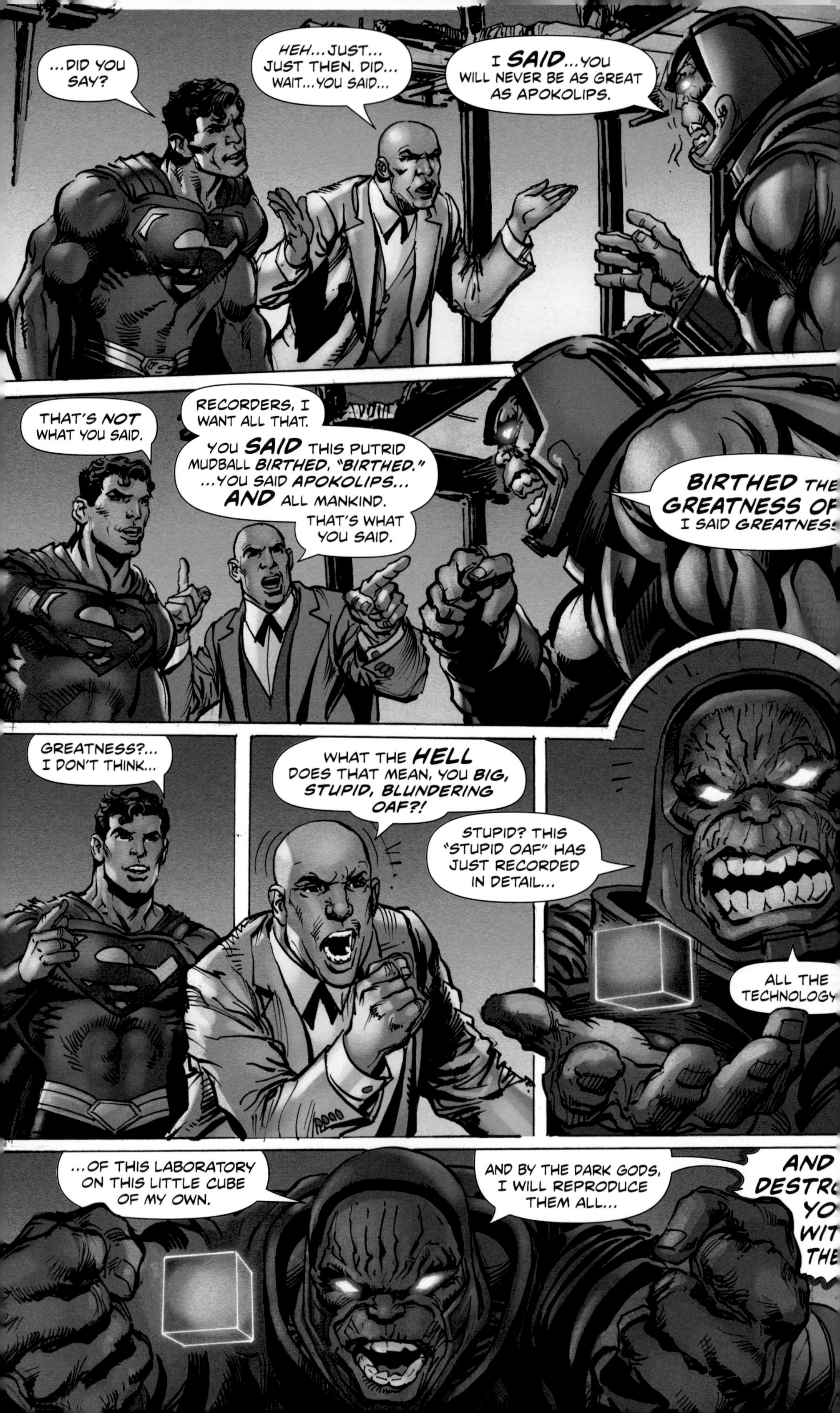
...DID YOU SAY?
HEH...JUST... JUST THEN. DID... WAIT...YOU SAID...
I SAID...YOU WILL NEVER BE AS GREAT AS APOKOLIPS.
THAT'S NOT WHAT YOU SAID.
RECORDERS, I WANT ALL THAT.
YOU SAID THIS PUTRID MUDBALL BIRTHED, "BIRTHED." ...YOU SAID APOKOLIPS... AND ALL MANKIND.
THAT'S WHAT YOU SAID.
BIRTHED THE GREATNESS OF I SAID GREATNESS
GREATNESS?... I DON'T THINK...
WHAT THE HELL DOES THAT MEAN, YOU BIG, STUPID, BLUNDERING OAF?!
STUPID? THIS "STUPID OAF" HAS JUST RECORDED IN DETAIL...
ALL THE TECHNOLOGY
...OF THIS LABORATORY ON THIS LITTLE CUBE OF MY OWN.
AND BY THE DARK GODS, I WILL REPRODUCE THEM ALL...
AND DESTRO YO WIT THE

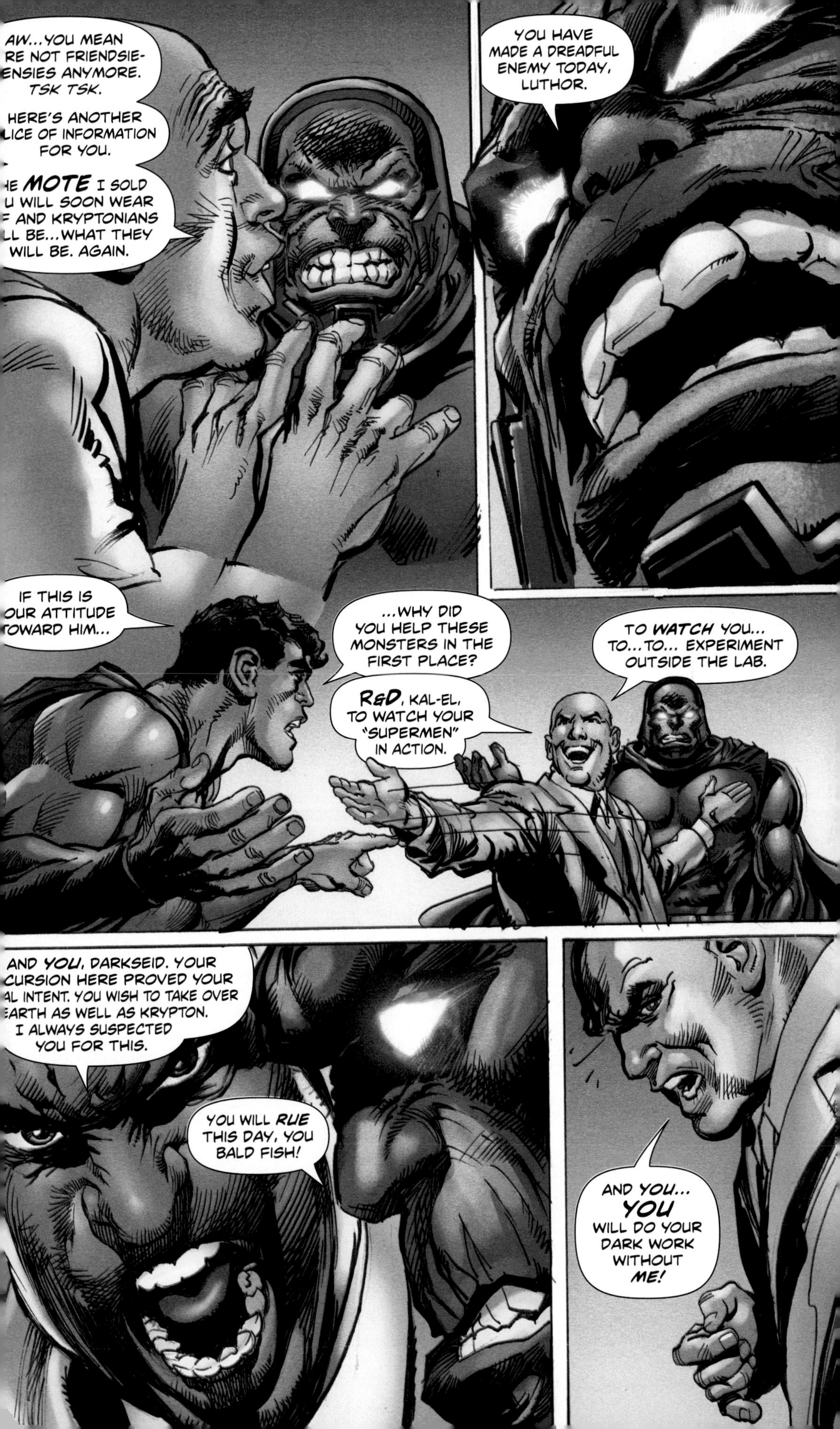
AW...YOU MEAN
RE NOT FRIENDSIE-
ENSIES ANYMORE.
TSK TSK.
HERE'S ANOTHER
LICE OF INFORMATION
FOR YOU.
HE MOTE I SOLD
U WILL SOON WEAR
F AND KRYPTONIANS
LL BE...WHAT THEY
WILL BE. AGAIN.
YOU HAVE MADE A DREADFUL ENEMY TODAY, LUTHOR.
IF THIS IS
OUR ATTITUDE
TOWARD HIM...
...WHY DID YOU HELP THESE MONSTERS IN THE FIRST PLACE?
R&D, KAL-EL, TO WATCH YOUR "SUPERMEN" IN ACTION.
TO WATCH YOU... TO...TO... EXPERIMENT OUTSIDE THE LAB.
AND YOU, DARKSEID. YOUR
CURSION HERE PROVED YOUR
AL INTENT. YOU WISH TO TAKE OVER
EARTH AS WELL AS KRYPTON.
I ALWAYS SUSPECTED
YOU FOR THIS.
YOU WILL RUE THIS DAY, YOU BALD FISH!
AND YOU... YOU WILL DO YOUR DARK WORK WITHOUT ME!

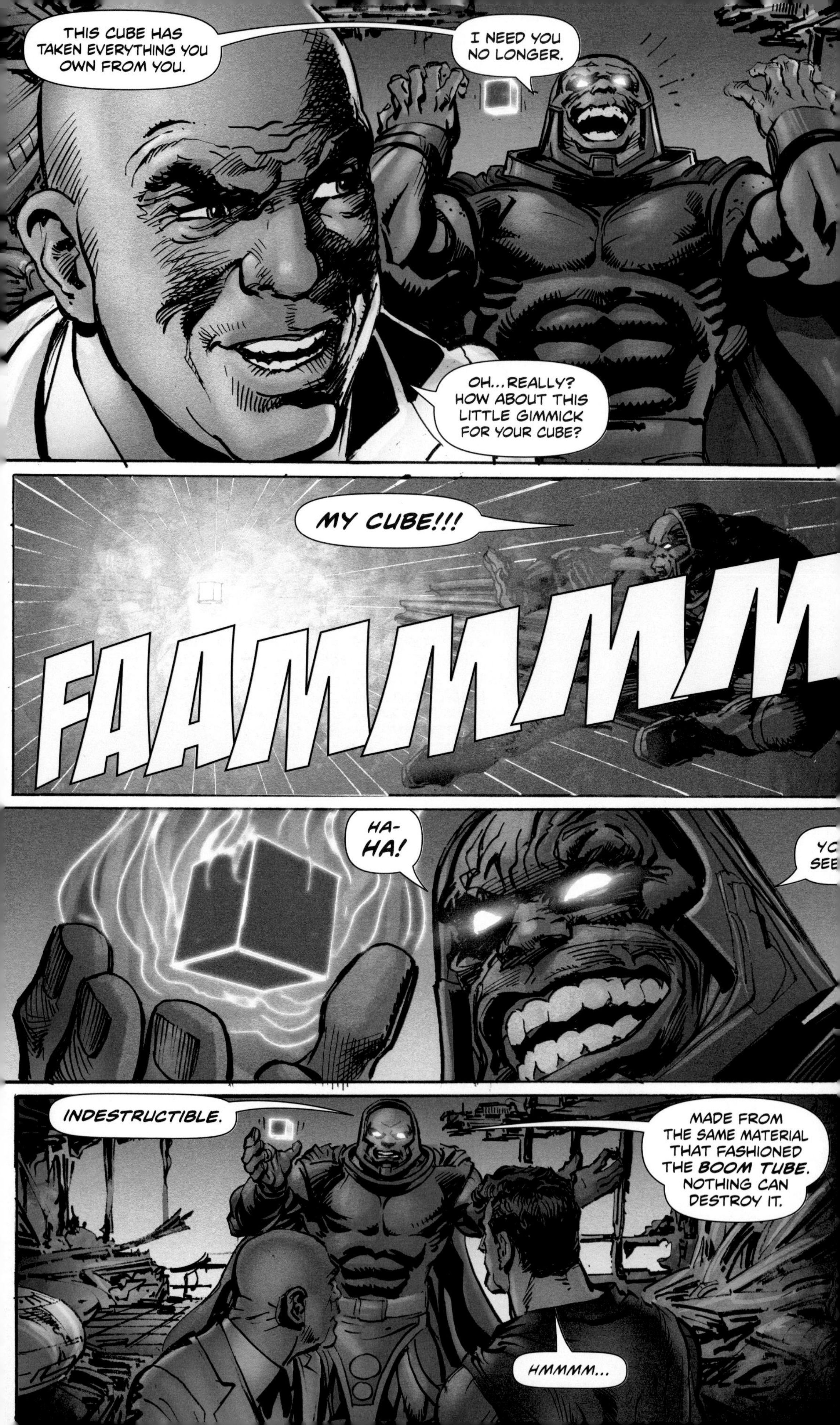
THIS CUBE HAS TAKEN EVERYTHING YOU OWN FROM YOU.
I NEED YOU NO LONGER.
OH...REALLY? HOW ABOUT THIS LITTLE GIMMICK FOR YOUR CUBE?
MY CUBE!!!
FAAMMMM
HA-HA!
INDESTRUCTIBLE.
MADE FROM THE SAME MATERIAL THAT FASHIONED THE *BOOM TUBE*. NOTHING CAN DESTROY IT.
HMMMM...

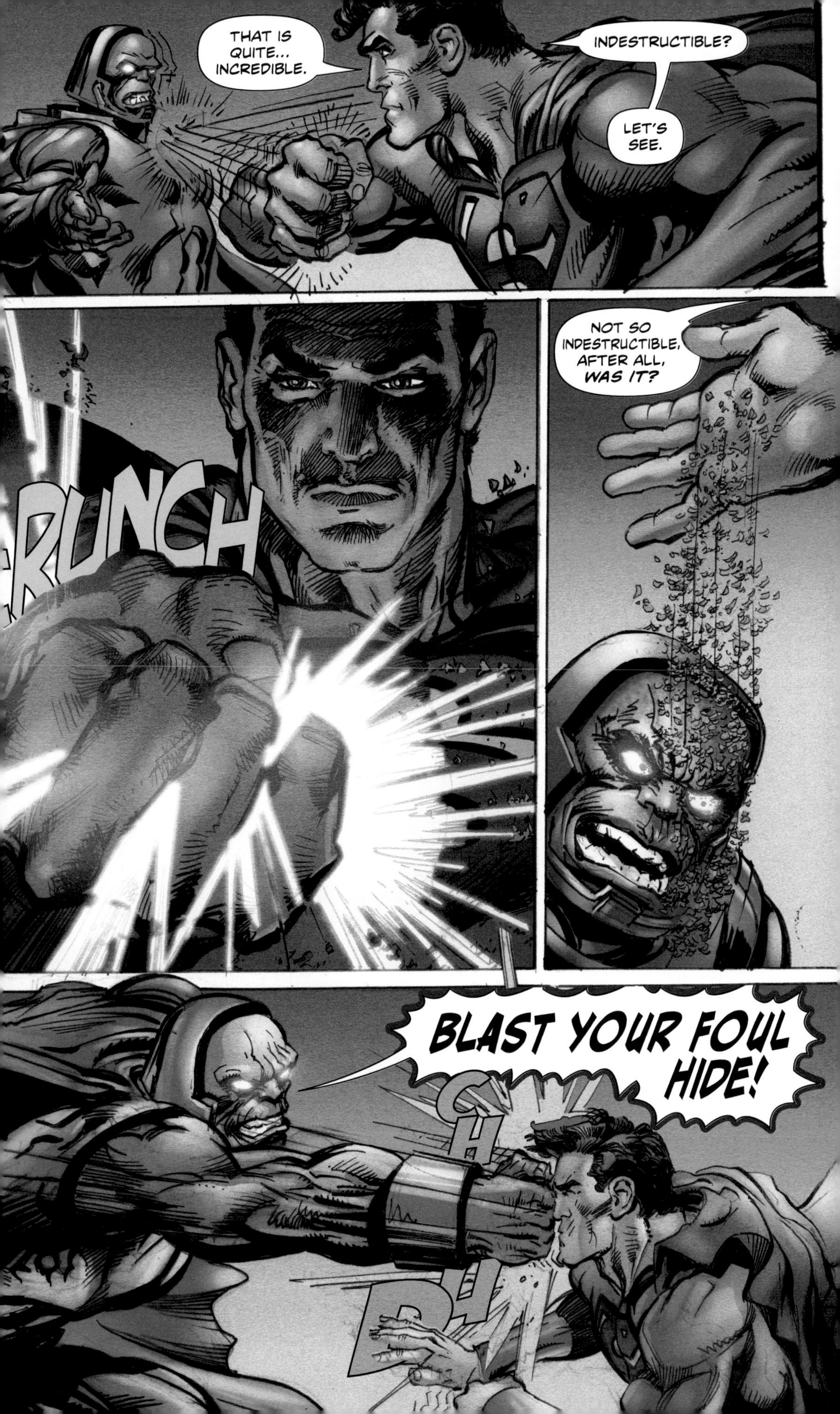
THAT IS QUITE... INCREDIBLE.
INDESTRUCTIBLE?
LET'S SEE.
RUNCH
NOT SO INDESTRUCTIBLE, AFTER ALL, WAS IT?
BLAST YOUR FOUL HIDE!

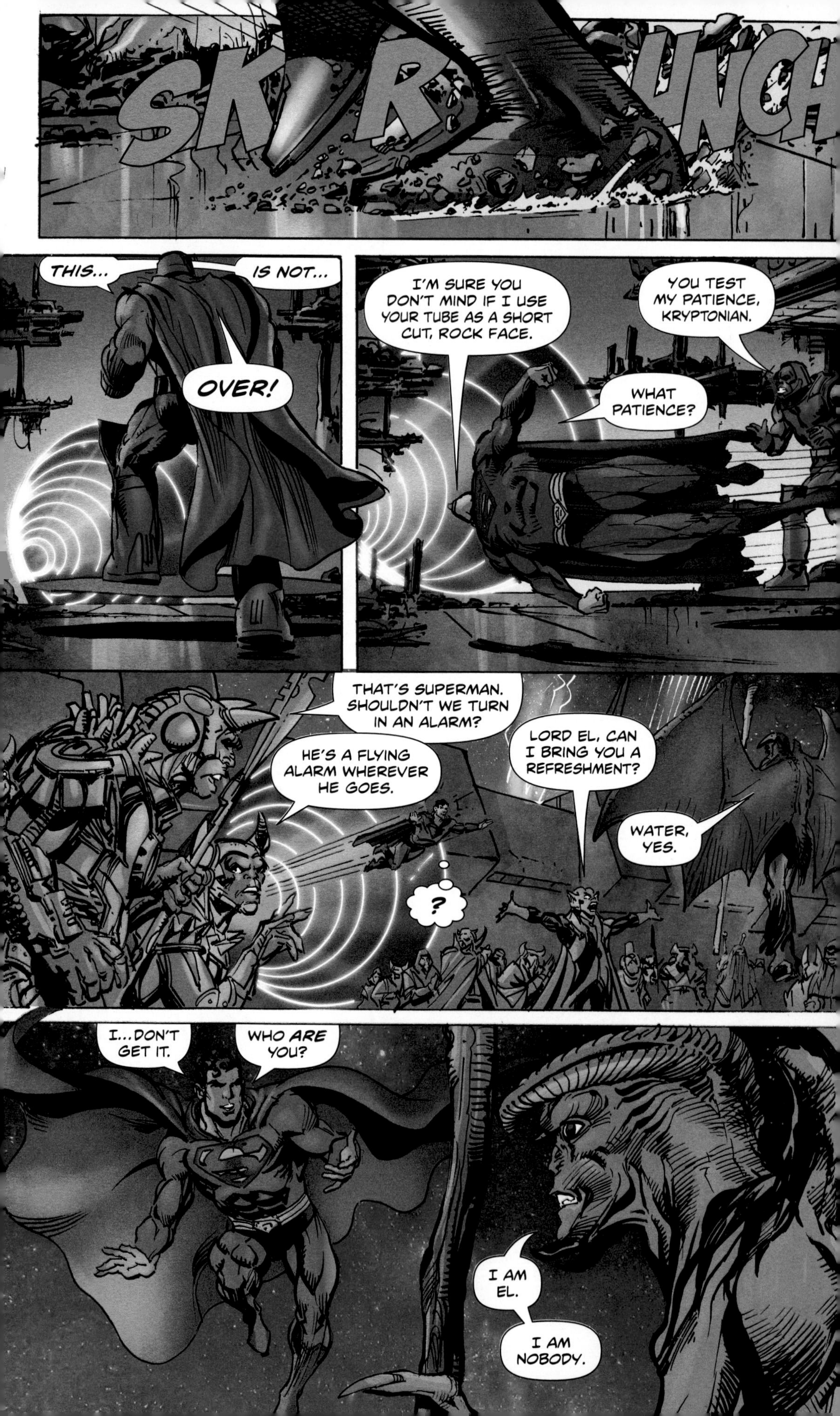
SKRUNCH
THIS...
IS NOT...
OVER!
I'M SURE YOU DON'T MIND IF I USE YOUR TUBE AS A SHORT CUT, ROCK FACE.
YOU TEST MY PATIENCE, KRYPTONIAN.
WHAT PATIENCE?
THAT'S SUPERMAN. SHOULDN'T WE TURN IN AN ALARM?
HE'S A FLYING ALARM WHEREVER HE GOES.
?
LORD EL, CAN I BRING YOU A REFRESHMENT?
WATER, YES.
I...DON'T GET IT.
WHO ARE YOU?
I AM EL.
I AM NOBODY.

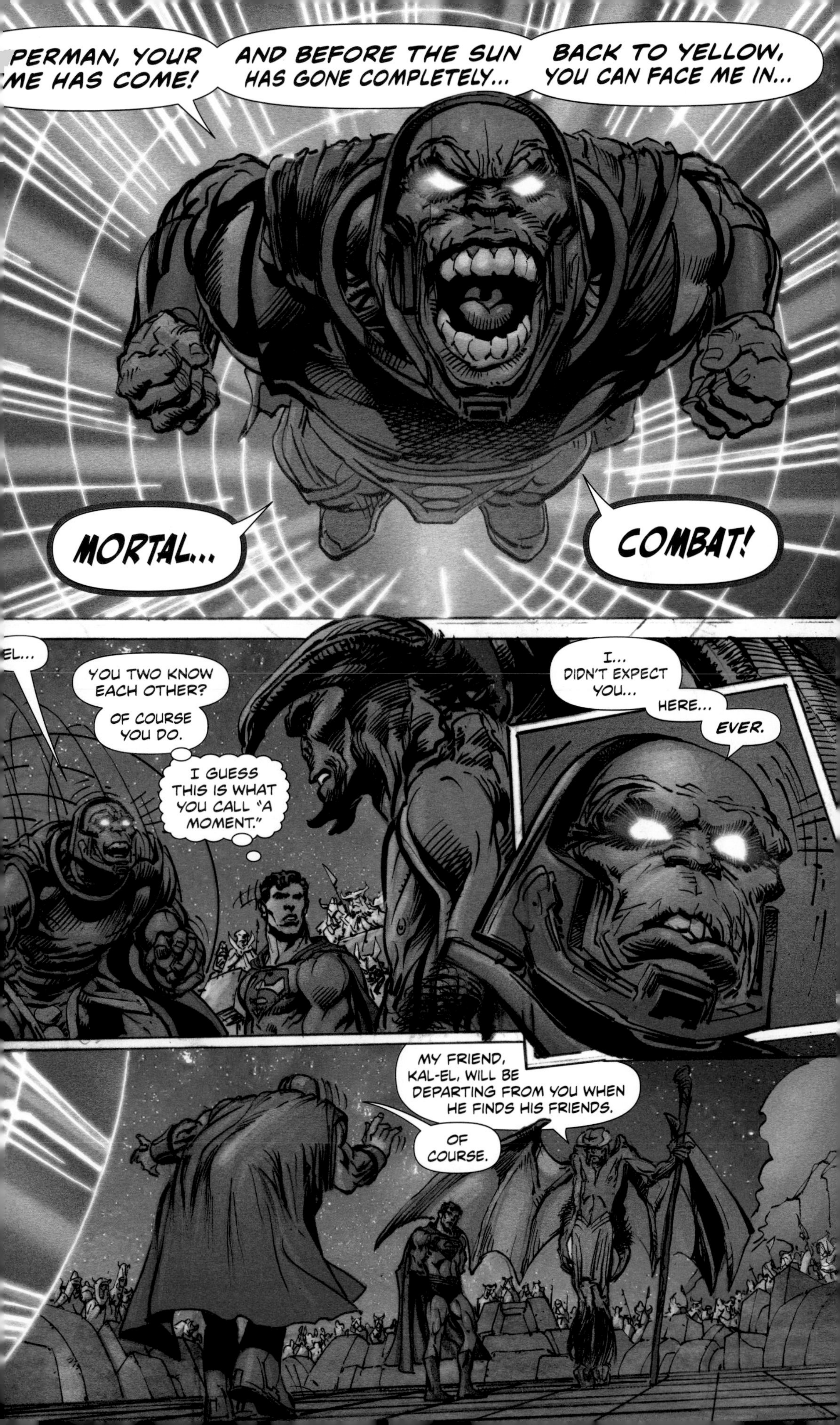
PERMAN, YOUR
ME HAS COME!
AND BEFORE THE SUN HAS GONE COMPLETELY...
BACK TO YELLOW, YOU CAN FACE ME IN...
MORTAL...
COMBAT!
EL...
YOU TWO KNOW EACH OTHER?
OF COURSE YOU DO.
I GUESS THIS IS WHAT YOU CALL "A MOMENT."
I... DIDN'T EXPECT YOU...
HERE...
EVER.
MY FRIEND, KAL-EL, WILL BE DEPARTING FROM YOU WHEN HE FINDS HIS FRIENDS.
OF COURSE.

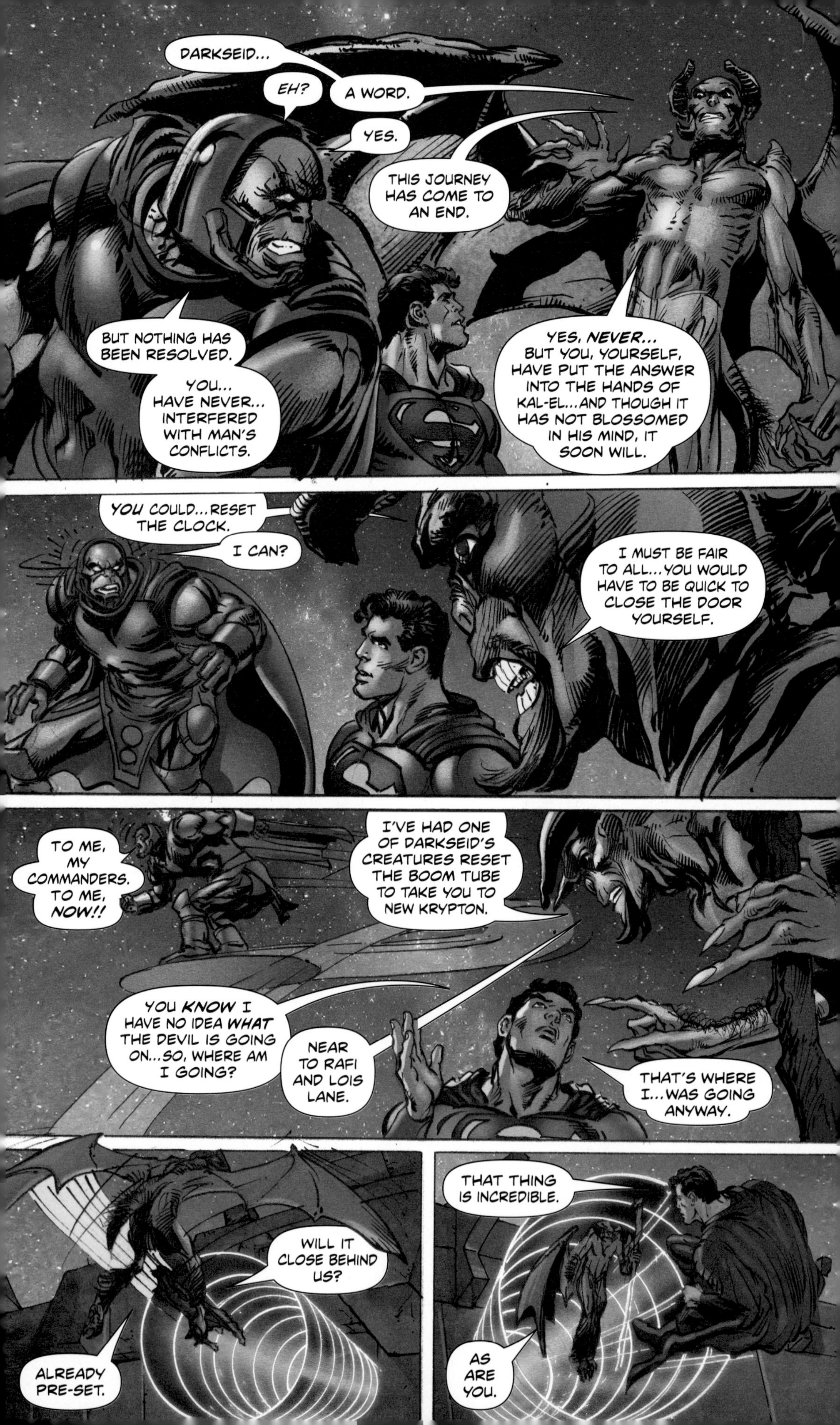
DARKSEID...
EH?
A WORD.
YES.
THIS JOURNEY HAS COME TO AN END.
BUT NOTHING HAS BEEN RESOLVED.
YOU... HAVE NEVER... INTERFERED WITH MAN'S CONFLICTS.
YES, *NEVER...* BUT YOU, YOURSELF, HAVE PUT THE ANSWER INTO THE HANDS OF KAL-EL...AND THOUGH IT HAS NOT BLOSSOMED IN HIS MIND, IT SOON WILL.
YOU COULD...RESET THE CLOCK.
I CAN?
I MUST BE FAIR TO ALL...YOU WOULD HAVE TO BE QUICK TO CLOSE THE DOOR YOURSELF.
TO ME, MY COMMANDERS. TO ME, *NOW!!*
I'VE HAD ONE OF DARKSEID'S CREATURES RESET THE BOOM TUBE TO TAKE YOU TO NEW KRYPTON.
YOU *KNOW* I HAVE NO IDEA *WHAT* THE DEVIL IS GOING ON...SO, WHERE AM I GOING?
NEAR TO RAFI AND LOIS LANE.
THAT'S WHERE I...WAS GOING ANYWAY.
WILL IT CLOSE BEHIND US?
ALREADY PRE-SET.
THAT THING IS INCREDIBLE.
AS ARE YOU.

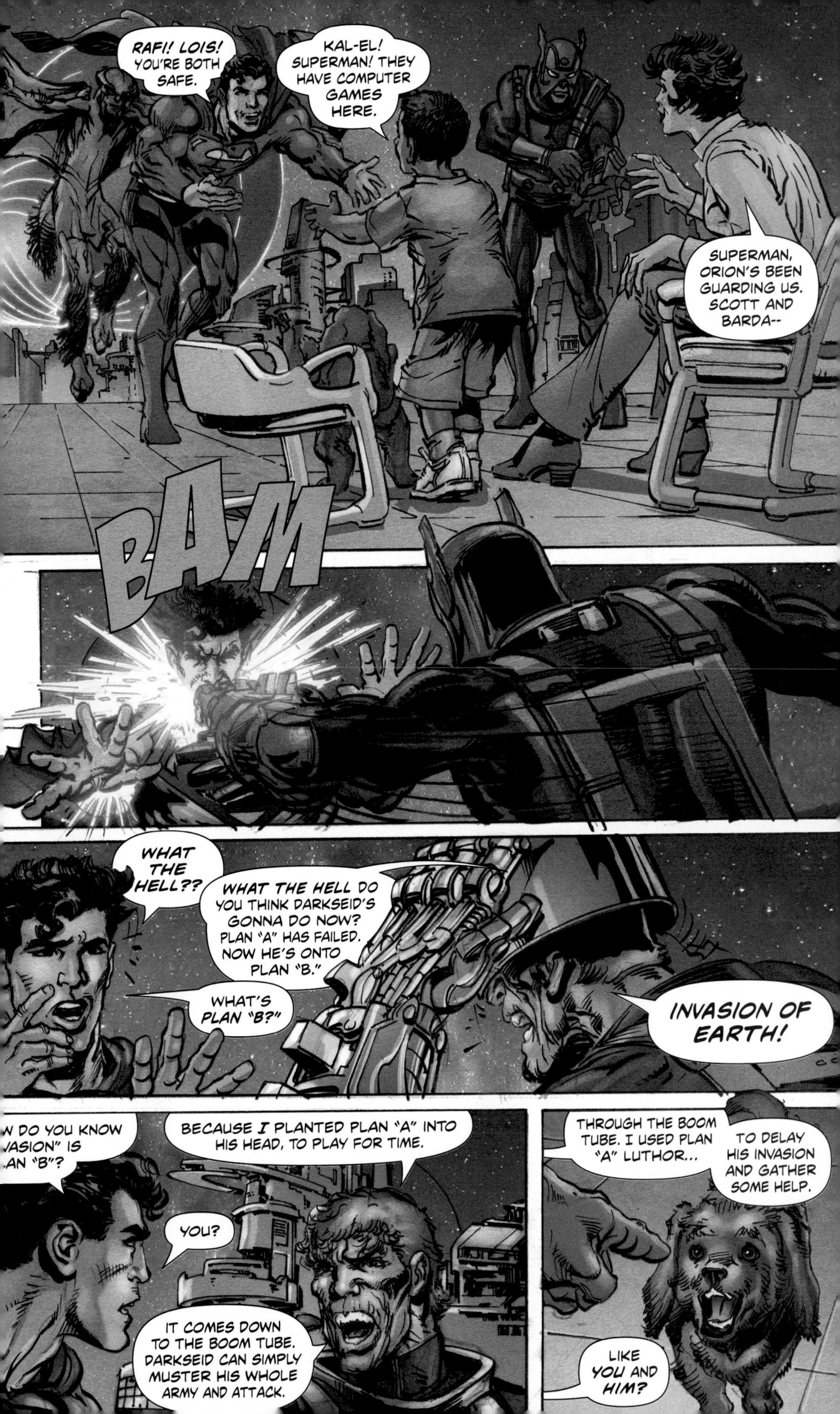
RAFI! LOIS! YOU'RE BOTH SAFE.
KAL-EL! SUPERMAN! THEY HAVE COMPUTER GAMES HERE.
SUPERMAN, ORION'S BEEN GUARDING US. SCOTT AND BARDA--
BAM
WHAT THE HELL??
WHAT THE HELL DO YOU THINK DARKSEID'S GONNA DO NOW? PLAN "A" HAS FAILED. NOW HE'S ONTO PLAN "B."
WHAT'S PLAN "B?"
INVASION OF EARTH!
W DO YOU KNOW VASION" IS AN "B"?
BECAUSE I PLANTED PLAN "A" INTO HIS HEAD, TO PLAY FOR TIME.
YOU?
IT COMES DOWN TO THE BOOM TUBE. DARKSEID CAN SIMPLY MUSTER HIS WHOLE ARMY AND ATTACK.
THROUGH THE BOOM TUBE. I USED PLAN "A" LUTHOR...
TO DELAY HIS INVASION AND GATHER SOME HELP.
LIKE YOU AND HIM?

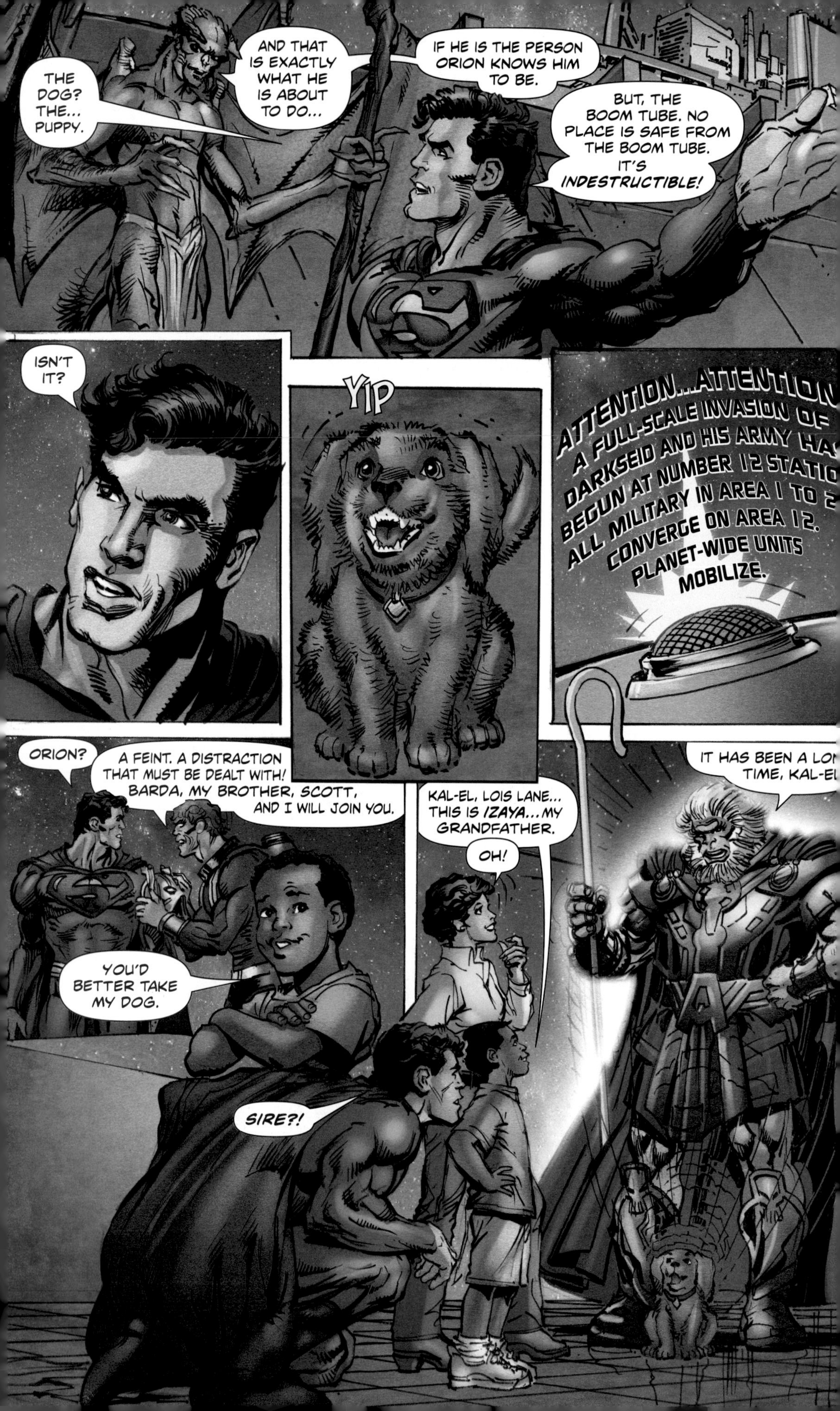
THE DOG? THE... PUPPY.
AND THAT IS EXACTLY WHAT HE IS ABOUT TO DO...
IF HE IS THE PERSON ORION KNOWS HIM TO BE.
BUT, THE BOOM TUBE. NO PLACE IS SAFE FROM THE BOOM TUBE. IT'S INDESTRUCTIBLE!
ISN'T IT?
YIP
ATTENTION...ATTENTION
A FULL-SCALE INVASION OF DARKSEID AND HIS ARMY HAS BEGUN AT NUMBER 12 STATIO
ALL MILITARY IN AREA 1 TO 2
CONVERGE ON AREA 12.
PLANET-WIDE UNITS MOBILIZE.
ORION?
A FEINT. A DISTRACTION THAT MUST BE DEALT WITH! BARDA, MY BROTHER, SCOTT, AND I WILL JOIN YOU.
YOU'D BETTER TAKE MY DOG.
KAL-EL, LOIS LANE... THIS IS IZAYA... MY GRANDFATHER.
OH!
IT HAS BEEN A LO TIME, KAL-E
SIRE?!

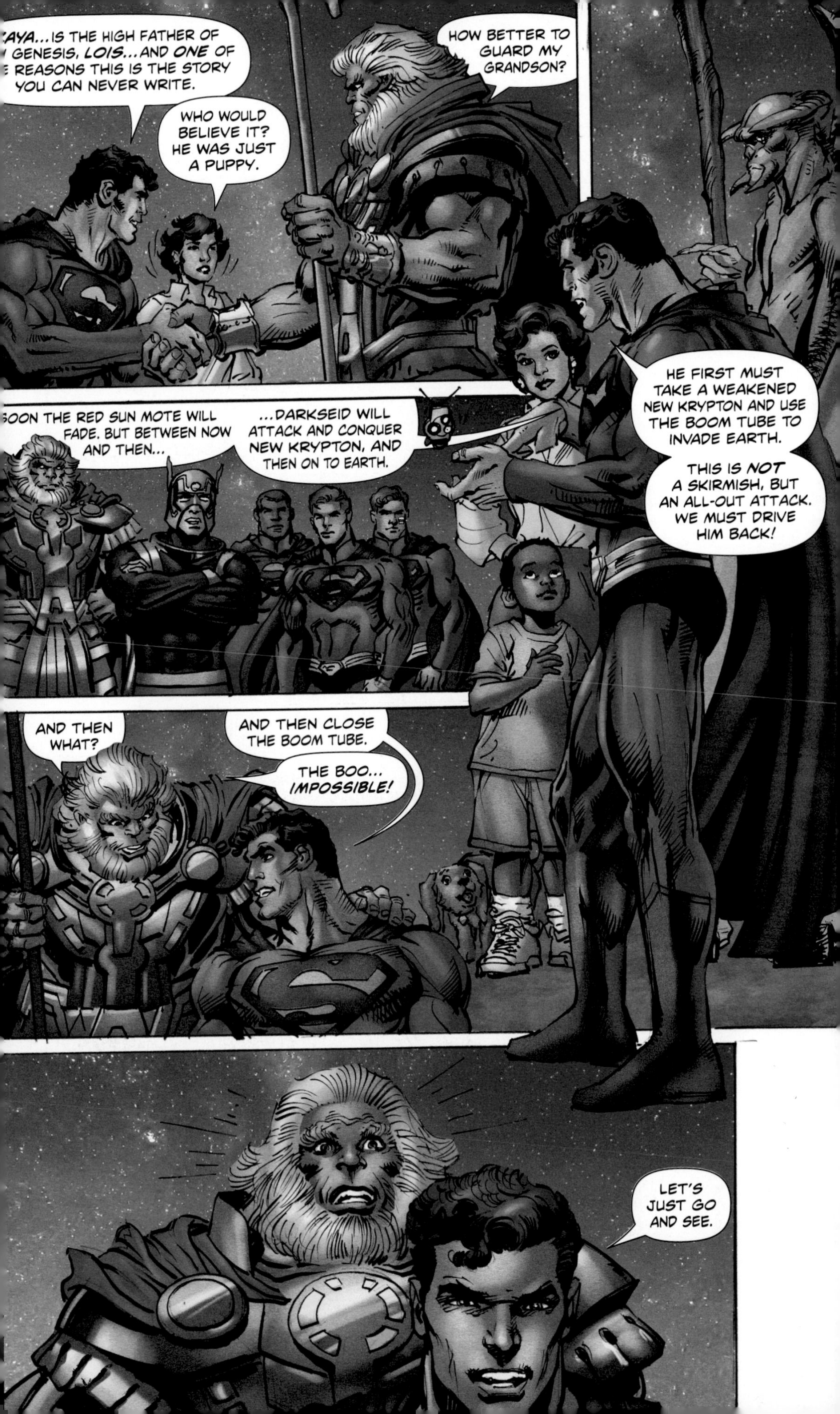

KAYA...IS THE HIGH FATHER OF GENESIS, LOIS...AND ONE OF REASONS THIS IS THE STORY YOU CAN NEVER WRITE.
WHO WOULD BELIEVE IT? HE WAS JUST A PUPPY.
HOW BETTER TO GUARD MY GRANDSON?
SOON THE RED SUN MOTE WILL FADE. BUT BETWEEN NOW AND THEN...
...DARKSEID WILL ATTACK AND CONQUER NEW KRYPTON, AND THEN ON TO EARTH.
HE FIRST MUST TAKE A WEAKENED NEW KRYPTON AND USE THE BOOM TUBE TO INVADE EARTH.
THIS IS NOT A SKIRMISH, BUT AN ALL-OUT ATTACK. WE MUST DRIVE HIM BACK!
AND THEN WHAT?
AND THEN CLOSE THE BOOM TUBE.
THE BOO... IMPOSSIBLE!
LET'S JUST GO AND SEE.

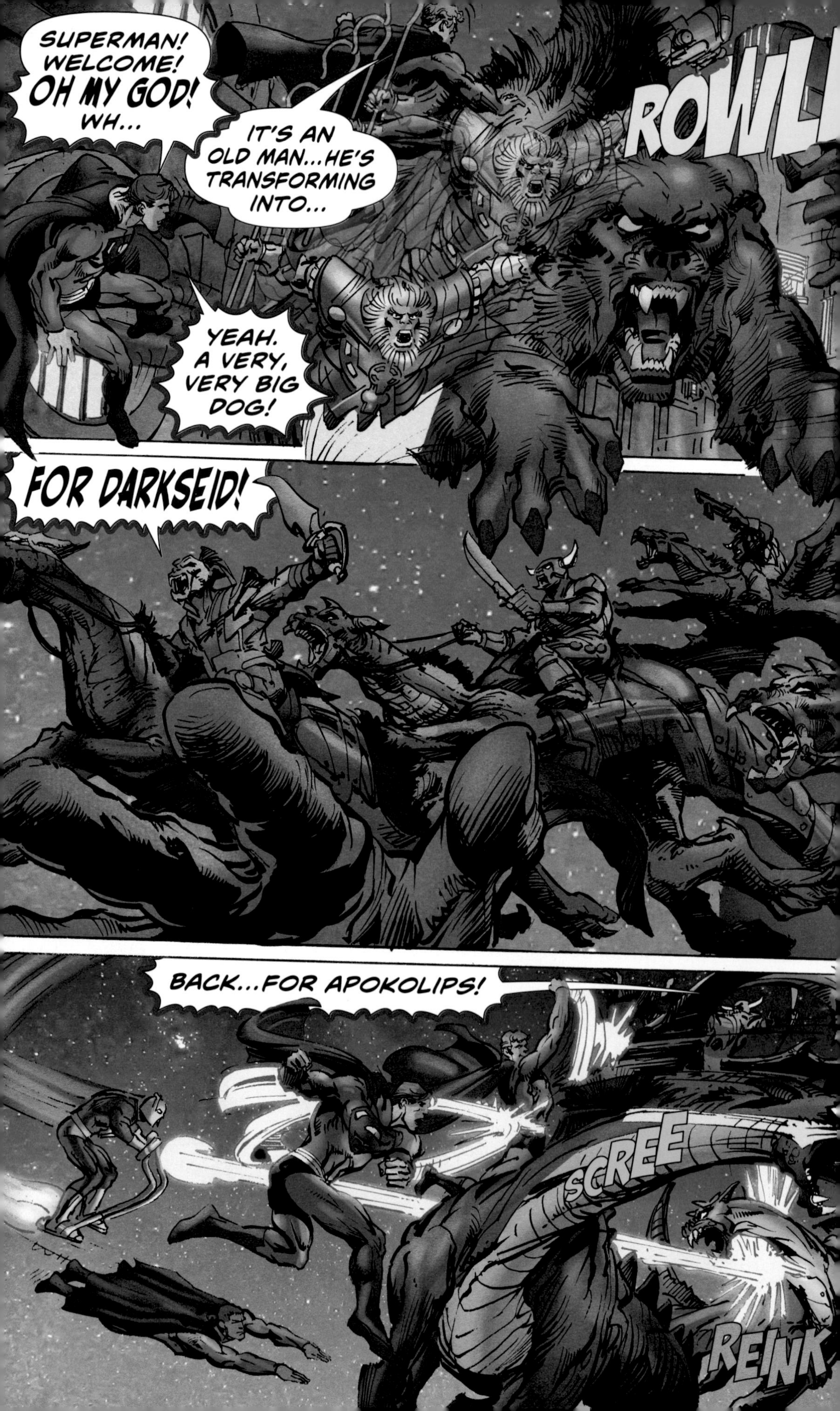
SUPERMAN! WELCOME! OH MY GOD! WH...
IT'S AN OLD MAN...HE'S TRANSFORMING INTO...
ROWL!
YEAH. A VERY, VERY BIG DOG!
FOR DARKSEID!
BACK...FOR APOKOLIPS!
SCREE
REINK

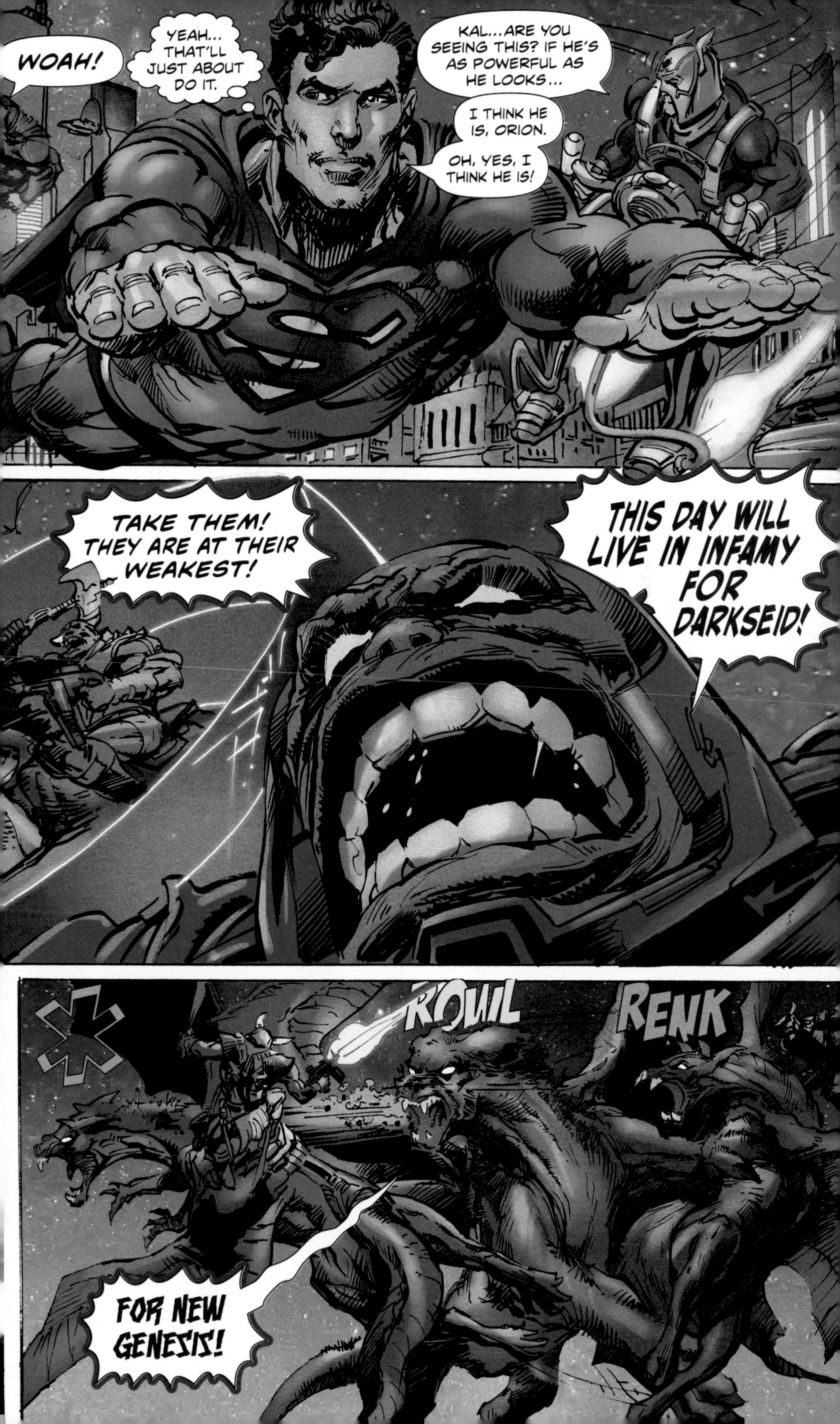
WOAH!
YEAH... THAT'LL JUST ABOUT DO IT.
KAL...ARE YOU SEEING THIS? IF HE'S AS POWERFUL AS HE LOOKS...
I THINK HE IS, ORION.
OH, YES, I THINK HE IS!
TAKE THEM! THEY ARE AT THEIR WEAKEST!
THIS DAY WILL LIVE IN INFAMY FOR DARKSEID!
ROUIL
RENK
FOR NEW GENESIS!

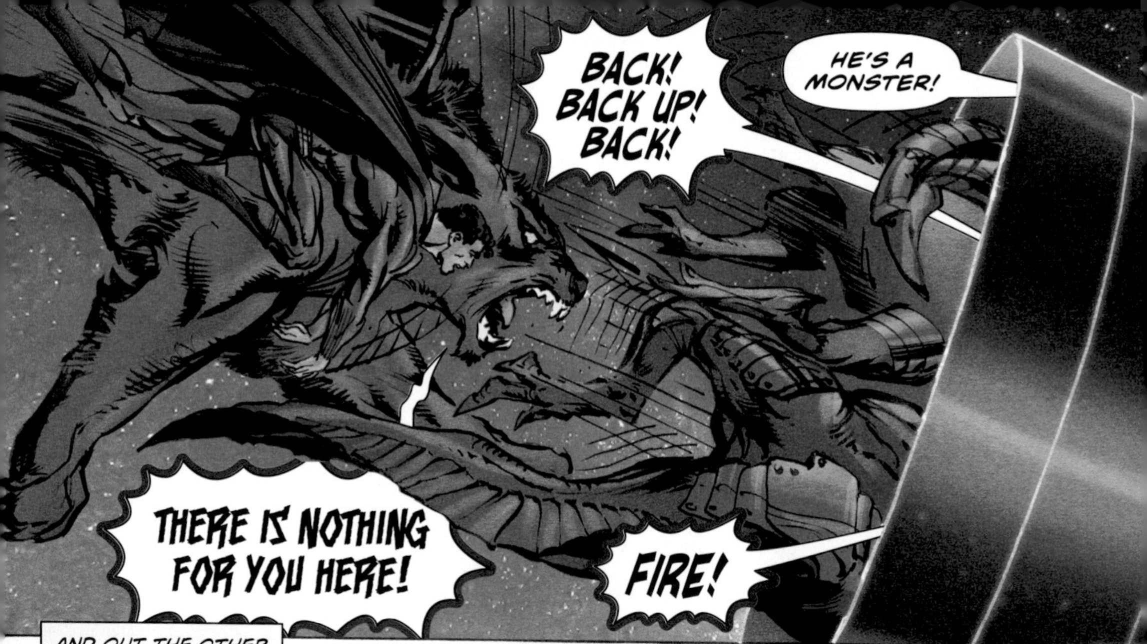
BACK! BACK UP! BACK!
HE'S A MONSTER!
THERE IS NOTHING FOR YOU HERE!
FIRE!

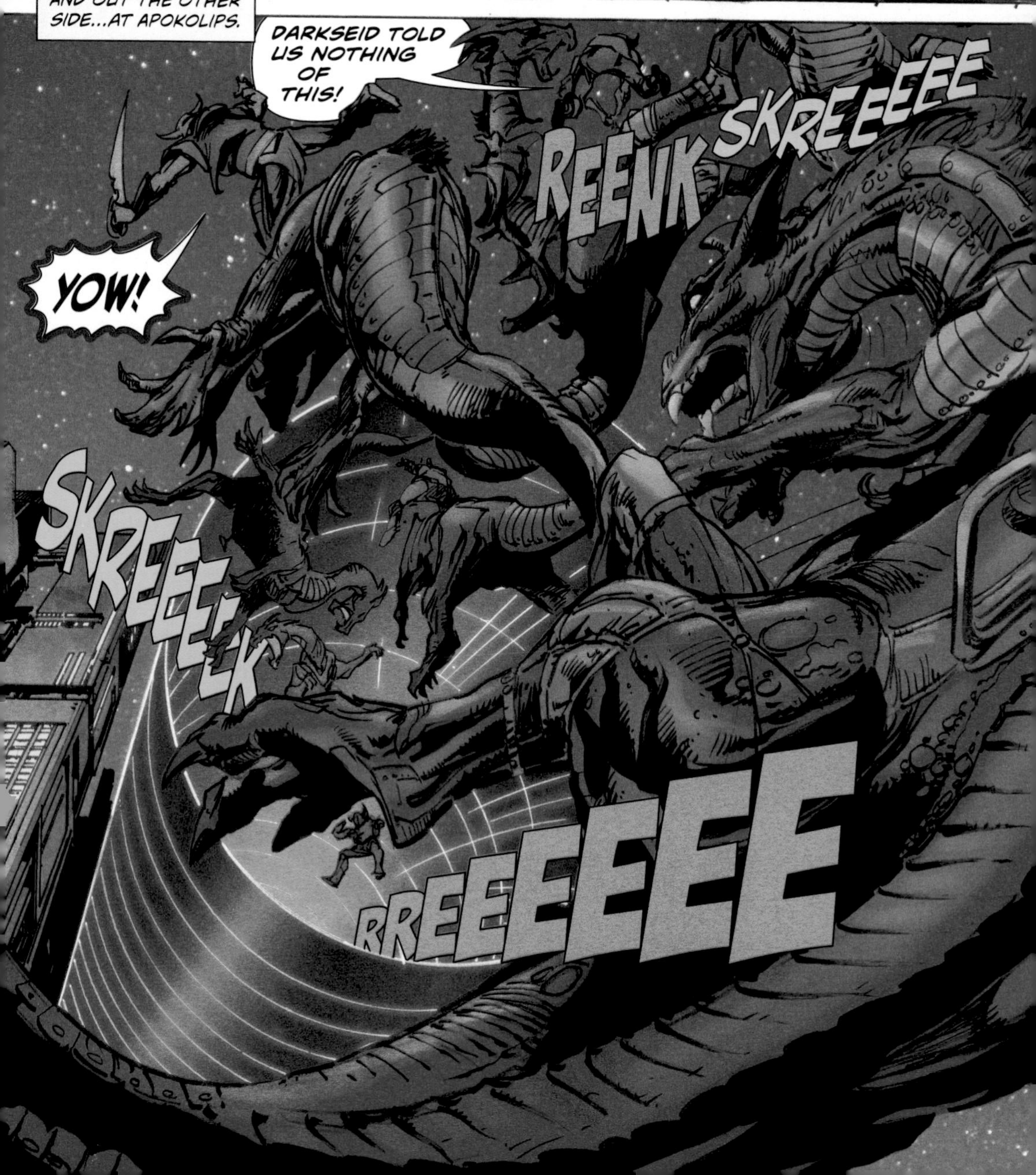
AND OUT THE OTHER SIDE...AT APOKOLIPS.
DARKSEID TOLD US NOTHING OF THIS!
REENK
SKREEEEEE
YOW!
SKREEEEK
RREEEEEEE

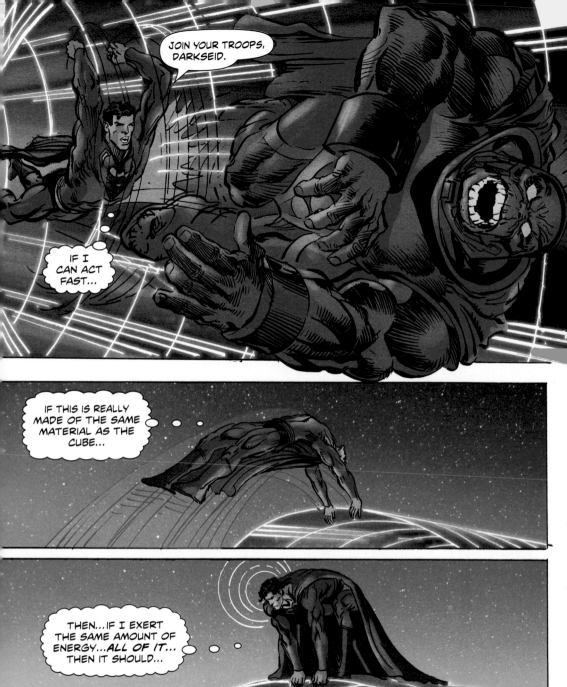

JOIN YOUR TROOPS, DARKSEID.

IF I CAN ACT FAST...

IF THIS IS REALLY MADE OF THE SAME MATERIAL AS THE CUBE...

THEN...IF I EXERT THE SAME AMOUNT OF ENERGY...*ALL OF IT*... THEN IT SHOULD...

...BEND...INWARD... VERY...TOUGH MATERIAL.

I'M ACTUALLY BREAKING A SWEAT... *UMPH*...

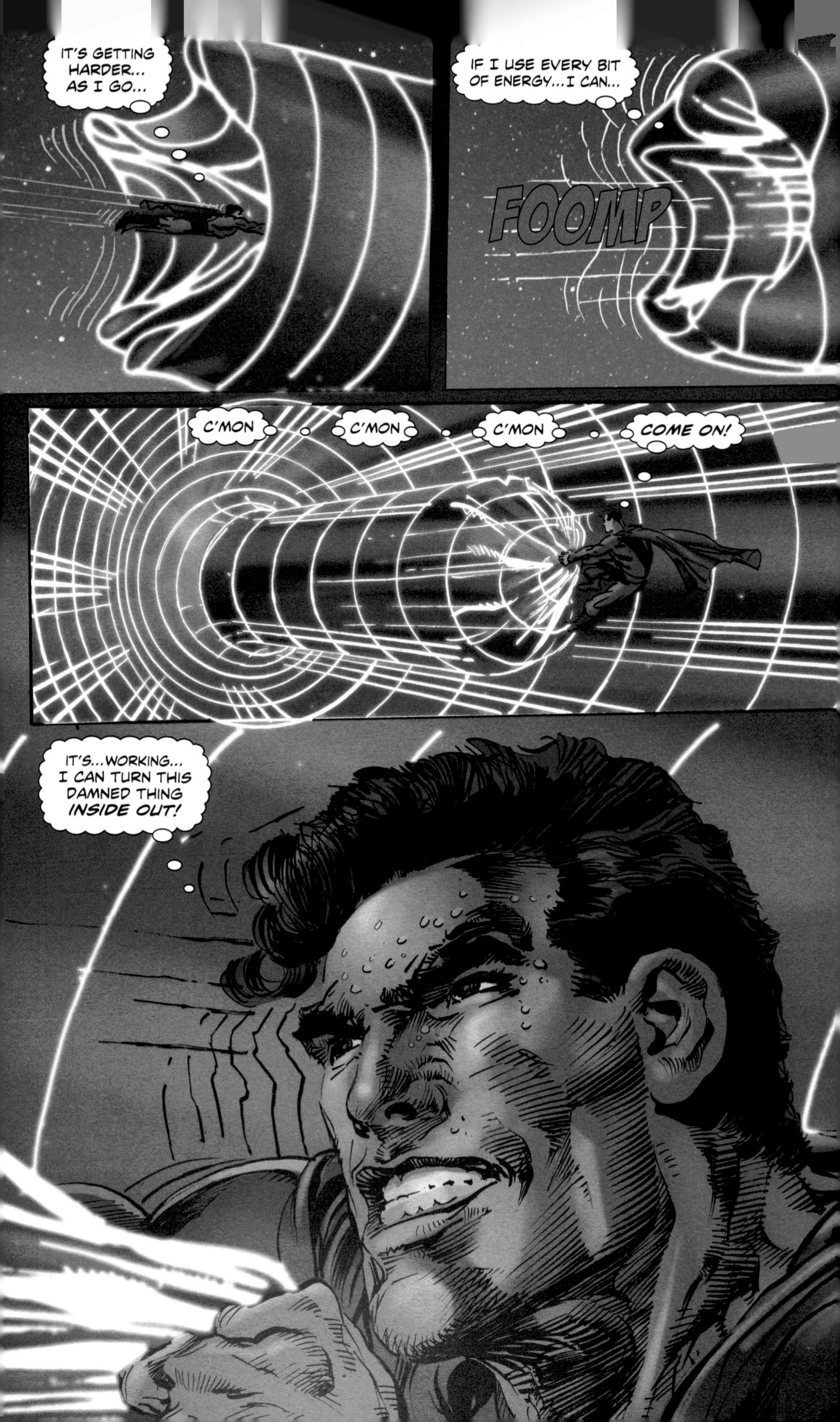
IT'S GETTING HARDER... AS I GO...
IF I USE EVERY BIT OF ENERGY...I CAN...
FOOMP
C'MON
C'MON
C'MON
COME ON!
IT'S...WORKING... I CAN TURN THIS DAMNED THING INSIDE OUT!

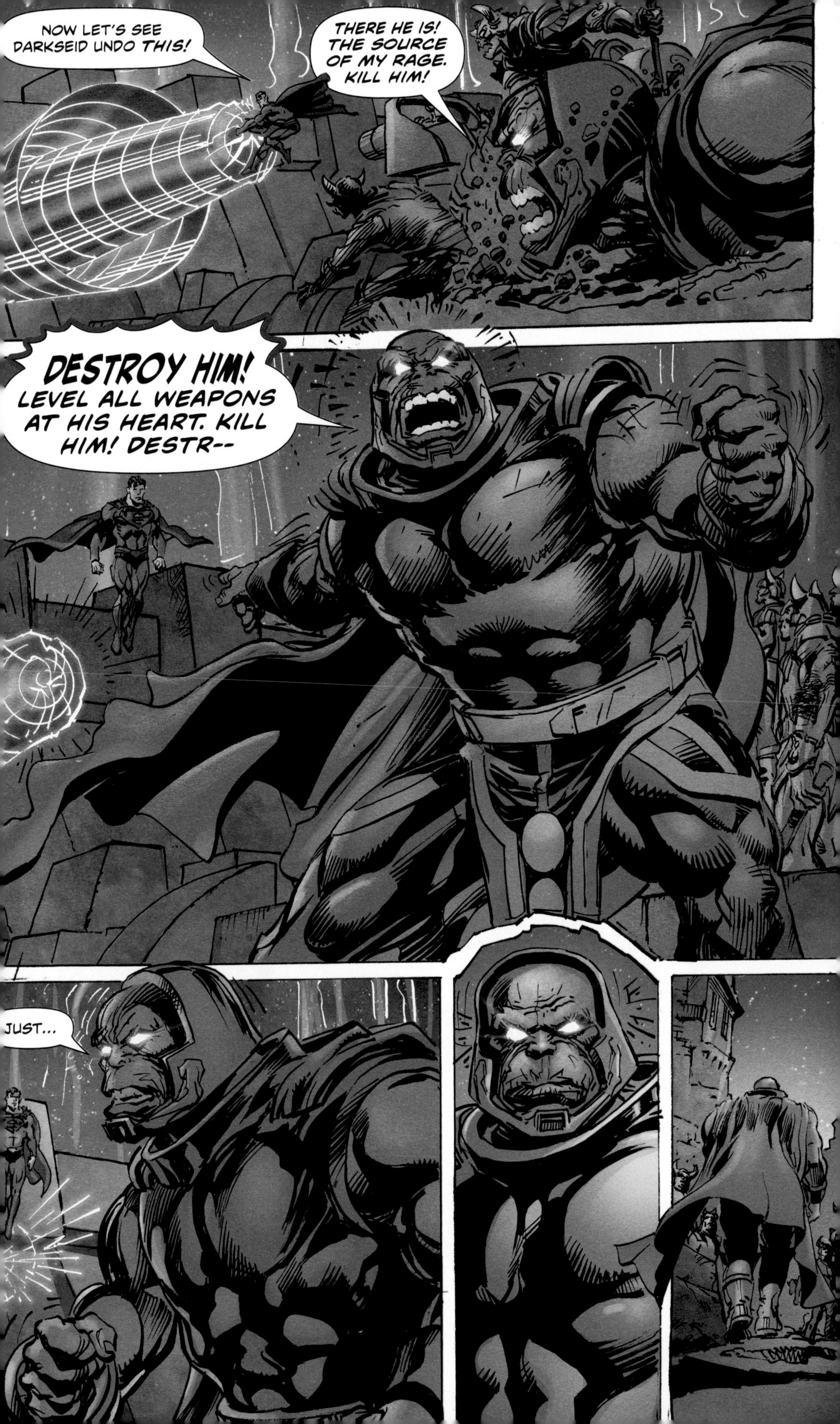
NOW LET'S SEE DARKSEID UNDO THIS!
THERE HE IS! THE SOURCE OF MY RAGE. KILL HIM!
DESTROY HIM! LEVEL ALL WEAPONS AT HIS HEART. KILL HIM! DESTR--
JUST...

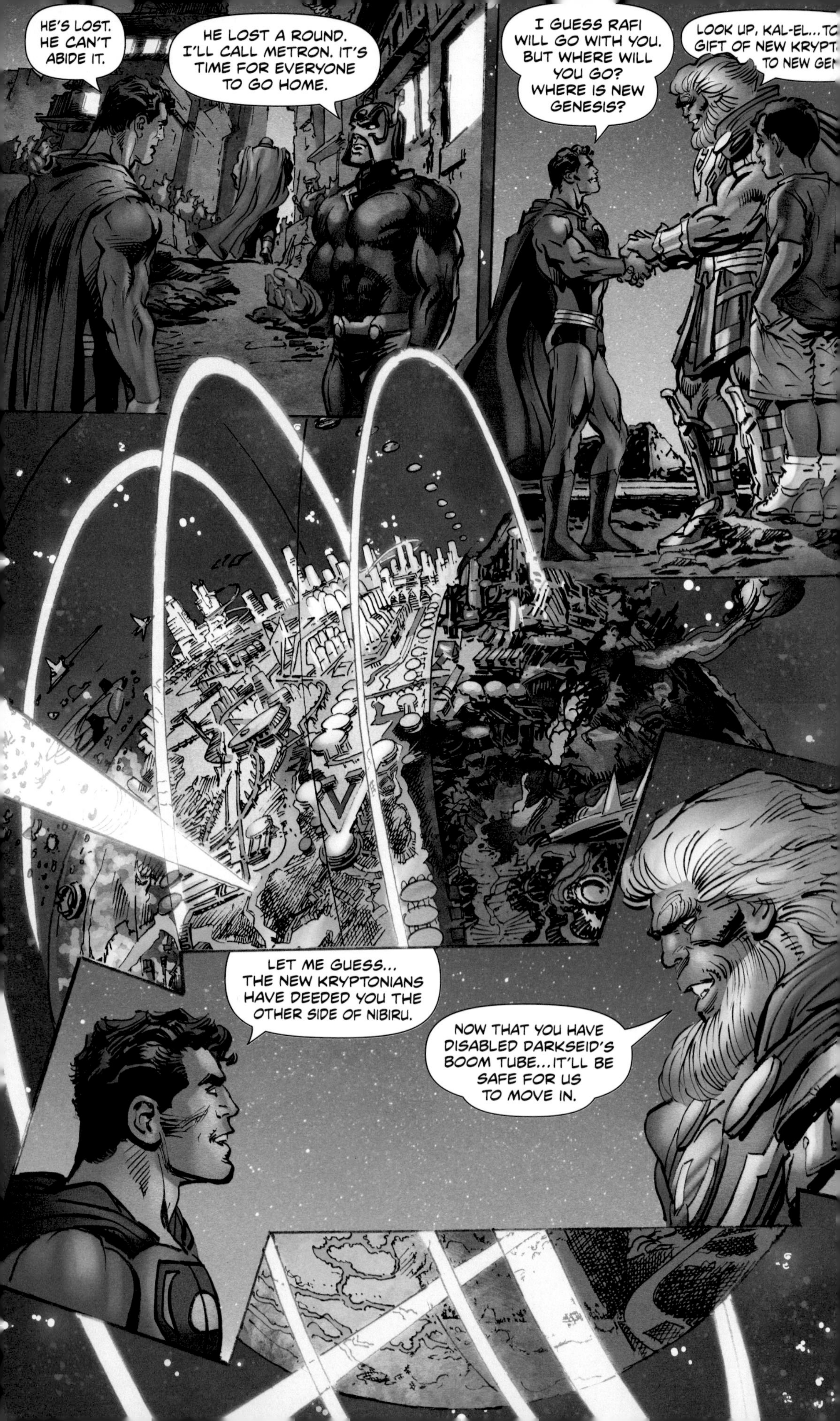
HE'S LOST. HE CAN'T ABIDE IT.
HE LOST A ROUND. I'LL CALL METRON. IT'S TIME FOR EVERYONE TO GO HOME.
I GUESS RAFI WILL GO WITH YOU. BUT WHERE WILL YOU GO? WHERE IS NEW GENESIS?
LOOK UP, KAL-EL...TO GIFT OF NEW KRYPT TO NEW GEN
LET ME GUESS... THE NEW KRYPTONIANS HAVE DEEDED YOU THE OTHER SIDE OF NIBIRU.
NOW THAT YOU HAVE DISABLED DARKSEID'S BOOM TUBE...IT'LL BE SAFE FOR US TO MOVE IN.

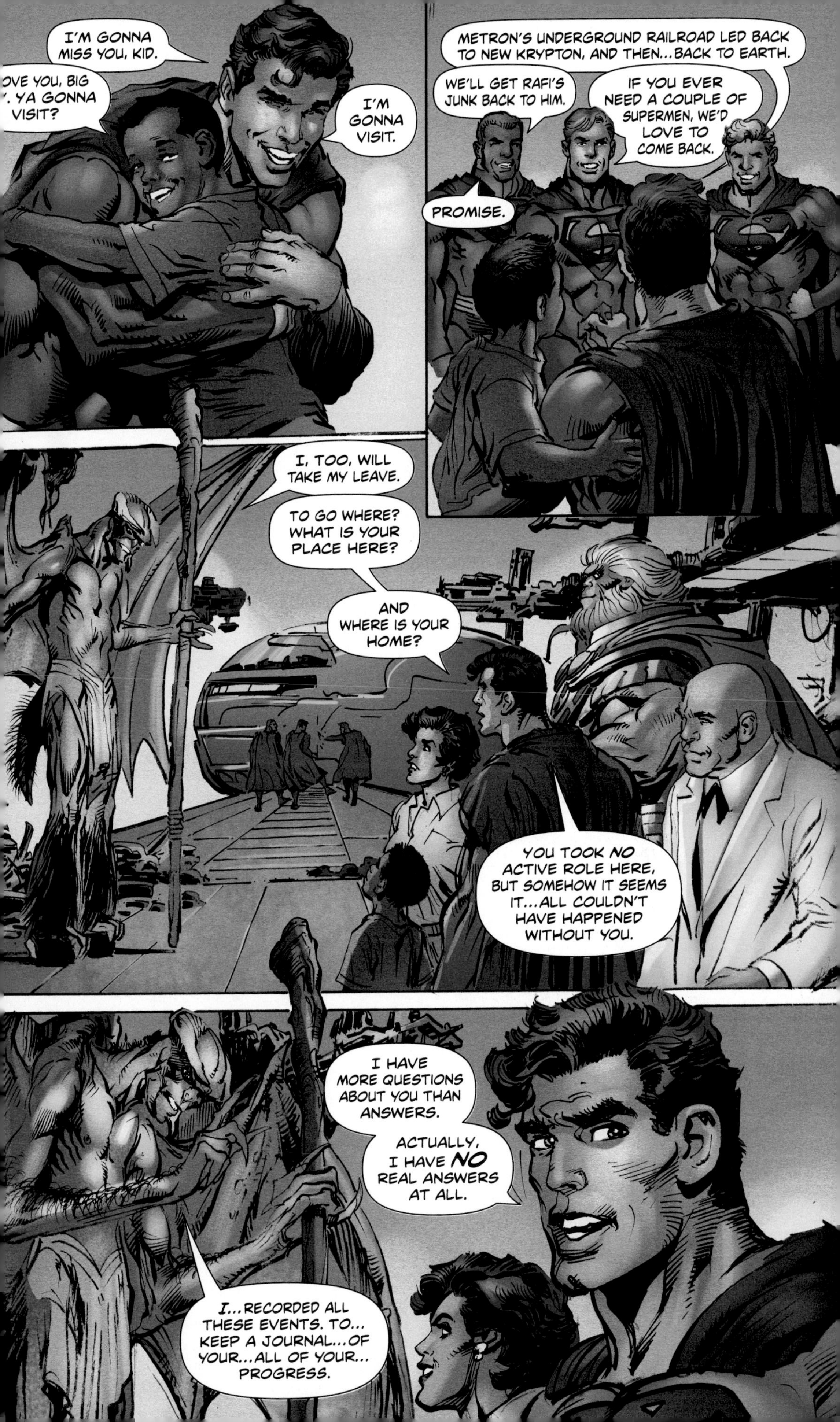
I'M GONNA MISS YOU, KID.
OVE YOU, BIG . YA GONNA VISIT?
I'M GONNA VISIT.
METRON'S UNDERGROUND RAILROAD LED BACK TO NEW KRYPTON, AND THEN... BACK TO EARTH.
WE'LL GET RAFI'S JUNK BACK TO HIM.
IF YOU EVER NEED A COUPLE OF SUPERMEN, WE'D LOVE TO COME BACK.
PROMISE.
I, TOO, WILL TAKE MY LEAVE.
TO GO WHERE? WHAT IS YOUR PLACE HERE?
AND WHERE IS YOUR HOME?
YOU TOOK NO ACTIVE ROLE HERE, BUT SOMEHOW IT SEEMS IT... ALL COULDN'T HAVE HAPPENED WITHOUT YOU.
I HAVE MORE QUESTIONS ABOUT YOU THAN ANSWERS.
ACTUALLY, I HAVE NO REAL ANSWERS AT ALL.
I... RECORDED ALL THESE EVENTS. TO... KEEP A JOURNAL... OF YOUR... ALL OF YOUR... PROGRESS.

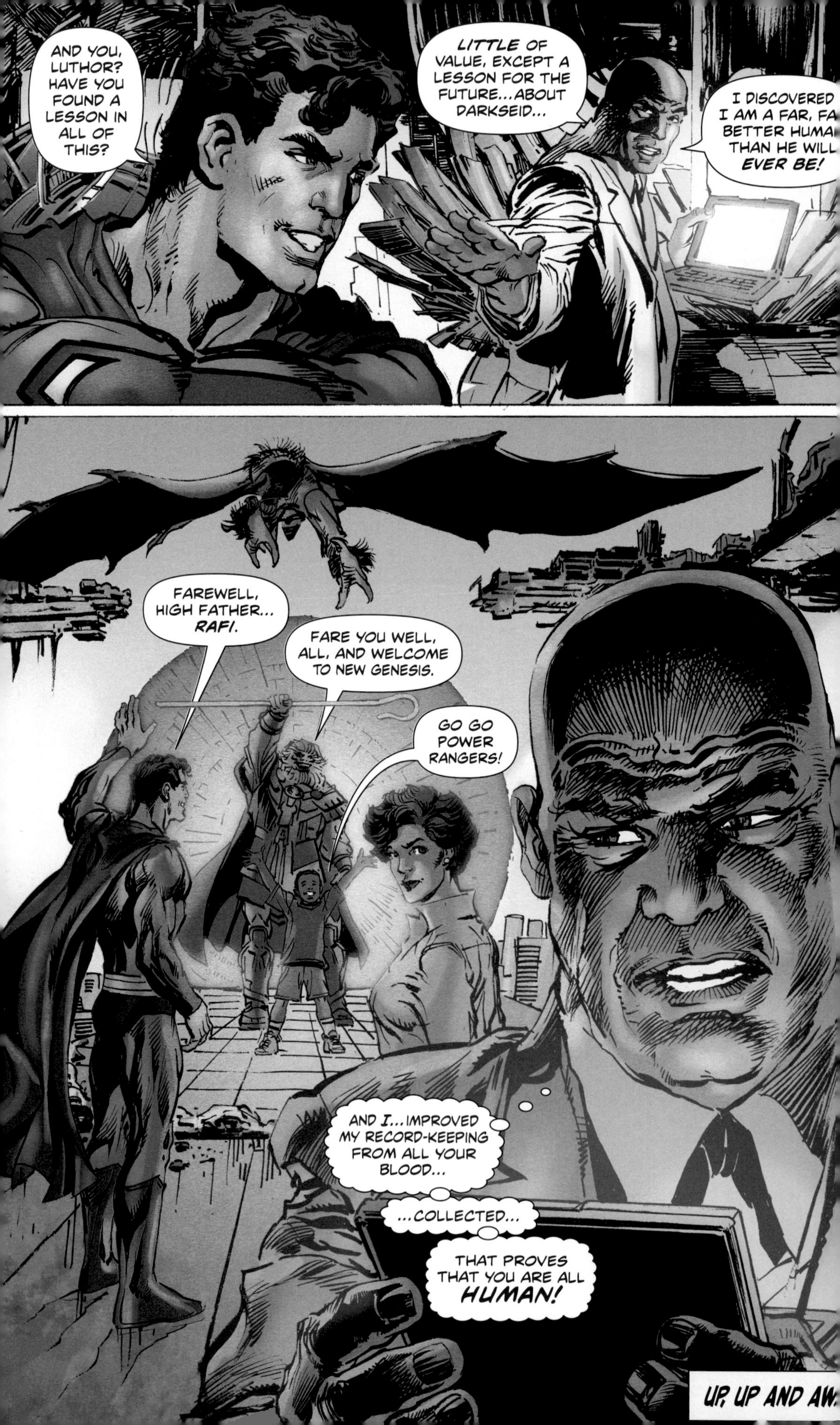
AND YOU, LUTHOR? HAVE YOU FOUND A LESSON IN ALL OF THIS?
LITTLE OF VALUE, EXCEPT A LESSON FOR THE FUTURE...ABOUT DARKSEID...
I DISCOVERED I AM A FAR, FA BETTER HUMA THAN HE WILL EVER BE!
FAREWELL, HIGH FATHER... RAFI.
FARE YOU WELL, ALL, AND WELCOME TO NEW GENESIS.
GO GO POWER RANGERS!
AND I...IMPROVED MY RECORD-KEEPING FROM ALL YOUR BLOOD...
...COLLECTED...
THAT PROVES THAT YOU ARE ALL HUMAN!
UP, UP AND AW

FROM THE WRITER OF *JUSTICE LEAGUE & GREEN LANTERN*

GEOFF JOHNS
with GARY FRANK

SUPERMAN:
THE LAST SON OF
KRYPTON

with RICHARD DONNER &
ADAM KUBERT

SUPERMAN
& THE LEGION OF
SUPER-HEROES

with GARY FRANK

SUPERMAN: BRAINIAC

with GARY FRANK

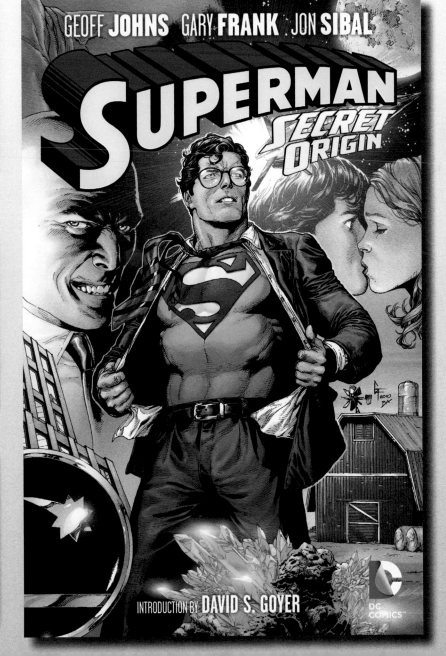

DC COMICS™

GRANT MORRISON
with FRANK QUITELY

FINAL CRISIS

with J.G. JONES, CARLOS
PACHECO & DOUG MAHNKE

**BATMAN:
ARKHAM ASYLUM**

with DAVE McKEAN

**SEVEN SOLDIERS OF
VICTORY VOLS. 1 & 2**

with J.H. WILLIAMS III &
VARIOUS ARTISTS

ALL ★ STAR

**GRANT MORRISON
FRANK QUITELY**
JAMIE GRANT

DC COMICS™

MICS™

"Welcoming to new fans looking to get into superhero comics for the first time and old fans who gave up on the funny-books long ago."
—SCRIPPS HOWARD NEWS SERVICE

START AT THE BEGINNING!

JUSTICE LEAGUE VOLUME 1: ORIGIN

THE NEW 52!
DC COMICS™
JUSTICE LEAGUE
VOLUME 1 ORIGIN
"WRITTEN BY GEOFF JOHNS, WITH ART BY THE GODLY JIM LEE, JUSTICE LEAGUE IS A MUST READ."
— COMPLEX MAGAZINE
GEOFF JOHNS JIM LEE SCOTT WILLIAMS

AQUAMAN VOLUME 1: THE TRENCH

THE NEW 52!
AQUAMAN
GEOFF JOHNS IVAN REIS JOE PRADO

THE SAVAGE HAWKMAN VOLUME 1: DARKNESS RISING

THE NEW 52!
SAVAGE HAWKMAN
VOLUME 1 DARKNESS RISING
TONY S. DANIEL PHILIP TAN JAMES BONNY

GREEN ARROW VOLUME 1: THE MIDAS TOUCH

THE NEW 52!
GREEN ARROW
VOLUME 1 THE MIDAS TOUCH
DAN JURGENS J.T. KRUL KEITH GIFFEN GEORGE PÉREZ

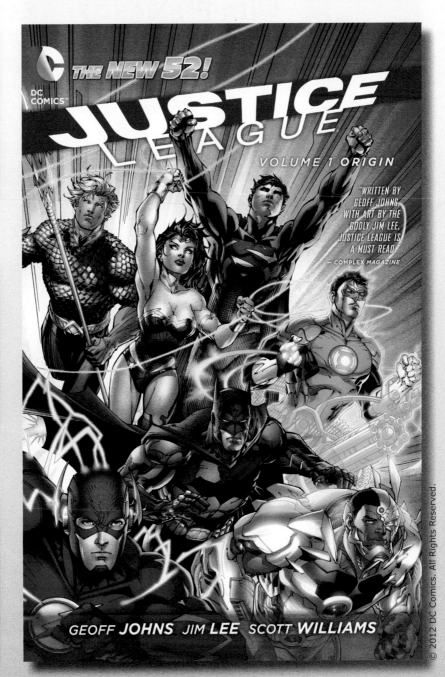

*"ACTION COMICS has successfully carved [...]
own territory and continued exploring Morris[...]
familiar themes about heroism and ideas."—[...]*

*"Casts the character in a new light, opens up fresh story[...]
ing possibilities, and pushes it all forward with dynamic R[...]
Morales art. I loved it."—THE ONION/AV CL[...]*

START AT THE BEGINNING

SUPERMAN: ACTION COMICS VOLUME 1
SUPERMAN AND THE MEN OF STEE[...]

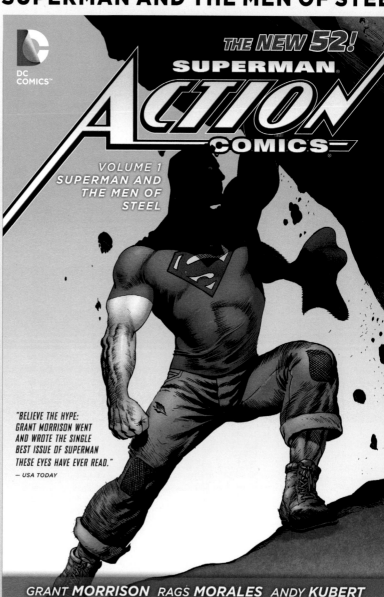

*"BELIEVE THE HYPE:
GRANT MORRISON WENT
AND WROTE THE SINGLE
BEST ISSUE OF SUPERMAN
THESE EYES HAVE EVER READ."
— USA TODAY*

GRANT *MORRISON* RAGS *MORALES* ANDY *KUBERT*